A HOUSE IN ST JOHN'S WOOD

A HOUSE IN ST JOHN'S WOOD

In Search of My Parents

MATTHEW SPENDER

FARRAR, STRAUS AND GIROUX

NEW YORK

Farrar, Straus and Giroux
18 West 18th Street, New York 10011

The photographs reproduced in this book are from the Lizzie and
Matthew Spender Collection, with the following exceptions:
frontispiece: by Ida Kar, 1957 © National Portrait Gallery, London
p. 32: courtesy of the Humphrey Spender Archive
p. 307: courtesy of Natasha Gorky

Library of Congress Cataloging-in-Publication Data
Spender, Matthew, author.
   A house in St John's Wood : in search of my parents / Matthew Spender. — First
American edition.
        p.   cm.
   Includes index.
   ISBN 978-0-374-26986-9 (hardback) — ISBN 978-0-374-71350-8 (e-book)
   1. Spender, Stephen, 1909–1995.   2. Spender, Natasha.   3. Spender, Matthew—Family.
4. Poets, English—20th century—Biography.   5. Critics—Great Britain—Biography.
6. Pianists—Great Britain—Biography.   I. Title.

PR6037.P47 Z845 2015
821'.912—dc23
[B]

                                                                            2015022210

www.fsgbooks.com
www.twitter.com/fsgbooks • www.facebook.com/fsgbooks

1   3   5   7   9   10   8   6   4   2

To my grandchildren:
Cleopatra, Aeneas, Ondina and Marlon

My father and me in 1950.

CONTENTS

ACKNOWLEDGEMENTS

I WOULD LIKE TO thank the following archivists and archives: The Astor, Lenox and Tilden Foundations of the New York Public Library; the Bancroft Library, University of California, Berkeley, CA; Isaac Gewirz at the Berg Collection of the New York Public Library; Chris Fletcher, Colin Harris, Charlotte McKillop-Mash and Judith Priestman at the Bodleian Library, Oxford; The British Library, London; William Hansen at Duke University Special Collections, Durham, NC; Callista Lucy at the Library of Dulwich College, London; Andrew Gray at Durham University Library (UK); the T. S. Eliot Archive, London, and Debbie Whitfield, secretary to the late Valerie Eliot; The Stefan Georg Archive; Kristina Rosenthal at the McFarlin Library, University of Tulsa, OK; the Fondren Library, Rice University, Houston, TX; Richard Ring at Trinity College, Hartford, CT; the Henry E. Huntington Library, San Marino, CA; the Harry Ransom Center, University of Texas, Austin, TX; the Karl Marx Library, London; the National Archives at Kew; the University of Warwick Library.

Among my friends and colleagues: Nelson Aldrich, Anita Auden, Don Bachardy, Simon Baddeley, Andrea Barzini, Theresa Booth, Keith Botsford, Katherine Bucknell, John Byrne, Joanna Clarke, Harald Clemen, Michele Cone, David Elliot, Jason Epstein, Natasha Fair-weather, Michael Fishwick, Graham C. Greene, Walter Gsottschneider, Stephen Guise, Henry Hardy, Frank-Rutger Hausmann, Selina Hastings, Oliver Herford, Immy Humes, Chantal and John Hunt, Alan Jenkins, Nicholas Jenkins, Michael Jordan, Paul Keegan, Annette Kern-Stähler, Stephen Lushington, Edward Mendelson, Caroline Moorehead, Dominique Nabokov, Ute Oelmann, Peter Parker, Antony Percy, Matthew Pintus, Tristan Platt, Sarah Plimpton, Bill Price, Robin Ramsay, Vicky Randall, Tom Rivers, Georgie Rowse, Giovanni Russo, Stephen Schlesinger, Giles Scott-Smith, Bob Silvers, James Smith, Jane Spender, Rachel Spender, Julian Stern, Frances Stonor Saunders, John Sutherland, Martino Tomei, Jason Toynbee, Polly Toynbee, Ed Victor, Roman Vlad, Jennifer Josselson Vorbach, Willi Vossenkuhl, Hugh Wilford and Zinovy Zinik.

With special thanks to the late Reynolds Price, with whom, after a gap of forty years, I took up the thread of a conversation as if it had never been interrupted. To my sister Lizzie, who waived her copyright to our parents' writings. To my cousin Philip Spender, who gave me several details I would otherwise have missed. Finally to Lara Feigel, Nico Mann, David Plante and our daughter Saskia, who read drafts of this book and gave excellent advice. And to Jonathan Galassi and Christopher Richards, my editors in New York; and Martin Redfern and Peter James, my editors in London.

NOTE

When quoting from letters or diary entries, I have retained the errors of spelling and punctuation. Some errors are mere laziness, such as 'wont' for 'won't', but others are indicative of the writer's state of mind.

A HOUSE IN ST JOHN'S WOOD

NATASHA'S LAST WISHES

My MOTHER DIED on 21 October 2010, at eleven in the morning, in her bedroom on the top floor of 15 Loudoun Road, the rented house in St John's Wood where she'd lived for the previous sixty-nine years. I heard the news on my cellphone driving along a back road in Tuscany. I rushed home, collected my passport and flew to London, where I arrived at about seven in the evening.

The house had been neglected since my father's death in 1995. A large crack ran down the external wall to the right of the front door. Squirrels nested in the roof next to the water-tank, and they'd reopen their hole every time we patched it up. I'd offered to make major repairs on condition that I'd be reimbursed after her death, but the lawyer told me, 'It won't happen. Buy her an umbrella.'

Downstairs in my father's study, my mother's attempt to organize his papers had replaced the creative untidiness of work in progress with the sepulchral untidiness of boxes ready to be taken to an archive. In the music room her Steinway was shrouded and the scores were shelved. In her last years she'd actually forgotten how to play. The back door from the kitchen to the garden, squeezed by subsidence, had been planed so many times to make it fit the frame that it was no longer a rectangle. The house was a tomb long before her death added an aura of absence to the surreptitious creak of decay.

Her live-in minder had packed a rucksack and was waiting with her boyfriend in the hall. As I kissed her cheek, I smelled the excitement of a witness who'd seen someone die. I wondered if the experience was as thrilling as observing a birth.

My wife was waiting for me in the piano room. We phoned for the undertaker. Then I went upstairs to say my goodbyes. I took a sketch-pad with me to make some drawings of my mother as she lay there. I'd done the same with my father and it had been a fascinating experience, but this time it didn't work. The drawings came out angrier and angrier. Was this my feeling, or hers? She herself just looked exhausted. The anger was in the drawings.

By her bedside lamp lay a curl of papers. In a desultory way I straightened them out. They were documents designed to exclude me from my father's literary inheritance. A covering letter showed that she'd arranged to sign these in front of the lawyer a few days later.

She'd been talking about this for years and I'd always told her she should do whatever she thought best. Would she or wouldn't she? There was an element of sadism in my detachment. In the background lay a battlefield. She knew I disagreed with her interpretation of my father's life. To her, he'd always been a pillar of integrity, and anyone who questioned this was despicable. I agreed about his integrity, but everything else about my father's life made me want to qualify her pure idea of him with the confusion of reality.

I'd always expected her to change her mind about cutting me off, but here we were. Dutifully, I took the documents to the lawyer the following day. Were we obliged to honour her wishes? The lawyer flipped through the papers and asked, 'Where's the signature?' I said that she'd planned to sign them in his presence – let's see – tomorrow afternoon. 'A lot of old ladies leave things just a bit too late,' he said. And casually he dropped them in the trash.

All other aspects of her Will were fine. She'd left everything to my sister Lizzie and myself. She hadn't created a foundation dedicated to protecting her husband from my interpretation of his life. The lawyer added soothingly that, as we were our parents' sole heirs, the literary executorship was of minor importance. So I calmed down.

It took us ten days to organize the funeral. Lizzie had just flown from London to Sydney and she needed time to recover before she'd fly back.

While I waited, I sat alone in the piano room listening to the shuffling of the masonry. I looked through the boxes next door but they contained nothing that interested me. Then I tried the door of the tiny room downstairs where my father used to store all the papers that he felt he couldn't throw away.

It was still untidy, but no longer the impenetrable chaos it had been during my father's lifetime. The correspondence had been sorted into slim files stored in alphabetical order. Among them I found two packages marked in my mother's handwriting, 'to be destroyed without opening after my death'. One was shut with a strip of Sellotape. The other had also been shut, but somebody had sliced it open. I took them upstairs to the piano room. After an hour of dithering, I began to read the contents of the open file. They were letters from Raymond Chandler to Mum. After reading two or three, I realized they were passionate love letters.

I rang the lawyer and asked if we had to obey her wishes. 'No,' he said. 'She had the right to destroy her property, you don't. You could, but if I were you I wouldn't.'

Raymond Chandler's supposed passion for my mother had become one of the great 'causes' of her old age. A biographer had come across some evidence in Chandler's archive and he believed that an affair had actually taken place. My mother went wild. Friends were asked to intervene. She who was so frugal spent hundreds of pounds on solicitors. In the end, the biographer gave in and the evidence was written up as a fantasy, but the letters I was reading in the piano room showed that their friendship hadn't been quite as limpid as she'd always maintained.

While my mother was alive, I'd accepted her assertion that she was in charge of the past. She was the keeper of the flame, my father's life belonged to her. She was obsessed by the thought that bad books would be written about Dad and lurk on library shelves waiting to ambush the innocent reader. Now, all those neat files would enter an archive. Wasn't it my duty to present my parents' lives in the best possible light, before hostile biographers started plundering them?

That's what I thought, but a month after I'd started writing, my mother came to me in a dream. She was furious. 'What makes you think you can write a book about us? For instance, what do you know about —' and here she mentioned someone I'd never heard of. I mumbled an answer. 'There you are,' she said triumphantly. I explained hesitantly that if a book is well written, whether or not it's the actual truth, it acquires a truth of its own.

In the background, my father sniggered. She asked, 'And what are *you* laughing at?' 'Well,' he murmured apologetically, 'it only goes to show what he thinks of literature.' I said that they were both dead, so they couldn't be offended. The dead have no feelings, I said. My father stopped laughing and I woke up.

I lay there thinking how curious it was that they should behave in character, even in a dream. When they were alive, if my mother was determined about something, my father always backed down. But I wasn't sure I understood what he meant about my thoughts on literature.

My father thought that literature should tell the truth. His poems were always built upon specific moments when life had been revealed to him in all its simplicity and nakedness. The poem had to bear witness to that vision and transcend the mere sentences of which it was made. The idea of truth was very important to him. In politics, which occupied a great deal of my father's attention, 'the truth' meant one must never tell lies in the name of a higher cause, or sacrifice the rights of an individual in the name of the collective good.

These truths are complicated. Both, I think, involve ideas about England. But since I left England forty-five years ago, and since I refused to discuss any aspect of my parents' lives with them while they were alive, what chance do I have of chasing the truth now?

At this point a memory comes back to me of my father's study while he lived: the books and articles finished at the last possible minute, stuck together with tape and paperclips. The galley proofs, the glossy sparkle of the published version. To write a book is to embark on a quest, and if in this instance I've made mine more difficult, so much the better.

I

A WORLDLY FAILURE

IT WAS W. H. Auden who taught me about adjectives. He stayed with us whenever he came to England. I was nine years old. Scene: 15 Loudoun Road, my parents' house in St John's Wood, eight-thirty in the morning. I was late for school. Wystan, with an air of having already been up for hours, was smoking at the breakfast table, bored or thoughtful, looking out of the window at the tangled ferns of the basement area. Mum and Dad were still in bed, in their bedroom with a large dressing-table on which lurked strange hairbrushes sold recently to Dad by a sadistic hairdresser who had persuaded him he was losing his hair.

I was in a panic over a test due that morning on what an adjective was.

Wystan looked surprised.

'An adjective is any word that qualifies a noun,' he said.

'I know how to say that,' I said. 'But I don't understand what it means.'

He looked around the table, discarded the cereals and found among the debris of the night before a bottle of wine. One object more memorable than the others.

'Ah . . . you could say, the *good* wine,' he said firmly. 'Its goodness *qualifies* the wine.' Then he thought for a moment, peering at the bottle. 'The wine *was* good,' he said, correcting himself; and added in a tragic voice, 'now all we have left is an *empty* bottle.'

That summer, my sister and I had been abandoned on an island off the coast of Wales. I'd liked it. Lots of puffins, a few cormorants and numerous placid sheep. On top of the hill in the middle of this island were three grass tombs of long-dead Vikings, and Bardsey Island had left me with an obsession with barrow-wights and the sinister mystery of Norse ghost stories. Hearing about this later that year, Wystan sent me from New York the Tolkien trilogy, *The Lord of the Rings*. I read it straight through.

Auden used to say that he knew where every detail of this trilogy came from and one day he'd write about it. Dad tried it once but he found Tolkien tremendously boring.

Once, Wystan and I wrote Tolkienish poems together, still over breakfast but a few years after the adjectives. I collected them and copied them into a notebook that I decorated with a heraldic crest 'with whiskers', as that kind of shading was called at school. Here are a couple of verses:

> God knows what kings and lords,
> Had their realms on these downs of chalk,
> And now guard their bountiful hoards,
> One night you may see them walk.

> They walk with creaks and groans
> Cloaks fluttering as they go by,
> They ride on enormous roans
> Which block out the stars and the sky.

Lines two and four of each verse are Auden's. 'Can I use them?' 'Of course.' I got the impression that words could be seized out of the air and given generously from one person to another.

My frequent readings of *The Lord of the Rings* always featured Wystan in there somewhere. The kind but didactic Wizard. In this earliest phase of knowing Wystan I intuitively grasped his own self-image as a young man, which was that of 'Uncle Wiz', an eccentric Victorian vicar with a bee in his bonnet about the Apocrypha. He didn't want to be taken seriously every inch of the way. He liked to pontificate, but he also wanted be teased about it in return. It was part of his longing for universal love, a very strong need he had.

Wystan knew a great deal about our family. There's a story of him running round and round the aspidistra at our house in Hampstead when he was a little boy. He was my uncle Michael's friend at Gresham's, Holt, the school they both attended. They were two years older than Stephen, who only met Wystan when they were under-graduates at Oxford.

At Gresham's, Michael and Wystan had sat through a memorable occasion when Harold Spender came down to give the boys a pep talk. My grandfather read the parable of the Prodigal Son, and when he came to the words, 'But when he was yet a great way off, his father saw him, and had compassion, and ran, and fell on his neck, and kissed him,' Harold looked lovingly at his son Michael, perched at the keyboard of the organ in full view. I think Wystan must have remembered this story because, without intending to, Harold had for a moment become 'camp'. Anyway, it was Wystan's story. My father was at the under-school of Gresham's at the time so he did not witness this memorable scene.

Having thus embarrassed his eldest son, my grandfather continued with a stirring sermon along the lines of 'On, and always on!' (It's the title of the last chapter of his autobiography.) There was a boy-scout element to Harold and he wanted to inspire these youngsters with manliness. But it did not go down well. It was just after the First World War during which many former pupils had lost their lives. Their names glowed freshly on the oak panels behind him.

'You killed him, my dear,' said Wystan over supper at Loudoun Road, around the time when we wrote the Tolkien poems together. And when Dad started laughing, he said firmly, 'You killed him by ignoring him.' Dad stopped laughing and looked annoyed. He'd never believed Auden's theory that sickness, or even death, comes from damage to the psyche: that heart disease comes from an inability to love, that cancer comes from 'foiled creative fire'. He called this aspect of Auden's imagination 'medieval'. In this case Wystan – smiling at Dad with benign condescension – was saying that the young Spender boys had killed their father with snubs.

I don't know why my father had such difficulties with his parents, but it might have had something to do with the anger of young people towards the older generation, which they held collectively responsible for the disaster of the First World War. How could anyone believe in the world of 'clean thoughts in clean bodies' after that? Stephen hated his father. He thought he was a failure. He was only seventeen years old when Harold died, so his relationship was frozen in an adolescent image where Harold was the hieratic statue that had to be toppled from its pedestal. If 'killing the father' is an essential part of growing up, Stephen did his early.

It was easy to mock this man who could never earn enough money to keep his family going and who yearned for unattainable positions of power. But the bitterness with which Stephen writes in his novels and his poems about 'failure' meant that, at some level, he subscribed to Harold's romantic notion of life as a series of peaks, of challenges, of high aspirations and magnificent achievements. 'Failure' was Stephen's way of defeating his father, but it also kept alive Harold's scale of values.

When Stephen was twelve, Harold stood as a Liberal candidate in a general election. My father remembered being hauled around Bath in a pony-carriage with his two brothers, each with a placard round his neck saying 'Vote for Daddy'. Harold lost, and the effect on Michael and Stephen was traumatic. Michael said: 'When they are very young, the children of a public man worship their father for being famous – a kind of god: but it's extraordinary how soon they get to realize it if he's a public failure.' Michael developed a stammer. He decided that his father was 'inefficient', which in his eyes was the worst thing a man could be. Stephen, instead, just couldn't stop crying. It confirmed his suspicion that his father was a windbag whose exhortations of 'on and ever on' were meaningless.

Harold Spender's wife, my grandmother Violet Schuster, came from a successful Jewish family that had emigrated from Germany to England in the 1860s. At the time of their marriage, the Schusters established a trust for Violet and her children – a long document camouflaging the fact that Harold wasn't allowed to touch it.

Violet was a delicate woman who gave birth to four children in four years, one after the other. She died in 1922, at home, on the kitchen table, after an operation to remedy complications deriving from a hysterectomy. For years she'd struggled with a condition that could not be named. Her death was a great shock. Until then she had been able to run the house (peremptorily) and accompany her husband on his frequent trips to Europe and America.

My father's dominant memory of her was of her complaints. Too much noise was coming from the children's room; they'd given her a headache. Because the details of her state of health were never discussed, he probably assumed that his mother was more neurotic than was the case. 'Hysteria', in Aristotelian terms, means blood boiling in the womb, and I'm sure that my father's incapacity, indeed terror, of anything resembling a woman's lack of control over her body stemmed from an unhealed memory of his mother's sufferings.

They all spent a fortnight in the Lake District during the First World War. Violet was in a bad state because of the death of her much loved brother in the trenches. The war was present even in this beautiful place. She noticed that Keswick had been emptied of its men, leaving behind only those who were working on the farms. She saw several Scottish soldiers on the train drinking desperately at the thought of having to go back to the front. 'A thin matchboarding separates us all from some terrible thing dimly known.'

In spite of her dark state of mind, they enjoyed this moment of escape. It was one of the few times when they were together as a family. Stephen chased butterflies, Humphrey collected crystals that glittered on the paths leading up into the hills behind the farm. When it rained, slugs sailed down the paths like barges on the Thames. Michael bonded with Harold and learned how to row a skiff on Derwent Water. Harold also taught Michael about climbing, and gradually they formed a team from which the others were excluded. Harold was a great climber. His guide to the Pyrenees is still read. There's even a recent translation into Catalan.

For the rest of his life, Stephen wrote and rewrote his memories of Skelgill Farm. A key moment took place when he overheard Harold reading Wordsworth's *Prelude* to Violet as they rested in deckchairs looking at the sunset. They were in deepest Wordsworth country; it was a predictable book to choose. Stephen, aged eight, understood 'Wordsworth' or 'Worldsworth' to have something to do with his father's metaphorical symbolism: the world was a word, and the word had worth – was valuable.

Stephen asked his mother why Wordsworth was a poet, and what a poet was. She said:

Wordsworth was a man who, when he was a child, ran through the countryside and felt himself to be a living part of it, as though the mountains were his mother, his own body before he was born. And when, in later life, while he was still young, he came back from many journeys to the lakes, he felt all those memories, which were one with the scenery, surge through his arms and legs and his whole body on his walks here, and come out through his fingers that held a pen, as words that were his poems.

After Violet's death in December 1921, Harold went into a decline. The finances of the household were now controlled by his mother-in-law, Hilda Schuster, with whom Stephen formed a conspiratorial relation-ship based on books and trips to the theatre and long conversations of a kind that Harold's self-righteousness precluded. Stephen's hatred of his father could have derived from a subconscious conviction that Harold was responsible for his wife's death, but in the many texts my father left, he stresses only the absurdity of his father's grief. 'I am a broken man,' said Harold over lunch, blinking at his children. 'You are all that your poor old father has left.'

In his autobiography, my father writes: 'it is no exaggeration to say that at the end his unreality terrified me'. In 1940, writing his novel *The Backward Son*, Stephen returned to his father's reaction to his wife's death. Harold's lack of reality has become a caricature. 'He saw what he had never seen – that he was a fool, and that she had a touch of genius. "The divine fire of Parnassus breathed on her," he thought, automatically trying to make this thought unreal.' (Harold published Violet's poems soon after she died, but he never claimed that she was an unrecognized genius.) 'It was she, he now realised, who had saved him; it was she who had made him, in spite of everything – he could grasp it now – a worldly failure. For he knew now that he would never succeed, he would never be in the Cabinet, he would lose his seat in the House, he would be despised.' (In this novel Harold is an MP, a role he never achieved in life.) 'His one saving grace which he could secretly cling to for the rest of his life was his sense of failure.'

'For one translucent instant of purely sincere feeling, he hated the children.' Well, one could reverse this thought. In the upset following his mother's death, one of Harold's sons hated his father.

By the time they caught up with each other at Oxford, Wystan was a young intellectual of astonishing self-assurance and Stephen was a tall clumsy well-meaning puppy who couldn't enter a room without tripping over the carpet. From the moment they met, Wystan treated Stephen like a younger brother, partly because he knew everything about the Spender family. He could see that Stephen's woolly-mindedness was a disguise, a reaction against his elder brother Michael's super-efficiency. In his wilful way, Wystan deduced that Stephen was the opposite of what he seemed. Auden believed that the characteristics his friends presented to the world were shields protecting qualities that were their opposites. Thus Stephen wasn't the hapless weakling that his persona projected. On the contrary, he was as tough as nails.

When they met, Stephen was in love with a young man whom he calls Marston in a series of poems he was writing about him. He'd slip these under the door of Auden's rooms at Christ Church as soon as they were fit to be read. My father at that time gave his poems to anyone who showed an interest, and he'd already acquired a reputation by the end of his first year at Oxford.

One day in 1929, a few days after he'd left with Auden a new poem and a diary entry about walking along the banks of the River Wye with Marston, Stephen received back a short note in Auden's almost illegible minuscule. 'Have read your diary & poems. Am just recovering from the dizzy shock. Come out all day Thursday. Shall order a hamper of cold lunch.'

On the Thursday, they set off by bus from Oxford in the direction of the Berkshire Downs. The bus let them off in the countryside. They clambered through a hedge, hopped over a little ditch and climbed to the top of the nearest hill. They ate egg sandwiches and cold roast chicken and drank a bottle of wine, looking out towards the West Country, which Stephen loved.

Auden said that the great strength of Stephen's writing was his capacity to describe whatever happened to him 'as though it had never happened to anyone before'. It was this quality that had made him dizzy. 'When you create your experience you are excellent. When you attempt to describe or draw attention to your feelings you are rotten.' He quoted from memory two lines from one of the Marston poems. 'Taking your wrists and feeling your lips warm', he said, was excellent. But 'Let us break our hearts not casually, but on a stated day', was bad, because the reader couldn't believe that the writer's heart was indeed breaking. On the contrary, it was clear from the poem that the writer was enjoying himself.

Auden said he was jealous of the Marston poems, but he added a word of caution: 'I console myself by thinking that you are hopelessly literal-minded. Actuality obsesses you so much that you will never be able to free yourself and create a work of pure imagination.'

For the first time, Stephen had been given a new idea about how he could use the material that the world threw at him.

> Until now, writing for him had been a kind of lottery. If he was emotionally stirred he wrote down the first words that came into his mind, clinging the while precariously to rhyme and form as a rider clings to a horse which is running away from him: then he hoped one day that such 'inspiration' and shots in the dark would produce a successful poem. What had happened now was that an experience had brought him in touch with more than an emotion – with a subject matter capable of crystallization in words.

To be a poet was not the same thing, he now understood, as writing good poems one after the other. There had to be a field of experience out there, a known territory, a vision. Violet had bound Wordsworth to a specific piece of land. Auden mapped out for Stephen poetry as a continent.

During that summer vacation, Stephen bought a little printing press, and in the basement of the family house in Hampstead he set up a group of Auden's poems. These were the first poems of Auden's to appear in print, a booklet of 'About 45 copies', as the title page casually puts it.

Auden visited the Spender household while this was going on. He asked to be included in the domestic arrangements; meaning a cup of tea for him too, please, whenever the servants made theirs (which was eight times a day).

Wystan told Stephen's governess – she'd become an important figure in the orphaned phase of his childhood – that Stephen's 'innocence' was, of course, the exact opposite of what it pretended to be. Stephen projected an image of himself as someone who was timid, considerate, over-generous and unsure. This was a result of his refusal to accept himself as he really was: ruthless, selfish and domineering. His generosity was purposefully asphyxiating. He forced people to reject him, so as to avoid the guilt he'd feel if he rejected them. He wrote self-confessional letters to his friends, apparently throwing the whole of his life at the recipient's head, in order to disguise the fact that he always kept something back. His love for Marston was 'symptomatic'. Marston had been chosen as a love object because he was untouchable, which of course meant that Stephen himself did not want to be touched.

Stephen's supposed capacity to be humiliated was a sham. Only love involved humiliation, and Stephen was not prepared to love anyone. 'One can't be physically intimate without revealing oneself as one really is.' In place of intimacy, Stephen cultivated an exaggerated view of his friends. Auden himself was 'the Sage'. To turn friends into myths was a way of not communicating with them. 'One does not reveal one's worse nature to a hero.'

One afternoon during this printing-press phase of their friendship, they went out for a walk on Hampstead Heath. There, Wystan learned that Stephen had no money problems, because he enjoyed an allowance of three hundred pounds a year. What! And yet he complained about being unhappy? Nobody, said Wystan dogmatically, had the right to be unhappy on three hundred pounds a year. He himself would kill for half that amount! In fact, would Stephen consider splitting it? (I can imagine my father laughing politely and changing the subject.)

'Are you a Verger?' Wystan asked Stephen abruptly. Stephen said he didn't understand the question. 'Are you a Virgin?' Stephen gave a vague reply. 'Well, presumably you must know whether you are or you aren't,' said Wystan. This particular problem was solved soon afterwards. And when Stephen put up some resistance, Wystan told him briskly, 'Now, dear, don't make a fuss.'

2

WITHOUT GUILT

As I SEE it, Auden's extraordinary matter-of-factness about sex liberated my father, but it was also a challenge. Stephen saw that the guilt that had been drummed into him as a well-brought-up schoolboy could simply be dropped. But if love was to be elevated into an acceptable or even a central part of his life, then with whom and on what terms? This Wystan couldn't answer – though he said that Marston wasn't the one. And pragmatic though he may have been in many ways, Auden himself did not solve this problem for a very long time. Christopher found Heinz, Stephen found Tony, but Wystan did not manage to create a permanent love until he found Chester in New York during the Second World War. In 1928, the war was not even remotely visible.

Auden, Isherwood, Spender: these were the three young writers who 'ganged up and captured the decade', as Evelyn Waugh put it years later in a grumpy mood. There's an element of truth in saying that they shared a programme, but as their writings are so different from each other's, it's hard to say if this involved life choices, or how life fits into art, or a desire to challenge conventional England, or a need to resist Fascism, or a mixture of all of these.

Auden left England in the early summer of 1928 as soon as he'd graduated. First, he found rooms in a quiet suburb of Berlin, but at the beginning of the following year he moved to the centre of town and began to lead a more adventurous life. He kept an interesting diary, which seems to follow a programme involving the relationship between love and sex. He sought adventures with the boys of the Adonis Bar and other *Lokalen*, with their wide assortment of different talents, and he kept his reactions under observation.

After numerous trials, Auden fell passionately in love with a sailor called Gerhart Meyer, 'from the sea / The truly strong man', as he appears in one of Auden's early poems. Gerhart's thing was to fuck a prostitute in Wystan's presence, and Wystan went along with this, even though the intention was clearly to make him jealous. With detachment Auden writes in his diary: 'What is odd is that when he could have any woman he liked from the Queen of England upwards, he chooses whores and not the prettiest either.' Auden does not want to feel jealous, so he tries to define jealousy to see if he fits into its parameters. 'Jealousy is of two kinds, the fear that I don't exist, and the fear that he or she doesn't exist.' Usually, writes Auden, he's not jealous – for the simple reason that he's so sure of himself he can never feel he isn't there. Therefore Gerhart, or category two, must be the case. Indeed, 'He seems to belong to another world and might go up in smoke any moment.'

This diary, which has never been published, shows how difficult it was for Auden to perceive reality. The right-hand page is for experience summarized as objectively and truthfully as possible. The left-hand page is for abstraction. In a letter written to my father at the beginning of the war, Wystan said that he needed a great deal of abstraction, in the shape of rules and theories, before he understood what he felt. 'My dominant faculties are intellect and intuition, my weak ones feeling and sensation . . . I must have knowledge and a great deal of it before I feel anything.'

Gerhart may have been a 'truly strong' man, but some of the boys of the Adonis Bar dressed up as sailors, took their lovers to Hamburg on the grounds that they were about to set sail, fleeced them for farewell gifts and then secretly took the train back to Berlin. From Auden's diary, it looks as if Gerhart was one of these – for in Hamburg, he suddenly vanished.

In another mood – this is also typical of Auden – he totted up the expense. He was missing his dressing-gown and a pistol, and he'd spent too much money on Gerhart's shoes. Not too bad, considering. But he became depressed. He took a day trip out of Berlin to look at the countryside. Observing the beautiful indigo sky behind the steel works as he came back, he thought: 'Country on a fine day always makes me feel Why do I bother about people. They are insignificant. But country is not enough.'

Auden's 1929 diary is one of the rare occasions where one can guess how his strange and exceptionally intelligent mind worked. Love, and sex, and writing, must surely be connected – but how? My father thought that they could be welded together into one gift, but he found by experience that although an adventure opened up new possibilities for his writing, the long-term prospect of love got in the way.

In the long vac of 1929, Stephen also went to Germany, but he stayed in Hamburg rather than Berlin. He also had a plan. 'I have always regarded my body as sinful, and my own physical being as something to be ashamed of and to be overcome by compensating and atoning spiritual qualities. Now I am beginning to feel that I may soon come to regard my body as a source of joy.'

At a party filled with beautiful uninhibited young people, he overheard the word *unschuldig*, and he assumed they were referring to him. It means 'without guilt'. Stephen latched on to this word as a talisman that would guide him through all his future explorations of love. Whatever he did with his body, it would be 'without guilt'. My father often talked to me about the German concept of the 'guiltless fool', with reference to *Parsifal*, for example. The guilt that had been drummed into him by his education was to be kept at bay with this word. It was his shield, his banner, his credo.

In Hamburg he went through one unsatisfactory night of love with his host, a rich and cultured young German who 'collected' writers. Stephen wrote about it in his diary, which he tried to turn into a novel as soon as he got back to Oxford. This was *The Temple*, the homosexual coming-of-age novel that failed to find a publisher for nearly sixty years.

By Stephen's own account, *The Temple* went through five major drafts over the next three years. It took time away from writing poetry and it delayed the publication of his first collection of poems with Faber for at least a year. At one point the heroine of *The Temple* was a girl called Caroline, but this proved impossible and the book returned to the viewpoint of a first-person narrator. Stephen's problem was that he couldn't get away from what had happened; and novels surely need to be pushed beyond a disguised version of real events. Auden had been aware of this drawback in Stephen's writing from the moment they'd discussed it on that famous picnic.

The Temple was Stephen's third attempt to write a novel. The first, 'Instead of Death', was a thinly disguised account of his first year in Oxford, including his meeting with Auden, who seems to have had a role in the book as a 'Lord of Death'. Louis MacNeice read this text, which has not survived. He thought the portrait of Auden was bad, but it was 'an exquisite example of Stephen's lust to mythologise the world in which he walked'. MacNeice told Stephen bluntly that he didn't recognize his Oxford. 'Oh that does not matter,' Stephen said, 'I am thinking of transposing the whole scene to a lunatic asylum.'

Stephen sent 'Escaped', his second novel, to Christopher Isherwood for criticism. He'd met Christopher in Auden's room in a scene that has been described so many times it's not worth mentioning, except to say that everyone behaved in character. Stephen was bumbling and enthusiastic, Christopher was clipped and professional. Christopher read 'Escaped' and responded with a tough letter. He'd seen some of the sections before as independent pieces, he wrote, and he'd liked them. But they did not add up to a novel and the last section was 'complete trash'. Stephen's narrator was mad, and Stephen himself was anything but that. Madmen were boring, wrote Christopher, because they had no connection with reality. The material was too close to the author. 'You are right down in the scrum with your characters, not up in the grand-stand.' He must learn the craft of writing. A novel had to add up to more than a paraphrase of real events.

Stephen was not offended. He took for granted that Christopher was the Master. In 1930, after Stephen had left Oxford (without having obtained a degree), he joined Christopher in Berlin and set about rewriting *The Temple*. Their relationship – Isherwood makes it clear in *Christopher and His Kind* – was that of 'teacher and pupil'. In their later reminiscences, both writers tinged these roles with irony. Stephen took Christopher's letters as if they'd been red-hot bulletins from a front where literature was being deployed like guns. Isherwood emphasized the huge difference in their relative heights, so the taller pupil would have to bend down to hear whatever words of wisdom the Master might be whispering. But the underlying fact remains: Spender needed to learn from Isherwood. This made him more patient, respectful, even deferential towards Isherwood than he ever was towards Auden. He even followed Isherwood's diet of lung soup and toffee, with dreadful results for his teeth.

Stephen saw that Christopher never paraphrased real events. He did something more mysterious: he made events happen. 'Christopher, so far from being the self-effacing spectator he depicts in his novels, was really the centre of his characters, and neither could they exist without him nor he without them.' Isherwood lived in a nimbus of his own fiction, like an illustration in a Victorian magazine showing Dickens at a table with Mr Pickwick and Mrs Haversham floating in the air above him; only in Christopher's case his characters were real people walking about in the same room as himself.

In the early phase of Isherwood's years in Berlin, he wrote about England. It was painful for him, because he had a profound hatred for that country, which he imagined to be populated by The Enemy – his word for the restrictions of convention.

On one occasion soon after they'd met, Stephen told him a funny story about a recent clash in Oxford between himself and the academics, the patronizing Wykehamists, the future Foreign Office mandarins. Christopher responded violently. He'd like to take all those beautiful places, like Venice or Oxford or Cambridge, and blow them up with dynamite. Not because they were ugly. On the contrary, they were beautiful. But on top of that beauty The Enemy had constructed good taste, appreciation, weighing things judiciously and ending up with nothing. 'The whole system was to him one which denied affection and which was based largely on fear of sex.'

It was a question of Them against Us. Real feelings were accessible only to the few, said Christopher. 'The poets, the creative writers, the healers, and a few simple people, workers who express themselves in their work, women who have been truly loved, saints and sensualists – are the lords of life. Everyone else is a slave, and the Happy Few who have really lived their experiences and made them a part of themselves, and who don't just discuss things and reason about them, know it.' The slaves could destroy the Happy Few. They could ruin your life, they could 'hem you in with rules and inhibitions which you almost persuade yourself to accept as necessary'. Stephen mustn't fall for it. He mustn't allow the formality of Englishness to smother his emotional life. 'In England, chastity is a puritan myth. It's a huge conspiracy to pretend that a whole side of human nature in ourselves and others doesn't exist.'

Stephen took what he wanted from this diatribe, but neither then nor later did he want to lose contact with England. Nor was he prepared to abandon art galleries and concert halls merely because The Enemy might form part of the audience. Christopher says of himself: 'He had grown to hate the gushings of concert audiences and the holy atmosphere of concerts.' This wasn't true of Stephen, who heard all the great pre-war musicians in Berlin or Salzburg, where he went for a fortnight every summer with Isaiah Berlin, whom he'd also met at Oxford. Isaiah at this point in his life was hesitating about a career as an academic, and he admired the courage with which Stephen threw himself into amorous adventures; and also, a little later, into predicaments that had sombre political implications.

During his earlier visit to Hamburg, Stephen had made friends with the German scholar Ernst Robert Curtius. Plump, cordial, slightly pompous but also affectionate, this man held the keys to German literature, which Stephen had never studied at school. It was also flattering that Curtius admired Stephen as a writer. 'It is a wonderful thing to meet a young poet, gifted as you are; a child of the sun,' wrote Curtius soon after they'd met. 'It has been an unlooked-for revelation.' He was sure that Stephen's energy would last, unlike that of most young talent. 'You have got power – "to run a factory on" – and purity (a purity of a new, much wanted kind). Both these things show in your verse as well as in your person.' The letter is serious in a very German way, as if their relationship existed beyond their individual participation in it.

The 'purity' of which he speaks took into consideration the adventurous life that Stephen had begun to lead in Hamburg. Curtius loved hearing about the bad boys who waited for clients in the bars around the docks of the huge industrial port. Stephen told one story about the experience of being robbed – Christopher later appropriated it in one of his Berlin stories – and Curtius just thought it was amusing. It was neither shocking nor tragic, this scene from the lower depths. It was merely absurd.

Later, thinking about this incident, Stephen tried to understand why he'd found it impossible to think of himself as a victim. Being richer and better educated than the robber, there was a certain Robin Hood justice in being fleeced by him. Even while he was being robbed, Stephen could pity the robber. Stephen's inner world was inviolable. Whatever was stolen, the robber couldn't take away the advantages that society had given him.

This generosity of exploitee to exploiter was a kind of selfishness, Stephen thought, as though the robber's faults were 'projections of my own guilt'. But being feeble about an unfortunate experience could also become a part of his professional equipment. 'Within this inner world even weakness could become a kind of strength. It isolated me and disqualified me from other kinds of work than poetic writing.'

My father's increasing interest in communism from 1931 onwards grew from his fascination with this vast, unfamiliar subculture. He thought that the poor and the underprivileged were in possession of some secret, and he believed without question that communism was on the side of the workers; whereas it was equally obvious that the Nazis were luring the unemployed into vast armies that would be destroyed in a future war. Curtius, who saw this change taking place in Stephen as a result of his life in Berlin, decided that this wasn't really a political revelation, but a form of sentimentality based on the attraction of the working classes.

It was after a visit to Curtius in November 1931 that Stephen wrote his most famous poem, 'I think continually of those who were truly great'. Its heroes were the great writers of German Romanticism that Curtius had so brilliantly brought before him. Stephen sent Curtius the poem as soon as it was finished, and Curtius placed it in the context of Stephen's recent enthusiasm for the workers. It was his best poem so far. It was 'both particular and grand', he wrote. It suited him much better than *Bolschewismus*. He was sure that, with his temperament of a poet and with his sensitivity towards beauty, Stephen would soon see through communism, in the same way that Whitman had seen through American democracy. 'Your politics are guided by your sense of eroticism and aesthetics.'

In Hamburg and later in Berlin, Stephen fell in love with various boys with whom, throwing caution to the winds, he attempted to create a long-lasting relationship. Being in love heightened his sensitivity to his surroundings, and from that mood his poems could spring. But he was also interested in creating a permanent relationship.

One of the first of these was Harry Giese, a pleasant somewhat dumpy young man (there's a photo in the Isaiah Berlin Archive in Oxford), and the only reason why they were together was that Harry had asked Stephen to take him away to the countryside, where he thought he could be happier. 'He has introduced Order into my life,' wrote Stephen to Isaiah. Harry managed their money (and was more frugal than Stephen), and their days were now blest with 'Regular Hours'. They met every day for lunch at a quarter to one, and after lunch they played a game of chess. 'The difficulty with him is that he won't ever leave me alone, and that bores me awfully.' He couldn't stand Harry's 'aura of respectability'. 'I imagined it would be very exciting to have a boy always, but, as a matter of fact, it is very bourgeois and ordinary.'

They planned to go off to the mountains for a while, 'to see if he is better when he has work'. And that was another problem. The boys who haunted the bars of Berlin waiting for an admirer were longing to be saved, but once this had happened, what next? No question of them spending the day indoors reading a book. In Munich, when Stephen went to the Alte Pinakothek to look at paintings, Harry refused to join him. He went window-shopping instead. 'He is bored in a rather hopeless kind of way, as boys from town often are.'

Harry Giese was mundane; but Stephen always hoped that one day a working-class crim would produce a poem from his pocket, 'magical with the mystery of the lights and silver balls of amusement arcades, or smouldering with the passion which chooses a different bed-mate from the pavements every night'.

After Harry, there was a seventeen-year-old Russian stateless boy whom Stephen calls in his letters Georg 101. I have no idea what the 101 stands for, but Georg might have been connected with the school for workers in the Karl-Marx suburb of Berlin where my father taught English for a while.

In 1932 there was a more serious adventure, though it sprang from a ridiculous beginning.

At this point Stephen had been living in Berlin for several months every year next door to Christopher, who was immersed in the material that later became his Berlin stories. But Stephen also kept his presence alive in London, which he visited frequently. Christopher, on one of his rare trips back to England, found that Stephen had been dining out on their Berlin adventures. He panicked. His material was being appropriated. He solemnly told Stephen that Berlin was no longer large enough to accommodate the two of them and their friendship was at an end. Instead of telling Christopher, Don't be silly, my father was so upset that he ran off to Barcelona to save a German boy who was miserable. They'd never met. Someone at a party in London told Stephen he should go, so off he went.

The boy in question, Hellmut Schroeder, turned out to be a narcissistic former waiter from one of the main hotels in Berlin. He was convinced that he'd been victimized by all the people who'd befriended him. 'It's as though all those crowds of people in the square here, and in Berlin, and in the hotels where I have waited, had slimed across me, leaving their tracks like snails.' The name 'Hellmut' means 'Light-strength', but in letters written back to Christopher in Berlin, Stephen said he should really be called 'Dunkelmut', or 'Dark-strength', such was the boy's melancholia. He'd even become unhappy if Stephen told him he was looking happier today than yesterday.

'I think that all he needs is to be liked,' Stephen wrote to Virginia Woolf, 'so as I like him extremely I shall stay here.' He preferred the days that were 'domestic'. Hellmut became gradually less sulky, indeed he attempted to respond to Stephen's kindness. They began vaguely looking for somewhere to live. House-hunting reassured Hellmut, because it suggested permanence. Yet there was something odd about Stephen's affection, something that Hellmut felt he had to challenge. 'We were very affectionate all of yesterday. Yet H. questioned me again, because he is always anxious to prove that I am fond of him, but that my fondness is unlike that of the hundreds of people who have been physically attracted to him.'

Stephen gradually became aware that, in spite of his efforts, he could not become close to Hellmut. He blamed himself. In a rare passage of analysis in his diary, he gives way to self-loathing. 'I have the stupidity & the intelligence, the openness & the tiresome subtlety of the educated savage.' There's a lot of Englishness packed into that one sentence, or at least the Englishness of a certain class and education of the time: 'The central regret of the person who is intellectual

& who realizes that intellectualism has no absolute moral worth is that he is dependent for this realization on his intellect. Therefore he wishes to prostrate himself to a class of people who are unintellectual.'

My father thought that the working class possessed a secret which had been eradicated from the bourgeoisie by education. The working class, having been exploited for the benefit of the bourgeoisie ever since the Industrial Revolution, had managed to keep alive their feelings. Their lack of sexual inhibition was a gift; and sex was the highest form of communication between people. Sex stood at the core of universal brotherhood. Though at an intellectual level he would acknowledge that women also faced the challenge of bringing their sexuality into line with other forms of freedom, to him the sexuality of men was more romantic, more moving. The breadlines consisted of queues of men; women were hardly visible.

In Barcelona, they tried to create a social life. Then Hellmut began to have affairs with other men. At first Stephen was upset, then he was merely bored. He realized he'd been stupid to think he could save him. 'Hellmut is a nice person, very hysterical, beautiful, uninteresting, sensation-mongering, and second-rate who has the incredibly petit-bourgeois mentality of most German homosexuals.' Stephen thought that Hellmut was jealous of him, 'because I am not completely petty and because I live very happily in a world that he cannot reach'.

Enter unexpectedly an alcoholic American writer called Kirk, sent by a friend of Isherwood's in Berlin. Where Hellmut was difficult, Kirk was impossible. What's more, they were jealous of each other. 'Hellmut is a homosexual of the "major unknown authors of our time" type, so that the arrival of Kirk led to all sorts of absurd dramas being performed.' Somehow the story fumbled its way to a conclusion without any casualties. Kirk eventually went off to Ibiza and Stephen sent Hellmut back to Berlin.

Because it dealt with homosexual acts, it was inevitable that Stephen's brave novel *The Temple* would be turned down. On one of these occasions – and there were many – Stephen wrote a revealing letter to his grandmother, who'd become involved in trying to place the book: 'To me the book has the significance of a vow that I made to my friends. I promised them that I would write absolutely directly about certain things, and I think it is right that I should fulfil my promise. I am writing and working and living for my own generation and, in that sense, being modern is a religion with me.' The conventional life of the 1850s was dead, he wrote. 'As regards sexual abnormality, I don't think that, or any other of the startling symptoms of contemporary society that so shock the English reader, are nearly so important as people imagine. My feeling is that if one loves one's fellow-beings, one cant be so very abnormal.'

He's hinting, I think, that *The Temple* was in some way connected to the stories that Isherwood was writing at the time. If the comparison is worth making, then his novel is more explicit, perhaps more courageous than the ambiguous and undefined 'Herr Issyvoo' of the Berlin stories. Christopher read several versions of the book but, having once written a ferocious criticism of a novel by Stephen, he kept his comments to himself.

Deep down, my father must have known that *The Temple* would never be published. Quite apart from its sex scenes, it was also libellous. I suspect he sustained himself through five rewrites by the fantasy that one day it would come out, and the book would be denounced to the magistrates and banned, and he himself put on trial for obscenity. At Oxford he'd met Radclyffe Hall, the author of the lesbian novel *The Well of Loneliness*, and he'd invited her to speak to the English Society. She'd replied with a letter of touching bravery describing all her troubles with the magistrates, which were long and costly. Stephen also admired unconditionally D. H. Lawrence, whose *Lady Chatterley's Lover* had also been banned. If he'd ever been arrested, he would have given a passionate speech in support of freedom of expression along the lines of the letter he'd sent to his grandmother.

3

SUICIDE OR ROMANTICISM

IN THE SPRING of 1933, near Piccadilly Circus, a few weeks after
he'd published his first volume of poems with Faber, Stephen met
Tony Hyndman. The book had placed Stephen firmly in the limelight
and critics were beginning to pay attention to a whole new school
of young British poets. He was full of confidence and, in his usual
impetuous way, Stephen immediately invited Tony to come and live
with him. They were together for the next six years; and at some
level they remained attached to each other for the rest of Tony's life.

I take the view that Stephen's desire to live openly with Tony in
the early Thirties was a brave attempt for the time. If the affair failed,
it was because Tony couldn't reach the role that Stephen had imagined for him. Though he was quick and sharp about London literary
gossip, he was unable to become a serious person. The initial attraction of Tony was, of course, the opposite of this. He was down to
earth, humorous, light-hearted. But since he never changed, since
he couldn't learn to love Mozart or Michelangelo (as it were), my
father lost his temper. By the time he ran off to fight in Spain, Tony
had become 'the son whom I attempted to console, but of whom I
was the maddening father'.

I remember Tony from my childhood, when he was not much older
than forty. He spoke with a slight Welsh lilt and was cheerful to look

at, with curly brown hair and a friendly smile. My father employed him in the garden whenever he was desperate for cash, which was often. Tony was full of compliments for my small self but touchy about his relationship with Stephen, which he implied had included a wealth of experience that had nothing to do with Mummy or me. This wasn't clear to me at the age of eight, but by the age of twelve I'd noticed that Tony wasn't a real handyman. He was too knowing.

Years later when he was planning his autobiography, Tony wrote that it must have been fate that had brought them together. 'To me, from the moment I left Hyde Park Corner I was alone. Every step towards the Circus, each pause at a shop window in case some gent might pick me up, all the moments of time, step and pace led me to you.'

They moved into Stephen's small flat in St John's Wood. After less than a fortnight they left England and toured Europe: Paris, Florence, Rome, then northwards to Levanto on the coast between Tuscany and Liguria. There, in a palm-secluded hotel above the sea, they went through their first major confrontation. Tony mentions it twice in his memoirs. 'In Levanto where I wept because suddenly all my resistance went. There was the urge to give, not to take; to protect instead of protection.' And again: 'What happened was inevitable, having got so far. "Will we always be friends" said Stephen one night: I broke down: never given myself to anyone before: it was complete: I wept with relief.'

Stephen remembered this occasion differently. According to him Tony said, 'I want to go away. You are very nice to me, but I feel that I am becoming completely your property. I have never felt like that before with anyone, and I can't bear it.' He probably expected Stephen to beg him to stay, but instead Stephen said he was free to go, if that's what he wanted. They'd meet again in London, perhaps. However, 'by saying this, I had deprived him of any reason for wishing to leave'.

In those days, working-class boys who lived with some 'gent', as Tony put it, assumed identities that had been worked out for them since time immemorial. They learned these roles in the bars and the barracks and the *Lokalen* where boys congregated. Gerhart Meyer, Auden's lover in Berlin, was a 'tough' boy. Harry Giese was the 'reliable ox' who wanted to be cared for. Hellmut Schroeder was a 'broken wing' boy, the misunderstood genius; and Stephen had followed the fantasy as far as it could go, given that Hellmut didn't actually produce anything. These roles formed a protective shell to disguise the fact that the 'boy' was in a subordinate position. It was a matter of pride. That's why, after Tony collapsed in Levanto, he never forgot. He'd revealed once and for all that he was Stephen's dependant. No amount of reassurance from Stephen could eradicate this mistake.

If you have a wide education you don't mind being humiliated, because you have nothing to lose. Everything important is in your head where nothing can get at it – as Stephen had realized when he'd been robbed in Hamburg. Even something as humiliating as scrubbing lavatories in jail won't affect your capacity to think, but if you are aiming to improve your social status, the faintest trace of public humiliation raises questions about rank and respect. Tony's position is therefore, to me, more poignant than Stephen's. And Stephen's generous offer of equality to Tony was self-delusional. It merely underlined the fact that Tony was not Stephen's equal.

Yet there was something in this unexpected confrontation that broke an inhibition in Stephen as well. He was made to realize that he could, after all, communicate with Tony in spite of the difference of class. This had never happened so far. As he wrote to Isaiah: 'When I was first here the very fact that I was with someone whose difference from me I had to accept & recognize made things very painful for me. Because till now I have always had that kind of relationship with people who were tarts or sneaks or liars or something, & all that was required from me was an attitude. This is quite different & was at first less noble and more difficult. However now we are both reaping the fruits.'

Back in London in the early summer of 1933, they tried to create an identity as a couple before their friends came back from their holidays.

Tony looked for a new flat or printed photographs in the kitchen of their rented rooms or did the housework. Stephen wrote to Lincoln Kirstein, the editor of the American magazine *Hound and Horn*, for which he'd contributed some poems and articles: 'I feel more & more happy with Tony & we are much surer of each other than before. Often with him I have a feeling that I have now everything that I've ever wanted out of life & am completely satisfied: I also feel often as if I would like to stop now & not go on.

Tony swimming in Lake Garda in the summer of 1936.

They found a new flat on Randolph Crescent, in Maida Vale. Then Tony went off to Wales to visit his family. 'It's horrid not having you about to kiss every hour while your [you're] tidying the place up,'

Stephen wrote to him. 'But it is lovely to look forward to our life together again.' He loved being with Tony. He wrote to Kirstein, 'He is one of those lucky people who knows he needs love all the time and who can accept it.'

Their existence as a couple was noticed by Virginia Woolf. 'I see being young is hellish. One wants to cut a figure. He [Stephen] is writing about Henry James and has tea alone with Ottoline [Morrell] and is married to a Sergeant in the Guards. They have set up a new quarter in Maida Vale; I propose to call them the Lilies of the Valley. There's William Plomer, with his policeman; then Stephen, then Auden and Joe Ackerly, all lodged in Maida Vale, and wearing different coloured Lilies.' The reference is to Oscar Wilde, who was often depicted holding a lily.

Stephen had met the South African novelist William Plomer while he was still at Oxford. Joe Ackerley went on to become the editor of the *Listener*, where he frequently commissioned articles from his friends. Virginia Woolf was right to detect something conspiratorial in the vision of all these male couples living openly together, but she was amused rather than shocked – though maybe there's an element of snobbery in there somewhere.

As soon as he thought he had a satisfactory draft, my father showed her a typescript of *The Temple*. Perhaps it was his way of proving that this particular Lily of Maida Vale was serious. She gave it her full attention on more than one occasion, but she did not think that it worked. *The Temple* includes a sex scene between two men, but that was not the reason why she told him the book should be abandoned. Virginia Woolf was not shockable in that way, however sensitive her literary persona might seem. Sex was an aspect of freedom; therefore it should not suffer any puritanical restrictions. As a subject, however, sex disturbed her. My father told me that he'd asked her once how important in a relationship she thought sex was. She said: 'It depends how highly you value cocks and cunts.' She had not dodged the question. She'd merely killed the subject.

In the spring of 1934, Stephen and Tony travelled to Yugoslavia via Venice and Trieste. By the middle of the month they were settled in a pension in Mlini, a small fishing village not far from Dubrovnik. The hotel's other clients were Nazi holidaymakers, but apart from that, it was a peaceful place where Stephen could work.

One day, there turned up at their hotel an American woman with her daughter, plus her daughter's nurse. The woman was Muriel Gardiner, a young psychiatrist studying in Vienna with a pupil of Freud. She and Stephen made friends. She told him about the suppression of the workers in Vienna early in the year. She'd been there. She could provide an eyewitness account – which Stephen incorporated into *Vienna*, a long poem that tries to blend politics and personal experience into one narrative, in order to make the point that in this particularly dark period of Germany's history private lives and public disasters were becoming inextricably tangled.

In Vienna a few weeks later, while Tony was recovering from an operation for appendicitis, Stephen and Muriel began to have an affair.

To Christopher Isherwood he wrote: 'I find the actual sex act with women more satisfactory, more terrible, more disgusting, and in fact more everything. To me it is much more of an experience, I think, and that is all there is to it.' This draws a line between himself and Christopher, who'd never had such doubts about his sexual identity. But there's a curious aspect to 'normal' sex. 'The effect is funny, because I find boys much more attractive, in fact I am more than usually susceptible.'

This is honest, but it's also strange. He loved Muriel, but a magnet drew him in the other direction. And Tony? Wasn't he the steadiest relationship at the moment?

He wrote about his confusion to William Plomer: 'As a "character" I am no good. I realized that when I saw that I was capable of feeling just the same about Tony, & being attracted by a woman, and wanting to go with miscellaneous boys. Obviously if I'm like that my relationship with Tony becomes the thing that is most holding me together and that I must most cling to; and Tony becomes the person whom I get to appreciate more and more. Beyond that there's really nothing but work, & pornography, silliness of all sorts.'

Muriel observed this confusion sympathetically and without creating a scene. She was a psychiatrist trained to observe, not to intervene. She loved Stephen and she did not wish to challenge his 'ambivalence', as he called his obsession with Tony whenever he discussed it with her.

As far as Stephen was concerned, Tony's reaction was more important than Muriel's. 'Tony has been terribly upset about this, although he was extremely generous about it, and never felt in the least resentful. In fact, he was very fond of her.' Tony was anxious that Stephen might want to get rid of him; and Stephen understood. He reassured Tony. 'Even if I married, it wouldn't form a separation, because we would want to live together for our whole lives.'

His relationship with Muriel faded because chance and politics prevented them from spending more time together. Then Stephen suddenly decided that he could not go on living with Tony. 'We had come up against the difficulty which confronts two men who endeavour to set up house together. Because they are of the same sex, they arrive at a point where they know everything about each other and it therefore seems impossible for the relationship to develop beyond this.'

Two men living together formed 'a substitute relationship in which each of the two expects the other to be something other than they are, because each of them is a substitute for something else'. Instead, a man and a woman living together could map out an area of reciprocal incomprehension that would allow their relationship to grow.

It's surely odd to suggest that heterosexual relationships work because they are based on mutual incomprehension, but he never went back on this view. It was even more odd that my mother, years later, defended this idea. I remember discussing it with her long after Dad's death. She told me: If you are two people of the same sex, each will know how the other is feeling just by the shape of your companion's shoulders as he (or she) gets out of bed in the morning. And, consequently, how the whole day will go. Whereas if two people of the opposite sex live together, there will be things that you'll never understand about each other, however close you become.

Mum told me this without seeing the absurdity of the idea. I wondered if Dad hadn't been trying in his mild way to explain away his preference for men with a joke. I also wondered how she'd have felt if she'd ever interpreted his idea that heterosexual love is based on incomprehension as a rejection of herself; but as far as I know, this never happened.

In *World within World*, he suggests that the attraction of working-class men was so unusual, it constitutes a gender of its own. 'The differences of class and interest between [Tony] and me certainly did provide some element of mystery, which corresponded almost to a difference of sex.' There are men, and there are women – and there are working-class men who are somehow in between?

I hear the ghostly voice of Tony murmuring in my ear, telling Dad: Steve, you've gone daft!

Lincoln Kirstein wrote from New York to say how upset he was that Stephen's relationship with Tony had failed. 'I had your companion-ship in my mind as a kind of standard where I thought there is practical friendship.' He'd met Tony in London the year before. (They'd all gone to the Zoo together.) 'Of course it was irresistible that it broke up. And I'm glad it happened as it did.' Meaning with-out recrimination. 'I'm so much in the same situation except its worse since I've no one like Tony.'

Earlier, Stephen had written to Kirstein: 'As far as homosexuality goes, it is for me utterly promiscuous, irresponsible, adventurous excitement: the feeling of picking someone up in a small village and going on somewhere else next day. This is very anti-social, but there it is.' Kirstein agreed. 'Its an uncontrollable unpolarized attraction which swells up around any one that looks in kind of a warm way.' The opposite, in other words, to faithful companionship. Kirstein wondered if he should give up the idea of living with anyone. 'I hate to think I'm completely separating a very important part of my life from its front source, but that's what seems to be happening.'

To Kirstein, casual affairs gave a sense of loss. 'The intensity of some super-charge is there, for waste. The waste is what is detestable. Also it's all confused with me in questions of class. I idealize the workmen and I can't stomach the boys I knew in college. In one way its suicide or romanticism, but in another it prevents me from being promiscuous and widens the range of my sympathies.' Kirstein had already eliminated the idea of living with a social equal. Now, living with a social inferior presented its own problems. But he told himself, at least desire for working-class boys had nurtured his sympathies regarding their predicament.

Stephen's separation from Tony took three years and it was as painful as any ending of a relationship could be. There was no separation between their private feelings and the dark progress of Fascism in Europe, corroborating my father's lifelong conviction that in the Thirties, in a most unusual way, private and public dramas became fused.

At the end of 1935 Stephen and Tony, together with Christopher and Heinz, sailed to Portugal where they had vague plans to start a writer's retreat. This failed early in 1936 and Tony and Stephen left for Barcelona, a city that Stephen knew from his days there with Hellmut. They arrived just in time to see the first phase of the Spanish revolution which, towards the end of the year, was challenged by the arrival from North Africa of a Fascist army bent on destroying it. Back in England, Stephen became engrossed in attempts to drum up support for the Republic; and, between one public appearance and another, he married his first wife.

I never met Inez Pearn. I remember staring at a portrait in an exhibition labelled 'Mrs Spender', painted in 1937 by Bill Coldstream, who later became the head of the Slade where I studied art. I must have been fifteen or so. I did not recognize my mother. I told Dad that it was a very bad likeness and he said, 'That's not Natasha. That's Inez.' This was the only time I ever heard her mentioned.

The portrait shows a tense though intelligent young woman trying to nestle deeper into the sofa on which she's resting. My father first met her at tea with Isaiah Berlin at All Souls one afternoon in October 1936. He'd come up to Oxford to give a speech in support of Spain. Seeing Stephen eyeing Inez intently, Isaiah joked that perhaps this was the woman he'd marry. Isaiah always blamed himself for putting the idea into Stephen's head – and he may not have been wrong. My father, intensely self-willed, had the peculiar idea that he had no will at all. 'I have no character or will power outside my work,' he'd written in 1929 in his Hamburg journal. 'In the life of action, I do everything my friends tell me to do, and have no opinions of my own. This is shameful, I know, but it is so.'

When Inez met Stephen, she was in the middle of two love affairs, one with Denis Campkin, who happened to be the son of Stephen's dentist, and another with a young up-and-coming Oxford communist, Philip Toynbee. This was a period when Oxford was polarized between those who wanted to intervene in Spain on the side of the Republic, and the 'hearties' who backed the British government's policy of neutrality. Toynbee was a glamorous figure, in fact he went on to become the one and only communist ever to be elected President of the Oxford Union. But if Philip was glamorous, Stephen was even more so. He was a famous poet, and his support for the Spanish Republic meant that he was constantly present at meetings – distracted and sometimes confused, but perhaps for that reason a useful supporter for the communist cause. A hesitant conscience was more convincing to the students than dogma.

Inez could never bring herself to end one affair before starting a new one. She was not confident in her looks, although 'she had the kind of drive and concentration on the other sex which leads to success. Those who were attracted to her thought her very pretty, those who were not found her ordinary looking'. This in a romantic self-portrait from one of her novels. It bolstered her self-confidence if a man fell in love with her, because it reassured her that she was capable of love. She suspected that love had been drummed out of her by her dreadful upbringing. Her father had died before she was born, and she was raised by her weak mother and a manipulative aunt. She was determined not to fall back into the dismal predicament of her childhood.

Inez Pearn a few weeks after marrying Stephen.

My father saw Inez just that once at Isaiah's, then a month later he invited her to a housewarming party at his new flat in Hammersmith, freshly decorated with the latest furnishings bought with the unexpected profits from the 'communist' book (as he called it) that he'd just written: *Forward from Liberalism*. Bentwood chairs and copper ceiling lights such as he'd seen in Hamburg in his earliest moment of freedom. There, seeing how attractive she was, he took her into a side room and kissed her. The next day he invited her to lunch at the Café Royal and proposed marriage.

She went back to Oxford in tears, and when she saw Philip Toynbee that evening, he was appalled to hear that she hadn't said no. Though he tried to persuade her not to go through with it, he knew that in the end Stephen would win.

In the contorted weeks that followed, Philip continued to sleep with her while Stephen stayed in London. At one point, to shake off Philip, Inez had a brief fling with Freddie Ayer, a young philosophy don. It didn't work. Freddie and Philip met and made friends. They agreed over drinks that it was important to them to give satisfaction to a woman in bed; yet in all this mayhem nobody was permitted to show jealousy towards anybody else. Jealousy infringed upon freedom; and 'free love' in those days was almost a political belief.

Stephen proposed to Inez on 13 November 1936, and they were married a month later in a registry office in London. 'I'm just not capable any more of having "affairs" with people,' he wrote to Christopher; 'they are simply a part of a general addiction to sexual adventures.'

The marriage had a devastating effect on Tony, who'd been joking and plotting with Philip Toynbee up to the very last minute, in the taxi as they went to the ceremony together. He left to fight in Spain two days after the wedding. He'd been threatening to do this for months. Stephen had been torturing himself with thoughts that if Tony went to Spain, he, Stephen, would be responsible. Tony couldn't make up his mind whether this interpretation was true or not. On the one hand it was good if Stephen suffered, because it would keep their relationship alive. On the other hand it took away Tony's autonomy as a man who was in charge of his own life – as someone capable of taking a moral decision to go and fight, unlike the pusillanimous Stephen.

Less than a month after Tony left, Harry Pollitt, head of the Communist Party of Great Britain, invited Stephen to the Central Office in King Street and proposed that he travel to Spain in order to trace the whereabouts of the *Komsomol*, a Russian ship loaded with munitions which had mysteriously disappeared on its way to Barcelona. It was an odd thing to ask. Finding the *Komsomol* was a problem that either could be solved easily, by asking the Red Cross, or else was very difficult, in which case Stephen risked being shot as a spy.

In Spain, my father's idea about how to find a missing Russian ship was to ask anyone he met in newspaper offices and in bars if they'd heard anything about it. Within a week of his arrival, three intelligence services knew about him: Republican, Fascist and British. At one point he wanted to cross the lines and ask the Fascists, but by that time his quest was well known and he was turned back at the frontier. It would have been embarrassing for General Franco if he'd had to shoot a British national.

The British authorities became interested. What was he up to? London sent back this message: 'Stephen Spender was born on 28.2.1909 and is a person of leisure and private means. He became a passionate anti-fascist as a result of travel in Germany, and has lately come to see in communism the only effective solution of world problems. His views are set out in his two recent books, *The Approach to Communism*, and *Forward from Liberalism* and he has also produced poems of considerable power. He is in touch with members of the international left-wing group in London, but has not, so far as we know, engaged in active politics.' The local officer in Gibraltar noted: 'Up till now, as far as we know, his communism has not been more than theoretical. It may be necessary to keep a sharper eye on him in the future.'

He went back to London none the wiser on the subject of the *Komsomol* and reported his lack of findings to King Street. Harry Pollitt then persuaded him to join the Communist Party, which Stephen did, writing a dramatic article for the *Daily Worker*: 'I join the Communist Party'. Then Pollitt sent him back to Spain to run a radio station.

By the time he arrived in Valencia, the radio had been suppressed.

At this point Stephen heard that Tony had attempted to desert from the International Brigade and was under arrest. He spent the following weeks attempting to save Tony and bring him safely back home. This enormous effort brought him into conflict with the communist commissars whose job it was to keep discipline among the volunteers. Sadistically, they restricted the occasions when they could see each other; though they didn't stop Tony from writing to Stephen – these letters being read by their censor. 'Oh my darling, it all seems so terribly unfair,' wrote Tony after one of these meetings. 'I don't think I could bear even to see you again only for a short while. Such short-lived happiness only leaves me more torn and miserable than ever. But do come if you can.'

Stephen went behind the backs of the commissars. He contacted the British acting Consul in Valencia, who was sympathetic, and the Spanish Minister of Munitions, Alvarez del Vayo. Stephen's reputation as a poet was a valuable commodity to the Spanish Republic, more valuable than the intransigence of the commissars, who naturally became furious when they realized they'd been bypassed.

Stephen could see Pollitt's point of view, which was that deserters from the front couldn't be treated leniently. But he also felt that, if he could save this one man from a fate he did not deserve, he shouldn't give up. 'What with your family and your friends, you have been more trouble to me than the whole British Battalion put together,' Pollitt told Tony on one of his visits to Spain. He promised Tony he'd be on his way home within a week.

Exasperated by endless meetings with Stephen to discuss the Tony problem, Pollitt cut through one conversation by asking Stephen a simple question: 'Is there any sex in this?' It was a key moment in my father's life. He did not tell lies. As far as he was concerned, he had no choice but to answer truthfully. So he said, 'Yes.'

The Spanish Civil War retained a personal element that vanished in the subsequent much larger European war. Even so, a confrontation discussing the sexual relationship of a deserter and his lover seems to me one of the strangest of all war stories.

Stephen last visited Spain to attend an international writers' conference that took place under the threat of imminent defeat. Groups of authors were driven in grand cars from one hotel to another. Speeches were made and delicious meals eaten. Stephen decided to challenge this opacity and ask the delegates for information about 'certain methods which were used in Russia and in Spain and were they prepared to say that they accepted full responsibility for these because they were inevitable and necessary?' Was it true that summary executions of members of the anarchist brigades by the communists were taking place behind the scenes? 'I wanted to know what was going on, and why, and who was responsible for it.' There was no answer. Instead, the question was attacked and Comrade Spender criticized for believing 'bourgeois propaganda spread by fascist agents'.

The writer Sylvia Townsend Warner, a member of the committee in charge of the English delegation, told him firmly, 'what is so nice is that we didn't see or hear of a single act of violence on the Republican side'. She saw Stephen as 'an irritating idealist, always hatching a wounded feeling'. She wanted him expelled from the Party immediately. 'She was concerned, she said, lest they were giving the wrong advice to their young writers: this was an issue of far greater importance than the fate of Spender.' The Hyndman case would provide all the necessary justification.

As soon as he got back to England, Stephen wrote a letter of protest to Harry Pollitt. He was being victimized in a smear campaign. 'When I was in Spain I discovered that the other members of the English delegation were occupied in acting as amateur detectives, apparently under the impression that it was their duty to "send a report to King Street". If any such report has been made, I think I should be allowed to answer it.'

Had Harry Pollitt betrayed him? 'I would like to remind you that on an important occasion when you asked me a leading question, I answered it truthfully. I am prepared to answer any other questions. But it is very painful to me that my confidential answer to your confidential question has been used to slander and prejudice people against me.' He was worried that his 'yes' on that fateful occasion might enter the public domain.

A few days later, Stephen invited Philip Toynbee to lunch at his flat in Hammersmith. Philip had visited Spain and the inevitable fall of the Republic was on everyone's mind. He'd also been seeing Inez in Stephen's absence, resisting her offer to leave Stephen and come back to him. In an aside, she spoke very bitterly about her husband. 'Stephen, she said, was utterly thoughtless and egocentric, unimaginative, going through the motions of generosity, but hopelessly ungenerous in his heart.'

The conversation at lunch was entirely about Tony: his stomach ulcers, the censorious moralism of the British commissars and the authoritarian role of Harry Pollitt. Stephen was panicking at the thought that he'd told Pollitt the truth. His 'Yes' meant that he'd descended to the level of sexual predator, with Tony as his innocent working-class victim. His own view of himself as an upright and honest man was under siege, for his position was dishonourable in the eyes of the CP.

Whenever my father thought that his integrity was under threat, he'd lash out in self-defence. He'd learned this at school, I think. He makes a comment somewhere in his journals: you can accept any kind of teasing or bullying at school, but there comes a point where you have to lash out, or sink.

After lunch, Inez and Philip were left alone. Inez, who'd been silent during the meal, told Philip wearily, 'It's like this every day!' When Stephen came back, he went on talking about Spain. 'Stephen very anti-Russian,' wrote Philip, who still followed the Party line, 'grotesquely & ignorantly.' Inez whispered to Philip in the background: We can now look forward to an article entitled 'I leave the Communist Party'.

My father abandoned communism after the Spanish experience, not just for political reasons – though there were plenty of those – but because the puritanism of the communists regarding personal behaviour was so great it constituted a political threat of its own. The communists were as repressed as the Victorians, Stephen wrote to William Plomer. It was inescapable. 'I believe in communism & wd therefore like to be a good communist, which means being a very normal & bourgeois person indeed. But now I know I can't manage to fit into this kind of life any more than the life which my parents wd have liked for me.'

If it meant leaving the Communist Party because of Tony, then so be it.

It is much best to accept the fact that I am not only a cad but that in the last resort I am prepared to act unscrupulously. If one accepts this, then there is quite a good working basis on which to adjust things as I don't want to make people unnecessarily unhappy although I have done so without meaning to & would now even do so knowingly if I thought it was necessary to break away from the new bourgeois trap in which I am caught.

It's a confused sentence. He's sorry about hurting people's feelings, he's a 'cad', but at the same time he'd fight 'unscrupulously' against the 'bourgeois trap' of communism. Yet all the while he still believes in communism as an idea.

4

A SLY SHELLEY

Tony came back from Spain in the late summer of 1937, and Stephen and Inez moved out of London to a cottage in Kent – perhaps to avoid him. Shortly after they'd arrived, Auden came to stay. He needed to talk about Spain.

Stephen described the background of the International Writers' Congress, to which Wystan had intended to go but didn't, because of visa problems. There had been a violent attack on André Gide for the book he'd written after his visit to the Soviet Union in 1935. Indeed, his *Retour de l'URSS* had divided most fellow-travellers from the rest of the Communist Party. Philip Toynbee, though for the moment he remained loyal, had written in his diary when the book came out: 'We must, must do something about it – protest first against the Trotskist label attached so readily to critics. Then try to extort a reply from the Soviet Government. All this of course inside the party.' Stephen had been shocked at the viciousness of the attack on Gide and the refusal to discuss the book itself. And they'd attacked him, too, over Tony. Was this the inevitable fate of all those who disagreed with the communists? Character assassination, rather than rational discussion?

Auden's view was: 'political exigence was never a justification for lies'. In spite of the complexity of Auden's mind, or perhaps because of it, he often insisted on following the simplest of rules. It eliminated

47

long moralistic arguments and much soul-searching; but to say 'lying is wrong' also struck at the heart of communist tactics.

One evening at the end of November 1937, Christopher turned up at Stephen's flat in Hammersmith. 'Stephen's affairs are in a fine old tangle. The triangle has turned into a quadrangle.' He's referring to Stephen, Inez, Tony, plus an offstage lover of Inez. 'Stephen said of himself: "I only really feel what my friends tell me I feel." He's worried about Inez and about Tony's future. He even claims to have shed tears last night for an hour. But under all his remorse, he's really laughing and naughty and very sly. A sly Shelley.'

To Christopher, there'd always been something absurd about Stephen's marriage. Absurd, too, for Stephen to pretend he had emotions while simultaneously saying they were wished on him by his friends. Meanwhile in front of Christopher, Stephen played down his capacity to love a woman. He did not want to be deflated by a sardonic remark.

Isherwood was planning to leave the country with Auden. They'd take a boat to China and write a book about the war in Manchuria. Christopher's life since Hitler came to power had been a restless shifting from country to country: Denmark, Holland, the Canaries, Portugal. His lover Heinz had been lured back to Germany and arrested and he was desperate. He did not want to live in England, the land of The Enemy.

In Shanghai they stayed with the British Ambassador. The late British Empire was hospitable. Auden had just won the King's Medal for Poetry and they were important visitors. Of the two Auden seemed the more important, and this made Isherwood uncomfortable. 'In China, I sometimes found myself really hating him – hating his pedantic insistence on "objectivity", which was merely a reaction from my own woolly-mindedess. I was meanly jealous of him too. Jealous of his share of the limelight; jealous because he'll no longer play the role of dependent, admiring younger brother.'

They visited the front line. Isherwood wanted to test himself. 'If I was scared in China – far more often than Wystan – I, at least, didn't show it. And, maybe, as taking those little risks was more difficult for me, I even displayed a kind of mild courage.' This was a good reason for being there: to test how they'd behave when war came to Europe.

In Auden's life there had been no equivalent, so far, to Heinz in Christopher's or Tony in Stephen's. Several times in the China adventure Auden became depressed by the thought that love might pass him by. He could observe love happen, he could briskly and cheerfully manage sex, but what about love? To love his neighbour as himself he could also manage, both as a Christian principle and as a vision of humanity. But love, in the sense of sex plus affection plus trust, hadn't yet happened.

They came back via a boat to Vancouver then a train to New York. Auden liked this new city immediately. New Yorkers belonged to their city in a different way than Londoners belonged to London. Auden had never liked London, and literary London took for granted that he belonged there and held certain responsibilities. After all, London had created his reputation. By comparison, New Yorkers seemed to him free from the burden of expectations.

Over their return voyage across the Atlantic, he was in a bad state. 'Wystan in tears,' wrote Christopher in his diary, 'telling me that no one would ever love him, that he would never have my sexual success. That flattered my vanity; but still my sadism wasn't appeased. And, actually – believe it or not – when we got back to England I wouldn't have him to stay the night, because I was jealous of him, and wanted to stage the Returning Hero act all to myself.'

Over the summer of 1938, Inez left Stephen; and although several times it seemed as if she'd come back, she didn't.

Stephen was devastated, yet in his autobiography he writes that their separation was 'the breaking up of something which had never been completely joined'. But if nothing had become 'joined', it was at least partly because he did not want it to. As he'd written to a friend soon after the wedding, 'I believe I married really because I recognized in my wife someone who doesn't want to become absorbed in someone else any more than I do.'

He'd suffered intensely to see that she was unhappy and to feel that he was the cause, yet her unhappiness lay beyond his capacity to cure. He hated this feeling and he did not know how to cope with it. As he wrote to Christopher: 'I feel that people can't exist without me. Also, I sometimes feel at the very mercy of people – that I cannot refuse any request they make; I now think that this is a [way] of being at the mercy of one's feelings.' Tony's presence must surely have been one of the reasons why the marriage failed; yet this was not mentioned. Stephen felt loyal to Tony, and if Inez had ever suggested this constituted disloyalty to her, he would have become outraged. Jealousy hampered freedom, and freedom was the most important of all political ideas. Thus Tony remained offstage as Inez fled to Wales and Stephen stayed miserably in London. Perhaps Tony hoped that after the separation, he might rejoin Stephen.

Inez left him, not vice versa, so in a sense she seized the initiative. After she'd left, Stephen poured out desperate letters to a mutual friend, and these are helpful in trying to understand what he needed from love. 'The fact is that one must base life on love and not on "being in love" – at least, that is the difference between Inez and me, that I have love which could last thirty years and she lives on being in love from day to day.'

What was his idea of love?

If a human relationship becomes more important than anything else in two people's lives, it simply means that there is a lack of trust between these two human beings. A relationship is not a way of entering into a kind of dual subjectivity, a redoubled and reciprocal egotism; it is an alliance of two people who form an united front to deal with the problems of the objective world. The problem of married people is not to become absorbed in each other, but how not to become absorbed in each other; how, in a word, to trust one another in order to enter into a strong and satisfactory relationship with the outside world.

Stephen, so apparently open in his emotions, always kept something back. Auden had noticed this from the moment they'd met. Now Inez took stock of this characteristic and concluded that they'd reached a dead end. Tactfully, she wrote that if she were to return to Stephen, 'although our affection is very solid, we could not get any further with our relationship and should both be profoundly dissatisfied'.

The outbreak of the Second World War in September 1939 coincided with the foundation of the magazine where my father worked for two years as co-editor together with Cyril Connolly. So eager was Stephen to have an editorial role that he handed over a flat he'd recently rented on Mecklenburg Square in order to provide *Horizon* with an office.

Connolly was a critic and writer who so far had produced one excellent novel, *The Rock Pool*, about expatriate bad behaviour in the Twenties. He was older than Stephen and belonged to the generation which placed fine writing above political commitment – a conviction that had been reinforced by the collapse of the Spanish Republic. By October, he'd settled into a wing chair covered with pink silk by the window overlooking Mecklenburg Square. He wore baggy flannels, a woollen tie and a tweed jacket, like a housemaster at a boarding school. 'His movements like his voice were indolent, one had the impression he should be eating grapes, but at the same time his half-closed eyes missed nothing.'

As an editor, he described himself as going through 'periods of intense energy, interspersed with long lulls of sloth'. He also confessed in an editorial that co-editorship with Spender had its ups and downs, with moments when each would be 'sullenly burning manuscripts in different corners of the room'. Stephen wanted more political articles, Cyril wanted fine prose, and occasionally there were tensions.

Nevertheless the editorials, usually written by Cyril, tackled difficult questions about war aims and choices. Should the techniques of propaganda as perfected by modern advertising agencies be incorporated into the war effort? Would National Socialism of a British kind have to be introduced here? Nationalism – you cannot win a war without patriotism. Socialism – you cannot expect soldiers to fight without guaranteeing benefits for the families they leave behind. The great British capitalists and landlords were potentially Fascist, he wrote blandly. But: 'below them come the enormous professional and commercial middle-class, which, though capitalist, could easily adapt itself to socialism, and which is morally and geographically anti-Hitler because it believes in Democracy, Christianity and the British Empire'. Cyril certainly believed in democracy, less so in Christianity, and not at all in the British Empire. But the message of *Horizon* was that England required major social changes if the war was to be won.

Auden and Isherwood had left England at the end of January 1939, nine months before the war broke out. Everyone at their farewell party knew they wouldn't be coming back.

In January 1940, thinking of this anniversary, Connolly wrote an editorial in *Horizon*. Their departure was perhaps the most significant literary event of the war so far, he wrote. 'They are far-sighted and ambitious young men with a strong instinct of self-preservation, and an eye on the main chance, who have abandoned what they consider to be the sinking ship of European democracy, and by implication the aesthetic doctrine of social realism that has been prevailing there.'

Cyril did not approve of the literature of 'social realism' so presumably his remark was meant to be supportive. Unfortunately the phrase 'self-preservation and an eye on the main chance' provoked endless repercussions. At cocktail parties all over London people asked: Is Cyril really saying that Wystan and Christopher are rats who've left the sinking ship? Questions were even asked in Parliament.

Stephen was away when Cyril wrote this comment. When he read it, he worried about how Wystan would take it. He immediately wrote to him. In his reply, Auden wrote briskly, 'of course I wasn't offended by the editorial which I thought was very fair'. He added, 'I wish you were over here, not because I don't support the allies – which in spite of everything I do – but because there doesnt seem anything that you cannot do just as well here as there.' Meaning write poetry.

He confirmed this position in a conversation with Louis MacNeice, who appeared in New York for a three-month lecture tour. MacNeice, in a letter that appeared in *Horizon*, tried to play down the controversy. He said that Auden had told him that 'an artist ought either to live where he has live roots or where he has no roots at all; that in England to-day the artist feels essentially lonely, twisted in dying roots, always in opposition to a group; that in America he feels just as lonely, but so, says Auden, is everybody else'.

Auden thought that the only obligation of a writer was to write. My father thought this avoided the issue. If Hitler won, writers in Europe would disappear – along with many of their readers. In his 'Letter to a Colleague in America', written for the *New Statesman*, Stephen wrote: 'I wonder how much of value can be created, even in America, if the conditions in which we are living are so completely misunderstood.' This was a tactful way of asking, how can one concentrate exclusively on writing while the Nazis are out there, threatening to destroy writing itself?

This evoked a private protest from Auden. 'Your passion for public criticism of your friends has always seemed to me a little odd; it is not that you dont say acute things – you do – but the assumption of the role of the blue-eyed Candid Incorruptible is questionable . . . What you say is probably accurate enough, but the tone alarms me. "One is worried about Auden's poetic future." Really, Stephen dear, whose voice is this but that of Harold Spender, M.P.'

Bill Coldstream, who'd painted Wystan in numerous long sittings and who'd known him since they were adolescents, was convinced that Wystan had fallen in love. Otherwise he would have come back. There were many reasons why Auden failed to return: a suspicion that England would make a deal with Hitler, a dislike of taking human lives, a strong reluctance to being roped into writing patriotic poems in favour of the British war effort, along the lines of 'Spain', a work he'd come to dislike for what he saw as its insincere rhetoric. But of all the reasons to remain in the United States, love came first.

5

MUTUAL RENAISSANCE

M Y PARENTS MET in August 1940, a fortnight before the beginning of the Blitz. Tony invited a young pianist from the Royal
College of Music to lunch at *Horizon*, just around the corner from
where they happened to be: my mother, Natasha Litvin, aged twenty-
one. She thought 'Horizon' was the name of a pub, not the magazine
where my father worked. She wasn't sure if she'd come. 'Oh come
on ducky, you'll enjoy it,' said Tony. And so she went.

Mum was living with her mother off Primrose Hill at the time,
in a flat with one sitting room, one bedroom, and a tiny room under
the eaves with a stove and a sink. She once told me that when she
was a child practising on the upright piano perched on the landing,
if she fell into a daydream, the door above her head would open
and Granny would lean out and whack her head with a saucepan
to get her going again. At this point however her childhood was
over. She was a scholarship student with a promising career, and
she'd been invited to practise on the grand piano of Ian and Lys
Lubbock, who lived near Coram Square.

Every morning she walked down past the Zoo and along Prince
Albert Road to the Lubbocks. Signs of war were everywhere. On
Primrose Hill, an ancient wood had been cut down to make room
for anti-aircraft guns. The animals of the London Zoo were being

evacuated to Whipsnade in Bedfordshire, protesting, in large canvas-covered trucks. The bombing was expected to start at any moment. The first thing she noticed as she walked into the *Horizon* office – my father's flat – was a long table against the wall, piled high with books and manuscripts. The larger room overlooking the square contained a wing chair covered with pink silk, a big horn gramophone with a stack of records running along the floor and a long trestle table set for lunch. Awed by these surroundings, Natasha knelt and flipped through Stephen's records: Schnabel's 'Beethoven Society' recordings of the sonatas, the Busch recordings of the Haydn quartets and Fritz Busch conducting Mozart operas at Glyndebourne. Her taste precisely. And casually propped against the wall near the records, a little Picasso watercolour.

She was briefly introduced to Stephen, but before she could ask him about his taste in music, they sat down to lunch. A crowd of about ten people in the small flat. Cyril Connolly, *Horizon*'s main editor, sat at the head of the table. Natasha was down near the novelist Rose Macaulay, whom she remembered as having kept her crumpled velvet hat on at table, complete with veil.

Looking at Stephen surreptitiously from a distance, Natasha realized this wasn't the first time she'd seen him. Three years earlier, in October 1937, she'd joined a group of music students at the Kingsway Hall in London during a rally on behalf of the Spanish Republic. By that time the Spanish cause was as good as lost, but this did not make Stephen Spender less of a glamorous figure. He described the young English poets who had fought and died for Spain: John Cornford, for example, and Julian Bell, the nephew of Virginia Woolf. ('Spender praised the representatives of culture who had lost their lives whilst fighting with the Spanish Government Forces,' wrote a listener from MI5.) Natasha admired Stephen's speech because, unlike the others on the platform, what he said was free from the usual bombast.

After lunch the guests mysteriously disappeared, leaving Stephen with the washing up. Natasha helped – and that was that. As a child

I often imagined this scene: the guests leaving with their fingers to their lips like actors miming silence in a film. He'd been depressed all winter and his friends were longing for him to start a new life.

Years later, she described how she looked when Stephen first saw her. 'He probably thought me rather demure, even old fashioned, with my hair parted in the middle and the two long plaits wound over the head in Victorian style.' This is typical of the way my mother saw herself: shy, retiring, perhaps at some level even anti-social.

After they'd tidied up, they walked around Mecklenburg Square, and then out to supper together, staying on until the restaurant closed, darkness fell and Natasha had to go home in a taxi. During their walk Stephen mentioned the death of a friend, and he stopped and shut his eyes in an unconscious expression of pain. This was what attracted her: his willingness to reveal emotions. Not many Englishmen she knew did that.

They were both tall, so there was no problem about keeping up with each other when they walked in Regent's Park next day. And the next. And the next. Less than a week later, in another taxi with the Lubbocks going from a cocktail party to their house to have dinner, a tipsy Ian leaned forward and told Stephen that he should 'take on' his wife Lys, not Natasha. Which suggested to Natasha that in the eyes of the world, she and Stephen had already 'taken on' each other.

My mother writes this regarding her first impressions: 'The sudden luminosity of spirit which possessed me from that first day, I remember as a kind of mutual renaissance shared with Stephen, in whom one could sense this tentative turning towards the light, whilst I also was moving away from a restless year I had spent in Hampshire as paying guest of Susan Lushington, where music had been the only solace from the troubled impermanence I had known since 1939 in both outer and inner life.' It's a long sentence. When it came to revealing her emotions, my mother wanted to cram everything in and move on.

With several other Royal College students she'd been evacuated to Ockham Hall, where Susan Lushington, a keen amateur musician, had offered them hospitality. 'Despite successful achievements at the College and beyond, in recovering from an illness I had been troubled about the value and direction of my daily devotion to music.' She was certainly something of a success. In March 1940, she'd performed Beethoven's 4th piano concerto with the Royal College Orchestra under Malcolm Sargent. Not the easiest piece in the world. But illness? I know nothing about this, but my mother once told me that she'd had a stomach ulcer at the age of twelve, which suggests stress.

Her fellow students were marrying or going off to the war, or both in quick succession. What was to become of her? She didn't want to live with a musician and she hardly knew anyone else. A musician 'would be confining, compounding of stress, and prone to shop-talk. Too narrowing.' She was not interested in politics. 'Public life, its battles, crowds and compromises were not for me.' She could see herself doing good in a quiet way, at an individual level. 'I was a kind of agnostic Christian, totally unconcerned with dogma, but fond of and admiring those selfless lives, whether historical or personally known to me, which combined a sense of the sacred with understanding, love and tolerance.'

In the few diaries my mother left she insists that an introspective life would have suited her best. The life she chose with Stephen was the opposite of that, but she wasn't incapable of presenting a brave face to the world. Quite the contrary. She was also a musician, so she knew how to perform.

My mother was the illegitimate daughter of Rachel Litvin, an actor of Jewish ancestry born in Estonia, who'd come to England with her family as a child. Her father was Edwin Evans, a well-known music critic and champion of contemporary French composers. Unfortunately, my grandfather was married when Ray became pregnant, and although he offered to obtain a divorce, my grandmother refused.

In these dire circumstances, Ray was helped via her friendship with Betty Potter, a fellow actor, whose powerful sisters took over my mother's birth and foster care. Bardie, one of Betty's sisters, even offered to adopt her, but Ray refused. Margaret Booth, married to the son of the shipping magnate Charles Booth, became Natasha's 'Aunt Margie'. In fact all the sisters became Natasha's elective 'aunts'.

When Natasha was a few months old, the 'aunts' found a foster-mother for her. Unencumbered, my grandmother did her best to continue her career. 'I walked with Miss Litvinne, mother of an illegitimate child, down Longacre, & found her like an articulate terrier – eyes wide apart; greased to life; nimble; sure footed, without a depth anywhere in her brain. They go to the Cabaret; all night dances; John Goss sings. She was communicative, even admiring I think. Anyhow, I like Bohemians.' Thus my grandmother depicted by Virginia Woolf, of the sharp eye and sharper tongue, in the year 1924, when my mother was three. The following year she saw Ray acting the part of an orphan in a play. She was not impressed. 'Poor Ray Litvin's miserable big mouth & little body.'

Throughout my mother's childhood, the Booth family at their grand house on Campden Hill, or at their even larger property at Funtington in Suffolk, took care of my mother and encouraged her musical gifts. Funtington was full of the Booth children, although they were slightly older than Natasha. There are photographs. She is with them. They are in a magnificent tree-house in a chestnut tree. 'The joy was to be allowed to join them there among the dark foliage, pulling the ladder up after us, impregnable in our leafy hideaway.' At Funtington there was a bedroom known as 'Natasha's room', which means that my mother must have spent most of her holidays there.

The Booths were obsessed by music. Everyone played an instrument and they could perform complex chamber pieces without the help of musicians from outside the family. Aunt Margie looked down the table one Sunday lunch and said, 'Oh good. This afternoon we can play the *Trout*.' This, to my mother, was incredible luxury – and she was right! Who today can play Schubert's *Trout* Quintet, and the performers are all related? Beyond their music, the Booths enjoyed what my mother calls 'a democratic radical classlessness going back to Bright and Bentham'. I'm not sure whether 'classlessness' is the right word, but the Booths stood at the head of a strong tradition of English socialism. And they were rich.

Little Natasha grew up in three worlds: that of her foster-mother Mrs Busby, that of the powerful self-appointed aunts, and that of everyday life at school. She learned to speak in three different accents and she was proud of the fact that she could alter these voices instantaneously. 'As I grew, so did my ability for chameleon changes of manner to suit the ambience in which I might find myself. Yet at the centre of this changing stream of consciousness and easy, reliable adaptation to frequent changes of scene, there was a certain unequivocal sense of unity, an intact sense of self.'

Until she was twelve years old, Mum hadn't even known that she had a father. By that time she was in secondary school and doing well. She loved her foster-mother and the Booth family stood in the background to give her a sense of security. Then suddenly my grandmother told her that she'd be leaving Mrs Busby and coming back to London to live with her; and that the following day she'd have to visit the person Ray had never married and ask him for money.

The next day Mum boarded the 74 bus from Primrose Hill to Earls Court to meet the unknown man who happened to be her father. A housekeeper opened the door and she found herself in front of a large bearded gentleman in a pair of carpet slippers. He neither hugged her nor shook her hand, but he was a musician, so he could talk about that. He showed her his scores stacked from floor to ceiling, talked about French composers she'd never heard of and took her to the piano and played a bright little sonata by Scarlatti.

'His speaking voice was rather flat, the accent indeterminate, his laughter rather ponderous, and much of his musical talk was above my head. Somehow the occasion was lifeless, for although his kindness was apparent, dutiful, impersonal, it was difficult to feel anything at all.' Then, sitting side by side at the piano, he improvised a theme and invited her to join in. Her earliest love for the piano had come from improvising for hours on end, so she added a second subject. And that was the closest she remembered ever getting to her father. An old man and a young girl at a keyboard, tapping at the notes.

My mother aged fifteen, photographed at
the Booth country house near Funtington.

Edwin Evans had no intention of marrying Ray Litvin, or even of seeing her again. He'd give her an allowance of some kind but, as he told his daughter when they said goodbye, he'd arrange everything through a solicitor. There was no need for her to come again.

Years later, Mum happened to perform in a concert conducted by Eugene Goossens. He looked at her speculatively across a dining-room table while he ran through a mental list of Edwin Evans' mistresses. Finally: 'Oh, now I remember! You must be the daughter of the Russian woman!' One of the many was the implication.

My grandfather died ten days before I was born, so I never knew him.

Mum told me years later that she felt very little when her father died, and she'd had to piece together everything she knew about him after his death by talking to composers who felt indebted to him. Francis Poulenc, for instance, whom she met in Paris in the late Forties. He told her many stories about Evans, but she did not write them down, and when I asked her about them, she'd forgotten. Igor Stravinsky told her that Evans was the critic who in 1913 had insisted on the first performance of *The Rite of Spring* in London, for which he was very grateful. He gave Mum a copy of a photo from his family album showing her father standing on a veranda in the South of France with Diaghilev and Picasso.

Stravinsky told her that Evans had been with him in a taxi in Paris when he'd found the solution to the last pages of *Les Noces*. He'd been working at it for months and he couldn't think of a way of ending it – four soloists, four pianos and a choir, a devastating piece. Then he and Evans happened to be travelling past the cathedral of Notre-Dame one Sunday morning when all the bells started ringing. Stravinsky stopped the cab and wrote down the deafening notes as dictation.

Among the photographs that my sister Lizzie and I inherited is a yellowed newspaper clipping showing our mother with Stravinsky in the streets of Salzburg in the late Sixties. Stravinsky walks with difficulty and she's helping him. It's a moving image, but it took me a long time to see why. Stravinsky is cheerfully tottering, and that's understandable, because he's ancient. Then I saw it. Mum's body language was unfamiliar. It was the affectionate willowy bending of a daughter towards a father.

On Saturday 7 September 1940, Natasha had lunch with a group of young architects in a flat overlooking the Thames somewhere to the east of the Houses of Parliament. They came out and walked along the Embankment. The air-raid siren started. They checked the nearest bomb shelter but it seemed dank and dirty. 'Returning to lean on the parapet of the river, we gazed around us, when we suddenly caught sight in the east of a vast number of planes flying upstream from the estuary, and glinting in the sky like a shoal of silvery fish.' They stared upwards without moving. In spite of warnings in the newspapers that the bombings were about to start, they had no fear. 'One could not readily imagine at first that this was, as anticipated, the start of lethal enemy action on London, for in our leisured mood, the beauty of the day and of the gleaming, steadily advancing planes was almost hypnotic.'

Stephen at that time was living with his younger brother in the country. He rushed up to London to take charge. He decided she should move out. He took her to Oxford and called on Nevill Coghill, Auden's former tutor. Coghill was an amateur musician and Natasha had already given a concert in Oxford, so he knew how she fitted in. Word went round. Within a few days Natasha was installed. The old Bechstein her father had given her was moved to a room above the Church of St Mary, opposite the Radcliffe Camera. It was a beautiful room to practise in, though the choir occasionally took it over for their own rehearsals.

In the early days of their courtship Stephen and Natasha did not live together, because my father did not want her to become roped into the divorce proceedings with Inez. They met once a week in London. Natasha would hitch a ride at the Headington roundabout outside Oxford. That roundabout became a symbol of the war: officers and soldiers and mechanics and students and professors – you never knew who'd be standing next to you or who'd offer you a lift. For twenty years after the war it was remembered with nostalgia as a moment when class faded, everyone was in it together, no place to sleep was a good place because all places could be bombed, so travel light.

The Blitz, at least in this early phase, was met with bravado. Once, under a bombardment, caught among a group of partygoers who refused to troop off to the shelter, Natasha was told, 'play something lyrical'. So she played some Chopin waltzes – 'Chopin, for heaven's sake, which I almost never played!' A couple of distinguished guests lurked under the piano, giggling and passing a bottle of champagne to each other, wondering if a grand piano would give them any protection if a bomb came through the roof.

Over the winter of 1940–1, Stephen and Natasha stayed for a fortnight with friends in an eighteenth-century house south-east from London, near Romney Marsh. Wooden poles had been raised against the German gliders that would come over in the expected invasion. The winter had turned cold and a heavy snowfall smothered the countryside. Everyone in the neighbourhood had relatives in the armed forces, but the snow had lightened the mood, for the enemy bombers were grounded. The house had a warm kitchen and a warm workroom and they ran from one to the other through freezing corridors. The whiteness was reflected on the ceilings; and outside, the shadows of low clouds skittered over undulating snow.

This was the first time that Stephen and Natasha had spent more than a day together. Stephen worked in the attic in his overcoat while Natasha studied the Schubert B flat posthumous sonata, 'with its devout quality reflecting an atmosphere of *laudate adoremus*, in tune with the advent of Christmas'. After a few days, their hosts disappeared and they were left alone. The 'Wittersham Interlude', as my mother calls it in her memoir where it occupies a whole chapter, was an important moment in my parents' lives. Each laid out the past for the benefit of the other.

Stephen kept thinking of the tattered members of the International Brigade who'd fought in Spain, friendless and badly equipped. He compared them with the British forces in North Africa, well trained, well armed and backed this time by an entire nation. This war was for England; but it was also a moral cause. 'Stephen's conviction [was] that all repressive despotism had to be opposed by decency and insisting on truth. He had seemed so mild when we first met, that coming to know his strong-minded refusal to acquiesce in any political coercion and lies was to recognise a centre which was steady, even steely, in his peaceable nature.'

My mother practising the Schubert B-Flat Sonata in the early years of the war.

They discovered that they both had feelings of guilt about the First World War. As she puts it in her memoir: 'So many of our generation had felt guilty for having missed the first war and for our existence as burdensome, as somehow responsible for the sadness and privations of our parents.' Natasha's guilt perhaps had more to do with the fact that she was illegitimate, but she resisted this thought.

Although at the age of twenty-one on the Wittersham holiday I had long since found a robust, even amused acceptance, of such relics of childhood, there remained a lifelong, lingering feeling of apology towards my mother for her lonely years of adversity. I had never entertained untoward feelings about illegitimacy, for it was clear that there was no reason for me to feel responsible for that, despite my sympathy for her moments of embarrassment. But I continued to feel a sorrowful indebtedness for the struggle she had bravely faced to support us both.

Stephen told her: 'As very young children they had been appalled to feel their noisy play to be responsible for their mother's bouts of illness, when she appeared looking over the banisters and declaiming, as Stephen said like Medea, "Now I know the sorrow of having borne children." After her early death at the age of 42 they felt partly responsible for their father's unhappiness, a burden they could not alleviate, and perhaps that they even had had a share in its origins.' Stephen felt he'd rejected his father, towards whom he'd shown no sympathy after Violet died; but this took time to emerge. Years later, after I was born, Stephen told Natasha: 'Our father must have been desolate after the death of our mother, and I don't believe we gave him any comfort.'

At Wittersham, Stephen spoke openly about Tony and Inez. My mother summed up what he said in a simplification which has a certain truth, though I don't believe it covers everything. He felt they'd failed, because he'd spent too much time working. 'His devotion to his vocation in poetry was an unforgivable distraction – a sort of infidelity – for he was a transparently monogamous temperament.' My mother cannot have found it easy to accept Tony and Inez, standing invisibly offstage throughout the Wittersham Interlude. But 'monogamy' was an admirable virtue. So was work.

He told her about his early years in Berlin with Christopher Isherwood and with his younger brother, Humphrey. She was prepared to forgive him. 'He had lived his life in phases, and the earliest one of juvenile wild oats shared with Humphrey and with Christopher had in a few years been discarded like an animal shedding its skin. His monogamous devotion to Tony had foundered for reasons I well understood, and his latest disaster with Inez was to a union which had never been properly joined.'

Natasha told Stephen that his unsuccessful relationships with Tony and Inez were not his fault. 'His assuming total responsibility for these failures was a far from wise interpretation, for Inez had been in a whirl of indecision, even on her wedding day, when she was still at Oxford.' So, exit Inez. As for Tony: 'The pattern of Tony's restlessness had been lifelong.'

She told him: 'From now on there is no question of blame. There is only us.'

'I look back on that brief holiday as a time of exceptional élan in the feeling that we had dropped our childhood like unwanted luggage.' They loved each other. Their guilts could be discarded. 'The resolve I shared with Stephen to banish both self-blame and, in the future, any projecting of it upon each other, and to replace it with serene understanding of its origins, was to enhance the feelings of release from the past and rejoicing in the present which pervaded those happy snowbound days.' He'd told her everything about himself. He was turning over a new leaf – or so she thought. But he might also have been giving her a warning: Don't expect from me more than I can give.

They were married at St Pancras registry office on 9 April 1941.

'As we made the responses, it was, as we later described it to each other, as if we were alone in some high place – a water-shed where our pasts flowed away into one ocean, and our future together was a stream flowing away to another great sea, as we stood there at its source.' Together, they would descend the other side of this mountain, leaving the past behind. 'Meeting in forgiveness and the miracle of marriage, I realised that it had been this acceptance of whole histories, reaching back into previous generations, which had been distilled into that one present moment, (almost a knife-edge), of the vow.'

Stephen wrote to Julian Huxley: 'being married to Natasha will be quite different from just living with her, as she is really a very remarkable person'. Her character was in its way deeply religious. '"Being married" means something to her. This has a revolutionary effect on me, because nothing alters me so much as someone expecting something real from me, and the desire not to disappoint her in any way.' This was part of his idea that he had no will of his own. He would try to live up to her hopes, because they were stronger than his.

My parents soon after their wedding.

For their honeymoon they went to Cornwall. There, he showed her the many versions of a poem on which he was working. She had no idea that it required so many revisions and restarts, but when he explained to her the idea of fidelity to an event, it related to what she was trying to do with her music. 'For the poet or the composer there is fidelity to some original subjective experience, which is private and ultimately beyond the interpreter, however inspiring a reading there may be.'

She thought that Stephen's creativity provided her with limitless support. 'This rich vitality struck me like the liberation of entering another country, another climate, for apart from the Funtington circle, my not unlively musical world had been much narrower in focus.' His world renewed her optimism. 'Overtaken by this sudden upsurge in vitality and sensibility, music was once more intoxicating, the capacity to realise the beauty of phrasing that one intended or imagined seemed limitless ... For me, the vast repertoire of master-pieces for the piano waiting to be mastered was no longer a daunting proposition, and one could set about wholeheartedly learning each single sonata.'

Walking in the countryside, there would be occasions when Stephen would become distracted. My mother read these as moments when he'd entered his interior world and she should not cross that boundary. 'We would be chatting, in the way of friends or lovers, of an acquaintance or a landscape and yet – at a certain moment one could feel his need of silence and guess that some analogy with a dramatic or poetic theme had seized him, and he wished to chase after it in peace.'

6

FIRES ALL OVER EUROPE

'FROM PILLAR TO post.' I hear my mother's voice with the expression she always used to describe a life with no fixed abode. For a while they rented rooms outside Oxford from the historian A. J. P. Taylor, whose wife was also a musician. They happened to be sitting in the garden together on Sunday 22 June 1941, the day when Hitler invaded Russia. Taylor tossed his spade in the air and shouted, 'No! He couldn't be that stupid!'

Hitler had occupied my father's thoughts for a decade. Now he realized that Hitler was just as much a prisoner of the war as everyone else. War was a machine that would grind on until one side or the other claimed victory. If England lost, Stephen had a suicide plan. He would swim far out to sea and drown.

During the Blitz the staff of *Horizon* was evacuated to Devon, where Cyril amused himself by fishing for shrimps with a net, standing in the water with his trousers rolled up. Stephen visited him there and wrote a beautiful poem about watching an air raid over Portsmouth, but otherwise he was absent teaching at Blundell's School. He'd planned to work as a teacher for a whole year, but he couldn't stand the conventions of discipline and left after one term – which he seems to have spent trying to persuade one turbulent boy he shouldn't run away.

Stephen's elder brother Michael had become an officer in RAF Intelligence early in the war. From this lofty position he could not resist ticking off his younger brother, asking if he was 'taking the war seriously'. Stephen sent an angry reply insisting his war work was valuable. It consisted of broadcasts, a monthly article for *New Writing*, his play set in early Nazi Germany, plus his poems, plus his editorial work on *Horizon*. 'You may notice that I wrote a considerable part of the last *Horizon*, which the Min of Inf [Ministry of Information] considers the most valuable propaganda of its kind we have in neutral countries.'

At that point, the most important neutral country was the United States, for England fought Hitler for two years before the US joined in, and any effort to encourage American participation was worth trying. He was going to talk to someone in the Ministry of Labour the following week. 'I am sorry to hear that if I want a job you won't recommend me for R.A.F. Intelligence,' wrote Stephen bitterly. 'But it is just as well to know to whom one may turn & to whom one may not.' Michael thought Stephen should join the war, but not in any responsible capacity. His elder brother despised Stephen's intelligence – a stimulating factor, I think, in my father's ambition.

A few weeks later, Stephen went through his army medical tests. He failed. By begging the doctors to change the result, he made himself eligible to join non-combatant units stationed in England. Thus in September 1941 Stephen joined the London branch of the National Fire Service. He often used to joke that he became a fireman ten minutes after the Blitz ended and left ten minutes before the first buzz-bomb fell on London.

He and Natasha moved to Cricklewood for his basic training and he did his clumsy best to become a well-trained cog in a vast machine. 'I had to undergo an extra week of training, owing to a neurotic inability to pass any examination whatever. This has led to my sinking naturally to the bottom of the social scale during the war.' He was never promoted above the lowest rank and he was only asked to fight a fire twice. The first time, the man next to him took over. The second time, 'surrounded by a lacquered screen of fire, I felt strangely at peace, settled in the centre of the element, as though rowing in wide circles for hours on end'.

Lucian Freud, Tony Hyndman and John Craxton on the roof of Maresfield Gardens during the war.

He'd never been in a work environment such as this. Too many men in a confined space, the radio perpetually tuned to the Light Programme, chickens in the courtyard, snooker in the back room and a small factory near by assembling bits and bobs of electrical equipment. He was fascinated by the pecking order of the NFS. Professional firemen of low rank had suddenly been put in charge of large numbers of Auxiliaries, many of whom would have far outranked them in civilian life. They gave their orders awkwardly, almost apologetically. In trying to work out why the situation was so charged, Stephen concluded: 'Working-class people have a somewhat limited view of existence because they are tied to such a limited and narrow situation in the world.' From this perhaps obvious starting-point, he went on to analyse why social resentments, though they existed, were muted because of the war, although potentially dangerous for the future.

After he'd completed his training, he was stationed in north London not far from where he'd lived as a child. He rented rooms from Ernst Freud, one of Sigmund Freud's sons. His connection with the Freuds came through Muriel Gardiner, who'd helped to bring over Freud and his family just before the war. She'd also helped to finance a clinic set up by Freud's daughter Anna. It took care of refugee children. My mother worked there for a while. She was entrusted with a little boy called Robert. She wanted to have a child herself, but was having difficulty carrying her pregnancies to term.

The house in Maresfield Gardens still kept a student atmosphere. The Bechstein, back from Oxford, was played, and Stephen worked in the attic whenever he could, seeing that he was on duty forty-eight hours out of seventy-two at the fire station around the corner. Ernst's son Lucian, whom Stephen had met when he was still a schoolboy, painted dead birds in one room. John Craxton, a young painter who'd studied alongside Lucian Freud, lived near by. Tony Hyndman was in and out of the house the whole time.

Tony had a proprietary interest in Stephen's new marriage, for after all he'd introduced the happy couple. It was cheeky of him to turn up, as he'd behaved very badly towards Muriel. In order to bring her daughter's nanny to England, Muriel had asked Tony to marry her, which he had, but then he'd blown a large sum of money that Muriel had given his new wife so she could buy herself a house.

By now, my mother had learned everything she needed to know about Tony. Out of respect for Stephen, she refused to be jealous. She merely put Tony on one side on the grounds that she was working. 'There was in Tony's nature a deep pool of idleness, even, paradoxically, a militant idleness, he wished to deflect the industry of his companions, to make them feel that their work was a slavish bad habit, an act of unfriendliness, that they were prisoners of discipline whereas it was superior to be free of it, unbuttoned, open to the experiences and the enjoyment that the moment had to offer.' My mother stunned Tony with music. She played that piano at him for hours on end. She slugged him with Beethoven. After a while, Tony would get bored and slope off.

The huge military mechanism needed to win the war had heightened everyone's awareness of how fragile life is. As if to satisfy a spiritual need, much larger audiences than normal attended concerts of classical music and the art exhibitions were crowded.

Peggy Ashcroft, an actor who became a close friend of my mother's, started giving poetry readings in 1941. Two years later Natasha began to be involved with the ENSA concerts, the Entertainments National Service Association. She says primly, 'My war work concerts demanded a larger repertoire of romantic salon music than I would otherwise have cared to learn.' Then in May 1943, coming back on a train from Cambridge where they both happened to have performed, Peggy and Natasha decided to pool their resources. Together with Stephen, and several other actors and writers, they founded the Apollo Society, a group of artists who travelled up and down the country performing poetry readings interspersed with music.

A line from T. S. Eliot would be read by Peggy: 'We have been, let us say, to hear the latest Pole / Transmit the Preludes, through his hair and finger-tips.' A Chopin prelude would follow, except the hair and finger-tips would be Mum's. The group discovered through trial and error that certain poets went well with certain composers. Shelley with Debussy, for instance. Such an unlikely combination. Only by performing them could they have discovered that they worked well together.

My mother stayed with the Apollo Society for twenty-five years, and it gave her a companionship she would not otherwise have had.

It was something she needed. Her quest for a career as a solo performer was otherwise an uphill struggle.

By the time Stephen joined the Fire Service, it had become so large that it faced the problem of what to do with the men when there were no fires. Noticing this, he wrote to the London Civil Defence Region suggesting the formation of debating societies. The idea was well received, and soon he found himself in the role of Area Organizer of Discussion Groups in No. 34 Fire Force.

The beginnings were simple. The firemen met and the organizer asked a question, such as What did everybody feel about Russia? It would be up to the men to come up with ideas. Then Stephen began to invite his friends to participate. These included Kenneth Clark, a key figure in cultural activities during the war, and Julian Huxley, the distinguished zoologist. Count Mihály Károlyi, former President of Hungary, told his audience that they should be lighting fires all over Europe, not putting them out. Stephen was teased about this by his fellow firemen for weeks afterwards.

My father's lifelong socialism included a desire to 'educate' the working classes in order to bring them up to the level that he and his friends took for granted. If his fellow firemen teased him about Count Károlyi and his other eccentric friends, it suggests that they knew what he was doing, recognized the class element and were good-humoured about it. Meanwhile it never seems to have occurred to Stephen that the spirit in which he followed this self-imposed duty was close to that of his father Harold, who'd spent most of his life engaged in good works of this kind.

Stephen persisted in applying to join various branches of political intelligence but without success. According to my mother, in one interview he was asked: 'and what kind of a degree did you get at Oxford, Mr Spender?' He explained that he had not taken his Finals. He had no degree. 'Oh? And so what exactly did you do with your time?'

This was the voice of conventional England at its most cutting.

Yet this world was in retreat. During the Second World War, England changed radically without anyone being fully aware of the fact. Food rationing was a logical step for a country under siege, but it was also a move towards a more egalitarian society. In other words, socialism. That bottle of extra-strong orange juice filled with vitamins was a benefit that transcended class, though the working classes added a teat and gave it to babies and the upper classes poured it into a tumbler with gin.

In November 1943, an internal vetting request regarding Stephen received this answer from MI5: 'Stephen Spender, like several other young and progressive thinkers, joined the Communist Party in the days of the united front because he saw in this the only way to combat fascism. His behaviour and writings of recent years show that he is no longer in sympathy with communism and in fact will have nothing more to do with them. There is no security objection to his employment by P.W.E. on the Continent.' The Political Warfare Executive was in charge of propaganda to Europe during the war.

In May 1944, Stephen was given three months' leave from the Fire Service. 'I don't think I shall ever go back,' he wrote to T. S. Eliot, 'because the Chief Regional Fire Officer has complained to the Regional Commissioner that my hair is untidy. Truly. They don't like my hair, and they don't like to say so . . . I am quite delighted, as I had never expected such recognition. It is like their deciding that, after all, Virginia Woolf is not quite suitable to be a Watchroom Attendant.'

He was discharged from the Fire Service a fortnight later and started a new job in the Political Information Department, the visible face of the otherwise secret PWE. The PID had an address – Bush House, the headquarters of the BBC – a phone number and paper with letterhead, which Stephen occasionally used for his private correspondence.

His first job was to file information on Italian Fascism. He did not speak Italian and he had no knowledge of Italian politics. Was he being tested, or was it just the usual confusion of Britain at war?

Of this peculiar period of his life, he told me one wonderful detail. In the corridor he bumped into Charlotte Bonham-Carter, who was working on aerial reconnaissance in the Italian section. 'My dear, I've just ordered a sortie over Verona,' she said. 'So beautiful, the Roman Arena! I simply had to see whether it was all right.'

I was born on 13 March 1945, at Queen Charlotte's Hospital in west London. My birth coincided with the explosion of one of the last German V2 rockets to land on the city. It fell near Maresfield Gardens, so it's just as well that Mum was busy elsewhere.

Soon after my birth my parents moved into 15 Loudoun Road, the house in St John's Wood where they lived for the rest of their lives. It stood at the head of long rows of terraces built down the hill towards Abbey Road. The view down the hill gave a feeling that the original wood of St John's Wood was not totally dead. Mum could sit at the piano and look out at greenery and dream of nature. As I grew up, I got to know the nearest trees as intimately as I knew my bedroom on the top floor. My thigh tingles at the memory of one huge pear tree, long gone, which several times I slid down in my shorts desperately clinging to the trunk.

I can just remember Loudoun Road in the early days, the walls unpapered and the floorboards without their fitted carpets. In my bedroom there was a lithograph in four panels showing a little boy bowling a hoop, by Pierre Bonnard. I loved it. But the key memory of my earliest bedroom is a light hanging from the ceiling whose nakedness was not covered by the lampshade. It was like living in a painting by Francis Bacon. In fact to this day I cannot separate the London of my childhood from Bacon's canvases, or vice versa.

The bombed London of my childhood smelt differently from how it smells today. There was a fine dust in the air – or at least so I remember – vaguely electrical with overtones of mouldy carpet. The war took a long time to fade. At the Church Street market they sold useful war debris, like a mile of tangled copper wire, or a gas mask

of crumbling rubber, or a primitive machine for turning old gramophone records into flower pots by warming them over a mould, or
a fireman's helmet with dents in it, or a liquid for giving colour to
black-and-white photographs. 'Our wonderful country makes the
best coloured pencils in the world,' said the woman selling this
potion, and a surge of patriotic pride would make us hand over a
threepenny bit, even if we had no photos worth colouring.

Down Baker Street, cheap shops squatted in the holes left by
grander ones that had been bombed . . . I can't remember the end
of the war, of course, for I was a mere babe in arms, but I can
remember the mood six or seven years later. I think I can understand
how deep the craving was to get out of recently besieged Britain as
soon as the fighting ended.

As France was liberated, Stephen became obsessed by the idea that
he should get to Germany as soon as the hostilities were over. If
only he could speak to Ernst Robert Curtius, he might find some
explanation for the disaster of the Nazis.

He was interviewed for this purpose by the Allied Control
Commission in November 1944. It went badly. He described this
interview twice, once soon after it happened in a letter to Julian
Huxley, and then six years later in his autobiography, *World within
World*. In the letter to Huxley, he said he'd told the interviewers that
he wanted to make contact with German intellectuals who would
be involved with literature and culture after the war. 'The interviewer
at the end of the table said: Do you think that after the Nazis there
can really be such a development? Among what class of people?'
Stephen mentioned Curtius, but his application was rejected.

Retelling this incident in *World within World*, he quotes this man
as having said, 'We can assure you, Mr. Spender, that after this war
there will be *no* culture in Germany.' This sounds like an after-dinner
improvement of the original story. But whatever was said, the interviewers were looking for trained officers to send to Germany for a

full two years after the war to help with reconstruction. Spender did not have the necessary qualifications.

In an unexpected turn of events, he was offered a candidacy for the Labour Party in the snap election called by Churchill for July 1945. Either he turned the offer down, or somehow the message didn't reach him because he was in Paris. But this non-event marks the beginning of a new phase in his life. In the future his political activities would take place within the system rather than knocking fruitlessly on the back door.

Labour won by a landslide, and it radically altered his position. He was commissioned to go to Germany and research its post-war intellectual life, just as he'd wanted. This resulted in a secret report that was only declassified recently. It makes interesting remarks about German war guilt and suggests that more should be done to educate the up-and-coming generation of young Germans.

His photographs show wrecked guns and downed planes and rude refugees sticking out their tongues at him as he floated past sitting in the back of a car with a corporal driving. Signs outside the barracks reminded officers to travel armed. They were warned that Werewolves, ex-members of the Hitler Youth, had been ordered to resist even after the surrender. The officers had to tackle huge refugee problems and there were ominous discussions in the Officers' Mess as to whether tensions with the Russians would lead to another war.

The car he was given suffered from a neurotic carburettor and sometimes he'd find himself in the countryside with nothing to do but listen to the larks singing in an empty sky. His driver became friendly with a German girl and Stephen was curious as to whether they'd become lovers. (They hadn't.) The black market thrived in the larger towns – which Dad seems to have enjoyed. He met a dodgy sergeant-major who could fix any deal, and became involved in complex negotiations to exchange a carton of cigarettes for an immense music box. This instrument became a part of my child-hood. *La forza del destino*, with supplementary arpeggios tickled by wee prongs touching nails stuck into a shiny bronze roller.

When Ernst Robert and Stephen were reunited at first all went well. Curtius talked openly about 'war guilt'. Yes, the Germans were responsible. There may have been excuses – their lack of democratic experience, their deference towards authority – but this did not alter the fact that Germany bore responsibility for the most abominable crimes Europe had ever seen.

It was exactly what Stephen had wanted to hear, but mixed up with his forthright opinions Curtius complained about his present situation. It was humiliating that the German army had been beaten by such amateur soldiers as the Americans, he said. And what were the Allies going to do about Russia? Where was the crusade against Bolshevism that was so obviously necessary? The triumph of Bolshevism would mean that culture in Germany would be utterly destroyed, he said. And could Stephen please get his suit back? It had been sequestered and he couldn't teach without it. Dutifully, Spender went where he was directed. Without a word, the officer opened a door into a room crammed with people whose condition was far worse than lacking a respectable suit.

Stephen began to feel that behind these views lay a peculiar self-ishness, as if Curtius was unable to see the European point of view, only the German one.

My mother was also touring Germany at the time, but they did not travel together. She was giving concerts for ENSA.

Once during her visit, she played two concerts on the same day in wildly different surroundings. The first took place in the concentration camp of Belsen in front of an audience of survivors. Later that same evening she played for a group of senior British officers in a baroque theatre attached to a castle.

At Belsen, she was warned that the ex-inmates could not endure anything profound, so she played short cheerful pieces on an upright piano. Even so, their reaction overwhelmed her, as if these listeners had no control over their emotions. 'Their applause after each piece was almost vociferous, there was an atmosphere of vehement pleasure, as if the music was a sign to them that they were indeed in the real world.' At the castle that evening, playing on a superb Steinway to a group of English officers who seemed completely detached from their surroundings, the response to a Schubert impromptu was 'courteous and much less demonstrative'. Somehow the two performances cancelled each other out. 'I remember the day's experience as imposing a profound recognition that only seldom, if ever, can one truly – entirely – enter into the lot of any other human being.'

My parents caught up with each other the next day by accident. The car taking Natasha to Berlin stopped by the side of the road to help a stranded vehicle, and out of it emerged Stephen. They spent a few days together in the devastated city. There's a dark photo in a family album of my mother wrapped in a coat standing in the middle of Hitler's Chancellery. An immense chandelier dangles from wires and three Russian soldiers scurry along in the background.

Over the summer, Stephen typed out his diary and began turning it into a book. He showed a draft to Cyril, who wanted to publish the Curtius material immediately. Stephen had promised to show the text to Curtius first, but he allowed himself to be overruled.

In January 1946, Curtius saw his words quoted in *Horizon* and he was appalled. He had received Stephen as a friend, not as an interviewer. If he'd known that Stephen had intended to publish his thoughts, he would have spoken differently. His remarks about German war guilt, in print, would make him seem disloyal to other Germans.

Stephen apologized several times. Curtius refused to accept his apologies and Stephen began to lose patience. 'Most people here have taken it to be a defence of your conduct since 1933, though perhaps you would not wish me to do that.' This was a hint that he thought there'd been something equivocal about the fact that Curtius had refused to leave Germany.

Curtius appealed to T. S. Eliot, who defended the German's

right to have seen the article before it was published. Eliot also thought that Stephen did not understand the position of Curtius within Nazi Germany. 'You discuss the reasons for his not leaving Germany after 1933 but I don't think that you attempt to justify his remaining there, you merely go a certain distance towards condoning it.'

My father insisted that Curtius should be held to his words. Remarks about etiquette were irrelevant. He wrote to Eliot that in his *Horizon* article he'd tried to give an idea of Germans such as Curtius, 'who have my sympathy, but whom nevertheless I regard as very dangerous unless their views can be dragged into the open and they themselves made responsible for them'. Eliot thought this was simplistic. 'It is very difficult for the majority of human beings to recognize any sense of collective guilt in which they are personally implicated.'

Stephen knew nothing about the condition of 'inner exile' adopted by those Germans who hated the regime but refused for patriotic reasons to leave Germany. They hid in curious places and kept silent. It was a German secret, a syndrome, an ailment. It could not be discussed without raising awkward questions about loyalty.

Stephen took the view that by teaching medieval Latin literature to his students, Curtius had evaded his responsibilities. He underestimated how tightly the Nazis controlled their intellectuals. Curtius belonged to a group of democratic professors who were under constant surveillance. In the mid-Thirties, he'd engaged an SS officer as his assistant, a certain Hermann Grimmrath. This man had protected Curtius until 1940, when he was sent to the Russian front, where he was killed. A colleague at Bonn University was denounced by a pupil and arrested, but by concentrating on Latin, Curtius avoided dealing with anything that belonged, as it were, to the present tense.

Eliot was closer to Curtius than Stephen, and he did his best to calm things down. He wrote to Curtius:

Against what damage he may have done you by it [the *Horizon* article], I can say nothing, for I am ignorant; but for the element of pure bad taste and stupidity I can plead. He is really a good and affectionate young man – though very callow for his years; but he has sometimes offended me – and, I think, others – by the tone he adopts. He is a Liberal, and therefore tends to intolerance and judging others; and he tends to take an unconsciously superior tone on the basis of very imperfect understanding.

The remark is ironic, but covers genuine irritation. The peculiar thing about the dispute is that, underneath, these three were in agreement that European culture was united. It wasn't a series of separate cultures divided by language and nationality. Only, Eliot thought the underlying unity came from its Christian roots, Curtius thought it depended on the structure of medieval Latin, and Spender thought – what? That it required to be invented in the immediate future?

Before he'd even set out for Germany, Stephen had hoped that he and Curtius might found a European magazine together. This plan had to be abandoned as a result of the quarrel. The idea, however, unexpectedly reappeared in a request from Information Services Control, one of the government bodies supervising Germany, to provide a blueprint for such a magazine. It was just the opening that Stephen had been waiting for.

7

THE PURITY WAS HERS

STEPHEN'S TWO VISITS to Germany had been preceded by several trips to France on behalf of the British Council. He had no idea what he was doing at these conferences, other than offering a supportive English presence. He occupied 'a role which I could not seriously be expected to fill but for which the audience accepted me as a token'. Vagueness, I think, formed part of his credentials. When he tried to check up on his duties, he was told by the Director of the British Council in Paris that he wasn't expected to do anything specific. Indeed, one day he wandered off and spent the afternoon with Picasso.

His connection with French cultural life owed much to his experiences during the Spanish Civil War, where he'd made friends with a number of French intellectuals who were also supporters of the Republic: André Malraux, Louis Aragon, among many others. He could renew his friendship with them at these conferences, though these were so crammed with intelligent people he felt it was 'impossible for anyone to do justice to anyone else'.

The problems of France were very different from those of Germany. In France, four years of occupation had left a feeling of disgust at the devious skills that everyone had had to learn in order to survive. The 'civic virtues' of the British were praised, meaning that in England goods were not distributed according to the rough rules of the black market. Of those he met, the communists seemed the least self-punitive about the war. A myth was being circulated that the communist partisans had liberated France by themselves, with no thanks due to Britain or the United States. Communism was far from over. It was the movement of the future, not the past. It was useless for Stephen to argue that, everywhere, communism had produced regimes governed by force from above. He was told condescendingly that French communism would be different.

Before sending Information Services Control the outline for a magazine they'd asked for, Stephen forwarded a draft to Eliot. In three single-spaced pages and thirteen numbered points, he suggests that it should concentrate on Germany's position within Europe. The consensus at the conferences he'd attended was that Germany must be reunited with Europe as soon as possible. He was also worried that France had come under German influence during the occupation. 'Germany has sown the seed of Nazi thought in the countries which are now victorious.' An international magazine would create a new sense of European identity, he argued.

Eliot, who'd had many years experience as the editor of the *Criterion*, wrote a dry reply agreeing with points 3, 4, 5 and 6, though he questioned points 1 and 2. But the real questions were: 1. Who would pay for such a magazine? 2. Who would write for it? 3. Who would read it? There's a touch of irony in numbering such obvious questions. I assume that Eliot was teasing the thirteen numbered sections of Stephen's rambling proposal. It was hard to imagine that any Germans would be prepared to pay for such a magazine in their present position, continued Eliot. 'The important thing is to get it into the hands of the right people, not to get it into the hands of a great many people.' He thought one might reasonably hope for a readership of perhaps eight hundred. (If this seems low, the circulation of Eliot's *Criterion* had been no higher.)

Stephen had already tackled the question of payment in the last paragraph of his proposal: 'The British Government, above all others, should encourage this scheme, because it is to the British that the continent looks more than to any other nation.'

His book on Germany, *European Witness*, came out in October 1946. Curtius saw that Stephen had not removed him from the text as he'd promised to do. He wrote Stephen a formal letter ending their friendship, with a copy to Eliot.

Even before this, my father had given up the idea of founding a magazine based in England and Germany. He'd suddenly become convinced that it should be published between England and France. He'd even found a young man in Paris who he felt could be his co-editor. Could he bring him to see Eliot? This project never materialized, but given his many contacts in Paris and his interest in the regeneration of European cultural life, Julian Huxley offered Stephen a job at the newly founded UNESCO, the cultural organization of the United Nations.

Huxley, the first head of UNESCO, was an old friend of Stephen's. Natasha remembered when Stephen had introduced her to him. They'd had tea in Julian's apartment overlooking the London Zoo, of which he was the Director. He'd scared her, because in making light conversation she mentioned that she'd seen an interesting bird in the countryside recently and he'd tried to pin her down as to exactly what kind of bird it was. 'It had blue wings' wasn't good enough.

UNESCO's main function was to promote international understanding via cultural exchanges. Defining culture, however, went against the American grain. President Roosevelt's plan to support painters and writers in the early Thirties had been bitterly opposed – not surprisingly, as the Artists' Congress and the Writers' Union quickly became communist front organizations. The American decision to participate in UNESCO was taken reluctantly, to forestall the possibility that it, too, might become a massive communist front.

The American representatives to UNESCO quickly formed doubts about Huxley. He was an atheist, which was unacceptable to most Congressmen. He also brushed away their hints that some of the people he was hiring were communists. A key moment occurred when Huxley obliged UNESCO to come to the rescue of Pablo Neruda, who as a communist was being harassed by the Chilean government. (Did Stephen encourage Julian? He'd known Neruda since the Spanish Civil War.) The cause of protecting intellectual freedom was impeccable, but the Neruda case was noted by the Americans as another black mark against Huxley, who was eventually forced to resign.

My father worked for UNESCO from the end of 1946 until March 1947. It required frequent trips to Paris from London. I haven't been able to trace much about his experiences at this time, but I note that somewhere along the way, his interest in Germany faded.

In the spring of 1947, my parents left England for a trip abroad in just each other's company. It was the first time Natasha had ever been to France.

At a party in Paris, Natasha saw her husband across a crowded room talking to an elegant young man. She asked the person next to her who this man was. The reply: 'Don't you know? That's Stephen's new lover.'

My mother stood up, and promptly fainted.

It was a terrible moment.

She'd misinterpreted the long conversation at Wittersham which had ended, 'There is only us.' Stephen had not put the past behind him, nor had fatherhood given him a new, deeper idea of marriage. He loved her – of that, she was confident. But whatever view he held of marriage, it wasn't hers; and now she was faced with the existence of a dark area of their shared life which she could never reach.

After a few days in Paris they continued by train to Italy.

The country was a mess and the black market flourished. Dollars and pounds were exchanged for lire at far above the official rate. One day in a hotel near Verona they needed the local currency, and my mother sent my father out to buy some – but not at the bank, she said, pointing down into the street from the window of her hotel. There, see? That man on the corner.

My father went out, came back, and they took a train to the next step of their journey. Once they'd settled into their carriage, my mother asked him how much he'd managed to get for his pounds. My father said he hadn't changed his money with the man on the corner, as she'd told him. He'd gone to the bank like everybody else.

Thereupon occurred a scene so wild that my father never forgot it. He told me the story at least twice. He was still upset about it forty years later. The scene ended, in one version, 'and she fainted dead away' – which seemed to me a lame end to a story he'd told with such obvious distress. But the other version ended, 'and she tried to throw herself out of the train'.

My father was terrified by this incident. It revealed to him an unpredictable area of her soul, and he had no idea how deep it reached. His mother had died when he was a boy and he always felt guilty about it, and as a result there was something about unhappiness in a woman that sent him into such a panic he was unable to think clearly. Or so I believe.

But, if it comes to that, my mother's emotions in this incident are also hard to understand. She may have been furious because he'd disobeyed her. Control was important to her. Or perhaps the incident derived from her chronic anxiety about money. But it came so soon after having fainted in Paris at the thought that Stephen still had lovers, I think some obscure form of self-punishment must have come into it.

Back in London, without telling his wife, Stephen discussed the problem with Anna Freud. Although my mother had taken lessons on childcare at Anna Freud's school until she'd become pregnant with me, she had not been analysed by her. Anna Freud gave my father her private impression. Natasha would probably benefit from analysis, but she was held together by such an immense effort of will, it might be dangerous to probe too deeply. There was a risk of damaging whatever made her function without discovering anything that could take its place.

It's unusual for psychiatrists to give off-the-cuff diagnoses of this kind – and here we are talking about the daughter of Sigmund Freud! Her message may have been: Natasha's predicament is certainly grave, but the best person to deal with it is you, Stephen. But my father interpreted it differently. He decided that his wife was held together in such a state of tension that an attempt to deal with any part of it would make the whole pack of cards collapse.

My parents, taken by a street photographer in Verona close to the time when my mother threatened to throw herself out of a train.

Whenever my father talked to me about my mother's character, it was entirely about her predicament as seen in this light. He never thought about how she saw him, nor did he consider that her moments of wildness might be a reaction to something he'd done. He had difficulty in understanding her feelings. They were hers, and she was responsible for them. This was true not just of his relationship with his wife, it has to be said. His entire effort was dedicated to understanding his own emotions, and those of other people were always mysterious to him.

As soon as I was old enough to form opinions on their relationship, he'd try to convince me that sometimes Mum had fallen victim to her emotions, and he and I should form an alliance to provide her with support. I resisted this desire to join a conspiracy. I thought we were missing two things: my mother's point of view, and an explanation why her outbursts made him panic.

My mother's feelings were revealed only after her death, hidden away in a diary written during a particularly stressful moment in her life, when my father fell in love with a young American ornithologist called Bryan Obst. Bitterly, she wondered why she'd accepted this predicament all her married life. Her harshest entries were written late at night, but in the morning she found her angry emotions had vanished. Her waking self was devoted to the image that their marriage was strong. Natasha at three in the morning was an entirely different person from Natasha at breakfast. She asked herself: Are the late-night entries the faithful ones, or those I write during the day?

I never questioned her daylight self, as it were, nor would she have accepted any form of criticism from me. Keeping up appearances in front of her children was a vital part of her sense of duty. She could complain to others now and again, especially to other women, but never to me. And, because appearances and therefore courage were involved, I knew that if I'd ever tried to find out what she really felt about my father's continued relationships with men, it would have been a far more destructive act coming from me than if she'd been challenged by a stranger.

For more about this tense period of their lives, we have to fall back on a short story my father started at that time.

In 'The Fool and the Princess', a man who wants to become a writer comes back from a tour of duty in Germany where he's fallen in love with a Displaced Person. There's no love affair, and he returns home to his wife. She of course guesses that something has happened. She's frightened. 'I suppose you've never been really happy with me,' she says miserably. I hear my mother's voice very clearly in this phrase. Such was her investment in her marriage, and such was her deep-seated lack of confidence, that she was prepared to blame herself for the fact that he'd fallen for somebody else.

He protests that he loves her. She suffers. They try to return to normality, but it's hard. 'The very existence of the deeper level where everything was forgiven, mind and body fused, made them more impatient on the level where everything was wearisome, mechanical and unforgivable. Yet they could not live always on the deeper level, of dreams, tears, acceptance and finality.' I read this as meaning: since deep down we are in agreement with each other, why can't we avoid these time-consuming confrontations? 'We' being Stephen and Natasha, not the characters in the story.

The narrator knows he's in the wrong, but he feels that his unconsummated relationship with the offstage 'Princess' has been good for him. 'He made an effort to shake off once more this self-satisfaction which parodied a change which he felt really an improvement in himself, parodied even his love.' He is guiltily aware that he can only understand how this situation is affecting *him*, and that although he loves his wife, her emotions are to him incomprehensible.

Left alone in the empty bedroom after one of these fights, he groans. 'Yet although it seemed to him that he was suffering, his suffering lacked purity. It proved to him that he was sensitive. All the purity was hers, hers moving downstairs, hers moving out into the darkness, hers if perhaps, she drowned herself in some river.'

The idea that the heroine of the story might throw herself into the Thames is, to me, a memory of the occasion when my mother had tried to throw herself out of the train.

Over the early summer of 1947, Stephen met the head of Sarah Lawrence College in upstate New York, who invited him to come and teach there for a semester. Thus he made his first visit to the United States.

My mother was preparing for a Promenade Concert at the Albert Hall, so Stephen travelled first. The day before he left, there was a major row. My father was still anxious about it next morning. From his cabin on the *Queen Mary*, he wrote his wife a long, self-reproving letter.

'What makes separation so bad is anxiety, regrets, feeling that one has not made enough of the time together, fears about what the other is up to, and so on. So let's both make up our minds that we are completely and utterly together, and then these few weeks can be spent in thinking about each other and feeling each other's presence.' This was one of my father's strangest fixations: that love thrived on absence, during which it could reach a more immediate level by the power of thought; and this imagined reality was more powerful than the physical reality of an actual person's presence. 'My anxiety about you is that you don't feel sure of me. But now there is no reason whatever for you not to be sure of me. You have your prom and your BBC concerts, I have my work, but you will soon be with me.' What does the word 'now' in this passage signify? That the row involved his recent Parisian lover, and that Stephen had promised 'now' to put this part of his life behind him?

'The root trouble with me is that I am self-willed, I am a rebel, I do not want to submit to god or to man, I do not want to be good. I still have some way to go before this can be changed, and I think the thing most likely to change it will be my book Autobiography and Truth which will really be about the subjects we were discussing yesterday.' He's referring to the book that later became *World within World*. 'My own idea that being good is being tame is childish and absurd. But sometimes seeing that one's attitudes are childish is not a cure of them, especially when temptations & excitement are involved.'

She was planning to become baptized; and that was good. 'I am sure that would be a great happiness to you. I also think that our Catholic friends are right in thinking that you are in a state of grace and that I am not.' She should 'go on and be Christian, if that is your fulfilment. In any case, I am sure it will not come between us.' I don't know if Mum went through with her conversion, but I don't think so. Perhaps she wanted to balance her relationship with Stephen with something else, then found that it wouldn't carry any weight with him, so she let it go.

He continues: 'It is so brave of you to play in the proms and to study the Bible and to pursue all your spiritual adventures.' There's something so vague about this, it's almost insulting. He corrects himself:

> I think of you all the time, in fact for me our marriage is a religion and I shall try to be a better observer of that religion than I have been because I realize now that appearances are very important as well as realities. For even when our relationship is authentic one has to make a great effort of creation and imagination the whole time to prevent its authenticity from being cheapened and thrown into apparent doubt.

He'd told his grandmother that to write about contemporary life was almost a religion to him, and now it's the institution of marriage that has religious connotations. Yet my father was fundamentally atheist. It's either an attempt to create a bridge with a certain aspect of his grandmother's temperament, or my mother's; or else it's a dramatic statement regarding his own commitment to her as a belief, a quest.

'But all I can say is that I love you, love you, love you, more than ever before, though I have always loved you, and if I have caused you to doubt it at moments I am very sorry and I ought not to have done so. I shall be living with you in my thoughts all this time when we are separated. In future let us do all we can to avoid long separations, though, of course, we cannot make absolute rules.'

8

AMERICA IS NOT A CAUSE

M Y EARLIEST MEMORY as a child is of rolling down the lawn
in front of the house in Scarsdale where we lived when my
father taught at Sarah Lawrence. It's not much of a memory. I vaguely
recall being plump and cheerful. My mother was with us; also an
English nanny who longed to go home. The only things that interested
the nanny were the sales in the department stores.

This was my father's first visit to the United States, and it represented
the beginning of a new axis in his life. America represented money,
and like many English writers he came regularly to the country on
visiting professorships or on lecture tours. Sarah Lawrence was a
good place to start. Among others, he met Robert Lowell, who came
for a visit, and Mary McCarthy, who taught there for a year while
she gathered material for *The Groves of Academe*. I don't know what
my father thought of his pupils, but when a Picasso lithograph he'd
brought with him disappeared, he complained to the President.
'Sarah Lawrence girls don't steal,' was as far as that went.

During this time there occurred a famous quarrel between Lillian
Hellman and Mary McCarthy. Hellman represented the unrepentant
Stalinist wing of the old American Communist Party, a position
which by this time McCarthy found physically repellent. She came
across Hellman speaking unofficially to a group of students at a

party where Stephen was present – not his own party, it seems, though later he remembered himself as being the host. Hellman didn't notice McCarthy, who looked no older than the other students. Hellman was speaking in a patronizing way about the writer John Dos Passos. In Spain, he'd 'sold out'. But then John had always liked his food, and there wasn't much he wanted to eat in the restaurants of Spain in the middle of a war. And so on.

McCarthy instantly recognized this as a piece of communist character assassination. The real background was that Dos Passos had seen the communist repression of the anarchist brigades in Barcelona, and he had been appalled, and had begun to say so. Hemingway had seen the same thing but he'd kept quiet. Therefore, back in the United States, Hemingway was hailed as the up-and-coming writer and Dos Passos became the victim of a whispering campaign.

Mary McCarthy's career in politics had much in common with that of my father. She was tougher and less romantic, but their early experiences with communists had a similar trajectory of well-meaning idealists led astray.

In *My Confession*, McCarthy describes the bizarre way in which, in 1936, she became an anti-communist. Until that date, she'd merely fitted communists into social categories. The literary communists, 'doing the hatchet work on artists' reputations', she held in low esteem. 'The forensic little actors who tried to harangue us in the dressing-rooms.' The silent types, evidently in charge of something (but what?), who were admired because their reticence suggested authority. The 'fellow-travellers' who remained outside the party on some tiny doctrinal point to appear intelligent. Apart from that she'd enjoyed reading Trotsky's autobiography; and that was about it.

Then came the news of Stalin's purge of his former friends in the Moscow Trials – which she had missed, because she'd been in Reno getting a divorce. Back in New York, because of something she said at a cocktail party, she found herself on a list of supporters of a 'Fair Trial for Trotsky' group. Once there, she found she was outside the

Party; and being outside, she felt the pressure of arcane, late-night persecution. This only made her dig in her heels. All of which, told in her ironic but precise way, is very interesting – but right at the end she adds a fascinating clincher: 'Those of us who became anti-Communists during that year, 1936–37, have remained liberals – a thing less true of people of our generation who were converted earlier or later.'

This is especially true of my father, and it formed a special bridge between him and McCarthy. Yet liberalism in England meant something different from liberalism in the United States. There had been, after all, a Liberal Party in England, and it had survived from the 1840s until the First World War, when it was overtaken by Labour. Stephen belonged to those liberals who'd joined the Labour Party via the circuitous route of left-wing politics, but to be a 'liberal' in the United States meant working outside the folds of either political party. These liberals had no constituency. This suited Mary McCarthy very well. She could stand outside practically everything yet still represent an idea. Spender, by comparison, was mainstream.

On their way back to New York, Natasha and Stephen stayed with the composer Samuel Barber at Mount Kisco. Barber had written a setting for Stephen's poem, 'A Stopwatch and an Ordnance Map', and he was a friend from way back.

Barber listened to my mother perform. Afterwards he told my father: she has a great deal of talent, but she's missing a piece of technique without which her career will be very difficult. But don't worry! There are piano schools where she can check herself in, like a car going into a garage. Six months later she'll re-emerge with everything in the right place. It's extremely boring, because it's purely mechanical, but without it Natasha will always have to work by straining her will.

My mother had given up the Royal College without graduating. She thought she was being badly taught. She'd begun to study with

Clifford Curzon, who in turn had studied with Artur Schnabel, the greatest Beethoven specialist of his generation. Clifford – he was my godfather, so I saw him at various times – could remember every word that Schnabel had ever said to him. But he taught interpretation, not mechanics. He could take a piece that Mum was studying and analyse a passage saying, Schnabel would have done it this way, Rudolf Serkin does it like this.

My father would sit restlessly in the background of these conversations, which went on right up to Clifford's death. Once, Dad took me outside the house, where in the open air he positively danced with irritation. I asked what ailed him. He said: 'Clifford lived for four years in Berlin, and he didn't even notice the Nazis.' To him this didn't constitute dedication to his art. It wasn't even absent-mindedness. It was horrifying.

Years later, Dad told me that he regretted the fact that they hadn't fitted the piano-garage into their lives, although I can't imagine how they could have found a space for it. The fact remained that my mother played the piano on her nerves, and her technique always lagged behind what she could comfortably do. In her time she played many difficult pieces, such as Prokofiev's Third Piano Concerto, Stravinsky's *Capriccio*, and of course the big staples like Beethoven's Fifth Concerto, *The Emperor*. And she'd always leave off practising until the last minute. Midnight on the night before, she'd still be thumping that awkward passage in the last movement. I once came out on to the landing from my room above the piano room and shouted, 'If you aren't ready now, you never will be,' whereupon a dreadful silence fell upon the house.

As a child I'd listen to her practising the same passage endlessly until her fingers went to the right places by themselves. Over the years it took a strange hold on me. As I lay on my bed upstairs reading a book, she'd go back and do those ten bars again and my eyes would go back and read those two sentences again. It was maddening. A book and a piece of music became intertwined into a mishmash of repetitions and stumbles. Words on the printed page acquired the emphasis of musical phrasing, a certain book would become associated with a particular composer. What I read and what I heard became one.

Stephen arrived in New York for his second trip to America early in April 1949. He discovered that many of Mary McCarthy's friends were bitterly complaining about her account of them in her novel *The Oasis*, which had recently been published in *Horizon*. He wondered: Is New York any less parochial than London? 'It is not surprising that people should be annoyed, but the feeling that the story somehow undermines the security of the characters described in it, is rather astonishing.'

The Cold War was a leading topic in the newspapers. It was becoming increasingly necessary to choose: Them or Us? Stephen looked down from his bedroom window at the streets of Manhattan and wondered, do we really have to become pro-American? What does this country have to offer? 'The cars as fertile as weeds; the anxiety of all the things in the shops to be bought. The creation of standards whose only nature is an ostentatiousness, which excludes people who do not share these. The anxious suspicious over-generosity of Americans.'

My father is taking up the cause of the rest of the world against the United States. I think his experiences in UNESCO might have affected him. The idea that even this institution had to become pro-American was hard to accept.

A few days later, away in the South, Stephen noticed a newspaper report analysing a recent conference that had been held at the Waldorf Astoria Hotel in New York. This Peace Offensive organized by the communists had been dramatically challenged by a group of liberals and ex-Trotsky intellectuals, including several of Stephen's friends. Mary McCarthy had been present, bringing an umbrella with which to defend herself against the Stalinists. Stephen read the story incredulously. Communism, the cause of peace? Nonsense! Nevertheless communism was still a 'cause', even if it entailed, in every country where it gained power, the loss of liberty for all except a few leaders at the top. 'America is not a "cause" in the same way. It is just America, with the American way of life and a rooted opposition to un-American ways, and tremendous waste, and a radio and a press and a movie industry, not to mention political parties, which advertise a commercialisation which is an insult to every race and class of people not directly involved in American ideas and interests.'

The fact that Americans insisted that their culture was superior to all others was agonizing to those non-Americans who had to chose between the USA and communism. 'America judges others by *her* values, *her* interests, which prevent her from either understanding or being understood.' The United States couldn't grasp that its culture might be unattractive to other nations. 'Not to see that the Voice of this America can never speak to the world – in fact, that it is only by learning the voice of the world of striving peoples that America can ever speak to the world, is a fatality which rots even America itself.'

This isn't anti-Americanism. It's exasperation with the choice of 'Them or Us', and a plea on behalf of many cultures that would prefer to choose neither. But to choose neither was not an option; and if the choice had to be made, of course it would have to be in favour of the United States.

Stephen was in the process of completing two important texts. The first was *World within World*, which he finished on a ranch in Taos, New Mexico, where D. H. Lawrence once lived. The second was his essay for *The God That Failed*, a compendium of memories written by key participants in the events of the Thirties, once communists, now repentant, some bitterly so. It was an influential book, made more powerful by the fact that most of its authors had not taken up the cause of the United States after they'd lost faith in communism. Indeed, my father's contribution includes this: 'Capitalism as we see it today in America, the greatest capitalist country, seems to offer no alternative to war, exploitation and the destruction of the world's resources'. If only communism worked, he wrote, it might provide an alternative to 'a mass of automatic economic contradictions'. My father's 'ambivalence' meant that he faithfully supported the United States while feeling ineradicable doubts about what that country stood for.

My mother and I weren't with him on this trip. We spent the summer of 1949 in Portofino, on the Ligurian coast of Italy. I was four years old and I remember my feelings at the time. I can even remember my father not being there, as a kind of latency, the state of expecting him to turn up, shared between Mum and me.

There's a photo of me aged four, fishing in the bay. My hat is large and floppy. My swimsuit is baggy. I remember the look of the water. Even when the day was calm and there was no wind the sea was never still. It lay a few feet below the edge of the port in glowing lenses beneath which tendrils endlessly traced the letter ess. At the beach, a sea urchin abandoned in my knee five long legs waving at the different points of the compass, patiently blundering through each other without tangling. They thought they were still in their carapace and were walking away from me – but what clever legs to do that by themselves.

I remember a race back from the beach, round the promontory and into the bay. I've done my best to raise it to the level of a trauma, but my life on the whole has been free of anything traumatic, so it remains just an instance of my mother behaving competitively. She had a strong competitive streak: the pursuit not of the thing itself but of the victory that winning represented.

The other participant was Alison Hooper, like Mum aged under thirty, both in cast-iron swimsuits made of some shiny material. There we were among the towels and trowels of the beach on the promontory, and Mum suddenly leaped up saying 'Race you home.' Whereupon Alison too sprang up, grabbed her towel and basket and started up the steps cut into the rock, of which there were rumoured to be a thousand. She took them two at a time and her calves flicked sideways as she ran.

Mum grabbed me, dropped me in the front of the rubber dinghy and started paddling. She shone with the gleeful sheen of early motherhood. Beautiful, with a child and a husband and a career, she was in the stage when the young mother says, Life, throw me a problem! There's nothing I can't solve!

As we set off in the rubber dinghy, our world withdrew to just her and me, the surroundings nothing but a pretty backdrop to our shared ambition, which was to paddle around the cliff and reach the edge of the quay first. So we paddled, she behind me steering and myself in front doing the best I could, with a little spade, not scooping the water but trying to hit it, except this element gave no resistance but took my hand in a brief flurry of bubbles.

Evidently we weren't going fast enough, for at a certain moment, round the edge of the rocks and with Portofino in sight, she said, 'Come on! You've got to paddle harder! There's a shark behind us!'

Immediately the friendly element of water and bubbles became dangerous. Why did I have to put my hand in there if a shark was waiting to grab it? The shark was behind us, and between me and it there was Mum, but she wasn't putting her hand into the sea and besides, she was armed. She could ward it off.

Now I couldn't paddle but only stab the water as if the shark was already there, under the bobbing rubber which obviously provided no defence except at least he couldn't smell us, but if my fist and spade flashed in and out fast enough, maybe he'd be discouraged and leave us alone. And now there were sharks all around us. I could see them under ends of the boats moored in the bay where the water was less choppy, backlit by rays that diffused into spangles of sunlight all around them. I knew these were the rudders of the boats we were passing because they were symmetrically poised and motionless under every boat, harder than any fish and more purposefully angled.

But they were rudders and sharks simultaneously, for my mother was in a state of anticipated triumph and paddling furiously and I was doing my best. 'Come on! Just a bit more!' And we won. We were on to the hard lip of the bay of Portofino just as Alison ran up, my mother waving a towel in the air and skipping to prove we'd done it.

My mother in north Italy in about 1949.

9

YOUR SINS OF WEAKNESS

THE CONGRESS FOR Cultural Freedom came into being between 1949 and 1950. It elevated and then nearly destroyed my father. It provided him with the magazine that he'd been trying to create since the war, and *Encounter* grew to become perhaps the most influential cultural magazine in English. But when in the mid-Sixties it turned out that both the Congress and all its projects had been financed by the CIA, the results for him were devastating.

Stephen had missed the foundation of the Congress, which took place in Berlin in June 1950. One of its most active promoters was Melvin Lasky, the editor of *Der Monat*. As a soldier in the US Army, Lasky had persuaded General Lucius Clay of the Occupying Forces to create this magazine. Lasky's ideas were clear and forthright. 'The mere announcement of fact and truth is not enough. The fact must illustrate, must dramatize, must certainly be *timed*; our truth must be *active*, must enter the contest, it cannot afford to be an Olympian bystander.'

When the CCF was founded, banner headlines in the newspapers declared 'Freedom has Seized the Initiative'. Two British delegates to the Berlin meeting, Hugh Trevor-Roper and Freddie Ayer, had no objection to promoting truth and freedom, but what freedom, on behalf of whom? Both Trevor-Roper and Ayer had worked in British Intelligence during the war. Trevor-Roper had written a book proving that Hitler was dead, for rumours that he had survived persisted for many months. Freddie, of course, had known Stephen since his first marriage. They immediately recognized that a semi-secret institution was being created. They wanted to know who would be in charge. The British government did not have the money for that kind of thing. Did this mean it would be an American operation? When they raised objections, they were told sharply, 'Don't rock the boat.' To which they sang out cheerfully, 'Whose boat?'

A few years before the *Encounter* scandal reached its climax, Freddie told us the story of 'Don't rock the boat.' My mother became obsessed by it. Surely it meant that the Congress for Cultural Freedom was a clandestine American operation? She brooded, but it wasn't exactly evidence. It was just another piece of gravel that refused to turn into a pearl.

Lasky, replying to a hostile article of Trevor-Roper's when he was back in London, wrote a fiery letter to the *Manchester Guardian*. The confusion of the Berlin conference, with its passionate fights between the delegates, was surely evidence of the kind of freedom to be pursued. 'We had invited them here precisely because we wanted to indicate the diversity of Western ideas, the rich individuality of democratic culture, and to make possible discussion, argument, criticism – if, in the end, a certain higher democratic unity.' Did the vague expression 'democratic unity' mean corralling a lot of people into one group in order to promote a single idea?

The main office of the CCF was set up in elegant surroundings in Paris, with Lasky living in a grand flat near by. The Russian émigré composer Nicky Nabokov also moved to France and joined the CCF. He'd met Stephen recently. The Director was Mike Josselson, who was born in Estonia and had moved to Berlin when he was ten, before emigrating to America. He'd worked as a buyer for Gimbel-Saks and had lived for more years in Europe than he'd lived in the USA. His attachment to European culture was as strong as his faith in that of the United States, if not stronger.

The American Committee for Cultural Freedom, which held its first meeting on 14 December 1950, was from the beginning beyond the control of the Paris office. It was perpetually torn by internal disputes. When Senator Joe McCarthy began his attacks on supposed crypto-communists in the universities and the government, most liberals in the American CCF wanted to resist, but the die-hard anti-Stalinists thought he should be supported. The liberals came to be defined as 'anti-anti-communists', a double negative that put them on the defensive.

Money was also a problem in the New York office. They looked with envious eyes at the CCF office in Paris, where visitors were taken out to fabulous meals. Diana Trilling deduced that, at least outside the USA, the CCF must be subsidized by the CIA, for the simple reason that the Paris office could afford expensive lunches and the New York office could not. Everyone knew that the CIA was prohibited from acting on American soil.

I take the view that at this stage it was no secret that the CIA was backing the CCF. Nor was it shameful. The vast subsidies of Marshall Aid had put Europe back on its feet, and here at last was an initiative involving culture rather than tractors. It was intolerable that young communists in Italy and France should believe the myth that communist partisans had freed their countries without any help from Uncle Sam, and any initiative challenging this illusion was to be welcomed. If you were a Fulbright scholar and you liked Italy and you were told you were a CIA agent, the best you could do was defend yourself with a joke. Oh sure; and don't forget John Wayne. He's also a tool of capitalist imperialism.

With regard to this early phase of the cultural Cold War, there were even some light-hearted moments. Jason Epstein, later one of the co-founders of the *New York Review of Books*, was commissioned to go to Nigeria on a weird mission. The Russians were building a deep-water port in Ghana and the CIA wondered whether, since they were there, the Russians would try to brainwash the young by infiltrating Stalinist textbooks into the high schools of Ghana and

Nigeria. He was met by two local agents with crew-cuts wearing identical seersucker jackets. So inconspicuous! But the local schools had excellent schoolbooks provided by the British and there were no signs of this particular plot by the Russians, so Epstein just spent time hanging out in bars with the local agents.

Can I really argue that the financing of culture was cheerfully taken for granted in 1951 and a dozen years later it had turned into a murky secret? I think I can. Shame comes into the picture. By the mid-Sixties, with the Vietnam War and the interference of the CIA in South America, it was no longer possible to be light-hearted about art shows and ballets whose ultimate sponsors were secret government institutions.

The English branch of the CCF, calling itself the Committee for Cultural Freedom, came into being on 11 January 1951. It acquired about forty members, most of whom were just names on the stationery. Stephen was ostensibly its Chairman, but he was frequently absent on lecture tours in the United States; or in Israel, which he visited for three months from March 1952 in order to write a book about the early days of the country. As far as Stephen was concerned, all that the English Committee achieved in its first two years was to give a few cocktail parties.

At the end of 1951, Stephen learned from Nicky Nabokov that the Paris CCF had recently purchased *Twentieth Century*, a British magazine languishing in financial difficulties. Stephen had a connection with this magazine, which he wanted to steer away from badly written political discussions that he found dull. Michael Goodwin, Secretary of the English CCF, thought he was in charge both of the magazine and of the Committee, and he became engaged in a struggle with the Paris office to maintain his position.

By now, Stephen knew that both the English CCF and *Twentieth Century* were subsidized by the Paris office, 'which, in turn, receives its funds from the American Federation of Labor'. Casually, almost indifferently, he qualifies this by adding: 'To many people, though, it seems that in fact its money comes from the State Department.'

If he'd followed up on this and tried to find out who was backing the CCF, would he have maintained a connection with it? I think not. But, by not asking, he could establish an understanding based on silence. What he wanted – literature – could run parallel to whatever it was the State Department wanted.

Stephen in a photo taken in Jerusalem shortly after he'd written a long entry in his diary about the intrigues behind the founding of Encounter.

Goodwin tried to convince his fellow committee members that they must resist any attempt of the CCF in Paris to give them orders. He bravely used the word 'dictatorship', and ran up bills at a grand restaurant, wining and dining those who he thought would help him in his struggle with Nabokov. At a certain point Stephen became so irritated with this behaviour, which eternally postponed the problem of improving the contents of *Twentieth Century*, that he resigned from the editorial board of the magazine – only to be told he didn't hold a post that he could resign. The same confusion existed in the English Committee for Cultural Freedom. Apart from the fact that Goodwin was Secretary and Treasurer, nobody seemed to have any official position at all.

Stephen wrote a dense summary of the infighting as he travelled by boat to Israel in March. He hadn't kept notes in his journal hitherto. The aspect that most interested him, in this retrospective moment, was Goodwin's personal ambition. 'He is, to me, a new type of person. Someone whose entire position rests in handling his own public and social relations.' And he and his cronies were not interested in publishing literature. A colleague of Goodwin's had written to Paris at some point, 'You continentals don't seem to realize that literature and poetry have no appeal to us English.'

For the moment, writing this on the deck of a ship travelling to Haifa, the whole intrigue involving Goodwin seemed to Stephen merely absurd. Politics don't come into his account. It was just a question of personalities. It was amusing to see how badly people behave. 'There is an idea for a novel in this somewhere.'

When *World within World* came out in April 1951, Auden wrote him an affectionate but critical letter from New York.

Have read World within World several times with increasing respect. The only criticism I have is that, while confessing your sins of weakness you pass over in silence your sins of strength, ie of calculation and coldness of heart; and nobody, my dear, who is as successful or can be as funny as you, is without them. The self you portray would never have got invited to all those houses and conferences. We love people because of their warmth and endearing weaknesses but we want to get to know them because of their powers.

This echoes a letter Wystan had written to him in 1942: 'I believe that you are a very strong, ruthless character. When you behave badly, it is not due to weakness of will but excess of will, unlike people such as, for example Cyril or me, who, when we behave badly, do so out of fright and a fear of independence.' This was consistent with Auden's bizarre categories of human types involving the truly strong, the weak, the man of Will and so on. Auden never reversed his first impression of my father. It was the same as the theory he'd told to Stephen's governess when he was printing Wystan's first book of poems twenty-two years previously.

Cyril Connolly also had doubts about *World within World*. It was a great book, but what about the man who wrote it? 'Mr Spender has always seemed to me two people,' he wrote in his review.

Let us call them S I and S II. S I is the youthful poet as he appears in Isherwood's *Lions and Shadows*, and to others who knew him in the early Thirties. An inspired simpleton, a great big silly goose, a holy Russian idiot, large, generous, gullible, ignorant, affectionate, idealistic – living for friendship and beauty, writing miraculous poems, expecting too much from everybody and from himself on whom he laid charges and responsibilities which he could never carry out. S II was shrewd and ambitious, aggressive and ruthless, a publicity-seeking intellectual full of administrative energy and rentier asperity, a young tiger sharpening its claws on the platform of peace.

The subtext of Connolly's review is that poets shouldn't become distracted by going on too many 'junkets'. This was the word they used among themselves regarding the friendly chore of attending conferences. Perhaps Cyril meant it as a warning.

We spent the summer of 1951 in Torri del Benaco, a small fishing village halfway up the eastern shore of Lake Garda in Italy.

We took over one entire wing of the Albergo Gardesana. Five rooms, including one for my baby sister Lizzie and her nanny. A piano hired in Verona followed us out. The brand-new railings of the brand-new staircase were cut down and rewelded to get the instrument up to Mum's room on the first floor. Such luxury would be unthinkable today; yet the hotel paid. The whole village participated in moving that piano. They were fascinated, and we were rich. A poet! Of international fame! Today, the fishing skiffs have been replaced by expensive speedboats and Torri is entirely commercial, but in those days there was innocent curiosity regarding these glamorous foreigners. It must have been baffling to think that words on paper could produce such wealth.

North from the hotel along the lake's edge, the way became blocked by houses flanking the shore. I was a nimble six-year-old and could work my way round them by jumping on curious stumps poking out from the mud. Someone told me that these were the remains of huts built on stilts in a prehistoric moment, and immediately the word 'prehistoric,' or rather 'pre-high-storic', acquired immense resonance for me. I imagined gorilla-like ancestors eating shellfish and staring out across the water, chewing morosely.

In the other direction, towards the wooden Lido, stood the remains of the towers that gave Torri its name. There was a long wall topped with swallowtail battlements. Lizards crept in and out of the flaking plaster of the lower levels, or ventured to cross the sharp gravel at my feet, not yet in those days covered with asphalt. The wall was so long I never got to the end of it.

After a week I made friends with a gang of boys my own age. I learned Italian quickly and took things at face value, as children do. The sole ambition of these boys was to grow up, leave school and earn money for their families. There was only one available opening: the tile factory a couple of miles down the road towards Verona. The tiles were made by mixing cement with coloured stones and pouring the mixture into long moulds which, after they'd set, were cut into slices like salami. Lots of dust, no extraction fans. It was considered unvirile to wear a mask, but the boys made hats out of old cement bags and wore them to protect their nicely oiled hair. These grinning playmates of mine were so proud of what they did. It was real work. The cement dust was corrosive and many of these early friends died in their forties. Start work at twelve and die at forty. The heroic period of Italy's 'economic miracle'.

Having to cope with the gang of small boys taught me a lot about leadership. There was one occasion as we were mooching around the edge of the port when we came across an unusual sight: two German boys our own age, complete with lederhosen and a proprietary look. My boys became very tense. This was only six years after the war, and it was the first sign they'd seen of tourists from the great black beast on the other side of the Alps. How dare they? Garbled memories of atrocities were poured into my ears. I had to do something. Well, to cut a long story short, I threw them into the bay, one after the other. Their self-confidence vanished and they paddled helplessly towards the shore in their wet leather shorts, like frogs. I felt guilty afterwards. It occurred to me, aged six, that leadership meant followership. I would never have done such a thing on my own.

All day my friends fished around the port with bamboo rods and filigree catgut and hooks as small as a baby's fingernail and bait made of spit and the inside of bread rolls. The tiny fish thus caught were cooked by the sun. A rock near by would become a board on which they rested until they stopped moving, then they'd gradually curl up, and later that afternoon the fisher-boy would eat them as if removing pieces from a game of chess.

The Albergo Gardesana had its own mystique, the opposite of dust and cruelty. There, all was order and cleanliness. Corridors of waxed marble floors and fresh plaster, dark and cold after the brightness outside. In the enormous kitchen I watched Signora Tomei bossing the cook as she made gnocchi at a wooden table, two at a time, one white pellet under each flour-dusted palm, the right going clockwise, the left counter-clockwise. The smells of freshly ironed linen and newly rolled gnocchi were as steadfast as columns in a church. The bossiness of la padrona. Her husband Commendatore Tomei had hair so firmly combed it seemed ironed to the top of his skull. The sacramental quality of service at table. The obligation to sit still, don't fidget, the food will be here soon. The waitress whose clothes were black and shiny and her white frilly apron stiff with starch. The binary quality of relationships, where to sit at table required manners that you could forget when you met Martino Tomei, their son, later in the street.

My father worked at a table on a balcony overlooking the lake. In the family album there are photographs of the American poets Robert Lowell and Allen Tate sitting against the background of the picturesque port, so his vivid and varied social life followed him even here. Over the water on the west side of the lake stood a beautiful mountain that looked like a fallen profile – of Napoleon, they said, though it could have been anybody. The sounds of the lake were soothing, but next door my mother was grappling with a late Beethoven sonata. I remember her warm-up pieces: Ravel's *Jeu d'eau* and Debussy's *Reflets dans l'eau*. Perhaps Mum liked their watery association with the lake.

In late June, a journalist came out from London to interview my father. What was his explanation for the sudden disappearance of Guy Burgess and Donald Maclean, the British diplomats who had defected to Moscow?

The Case of the Missing Diplomats was perhaps the worst secret service disaster of the 1950s. Nobody knew quite what they'd done, and indeed even today the actual damage has not been quantified, but meanwhile the various agencies of the United States were furious that two such obvious liabilities had been allowed to spy for the Russians for so long. It was living proof that the Brits were 'soft on communism'. Meanwhile in the English popular press, the 'old-boy network' of upper-class clubmen was held responsible for having protected them from exposure and arrest.

Stephen knew Burgess and liked him. He knew Maclean only by sight. Seeing that the journalist from London had made a long journey, my father spoke openly about Burgess, explaining that everybody was completely at a loss for an explanation. 'Everybody' included Stephen's friend the poet and literary editor John Lehmann, and in his innocence my father showed the journalist a letter he'd just received from Lehmann saying how puzzled they all were. The journalist asked if he could borrow it, promising to keep it confidential. Off he went, and a few days later the letter appeared on the front page of the *News Chronicle*.

Stephen's friends in London were furious. How could he have been so naive? Robert Kee was overheard talking about it with James MacGibbon, his partner in the publishing firm they co-directed. Jean, James' wife, was on the other line. James said: 'what on earth did he think he wanted to take it away for if he wasn't going to—' And Robert: 'absolutely typical Stephen'. And Jean: 'he's never quite grown up'.

This, according to my father's MI5 file – for of course the Missing Diplomats caused a major disruption among the security services. Anyone who knew them was now under surveillance. MI5 knew that one of the last telephone calls that Burgess had made was to 15 Loudoun Road. He'd been looking for Wystan, who was staying with us, but he was out for supper. My mother passed on the message but Wystan did nothing about it; and that was that.

Burgess had hoped that he might take Maclean to Prague, drop him off, and then lie low in Wystan's house on Ischia for a few months – as if the Italian police wouldn't have noticed. Auden was thus involved. In the same letter to Stephen in which he discussed *World within World*, he went into the Burgess case. 'I still believe Guy to be a victim, but the horrible thing about our age is that one cannot be certain.'

The word 'victim' suggests he thought Burgess might have fallen foul of some intrigue at the Foreign Office. On the other hand, what if it was all true and they really were spies? A week later, Wystan wrote again to Stephen: 'I feel exactly as you do about the B–M business. Whatever the real facts are, they are unintelligible; even the word betrayal becomes meaningless.'

Betrayal becomes meaningless? This could mean that, without knowing the facts, it's impossible to know what Burgess had betrayed. But the 'facts' are also 'unintelligible'. I think Auden means: in the Thirties Burgess shared with all of us a series of principles that belonged to the times. It was 'meaningless' to state that this idea had been 'betrayed'.

Burgess may have done things regarding which, if they knew the facts, his friends might disapprove, but this would not constitute 'betrayal'.

Cyril Connolly also knew both men, shared their background and was obsessed by their defection. Just the day before they'd disappeared, he'd had lunch with Donald Maclean at his club near the Foreign Office. They'd emerged late in the afternoon, 'into a little pin-striped shoal of hurrying officials'.

Cyril had been following the deterioration of both men in recent months. Had they left clues about their plans? Should he have guessed? Should he have done something about it? He went to great lengths to establish their movements in the days before they left. Was it prearranged, or had they taken fright? Had they been tipped off that they were in danger of arrest?

Connolly talked it over with John Lehmann on the telephone, and was duly eavesdropped by MI5. Lehmann thought the most plausible explanation was that someone, probably in the United States, had been about to reveal embarrassing details about this Thirties background of sympathy for communism that they all shared. Lehmann: 'It is very difficult to understand it otherwise isn't it?' Connolly: 'Yes, very.' Perhaps the implication is that, if this particular betrayal had stayed an English problem, it would have just simmered away in the background without anyone making a fuss.

Dad went back to London in July for the opening of a play he'd written for the Festival of Britain. Mum went with him as she had three concerts to perform, one at the Wigmore Hall. As I seemed happy in Torri, they left me behind. They weren't gone for more than a week, but because the hotel would have seemed lonely without them, I was entrusted to one of the big sailing boats which in those days still worked their way up and down the lake. The red-haired brother of one of the maids who occasionally took care of me was the skipper.

No cabin for me, just a throbbing hatch beneath the deck at the front of the boat smelling strongly of tar and diesel. Bed was a blanket spread over a coil of rope tied to the anchor. I felt the coils moving beneath me when I slept, and the delicious perfume of oil and tar warmed my dreams.

But I also remember feeling lonely in the square of a strange town at the upper end of the lake – perhaps Malcesine. This wasn't my village. My village was Torri. This village felt stranger than London, stranger than any town I'd visited, because my parents hadn't brought me there, while Francesca's brother sold his coal or did whatever he had to do in one corner of the piazza within a circle of gesticulating men.

On 9 July, Stephen was in Oxford for the first night of his play.

Back at the White Lion Hotel, an intelligence officer was waiting to question him in relation to the missing diplomats. This was William Skardon, a senior interrogator from MI5. They missed each other. Instead of spending the night, Stephen took the train straight back to London without going to the hotel where Skardon was waiting for him. MI5 decided not to reschedule this meeting. 'At one time it was thought that it might be worthwhile interviewing Stephen but after further consideration the idea was dropped as it was thought he could produce no further information.'

This is what Spender's MI5 file says. I don't believe it. My father told me that in fact he *had* been interrogated. He was asked if he was aware that Guy Burgess was a communist agent. And he'd said: Yes. 'Whenever Guy got drunk, which was almost every night, he'd tell us he was a Russian spy.' Why hadn't he reported this information to the appropriate authorities? 'I thought that if we all knew, you must know, too.'

There is something very cosy about this story. 'We' and 'You' were social groups that overlapped. Somewhere in the background lay a reservoir of shared experience. Although I could be wrong, I think my father's MI5 file is full of jokes. What significance would it otherwise have, to say that he'd never grown up? This suggests that the higher levels of those who kept an eye on him knew him. Had made up their own minds about him. Liked him, even.

Faced with Stephen's devastating frankness, especially after his gaffe involving the *News Chronicle*, it's easy to imagine what Skardon might have said next. 'I think on the whole, Mr Spender, we'd better forget that this meeting ever took place. And may I suggest that from now on you say as little as possible about Mr Burgess.' Skardon saw that Stephen, whatever his other virtues, was incredibly indiscreet. It would not have helped to dampen the scandal if MI5 interrogated him and then found their ignorance of a fact known to all – that Burgess was a Russian spy – spread all over London in a series of amusing after-dinner stories.

My parents came back to Torri and our hotel life resumed.

'I never knew where to find you,' Martino told me recently, for it was his job to look for me at mealtimes. 'You did not frequent the best youth of Torri,' he said, grinning. There was a big drain by the side of the other tile factory, the one near the church, channelling the overflow from one level of the village to another. I could slide down it but Martino was too big. Anyway, sliding down drains would not have suited the son of Oreste Tomei.

Torri wanted to improve itself. Everyone felt there was much to learn from these distinguished foreigners. Memmo the greengrocer heard that the great Spanish guitarist Andrés Segovia was coming for a holiday, so he practised and practised, and when Segovia gave him a lesson, the entire village stood in the street outside silently listening.

Torri was fascinated by the distinguished foreigners who appeared there for holidays. André Gide, for instance, who brought with him from Paris a particularly unruly boyfriend. The day after spending turbulent nights with the lads of Torri, Gide would listen to the complaints of the boys' parents. On his desk lay a stack of fresh banknotes. According to the degree of scandal involved, Gide would take some from the top and hand them over without a word. This was told to me by an old man whom I saw when Dad and I visited Torri for the last time several decades after Gide's visit. He now sold gas appliances, and nothing remained of his cherubic former self except his long curling eyelashes. It was a lesson for us all, he said. At the time, we just enjoyed exploiting him; and we despised him. At this stage in my life, he said, I have only gratitude for the example of good manners given to us by il Maestro Gide.

Mr Spender often went away to Verona, Martino told me. Once, he missed the bus. Martino found him at the edge of the water looking down. And he was always forgetting his papers. He asked Martino to remind him when the bus left and to make sure he didn't forget his briefcase.

This man, he said, pointing at one of the photographs on the table in front of us. It showed me as a confused six-year-old, Dad a cheerful forty, my mother in the background with her eyes tight shut – she hated to be photographed – and next to her a wiry young man whom I'd assumed to be Martino, except of course the son of the owner of the hotel would never have sat down with the guests. A striped awning screens us from the sun and above us the bougainvillea thrives. A tray of peaches in a cut-glass bowl suggests the meal is over. The wiry young man has a cautious expression as if he were calculating something.

Lunch on the terrace of the Albergo Gardesana, summer 1951.

This man used to work for the main tourist office in Verona, said Martino. It was thanks to him that your father decided to come to Torri. They knew each other, because he was engaged to an au pair girl who used to take care of you.

This man . . . and a long pause. Martino couldn't speak further.

I explained that I was in an awkward position. My parents' archive was about to become available to the public and there was a chance that a scandalous book could be made out of their life together. I wanted to write my own version first. I thought that their marriage had been solid and happy, but now and again my father lost his head over some young man; and this had made my mother miserable.

Martino smiled.

She used to stop playing the piano as soon as your father left, he said. She'd come downstairs and sit under the awning nearest to the lake, away from the other guests at the hotel. She'd just sit there reading a book. Now and again she'd look up and stare at the water. I remember it so clearly! As for your father – who am I to say what happened? He might not have taken the bus into Verona in order to meet someone. He was a very cultured man. He might have just wanted to look at a church.

IO

DON'T YOU EVER TELL A LIE?

WHEN WE CAME back from Italy in the autumn of 1951, we brought two young women of Torri with us to help in the house: Francesca, the sister of my skipper, and Idelma, who lived in a house above the village. My mother immediately showed them the brand-new washing-machine in the basement. They looked at it phlegmatically and said, O Signora, we'd much prefer to have the Lake of Garda outside the back door.

This was the most luxurious phase of our house in St John's Wood. *World within World* had been nominated for one of the book clubs and my father was feeling rich. The parquet floor of the front hall of Loudoun Road was scrubbed and polished every day by Francesca and Idelma, who lived in a room so small that less than two feet separated their twin beds. In the evening, pre-television, they sat side by side on one bed and read *fotoromanzi*, sentimental comic books, except instead of drawings there were photographs of actors miming the stories. The male actors were sultry and the female ones were often in tears, looking up at the top of the page for a solution to descend on them like the heavenly dove.

My father's study faced the front of the house, and his work table stood in front of the window of crinkly Victorian glass. Against the wall on the left stood a tall glass bookcase with two handwritten signs on it: 'Precious Book Cupboard' and 'Do Not Open (Dangerous Glass)'.

Up a steep staircase with wobbly banisters were three bedrooms: my sister's, my parents' and my own. The bathroom was decorated with yellow tiles dating from the Twenties. My parents' bedroom held a large framed mirror with, on the left, special brushes for Dad's hair sold to him by the sadistic barber who sent him home every month with a different-coloured rinse. Large framed reproductions of Blake's illustrations to Dante hung on the walls. They were gradually replaced by watercolours by John Piper, whom Dad knew from ages back.

My nickname as a child was Smashy. I liked guns. There was a silver six-shooter in an embossed holster. The only time my father ever spanked me was when I hit a visiting professor over the head with my pistol. I thought that since he was American, he'd appreciate this cowboy greeting.

My bedroom measured eight feet by ten. Two built-in cupboards, one Heal's cabinet containing a diorama of my war toys lit by tiny bulbs imitating bursting shells. My sister Lizzie's room was larger and looked south over the beautiful gardens between Blenheim Road and Marlborough Place. Once, our nearest neighbour Colonel Macintosh came over to complain. He said solemnly to Dad, 'I am old enough to be your father, and your father's father.' He said I'd chucked one of his pears at his cat. His pears fell into our garden and one could stick a bamboo into them and launch them and I didn't really mean to hit his cat, especially with the Colonel in a deckchair near by, but these things happen. My father was polite and when the Colonel left, he sniggered. Colonel Macintosh belonged to an imperial past and he had a handlebar moustache, and of course Colonel Macintosh always wore a Macintosh.

That autumn, my mother concentrated on four sonatas by Beethoven, two early, one middle, one late. My mother was a Beethoven specialist, and throughout my childhood I eavesdropped on the sonatas she practised.

She often talked about Beethoven, always in hallowed tones. She told me that when he wrote 'Must it be?' above a theme in one of the late quartets, it referred to his growing deafness and his search for spiritual strength in the face of adversity. The counter-subject, 'It must be!', signified peace of mind acquired with an immense spiritual effort. Years later, I discovered a short theme by Beethoven which he wrote in the margin of a letter to one of his friends. 'Money! Must it be? The old lady wants the rent again.' Much less spiritual, this brisk little piece told me something about my mother. I saw that Mum had wished on to Beethoven some of her own interior needs. She was attracted to the idea of spiritual struggle. Instead, whenever I think of Beethoven – which is often – I think of Mum: cantankerous, moody, bossy and high-minded, and on some occasions down to earth. The real Mum, not the spiritual Mum. This is how she played him, and I liked it a lot.

As a child, if I kept quiet and promised not to disturb her, I was allowed to take my toys and play under the piano while she practised. All I could see of her from this angle were her legs. The music came down among intense clicks and burps as the keyboard shifted slightly, allowing the hammers to hit two strings instead of three when required. Loudness, and the lateral movement of the wood-and-felt mechanism, were controlled by Mum's feet. The lattice heaven above my head squeaked, sighed and thrummed beyond the music. With all this noise, I couldn't understand why, down on the carpet, with the occasional movement on my part of tin soldiers, Mum would tell me sharply in mid-bar, 'Quiet!' Or even 'Quai . . . Ett!' if the music so dictated. But I learned that silence was vital whenever I nested, as it were, in Beethoven's belly.

My mother often tried to teach me how to play the piano. Small self sitting on her knee, her two arms on either side of me, her breasts against my shoulders. Her wrists parallel to the floor, fingers splayed, each finger as alert as every other finger, and the thumbs also trying to be alert and nimble though the angle suggested they rode side-saddle. Off we go! All I had to do was plonk my index finger on the note to the left of the two black ones which, at the height of my chest, would have transfixed me had they extended themselves into railway lines. When things went wrong and I missed my cue, my mother said 'Count' into my right ear, or joggled me with a throb of her upper thigh; and on we went. 'Come on. Count! It's not too difficult. You're on the first beat of every bar.' The bars weren't the ones recently cemented into my sister's bedroom window to prevent her falling out, though these were five, like the staves of music we were staring at, and horizontal, and vaguely musical, in that green leaves in the garden seen through the bars on rainy days made musical sounds.

Many times, my mother tried to explain to me how music worked. She drew on a piece of paper a thing called 'the rose of fifths'. I could see that indeed it was a rose. Each petal, indicated by a swift round shape, contained its botanical name: F sharp or, coming round the other way, G flat. I could grasp the principle of two and a half, or tone tone semitone. Maths ruled the universe, and this was maths. Only, I couldn't grasp what was wrong with the octave that it was so uneven. After a while you found yourself in someone else's territory.

I never learned to play the piano. Recently, as second clarinet in our wind quartet, I decided we ought to take a lesson from a professional. She listened politely to a whole movement and at the end she said, 'Matthew, why is it you have trouble in counting the beats in held notes? You're always in such a hurry to move off.' I explained about my mother, and the terror of hearing the word 'COUNT' slapped into the back of my neck. The teacher said, 'Are you sure you really need me? Wouldn't you be better off with a shrink?'

We spent the summer of 1952 at Torri, but this time I was left alone for longer. I stayed with Idelma's family in her house on the hill, sharing a room with a boy my own age. He had one gift I envied. He could tell the time by the sun. If I asked the time he'd look at the sun and say, 'Twenty-two minutes to three,' and that would be it. I had the watch, he had nothing, but his knowledge was superior. He also managed the goats, keeping them together by throwing stones at them as accurate as punctuation. He was in charge of the natural world and when the sun set, his hair rose up and turned into flames.

Beside the wood where a big green lizard lived there was a small field that suddenly filled with flowers. Peasants appeared at either end to cut them and send them off to the market. As these two groups drew together, they began to quarrel. Who had the right to cut which flowers? It was at this point, I think, that for me Italy lost the distinction between fantasy and reality. What could be more extraordinary than a hillside of angry peasants surrounded by flowers, some cut and bound in sheaves, some about to be cut?

My father came for a visit while I was staying with Idelma. As I took him up the hill to have lunch, I showed him the cemetery and talked about our local life. 'That's Idelma's aunt. And that's her cousin over there. Such a pity she died young, she looks so nice in the photo on the gravestone. You notice that some of the graves have little lights? Those are for the good people of Torri. Not many of them were good,' I said, 'because there aren't many lights.'

Idelma and family gave us a wonderful meal, so good that the finest restaurant would have been proud of it. This led my father to reflect on poverty. If this was the way they lived, with their ancestors in the nearby graveyard and delicious food on the table, then the Locrini family could not be called poor. Well, they were poor, because they had no money, but culturally speaking they were rich-poor. And there were plenty of people in the world who were poor-rich, who had money but were miserable.

He confided these thoughts to his diary, but he mentioned to my six-year-old self that we'd had a most wonderful luncheon. Oh, I said. Don't think we live like that every day. Mostly it's polenta with mince-and-tomato sauce, I said. Or polenta with just a chopped anchovy and some parsley to give it flavour. Or – and usually – polenta.

Early in 1953, Stephen travelled to Cincinnati, where he had been appointed to the George Elliston Chair for Poetry. In the background lay his determination to create an international magazine of which he would be the editor. It was an idea that he had pursued, at this point, for nearly a decade.

It hadn't been easy for him to obtain a visa in London. The American Consul asked him if he'd ever been a member of the Communist Party and he'd said, 'Yes, for about ten minutes in 1937.' The McCarran Act of 1950 prohibited giving visas to communists, even if they'd repented and changed their views. The Consul smiled and said, 'Mr Spender, don't you ever tell a lie?' It became one of my father's favourite after-dinner stories.

In Cincinnati, Stephen made friends with the Southern writer Allen Tate. There was a plan that Stephen and Allen would found a magazine together. This had been in the air since Stephen's first visit to the United States and he wanted to consolidate.

Tate had a heightened sense of the South as a 'subject'. He saw himself as a lonely figure resisting the pressure of Northern critics to steer Southern writers towards 'a literature of social agitation', as he put it with an air of disgust. Unfortunately, Tate's nostalgia for the South was not shared by Stephen. In his first visit to the South two years before, Stephen had been shocked by how much his hosts had talked about what he calls in his journal 'all the old business', meaning the South before the Civil War. 'Hatred of the bankers, the Negro problem, struggling with poverty, consciousness of the "hill billy country", and the "Old Kentucky home". Not to mention the in-eradicable resentment of Southerners against the Yankees for having put Negroes in charge of Whites in the period of reconstruction.'

If this magazine had ever been launched, would Tate and Spender have managed to create a bridge between England and the Southern United States? How many sympathetic readers would it have gained in New York? What would British readers have made of White Supremacy in literary form? The plan only goes to show how keen Stephen was to edit a magazine, anywhere, on any terms.

Though Tate was in several respects out on a limb, the two men got on well. I remember being left with him on one of his visits to London. He and I were put in the piano room by ourselves, because Dad wanted Tate to read to me 'Brer Rabbit and the Tar Baby'. Which he did with great relish, with all the different accents. It's considered today to be a viciously racist book, but as a child I just listened to this strange man with a funny moustache enjoying his own ability to perform. I liked it, though there'd been a moment of panic when Dad had left the room. I could see from the shape of his shoulders that he thought, 'Rather you than me!'

While my father was in Cincinnati, Mike Josselson, the head of the CCF in Paris, wrote to him saying the American CCF was planning to found a magazine. Irving Kristol would be one of the editors. Stephen immediately wrote to say that the English CCF had already made a plan, which he'd discussed recently with Allen Tate. Tactfully, he wrote to Kristol, 'Perhaps you could let me know how matters stand?'

Kristol wrote back saying that in Stephen's absence the heads of the English CCF had had several discussions with Josselson in Paris. It was a choice between two rival proposals. In one, the magazine would be based in New York, in the other the base would be London.

Before it even existed, Stephen started asking his friends for material for this future magazine. His access to great literary figures established his claim that he should be one of the editors. Eliot, one of the first authors whom Stephen contacted, wrote saying he hoped Stephen would 'draw an adequate salary, and that the magazine is to be comfortably subsidized'. (How like a fragment from a poem by Eliot are the words 'comfortably subsidized'!) Eliot could not let him have any of his own work to publish at the moment, unfortunately, but he thought that to mix politics and literature was a good idea, especially as contributors such as Isaiah Berlin and Raymond Aron would mean they would be dealing with politics 'on the highest level'.

Soon, Stephen wrote to Irving: 'it looks as if we are both to be employed by the British Committee'. Again, the phrase is casual. It suggests that in the background the negotiations between the American CCF, the Paris office and the English CCF had tilted in favour of the British; and that he was not directly involved in the process.

There's another revealing phrase in a subsequent letter to Kristol. Stephen had put forward suggestions for two political articles. One was to cover the current state of socialism in the United States. Stephen says apologetically about these: 'Not my branch but you might like them.' This implies that Stephen was to concentrate on literature and leave the political articles to his co-editor. Which indeed became the case. His subsequent role with all three co-editors, Irving Kristol, Dwight Macdonald and Melvin Lasky, was that he was in charge of literature and they were in charge of politics.

An article on socialism in the United States was a good idea, but the proposal was naive. The word 'socialism' was liable to give most Republican readers in the United States stomach cramps. It still would. The suggestion came straight from the heart of British social democracy. It pays no attention to what could be discussed in a magazine aiming for a wide readership in the United States. Nevertheless, it begs a question. If *Encounter* in its entire career gave scant coverage to the major problems of the United States – issues of race, Civil Rights, the Vietnam War – was it perhaps because somewhere or other, perhaps in the desk of Stephen's American co-editor, there was a list of subjects that were taboo?

Meanwhile my father's idea of a magazine had undergone a change since 1946. The magazine he'd wanted to start with Curtius was intended to have been more political than literary, judging by the draft proposal he'd sent to T. S. Eliot. By the time *Encounter* was founded, he'd become more interested in promoting literature. Politics were divisive and time-consuming, and his ambivalence about America as an 'idea' meant he wasn't the right person to act as a promoter of its values.

The first issue of *Encounter* came out in October 1953. The most remarkable thing about Irving Kristol, Stephen's co-editor, is the trajectory which took him from the extreme left to the extreme right of the political spectrum. Along with many other New York intellectuals, he was educated at City College, where he thrashed out with his classmates every single permutation of left-wing political theory; and yet he ended up as one of the founders of neo-conservatism.

'Irving Kristol fascinates me,' wrote Stephen in his diary after they'd worked together for a few months. 'He looks rather like a caterpillar which has pale bright blue eyes placed rather flatly in his head.' He was always in the office by the time Stephen arrived, and his ideas of how a magazine should be edited were quite unlike Stephen's. He ruthlessly rewrote the political articles as they came in. 'He regards a contribution as a chassis to which he then adds the coachwork. He loves doing this. He will arrive at the office saying that he has been up all night "editing" Nathan Glazer's or Leslie Fiedler's piece. "Hope he won't mind," he says. Then adds, reassured, "Nah, he won't. He does the same to mine."'

Kristol's view of Spender was the mirror image of this. 'There was always the possibility of friction, a possibility that was realized less often than I had feared. A poet, a man of letters, and a gentleman, Stephen was absolutely no kind of editor. I ran the magazine, he made contributions to it.'

I don't believe my father ever took an interest in Kristol's intellectual position. He recognized the general flavour of it, which at the time was that of a New York repentant-Trotskyite-but-still-somehow-Marxist Democrat. To my father, it was all just sectarianism. He'd seen endless backbiting of this kind before the war. What stuck in his throat was what Irving actually did, which was to take someone else's prose, put it on his desk and start hacking.

By this time I was a traditional English schoolboy with grubby knees and a uniform who went to the Hall School, a three-ha'penny bus ride up the Finchley Road from us.

If I walked to school instead of taking the bus, the route took me past a bomb-site that was being turned into a secondary modern school, one of the first and largest in London. After the site had been cleared, a truck arrived laden with ceramic stand-up urinals. With the help of friends, we made a tunnel out of these white and glittering masterpieces. And after we'd discovered a dead bird teeming with maggots, we called our magnificent temple the Maggot Place. There we could do useful boyish things such as throwing shards of broken glass like boomerangs and watch them curve round in the air and come back at us.

Our education was still deeply immersed in the British Empire even in the mid-Fifties. We schoolboys were dimly aware that the Empire was over in spite of what we were being taught. Troops from the Empire had taken part on our side in the Second World War, especially in the Far East. Were they to go back to knuckling their foreheads at the Brits afterwards? Yet we were told about the Indian Mutiny and the Black Hole of Calcutta, how those naughty natives had shut our tall blond officers in a hole and held torches to the entrance so that they all died of suffocation.

Behind the teacher's head the world stretched out its indented silhouettes against a background of soothingly empty blue. London was dead centre. Well, that was just a coincidence to do with map-making, but even so the composition seemed beautifully balanced. A thread of pink ran from country to country all the way around. These were colonies or Commonwealth, they were ours and they were contiguous except for a small bit centre right. Yemen was pink; but Iran? Afghanistan? Why couldn't we take over the missing chunk and make it finally true that the sun never sets on the British Empire?

I read G. A. Henty, given to me by my father who remembered the novels from his childhood. *With Clive in India, With Wolfe in Quebec.* After a while I got the hang of it. Young well-born Englishman finds faithful batman, saves his life and has him as a loyal supporter ever after, always in the background holding the tea things as the hero wrestles with fuzzy-wuzzies. They were not equals, these two adventurers, either in martial spirit or social graces, but they were loyal to each other through thick and thin. The hero's lot was solitary, except for this servant's steadying presence. An odd image of binary solitude began to appear. There were no women and only a few companions to talk to.

My father often gave me books he thought I should read. One of these was Homer's *Iliad*, not in a version toned down for children but in Fitzgerald's translation which had just come out. I read it from cover to cover. There's a battle at the beginning and a battle at the end, both so horrifying, no more vivid description of battle has ever been written. I loved this book. The death of soldiers by spear-wounds seemed to me magnificent, a moment of intense feeling dipped in red.

Our Latin teacher at the Hall had been a sergeant in the First World War. He mixed the campaigns of Julius Caesar with reminiscences of his life in the trenches. The Roman *gladium* or sword was the same length as the regimental bayonet, he said. Some of us didn't like the idea that war was, and has remained, nasty. *Sine mora*, meaning 'without delay', was once translated by the boy next to me as 'without morals'. Mr Rotherham thought this was the funniest thing he'd ever heard. He leaned back in his chair and his fat, comfortably buttoned waistcoat appeared above the edge of his desk. Without morals! I wish I could say that I was the one who'd thought of this brilliant mistranslation, for it surely indicates doubt regarding Caesar's joy in killing the early French.

On 9 January 1954, Peter Wildeblood, a political journalist, was arrested and charged under the laws prohibiting homosexual relationships. This followed the similar arrest of Lord Edward Montagu and Michael Pitt-Rivers, who'd been caught in a tent with two boy scouts. These became key cases. It took ten years or more, but the public debate over these trials eventually led to the creation of the Wolfenden Committee and the abolition of the laws against homosexual relationships.

Wildeblood took the courageous decision to state in court that he was homosexual, instead of becoming involved with the contortions of proving that the police had faked the evidence against him. Inevitably, he went to jail.

In the book he wrote about his experiences, he suggests that the impetus to prosecute British homosexuals had come from the FBI. At the time of his arrest, he was the Diplomatic Correspondent of the *Daily Mail*. He'd received information that purges were taking place in the US State Department. The administration wanted to weed out homosexuals from key government jobs on the grounds that they were security risks, and the British authorities were about to do the same. He quotes a newspaper report: 'Special Branch began compiling a "Black Book" of known perverts in influential Government jobs after the disappearance of the diplomats Donald Maclean and Guy Burgess, who were known to have pervert associates. Now comes the difficult task of side-tracking these men into less important jobs – or of putting them behind bars.' This suggests the arrest of Montagu, Pitt-Rivers and Wildeblood took place in the context of a security shake-up.

Stephen met Wildeblood soon after he came out of prison. 'I asked him whether to be arrested and tried must not be overwhelmingly shameful, however convinced one might be that the law had no right to judge this offence. He said that at first he felt very shaken, but as soon as he discovered the methods of the police, he was filled with such indignation that he ceased to feel concerned with any moral guilt on his side.'

I don't believe that my father was worried about the 'shame' that he himself might face if he ever found himself in the same position; and he certainly was not going to allow fear to shape his own life. He had a right to pursue his own desires. Sex was one aspect of political freedom. The idea of arrest was just something that had to be accepted, like car accidents or cancer. In the clubs where homosexuals met, the custom was never to mention the name of someone who'd ended up in prison. He was merely 'away'. And when he came back, everyone would pretend he'd never been absent.

In the Fifties, the police took the view that, whatever the law said, if two men lived together as a couple within their own premises, they should be left alone. Respecting people's privacy took precedence over the repressive laws. The police were less tolerant about soliciting in the street, but it was difficult to read this as persecution. Wilde-blood initially believed that his arrest was evidence of homophobia in the judiciary, but after much research he decided it had more to do with promotion than with prejudice. Promotion depended on the number of arrests an officer made, and it was easier to catch a homosexual than a thief. As a fellow prisoner told him when he was in jail, 'Why should they climb a tree to catch a burglar, when they can pick up people of our sort like apples off the ground?'

The painter Francis Bacon, a close friend of Stephen's, said of the Montagu case, 'Never trust a boy scout.' This remark was widely quoted, for boy scouts of course are supposed to be protectors of all that is finest in British values.

That summer, my sister and I were taken to Wales for the holidays. She was four years old and I was nine. Our parents must have stayed with us for a while, because a draft fragment of *The Temple* is signed at the bottom, 'Bardsey Island, 1954'.

It was a strange place to leave two small children: a bird sanctuary off Anglesey, total population fourteen. Our hosts were a woman artist aged forty and her lover, a Breton fisherman who was there for the fish. He wore a knitted cap and striped jumper and he was gone for most of the day.

We lived in an old brick vicarage with a walled garden to shut out the wind. Here, two hardy Siamese cats raided a small flock of racing pigeons. These birds didn't belong to the house. They bore the names of their rightful owners on plastic bands around their legs. They had been blown here in a storm during a race – blown all the way from Yorkshire where the fanciers trained them.

The bay contained an area of darker water with fewer white-tops, just the occasional wedge of wind from the shore sketching powdery lines upon its surface. The Breton fisherman once took me out there in his boat. His fish-hooks were made with any decorative material: feathers, coloured wool, tinsel left over from the Christmas tree. When the mackerel ran, he said, they took anything. Sure enough we passed over a shoal and he and I took out from the sea regularly spaced intervals of fish, like socks from a wet chest of drawers.

Four of the fourteen inhabitants of the island were ornithologists. They wore identical clothes and were uniformly thin. Their overcoats in cold weather were shut with wooden toggles and they lived in a disused lighthouse. One day I took them a seagull covered in oil. Its shiny black eye, so lively, contrasted with the matte black of its tarred and useless body. The ornithologist took it from me, said thank you politely and, whirling the bird around his head, smashed its head against the parapet. The bird flapped once or twice and died. When I got back to the vicarage I was told never to get tar on my shirt again.

The hill was topped with four barrows filled with dead Vikings. The Breton fisherman told me frightening stories about how the Vikings wouldn't sit still in their graves. He wanted to keep me close to the vicarage, but though I was scared, I still hung about the barrows, on which one day I found a perfect circle of horse-mushrooms. There was also a dead sheep. His worn white skull poked through his own fleece, which hung around him like a bed jacket.

On the wall near the old lighthouse was an object which fascinated me: a glass bottle filled with ants. Moss had grown over two-thirds of its roundness, but inside I could see tunnels with insects wandering up and down, twittering their antlers. Grubs in their white pith shells moved when joggled by other ants. I watched this vase of jewels for hours, but one day, to my shame, I smashed it with a stone. Immediately I ran from the field as if giant hairy whiskered ants with shields and bucklers might billow out of the wall after me. But the landscape remained indifferent. The seagulls mewed as usual and the wind did not soften.

I felt badly about this act for years. To destroy something beautiful was surely evil. Yet the ornithologist had killed a bird, which was just as beautiful; and moreover it was bigger. The two acts, pinned together by the crumbling lighthouse that was never lit, were part of the same thing.

Baths were obligatory. A galvanized iron tub was half filled with cold water, topped up with a hot kettle, and into it I was dropped. The iron had a raspy bottom and the usual cuts down this small boy's legs, painted with gentian violet, itched in contact with the water.

One day when I came in for my bath, I found it full of lobsters. The tub was their temporary home between the large cold sea and the small boiling pot in the kitchen. The water I was scrubbed in was sea water. That's why it itched. No longer fancying the rasping iron tub, I refused to get in, but the Breton sailor was fed up with me. He removed the lobsters and put them casually on the floor. His huge hand came down from the ceiling. Then he left the room.

I clung to the sides of my sinking ship and looked out at the lobsters prowling around, occasionally bursting into wild clacketing in protest at the unusual feeling of flagstones and air. Their legs were like the oars of Viking ships. They crawled, they paused. They were blue. In shadowy corners they ceased to exist. Lit by the dwindling fire, it was certain they were waiting in cunning stillness for me to leave my bath – their bath, their hidey-hole of salt water that smelled of iodine. And at that moment, I finally missed my mother.

When, at the age of thirty-five, I tried to tell the lobster story to Mum, she jerked the steering-wheel in fury and shouted, 'We've heard this story of your miserable childhood from soup to fish. You were a much loved child, and if you choose to remember differently, it's no bloody business of anyone but you.'

Actually, I sympathized. By that time I was a parent myself and it had occurred to me that childhood belongs to the child, miserable or happy as the whim takes the little bleeder. If I'd ever felt abandoned at having been dumped on a Welsh island while Mum prepared for a concert in London, time had qualified the trauma of the lobsters and turned it into a funny story – a story which even now was in the process of being reshaped by the complaints of my proto-adolescent daughter. But Mum was driving too fast. We were negotiating a wicked gap in the Alpilles between Saint-Rémy and Maussane. Carved square stones edging the gully were flashing past the window much too close. The curves were cantilevered the wrong way and the flexible pines that used to protect the sides had burned down the year before. A bitter scent of herbs blew into the car but I did not feel we should die in this place. I told her that if she didn't slow down we'd have to get out and walk.

II

DREAMING ONE'S WAY
THROUGH LIFE

W HEN WE CAME back to London from Bardsey Island, we
brought the two Siamese cats with us. Mag and Fitsi were their
names, and all day they chased birds. They were so wild Mum decided
that they had to live in the garden. A speech from Shakespeare's *Henry
V* that I was learning at the time has the line 'What feats he did that
day'. I always thought of this as 'What Fitsi did that day'. Fitsi, the
bird-slayer. She killed my canary. Dad wrote a poem about it.

Tony Hyndman was given the task of building a hutch for them
in a corner of the garden. He was often around the house at that
time, his life being in one of its down moments. I enjoyed watching
him working on this simple carpentry job and we began to make
friends. He could say the weirdest things. Such as, slyly: 'Well,
Matthew, and so there *you* are. Who ever would have thought of
Stephen as a family man.'

Tony insinuated that the work he was supposed to be doing was
a mere formality. Pulling weeds? Hutches for cats? 'They're half wild
anyway,' said Tony disparagingly. 'They'll never stay here,' he said, as
if he knew a thing or two about freedom. 'Stephen should just have
said no to bringing them back.'

I said nothing. I felt he was trying to form a conspiracy between us regarding Dad, and I resisted. He was crouching over the boxes. I was on my feet in my neat Hall School uniform with a Maltese cross embroidered in black thread on a pink blazer. I was looking down at him and he was looking up at me.

His own deferential pose annoyed him. He stood up abruptly.

'Got any money, Matthew?'

The question took me by surprise. 'No.'

'Nothing at all?'

'I've got half a crown. My pocket money.'

'I don't suppose you'd consider handing it over, would you?'

'No.'

'I thought not. Well, it was worth trying.'

And he grinned.

His grin put me on the spot. If I'd grinned back, it would have placed us in an equal position with regard to my father, the dispenser of half-crowns. We were both my father's dependants, otherwise he'd never have dared to ask.

When Dad heard about this, he was so furious he rang Tony and told him never to come round to Loudoun Road again. His anger gave me another clue. Cadging pocket money off his son was low, certainly. But Dad's anger showed there was more to Tony than a reluctant gardener. It showed that Tony had some claim over him.

Tony could ask Stephen for money. He wouldn't say no, though he wanted Tony to work for it, but cadging his son's pocket money was unacceptable. My father was an extremely tolerant man, but if he felt someone was attacking his persona he reacted violently. In this case he evidently thought that Tony had overstepped the line.

Tony at that time had been through some bad years, and it wasn't certain he'd ever pull himself together. A lover in Paris had introduced him to drugs. He'd stolen from his friends, and as a result he'd been arrested at various times. Eventually he was taken in by an Order of Franciscan Friars in the East End of London, but in the end – I think this was a few years after the pocket-money incident – he betrayed them too.

From time to time in the late Fifties, Loudoun Road was burgled; and without anyone saying anything, it was assumed Tony was responsible. 'An inside job', as the police would have said. I lost two clarinets that way, one after the other. Bandsmen in the army always needed clarinets. Mum on these occasions would go around the house and make sure the locks were in working order, then she'd claim the insurance. She was good at insurance claims. It was part of her frugality.

In the autumn of 1954, my father toured India as a representative of the Congress for Cultural Freedom. He was immediately faced with a problem that caught his imagination. Several students told him that the United States was behaving very generously with its wealth, but the way in which it spent its money showed that its gifts were not disinterested. Therefore, the recipients did not have to feel grateful. They could take the money and reject America with a clean conscience.

Stephen wondered for several days whether 'disinterested' charity was possible. As he put in his journal: 'an act "outside" historical materialism and therefore disproving of it'. American largesse was a bribe, and to be bribed was to be insulted. 'Just as in the old days your English old ladies used to collect six pennies in order to clothe the poor natives, so today the Americans think that they can distribute a lot of money with which, ultimately, we'll buy not loin cloths but refrigerators, we'll resist Communism.' He added: 'resolved to see that *Encounter* really is disinterested'.

Indian independence was recent history, and Indian intellectuals were aware that the United States was taking over from the British. It made them uneasy. The Americans could unexpectedly choose to support some other local politician or political group. Several times Stephen had to listen to nostalgic speeches about the British in India. 'Prof. Guptan Nair wishes that the British would try to use more political influence in India instead of leaving this to the Americans.'

On 24 October, in Sri Lanka, Stephen was taken to a beautiful Buddhist temple by a charming young man with an impossible surname. In the distance, he glanced at the young women in turquoise saris working against a background of dark-green fields. Beautiful! Afterwards, they had tea. The young man 'strongly attacked the Congress. I defended it miserably. He and a Turkish anthropologist consider my sincerity compromised by the Congress backing, and recorded their disappointment.'

In Madras, Stephen found himself in the opposite predicament. 'As soon as I arrived I was handed a printed sheet with information about the institution called Democratic Research. The sheet said the purpose of this was anti-communism.' His host gave a speech saying that the aims of this group ran parallel to those of the CCF. Stephen felt he was being forced into taking a stronger anti-communist line than he wanted. 'I refused to let him get away with this, saying in my own speech that I had never heard of Democratic Research but felt that, as an aim, it was unexceptionable provided it was objective and did not attempt to make propaganda.' He'd hardly defended himself in front of the two young men. He'd have looked worried and said 'yes' and left it at that. But if he were cornered in public, he'd fight. 'I am wretched about these National Committees of the Congress, in Australia and India.'

Throughout this time, he was also giving speeches on behalf of the British Council and the PEN Club. It made him an ambiguous representative for the Congress for Cultural Freedom: doubting its propaganda, and speaking on behalf of other associations.

Perhaps to escape from the stresses of all this, he took time out to visit the studios of local artists. He liked painters and always listened respectfully to their explanations of their work. Two of those whom he visited were Jamini Roy and Newton Souza. He bought several of their works, and they were grateful for this. Because he carried the aura of so many institutions on his shoulders, it gave them the air of having acquired that mysterious thing, an 'international' reputation.

Whenever Dad was away for a long period of time, Mum would fade. It was hard for her to establish a rhythm if my father wasn't there, for his expansive social life gave her something she had to fit around, like a vine around a tree. Alone in the house, there were moments when she would get to the piano room and just sit there.

Her natural pessimism wasn't based on anything philosophical, such as the transience of human glory. It was more of the variety of 'I told you it would end like this.'

Once, in the kitchen when I was about nine years old, as my mother was telling me off for something I'd done – or perhaps not done – the cupboard behind her, containing all our family plates, slowly came away from the wall. Dishes began to fall out, cascading past her head. I waited for her to turn, lithe as a snake, and push the thing back in place. But no. She stood there with head and shoulders bowed while porcelain halos travelled past her and shattered on top of one another on the painted cement floor, as if all her life she'd expected this to happen.

Auden wrote a poem once, containing the line 'And the frowning schoolgirl may be dying to be asked to stay.' When I first read it, I assumed he was thinking of Mum. He was in and out of the house so often. It was definitely her. I could see that my mother's frown might have even been attractive when she was a schoolgirl. Hands behind her back, her breasts pushed forwards with the indifference she always seemed to have about her body, a dark pigtail falling down the back of her frock; frowning yet longing for affection was a perfect description of her. The will to be loved was part of her conviction that she would surely be rejected.

My mother's will to be loved consisted of a kind of expectancy. She could charm, she could amuse, she liked being admired, but her standards were so high that whoever was on the receiving end of her approaches – and they were rare – had to accommodate himself to what she was. She knew this was brittle, but she couldn't help it. She knew she was all-or-nothing; and anyone who treats the Other in this way must accept the high risk of rejection.

141

My father's will to be loved had two aspects: a magnificent gener-osity of spirit that exploded in any social circumstances, hoping to strike a spark from whomever was on the receiving end. And a totally different spirit which was exclusive, binary and secret, a shared understanding which – and this was most mysterious – didn't neces-sarily require the presence of the Other in order to flourish. Indeed, too much of the Other got in the way.

In the background, so far back that my father cannot have been aware of it, the Information Research Department kept an eye on *Encounter* and shielded it from too much interference from its American owners.

The IRD was an affiliate of the Foreign Office set up to work in collaboration with the BBC. Its main job was to transmit news bulletins towards the Soviet bloc. The news had to be reliable, so the mechanism of debriefing refugees, analysing foreign newspapers and other aspects of intelligence work was involved.

One of its guiding lights was Christopher Mayhew, whom Stephen may have known at least by sight, as he was a friend of Philip Toynbee. Mayhew had seen Russian propaganda at close quarters and he decided it had to be challenged. He thought that 'social-democratic Britain was better placed than capitalist America to take the lead'. It would have to be secret, because anti-communist propaganda 'would be anathema to much of the Labour party'. Mayhew was a member of the Labour Party leader Hugh Gaitskell's inner circle, in a position to help set up a department within the Foreign Office, in contradic-tion with the left of his own party, and in secret.

One of the tasks of the IRD was to persuade its American coun-terparts that, when it came to propaganda, it was a bad idea to be too aggressive. An IRD 'draft brief' of 1953 defines the British position.

We regard the Stalinist communists alone as the enemy, and all other shades of political opinion and peoples, other than fascism or Nazism, as potential allies. In policy therefore our aim is to drive a wedge between communist parties and those most likely to support them, i.e. leftwing socialists, pacifists and certain intellectuals in Europe, and nationalists in Asia, the Middle East and Africa. We make no emotional appeals to those already converted, and we regard propaganda issued by right-wing elements as dangerous to us and helpful to the enemy.

The US intelligence officers who came once a year to review the situation insisted that the Brits were 'soft on communism'. Curiously enough, the American Committee for Cultural Freedom took the same view. *Encounter* 'has created an especial resentment and dissatisfaction for its apparent unwillingness to offend what it presumes are English sensibilities with explicit anti-communism'. *Encounter* should have become 'a counterweight to the *New Statesman & Nation*, both as regards forthright opposition to Communist totalitarianism and support of America's role in the free world'. Instead, it had allowed itself to become distracted by publishing literature, 'often of questionable merit'.

But the ACCF continued to be divided by constant bickering over Senator Joe McCarthy, whose self-appointed task it was to conduct a crusade against communists inside the institutions of the US government. Some ACCF members drafted letters to university presidents about teachers who'd lost their posts, while others said Senator McCarthy was doing a fine job. Arthur Schlesinger, a noted liberal historian later connected with the Kennedy administration, resigned from the ACCF in disgust. 'I had assumed that we were writers, artists, professors, intellectuals, people who have made, or hoped to make, some contribution to culture and had therefore an especial stake in its protection.' An association such as theirs should not be so sectarian. 'We have better things to do than pay off old scores.'

Now and again among the minutes of their general meetings Auden appears. The only time he registers an opinion is when the

ACCF commissioned a book on Soviet Russia and then found it couldn't pay for it. Auden says that if articles had been commissioned and written, they should be paid for, whether or not they were published. Typical Auden! The rules were there to be respected. Everything else could come later. The question was academic, as there was no money. Fractious to the last, the ACCF died for lack of funds.

12

SCANDALOUS GOSSIP

O N THURSDAY, 21 April 1955, Raymond Chandler came into our lives.

My mother sat next to him at a party given by Jamie Hamilton, who was both my father's publisher and Chandler's. Grey-faced, drunk, slow in speech, he 'yammered' at her – as she put it – on the theme of 'The Blonde' in American culture.

If she did not already know the background, Yvonne Hamilton would have told her afterwards. Chandler's wife Cissy had died late in the previous year and he was desperate. He'd tried to commit suicide not long before – the most incompetent attempt ever, in a bathroom with a pistol, missing with two shots and with a policeman outside politely knocking on the door.

Natasha picked up on his underlying unhappiness. She invited him to dinner at Loudoun Road on the following Tuesday. She enlisted the support of Alec Murray, an elegant fashion photographer, and Jocelyn Rickards, a painter and costume designer, two fans of his who she thought would amuse him. He'd told her at Jamie's, 'no literary heavy-weights', and these two were no threat.

Chandler was drunk again at this first visit to Loudoun Road but he assured the company that he never suffered from hangovers, as if this were the problem. Alec and Jocelyn drove him back to the Connaught Hotel.

Next day, in his thank-you note to Natasha, Chandler wove a fantasy around Jocelyn, with whom he'd just had lunch. Far from having taken off her clothes as he'd hoped, she'd 'outmanoeuvred' him with an affectionate hug in Bedford Square. He'd gone on to share a few Scotches with another woman whom he'd met on the boat coming over, and in his letter he made another joke about sharing a drink and sharing a bed. Would Natasha like to come to supper with him soon? He had an arrangement with the head waiter at the Connaught so that he was always served the most interesting wines.

All of which sounds like a pass so outrageous that it couldn't be real. If it had been, my mother wouldn't have gone, but she was curious. She went, and thereafter they met frequently. Lunch for just the two of them at Boulestin or La Speranza was a rare luxury for her. The only drawback was Chandler's despair, but for my mother that was an attraction. She saw herself as a saviour of desperate people.

After one meeting at the Connaught, she witnessed Chandler break down in tears of self-pity. She wrote him a letter of support, which he later destroyed. He regretted its loss: 'it would have been a comfort in bad times to be able to show myself that a greatly adored person once felt about me like that'.

A fortnight later Stephen came back from a party for Louis MacNeice, which had been followed by a broadcast for the French Service of the BBC, and found Chandler on the sofa assuring Natasha what a great genius she was in her music and how she should work harder at it, and that Stephen – Ray turned to him – should be more supportive. As he pursued this theme, Ray said knowingly: 'Stephen knows quite well what I'm talking about.'

Next day Stephen and Ray went together to the BBC to listen to my mother playing the Mozart C Minor Concerto with the Glasgow Symphony Orchestra. 'Orch bad', says Chandler's diary. That evening Chandler again took up the theme of my father's lack of appreciation for my mother's talent. My father, exasperated, wrote in his journal: 'he has the drunkard's sense of moral superiority, and his way of finding a wound and rubbing salt monotonously into it'.

This is reconstructed from documents, but I was also present at the time. A memory of Chandler slumped on the sofa comes into focus, smiling good-humouredly, leaning attentively towards my mother. Not that I was old enough to be included in grown-up dinners. I passed the peanuts at cocktail parties – the classic observation post for the children of writers in the Fifties. Chandler disapproved of children, which only made him more interesting. It was fun to be scowled at and smile back.

Mum took him to a hospital for a check-up. Bottles of Scotch fell out of his pyjamas when she unpacked his bags. When he was asked to leave the Connaught, she helped him to move to a furnished flat on Eaton Square.

Natasha told Stephen: 'it's no good dreaming one's way through life'. The remark disturbed him, but not because Natasha was giving him a warning as to her state of mind. Was she saying that she dreamed of living a different life? Or did she feel that her relationship with Chandler was dragging her into something that depended, on both sides, upon fantasy? If so, Stephen paid no attention. He turned it into a 'poetic' thought for the benefit of his diary: what's the difference between 'dream' and 'vision'?

My mother always saw herself as the pragmatic member of the family, the one with her feet on the ground. But real pragmatists don't think of themselves as such. They either are or they aren't. My mother wasn't. Have you bought the aeroplane tickets, Dad would ask? 'Yes of course.' But 'Yes' in this case meant she hadn't, she felt guilty, but she would buy them immediately and Dad would never know. So it would be all right to have told a lie. Which is fine, except then she'd forget to go out and actually buy the tickets.

On 24 July, Chandler came to dinner and refused to stay behind with the men when the women went upstairs to 'powder their noses', as was the custom at the time. The men talked downstairs of the railway workers' strike and the policy of the Trades Union Congress. Back upstairs on the sofa in the piano room, Ray entertained the ladies. 'Psychologists think neuroses begin in childhood, but I pick up mine as I go along.' I have a memory of this moment. Chandler slumped so deeply among the pillows and the women he seems part of the upholstery.

He was too much for one person to handle alone. Apart from Natasha and Jocelyn and Alec Murray, there were Alison Hooper (with whom we'd run that race in Portofino), and the novelist Kay Cicellis, and perhaps others. My mother, in the article she wrote about Ray years later, described this group as a 'shuttle service', and the expression is typical of her desire to demonstrate her practicality. It suggests something between home nursing and a taxi rank.

In retrospect, she saw what she did for Ray as purely humanitarian, as saving someone from self-destruction. Alison Hooper's name for her was 'Stern Daughter of the Voice of God', from Wordsworth's 'Ode to Duty'. According to Alison, Mum was 'essentially a Cause-girl', if not at times even 'a Mother Superior'. She threw herself into the quest of saving Ray with all of her 'awful power', wrote Alison, quoting Wordsworth – although perhaps with a friendly topspin.

And was there sex between Natasha and Ray? No, there was not. 'Stern Daughters of the V. of G. do not go in for affairs with crapulous old men,' wrote Alison firmly to Chandler's biographer years later. Instead, there was something more interesting and more complicated: a love affair that existed in each other's mind, a test, a duel – and since it was preordained that Chandler wanted to die, it was a duel to the death. Thus Mum would be summoned to the Connaught at three in the morning with a message that unless she arrived in half an hour, there'd be 'a mess like strawberry jam outside on the pavement'. It was comic, but he also meant it; and she'd get out of bed and go.

The Paris office of the Congress for Cultural Freedom had accumulated objections to Irving Kristol over the winter of 1954, and during the following summer they decided to fire him. He suspected that Stephen might have had something to do with this move, 'for reasons I no longer recollect, and may never have comprehended'. He wasn't too upset. He was fed up with the pusillanimous Brits and wanted to get back to New York.

Charles Turner, Hansi Lambert, Lucy Lambert, Stephen, Nicky Nabokov and Samuel Barber on the terrace of Hansi's chalet in Gstaad in the year when we went for a Mediterranean cruise together.

In late July 1955, there was a full meeting of the Congress in London to discuss his replacement. Melvin Lasky came from Berlin, Mike Josselson and François Bondy, the editor of *Preuves*, came from Paris, with Nicky Nabokov who was in charge of the musical programme of the CCF; then Dwight Macdonald himself, the possible replacement; and, in London already, Irving Kristol – who seems to have been perfectly happy to discuss his replacement – and Stephen.

Of these people Mike Josselson, Nicky Nabokov and Mel Lasky were probably aware that the Congress for Cultural Freedom was subsidized by the CIA. But although this sounds conspiratorial, the line connecting Paris to Washington was elastic. Mike Josselson's position was that of a European rather than an American. He understood and respected the independence of the intellectuals he was employing. There was no question of telling them what to do. If worse came to worst, someone might have to be replaced, but until that happened he had to be trusted. Nicky Nabokov, for example, was a key link to European music. Without him, it would have been difficult to have organized the big festivals which were the CCF's showcases of Western culture. But he was also hard to control, for his feud with Soviet Russia, and with Russian music, was personal.

Encounter was only one of many magazines which the Congress for Cultural Freedom was sponsoring. Post-colonial Africa, India, the Far East, were all places which were being targeted by communist propaganda, and the CCF needed to support local initiatives providing intellectual resistance; or start such initiatives itself. This could mean anything from giving money to a magazine that was in difficulties, to founding a new one, or starting a project involving a theatre group. These plans could become very detailed. Jennifer Josselson, Mike's daughter, remembers a discussion during which her father went over a project to build a theatre somewhere in sub-Saharan Africa: 'if we are building a theatre, let's put it near a market-place where people will have a better chance of going to it'.

Keeping an eye on the activities of the Paris office was John Hunt, who had been sent out to take over should Josselson succumb to a heart attack, which at times seemed imminent. When he arrived, Hunt had had little experience of the kind of meetings he now attended. His found them stimulating but very chaotic. As his role was that of an observer, he could join in the discussions and make suggestions, but he could not tell the others what they should do.

Regarding the independence of the sixteen or seventeen magazines that the CCF ended up supporting, John Hunt told me recently that they were satisfied if 60 per cent of published articles were in some way pro-American. In the case of *Encounter*, the proportion was always higher, so there was no question of interfering in the way it was run.

While the others wondered whether Macdonald might be too maverick to be put in charge of the politics of *Encounter*, Stephen concentrated on his views on literature. 'My colleagues certainly have one characteristic in common,' Stephen wrote in his diary after a hot three days of discussions, 'They are all Philistines. They dislike poetry and distrust everything which has high standards.' As for Dwight, 'his knowledge is so patchy, his self-assurance so great'. For instance, one of the things they discussed was whether they should run some articles on contemporary television. Stephen suggested that it would be interesting to write an article about television in Russia. Dwight said, 'Do you mean to tell me that they have television in Russia?'

The committee felt unable to come to a decision. Dwight was just too unpredictable. As Kristol put it later, 'Dwight has spent a fruitful life and a distinguished career purposefully being a security risk to just about everyone and everything with reach of his typewriter.' He was accepted as a 'roving editor' for a year.

Ten days later, from 5 to 20 August 1955, my father and I went away as the guests of Hansi Lambert, a Belgian woman from an old banking family related to the French Rothschilds. Hansi kept an important political salon in Brussels at the time. Mum stayed behind with Lizzie while we sailed around the Mediterranean in a long sloop dated 1904. Dad kept an intermittent diary, but he never wrote it up properly, which is a pity as the interaction of the guests was as tense as a who-done-it by Agatha Christie.

Léon Lambert, the son of Hansi, fell in love with Chuck Turner, the friend of Sam Barber, but Chuck wasn't interested and Sam became irritated. Emile de Staerk, assistant to Paul-Henri Spaak who was one of the founders of the European Union, spent so much time talking to the men that Lady Kitty Farrell got bored with all of them and turned her attention to the captain. The Lamberts found it impossible to stay anywhere for more than a few hours and this in turn annoyed the captain, as the crew could never go off duty. Getting provisions was difficult and the boat had an unusual appetite for water. There was a humiliating moment when at some remote island Cécile de Rothschild's yacht took their boat's promised supply of water and they had to wait four hours for more to accumulate. That evening Hansi murmured, 'We've always been the poor relations.' Which greatly amused the writers and the musicians, whose money problems were of a much humbler kind.

Cyril Connolly was on this boat. I remember him well. Cyril, with his ironic voice that somehow managed to be both neutral and facetious, teased everybody, beginning with himself. Dad's diary includes Cyril's running commentary on himself as he took too many grapes for breakfast. It ends with Cyril advising himself out loud to put the skins and pips on Stephen's plate so that when the Lamberts joined them, they'd think that Stephen was the greedy one.

I remember one devastating remark of Cyril's. It became one of Dad's favourite stories, though for some reason he didn't put it in his diary. Léon, bored with having to listen to the mixture of gossip and idealism from Stephen, Cyril and Sam, said that he had a good mind to give up his bank and sit around for the rest of his life, just talking, like them. Cyril said, 'Please don't do that, Léon. If there's one thing sadder than a banker, it's a banker without his bank.'

I was only ten, and frequently I got in the way by humming and hopping and fidgeting. Cyril said I was as irritating as a fly, and as flies needed to be swatted, he was going to roll up a magazine and swat me. The only question was which magazine could be spared for this messy task. The Lamberts thought this was very funny, but one day I said something sharp to Cyril and he stopped. He didn't frighten me. I could see in his small eyes surrounded by fat a nervous child peeking out, hoping not to be rejected.

On the Lambert yacht in a photo taken by my father.

My father gives a more high-minded version of this clash of wills. According to this, Cyril was complaining about a reader of *Horizon* who'd told him she couldn't understand his magazine. It seems that I piped up, 'You should have told her that you make it as clear as you can.' My father wrote that since my remark was sensible, Cyril treated me thereafter as an adult.

At the very end of the diary, my father writes this:

At Poros, I had a walk with Matthew, in which we had a very inter-esting conversation. He told me that he had three great worries in his life. I remember two of these, and forget the third. The first worry was that people at his school told him that during the war I had been a Communist, and against England. He wondered whether I could not resolve this problem by giving him a signed document, in which I stated that really I had been a member of the British Secret Service. I told him I had not been a communist during the war, nor a member of the Secret Service. The second worry was about our being in debt. He was afraid that I might die suddenly and leave a lot of debts, which couldn't be paid, and then they would have nothing to live on, and the television would be taken away.

I mentioned the British Secret Service? Aged ten? Was I already aware of something odd about my father's background? I remember this conversation, especially the bit about who pays for the TV if Dad dropped dead. But the Secret Service?

The boy who'd made me nervous about my father's behaviour during the war was called Cunningham. For a while, back at the Hall, he'd become the bane of my life. Whereas in carpentry class Cunningham was making a Wellington bomber, I struggled week after week with a hexagonal teapot-stand. I was jealous, also admiring, and so it was a surprise when he called me out. 'My father says that your father was a coward in the war. He ran away! What are you going to do about it?' Boys gathered round. A fight, a fight!

I had no desire to punch Cunningham or be punched back. I reported what he'd said to my father. Dad said mildly, 'He's mixing me up with Wystan. Cunningham? I suppose he must be the son of Admiral Cunningham.' And what had Wystan done in the war that made Cunningham so upset? 'Oh,' said Dad vaguely, 'he just stayed on in America.'

I was entirely on Cunningham's side. Wystan should have come back and dressed himself in martial khaki. Conduct unworthy of an

Englishman. Behaviour incompatible with the standards of the *Beano* and the *Dandy* and the *Wizard*, copies of which I read by torchlight under the sheets.

Over August 1955, while Dad and I were away on the Lamberts' yacht, Mum prepared for a concert alone in Loudoun Road.

Chandler was attentive, perhaps too much so. My mother was nervous and sometimes she didn't have time for him. He wrote later: 'I remember those awful days late last summer when you were breaking yourself in half trying to build a programme and would go to bed exhausted and cry. That was before you knew you were really ill. And I wasn't allowed to see you or even telephone you, for fear of distracting what little energy you could summon up for your "instrument".'

She was ill. It was hard to keep going. Whenever she did see Ray, she complained about her relationship with her husband: his spend-thrift attitude to money, his impracticality, his infatuations with young men. It was exactly what Ray wanted to hear, as he was fascinated by illness and he loathed homosexuality. A year later he wrote: 'I think you should have left Stephen long ago, but I have gone into that, and I know one does not always have a free choice. And it is always possible that you are much fonder of him than you have ever admitted to me.'

She also complained about money. When he'd first invited her out, she told him she 'didn't have tuppence to her name'. She said she could never hear a knock on the door without a flicker of fear that it might be a creditor with an unpaid bill. It was an anxiety held over from her childhood. Chandler said it was monstrous that she didn't have her own bank account, and he gave her a cheque so that she could open one. Later it emerged that she'd carried this cheque around in her purse for months without cashing it. This fascinated Chandler. There was something erotic about it: his cheque, her purse.

On 9 September, my mother learned that she had to have an

operation – of what kind, I do not know. Chandler wrote in his diary that the day scheduled for this procedure was 'the fatal day': 12 December, the first anniversary of the day on which, the previous year, his wife Cissy had died. The coincidence preyed on him.

My father decided that what his wife needed was a holiday; and Chandler was evidently falling to pieces. Maybe the two of them should just go off for a holiday by themselves? Obviously Stephen was exasperated. He probably needed the house to be empty so that he could work; or maybe he was just bored with Chandler. But he also hated illness, especially in women. Meanwhile Natasha wanted to save Ray, and Ray thought he was going to save Natasha.

So off they went. They stayed at the Albergo Gardesana at Torri del Benaco – our family hotel, as it were. What about the scandal, asked Ray? Stephen told him, 'my friends won't misunderstand me and I don't care about the others'. What could be more high-minded than that? They had separate rooms and Ray took care that they had separate bills, though of course he paid both.

Natasha tried to keep Ray busy with sightseeing: Verona, Venice for the night (there's mention of difficulties in finding a hotel on the Lido). If this was a rest cure for my mother, then 'gallivanting' (one of her favourite words) was hardly the right recipe. Ray was drinking, and she thought that keeping him on the move was a way of separating him from the bottle – and to some extent this worked. But she was out of her depth.

They got back to London in the last week of September. Chandler's residential permit had expired and he should have been on his way back to America. On the 27th, he had lunch with Ian Fleming, who gave him a copy of *Dr No*, inscribed 'from Private Fleming to Sergeant Chandler'. (Ray gave it to Natasha, and she sold it years later for a colossal sum.) Ray also had lunch with Eric Ambler at the Garrick Club. Ambler at that time was more famous than Ian Fleming, but Chandler was the leader of them all.

Finally, he went back to New York.

In November 1955, obsessed by the imminent operation my mother had to face on the anniversary of Cissy's death, Chandler came back to London in order to give her another holiday. This time they went to Tangiers. They stayed in a hotel with two separate bedrooms, sharing a bathroom and the living room. There was one kiss, it seems. He mentioned it eighteen months later as a rare and treasured moment.

Once again, her idea was to keep him on the move. They went for a walk in the old part of town, quarrelled, she stomped off and when Ray finally caught up with her, he got stuck in some mud. He remembered it because of the laughter of some nearby Arabs. I can just imagine this scene. Whenever my mother became irritated, she would walk off briskly into the distance; but she expected to be pursued.

She thought she was taking care of him. He thought he was taking care of her. 'As nanny my greatest problem was to keep her from exhaustion,' he wrote to Jamie Hamilton. To her, he grumbled later about 'the endless prowling of bazaars when you knew I could hardly stand up'.

They came back a few days before her operation, which my mother always insisted subsequently was 'routine'. Ray spent the evening with Stephen at Loudoun Road, and Stephen had to stay awake half the night to calm him down.

At this point it finally dawned on my father that the situation had become equivocal. The fact that he'd made no comment earlier suggests that he'd never considered Ray to be anything more than one of Mum's 'causes'. In an attempt to regain the initiative, Stephen wrote to Ray to ask if he could pay back some of the money Ray had spent on the various trips they'd made together, not to mention the operation Natasha had just been through – for which it seems that Chandler had insisted on picking up the tab. Surely he owed Ray something in the region of six hundred pounds?

This letter confused Chandler. At first he thought he was being rejected. Hadn't he been giving Natasha a holiday? Or alternatively, if she'd saved his life, wasn't his gift to her a legitimate expression of gratitude? 'I think it is absolutely true that Natasha gave me something to live for when I was in a very despairing condition, but I like to think that I should have acted the same.' Repayment for kindness didn't come into it, he decided. It was a matter of principle for him to help a woman in distress.

Chandler brooded about Stephen's offer for several days. In the end he decided that it put him in a position of power, because Stephen couldn't afford to hand over six hundred pounds anyway. He didn't have that kind of money. 'In all these things you have acted with immense dignity and generosity,' he wrote, with a smidge of condescension that would have maddened Stephen. 'You have exposed all three of us (I don't matter, because I don't care) to the possibility of scandalous gossip.' This implied that beyond their intimate circle they were seen by London society as a love triangle. Ray could now address Stephen as man to man. 'My only fear now is that the damn girl will get so well and so strong and so vibrant that we will all lose her to her music.'

Mentioning money made things more complicated. My mother thought a great deal about money. Its lack had been a constant anxiety throughout her childhood. She always wanted to save, while my father's attitude was if a cheque was in the post, he could go out and have lunch with his friends. But Chandler was strange about money, too. Though rich, he was blowing his capital very quickly. He had 'the incredible frivolity of those about to die', as Proust puts it. It gave him a secret pleasure to buy my mother jewellery, and watch her wear it, and take out an insurance policy in case she lost it, and remind her when the premium was due, even as my father was attempting to repay what he thought he owed Chandler, in instalments, through a solicitor, so that they didn't have to talk about it when they met. Trying to keep things under control, when Dad saw a diamond necklace around Mum's neck he made her take it straight back to Asprey's.

These skirmishes between the two men ended shortly before Christmas, when Chandler had to go to hospital to recover from a binge. This allowed Dad to forget about Ray. If he was ill, his manipulations descended to the level of symptoms.

When Ray came out of rehab, Natasha found him a furnished flat around the corner from Loudoun Road. This proprietary move on her part meant that the other members of the 'shuttle service' dropped out. She was assuming responsibility for him. In retrospect she thought she should have found a live-in nurse. She wasn't really up to taking care of him by herself.

Loudoun Road lies on an east–west axis, which means Stephen's study got the sun for the greater part of the morning and Natasha's piano room was lit in the afternoon. Carlton Terrace, where Ray was now staying, runs north–south; and number 49 faces north. No sun. I remember Ray's flat as dark and horribly furnished. In his letters he said he hated it and it's hardly surprising. The windows were dusty, there was a three-bar electric fire and a wing chair, and not much else.

He reminded her later of the times when she'd come round, thrown herself in that chair and said, 'What heavenly peace,' as if he represented an oasis of tranquillity. Which he didn't. But by saying that he did, she was helping him to reach out for it.

In February 1956, she went off to Switzerland to convalesce from the operation as a guest of Hansi Lambert. Chandler missed her. Was it really so great to sit in a grand house and be waited on by servants, he asked grumpily? Meanwhile he was taking his meals in Loudoun Road, where Francesca cooked for him. (He had his difficulties with Francesca.) Dad was away somewhere and his only company was myself and my sister. Once, I came in to supper with filthy hands and he asked how was it possible to get hands so dirty in just one day? I immediately apologized and went off to wash them – which he said in a letter to Mum was 'rather nice'.

Her letters to him from Gstaad, which he later threw away, were gloomy. Their secret name for that mood was 'Maudie', which I suppose comes from 'maudlin'.

While she was away, Stephen wrote another letter to him about money. Ray couldn't believe that Stephen was worried about what people might think. 'You cannot be damaged in reputation by anything to do with money,' he wrote to him reassuringly. 'If there is damage, it has already occurred, and was inevitable from the time I was sent off to Italy with Natasha.' All this sounds as if he's trying to provoke Stephen, but here he adds an unusually submissive sentence: 'I have always had someone to care for and protect. It is part of my excuse for living.'

Feeling better, Ray went back to teasing Stephen. He wasn't really making a real offer, was he? He was just appealing to be let off the debt on the grounds of poverty. What would happen if Stephen couldn't send an instalment to his solicitor? Would Stephen's solicitor dun him on Chandler's behalf? No! 'The whole idea is a fake.' Better for Stephen to give up one of his live-in maids, Ray wrote sarcastically – a low blow, since Francesca had been feeding him regularly.

Beneath this skirmish lay a deeper chasm to do with the profession they were supposed to share. Chandler disapproved of writers who failed to earn money by their writing. 'I regard financial failure as essentially a moral failure. People should have the strength to live in the world of their time.' The writer should understand the culture of his age and invent a work of art that was truly contemporary. Shakespeare in our age would have written for television. 'He would have taken the false gods and done them over.' To write a few weak verses for five friends living in Chelsea just wasn't good enough.

Chandler's early work consists of short stories that took him months to write and did not earn much when they were published, so his toughness on this subject is worthy of respect. But in my opinion he's striking a pose, not providing an argument. At this late stage of his career, his wealth came not from his novels but from Hollywood. In the film industry, there is work and there is money and there are films, and sometimes the writer wins. More often he loses. Sometimes all that remains of the writer is one gag immersed in a script written by others. The connection between money and words is tenuous, and the idea of Chandler taking on the false gods and producing marvels is only a fantasy.

My father was never competitive in this way with any writer, but it has to be said that he had no opinion at all of Chandler's work. He didn't like detective stories, and that was it. My mother tried the Marlowe novels, but there was something about Philip Marlowe's attitude towards women that she found unreal: a mixture of chivalry and sadism, neither of which she found attractive. Neither of my parents responded to the idea that Raymond Chandler had given the city of Los Angeles an identity it would not otherwise have; and that this gift has a touch of genius about it.

A week after trying to unravel his debt to Ray, Stephen went off to Venice for a congress involving Sartre, Merleau-Ponty, Silone and other serious European intellectuals. He was at the height of his involvement with power.

Two days after coming back, he gave a supper for Charlie Chaplin. Ray wasn't invited, and it rankled. Passing the peanuts, I remember Chaplin moving his legs in a facetious hop when he leaned against the piano, as if the shiny Bechstein needed taking down a peg.

On 10 May, the Spenders gave a farewell party for Ray before he flew back to America. He appeared with presents for us children. He was benign: this was his family. He wasn't the only guest, however, and there was a limit to the amount of attention my mother could give to him. After lunch, he was packed into a taxi by himself to catch his plane at Heathrow. It seemed ominous. In November of that year, by that time back in California, he wrote to Natasha, 'when I left England last May I knew I had lost you, since, if I hadn't, you would never on any pretext have let me go to Heath Row without you'.

13

THE IRRESISTIBLE HISTORIC
MIXED GRILL

ARLIER IN THE year, on 26 February 1956, the Soviet leader
Nikita Khrushchev gave a speech at the 20th Party Congress
during which he'd denounced the crimes of Joseph Stalin and the
'cult of personality' with which Stalin had surrounded himself. This
speech is often taken as marking the end of the first phase of the
Cold War. The Soviet leadership had acknowledged the most
appalling crimes. The communist parties of France and Italy lost a
great many members, and those who remained were tied to die-hard
Stalinists who defended the indefensible. It became clear that in
neither country would the respective communist parties ever gain
power via the ballot box.

Towards the end of the year, the governments of Poland and
Hungary attempted to break free from Russian control. The Polish
attempt ended badly, the Hungarian attempt disastrously. It was
suppressed by the Russian Army at the cost of many lives.

When all this was over, Stephen was invited to visit Poland. He
got on well with the members of the Polish Writers' Association,
and at the end of a banquet in his honour he was told he could talk
to any writer he wanted, even if that writer was languishing in jail.

It was an interesting offer, tinged with irony. Perhaps the idea was to show that, even within a repressive regime, a degree of liberty existed.

Stephen got up and told this audience of colleagues that there was one person he was curious to meet. He would like to meet a communist. There was dead silence. Then a voice from the back called out, 'Vous êtes arrivé trop tard, Monsieur.' You've arrived too late, Sir. It became one of my father's favourite after-dinner stories, but it shows that even after the disasters of Hungary and Poland he still thought of communism as an 'idea'.

In the newspapers, this was the great moment of the so-called 'Kremlinologist'. Academics, Foreign Office mandarins plus recent refugees from Russia guessed what was going on behind those vast red walls of Red Square. Khrushchev's policies swung forwards and backwards. He visited foreign countries and proposed arms limitations. Was this just a ploy? He denounced the 'cult of personality', but he himself was a personality of monumental proportions. To whom was he responsible? The Party? The Politburo? After he had eliminated the remaining Stalinists in the Politburo, was he going to become another Stalin?

Kremlinologists might have had some idea of what was going on in Moscow, but most Russians had none. And the West had no idea what it meant to live under such a repressive regime. Politics could not be discussed, opinions had to be camouflaged even from close friends. To readers in the West, George Orwell's *Nineteen Eighty-four* was a sinister fantasy. To Russian readers, it was stone-cold reality.

By the mid-Sixties, Russia subsided into a series of vast interlocking bureaucracies incapable of taking decisions. The Politburo met for long inconclusive discussions about what should happen next. Huge black cars floated round Moscow late at night giving the impression that something was about to be decided. The idea of taking over the world developed in a vacuum. Russians went wherever Americans had not yet arrived, while some dissidents in Moscow nursed the crazy fantasy that one day they might be liberated by

American bombs, followed by an invasion. I remember Joseph Brodsky talking to us about this: American GIs walking around Red Square handing out cigarettes to the grown-ups and candy to the kids.

One of the vast bureaucracies was in charge of cultural matters. 'Events' had to be organized. It was important that they occur, but nothing was supposed to take place that might tie the department to a future course of action. 'They were mere embellishments on the ideological façade,' as the novelist Zinovy Zinik, who was born in Moscow, told me recently. 'Every Soviet citizen, from the Politburo members to the plant workers, were prisoners, subject to the prison regime's code of behaviour and regulations; and then Stephen Spender turns up at the prison gates and demands from these prisoners a sincere public response and active participation in the life outside.'

Thus Stephen raised the banner of free speech and the right of fellow writers to communicate directly with each other. Chance of success, zero. 'The Writers' Union, founded in 1934, was a Stalinist institution for the regimentation of thought,' said Ilya Ehrenburg to an interviewer in the post-Khrushchev phase. But, throughout the Cold War, my father continued to hope that somewhere within the folds of Soviet bureaucracy there was someone with whom he could talk.

The Venice meeting over Easter of 1956 was one of those complex affairs where nothing serious is discussed, but much takes place beneath the surface. There was a group of European communists, another of liberals, and an official Russian delegation which nevertheless did not seem interested in representing the point of view of communist orthodoxy.

After it was over, Stephen wrote a novel about the event, amalgamating it with another similar meeting held in Milan in July. *Engaged in Writing* includes thinly disguised portraits of Sartre and Malraux and Silone, who are involved in an arcane ideological wrestling match while the representatives from Russia observe them with detachment, clothed in the mystic virtue of survival. Everybody knows that thousands of Russian writers have been sent to jail, or shot. Yet 'In spite of everything that had happened, the Russian delegates still had the aura of a priesthood not wholly discredited.'

> What seduced the Westerners most of all was that which they least admitted: an insatiable curiosity about what was happening 'over there'. There was a great dish, and what hid it was not so much an iron curtain as a silver cover. Under this, they knew there to be a course consisting of the irresistible historic mixed grill: revolution, murder, personal power, oppression and a sauce of reform. The steam of gossip shooting out on all sides was sanctified: every rumour a specimen, sniffed over.

There were intrigues that Stephen doesn't go into. Though he notes that the French delegates were particularly opaque, discussing subjects such as whether a discussion can itself be discussed, he doesn't mention the fact that the French and Italian delegates had to accept that, in their own countries, their respective communist parties dominated the selective processes in the arts festivals and the choice of novels to be published. There was no question of challenging mechanisms so powerful. The best these intellectuals could do was to flirt with the possibility of disagreeing with them.

In the end the hero, the Spender substitute, can stand it no longer. 'Dipping deep into the bran-tub of a past which seemed stuffed with different personalities marking different stages of his career, he adopted the manner he had used when most of those had been in their revolutionary prime.' This was the great unmentionable fact: these middle-aged Europeans shared a past during which they'd all believed in communism; and they faced three Russians who, by the fact that miraculously they were still alive, represented the awful consequences of that belief. Flamboyantly, he resigns. The gesture is treated with sympathy, for deep down the other representatives –

who of course wouldn't dream of abandoning their roles – recognize he's done the only honest thing possible.

Alone in a gondola, he remembers a sudden revelation he'd had during a previous meeting four years earlier, in a castle in eastern Europe where they'd sipped a lot of wine. Drunk and lonely, he'd caught a glimpse of a young man tending some vines. 'Lake below, mountains above, and between the lane of turreted leaves, the human form – the labourer in the vineyard. His dark-tanned trousers formed a pedestal of bark, split, stripped at the navel, peeled to reveal the bare torso of the burned sun-god, Apollo carved in wood, breast of lyre, mouth coining song.'

The image is a poem. All it needs is to be written down.

There the poem was so clear, so complete, simple as a single line, luminous as the day. It was perfect in his mind, he saw it clear and whole. He knew it as though he had been born with it silver in his mouth, and it would be scrolled within his hollow bones when he died. And yet it was at this exact moment that he realized that the virtue which could enable him to write it had gone out of him. There was no form, no rhythm, only the perfectly clear idea. The rhythm that can no more be defined than the unstated revelation in the shaping of a single letter of handwriting, had gone.

There was a price to be paid for attending congresses. If you believed that a fragment of life was the basis of a poem, the rare fragments that appeared in the life of the junketing poet would be crushed by the weight of congressional banalities and that poem would not be written.

On 8 July 1956, Stephen joined Nicky Nabokov at his château not far from Paris. Nabokov had asked him to write the libretto of an opera for which he'd compose the music. It was about the assassination of Rasputin, the mystic who acquired an unusual power at the court of Tsar Nicholas II, through the Tsarina. Nabokov had known many of the people involved in this dramatic incident.

Stephen's contribution to the libretto was limited to adding words to an idea that Nicky had already mapped out in the smallest details. 'He dictated to me the entire action of the play, with all the scenes, all the positionings of characters on the stage, the outlines of every piece of dialogue, from the first moment to the last. He has a capacity for grasping an idea in its concreteness from beginning to end, which would be genius if it goes with a corresponding creative grasp in every detail of the music.' Stephen sounds bemused. Nevertheless, 'It was very pleasant to be alone with him and not in the usual tangle of committees and dinners.'

One evening, probably during this visit, Nicky and Stephen were having supper alone together. At a certain point Nicky swept all the food and the cutlery off the table in front of him and buried his head in his arms. Glasses and porcelain lay broken around his feet, but he paid no attention. He was weeping uncontrollably. Through this muffled, histrionic, drunken, self-pitying heap, Stephen saw the full extent of Nicky's grief; how deeply he missed that idyllic pre-revolutionary world, how impossible it was for him to forgive those who had destroyed it.

In his long relationship with Nicky Nabokov, my father admired the intensity of his hatred for the Bolsheviks, because it was so honest. Nicky wasn't mourning a lost society that had pampered the Nabokov family. He was a fighter for a civilization that had been violently destroyed. Stephen often felt that his own position as a social democrat or wishy-washy liberal, or whatever it was, didn't amount to much. He wanted the working classes to be treated better than they had been, but beyond that, it would be hard to say what political aims he had in mind. And he often felt that communism was a 'cause' in ways that the capitalist West was not. Without occasional extremists like Nicky Nabokov, the other side would have had all the energy.

By this time Raymond Chandler had settled into a hotel back in California. He'd had a bad fall and been hospitalized for malnutrition due to alcoholism, but he was pulling himself together. He described his room. From the window, all he could see were women's legs. Presumably he was near the swimming pool. He didn't know if he liked those legs or not. They were distracting.

He wrote to Natasha regularly. He wanted to entice her to join him. He felt that she'd done a good job in helping him, and he indeed felt better, but as for being cured, 'I think I was fooling myself out of my great love for you.' This was a compliment, but immediately he adds: 'I don't suppose that from the citadel of family life you could appreciate the forlornness of my life.'

He wanted her to join him, but she would have to leave behind her family. 'In my own mind I have to divide you into two people. It is surely not that I love you less, nor that I admire you less as an adorable hostess and a sweet, devoted mother. But I must love you in sunshine and clean air – and alone.' Those damn children, for instance. Too spoiled! 'Any time a five year old child is allowed to dominate a dinner table and outtalk everyone else and I get reproved by you for not answering an unintelligible question the little brat fires at me – any time that happens, there is something wrong.' (Not me! The child was Lizzie. She was six, I was eleven.)

He was wondering whether he should leave Natasha something in his will. Like giving jewels, he enjoyed this fantasy. He wrote to his lawyer that he wanted Natasha to inherit his copyright, but added that it was important that Stephen didn't get his hands on it. 'He is the sort of man who, if he had fifty pounds, would spend it on a painting instead of paying the grocer's bill. He is good to his children and loves them. But he is not a normal man. He is not like you and me and his judgment is very faulty except in his proper sphere of pretentious and anaemic writing.'

Ray's opinion of my father's writing had started high. In 1949 he'd written to Jamie Hamilton: 'I like this fellow Spender very much. In fact I like him better than Auden, about whom I have always had reservations.' But when my father's autobiography came out in 1951, Chandler was shocked. Was this the kind of book that a man with a wife and two children should have written? Surely it was irresponsible, to say the least? Then he found out the interesting fact that, six years after publication, my mother still hadn't read it! This was a godsend, of course. Whenever she tried to defend her husband, all Chandler had to say was 'Have you read "World within World" yet?'

Publicity photo taken before my mother's concert tour of the USA in 1957.

Chandler found an apartment and began to bring from storage some furniture from his old house. He hadn't seen these pieces since Cissy died. But he hesitated to move in. An apartment – and alone? 'I don't know when I have been so unhappy. There was just about a month between your letters and though you said there were others they have never come. I have been so lonely that my life was almost unendurable.' He was bored with California. Even if Natasha came to join him, 'I can't see how I can count on having you for more than a couple of months a year at most, and what the hell do I do with the other ten?'

My mother hated writing letters, and she was not above pretending to have written one when she hadn't. Ray sat in the hotel and waited. Finally a letter from her came through.

He made the mistake of taking it to the new apartment where he was surrounded by Cissy's belongings. He opened it and read. 'It was hellish with the furniture, almost like reading the letters of someone very dear who has died.'

Did she understand what this implied? It wasn't just a question of Ray asking her to abandon her husband and children and come to California. He had a role for her in mind, and it had something to do with his dead wife. Cissy had also played the piano, and Cissy also had needed doctors. Chandler seems to think that the only thing that would hold him together was if he had my mother in La Jolla. Only then would his life become sober and solicitous. She would be ill, he would bring her meals in bed and write at night, as he had done with Cissy. He would care about his life, because he would be caring for her.

It was worse than impossible. It was downright sinister.

In October 1956, the Egyptian government nationalized the Suez Canal. England and France decided to invade the country to reimpose their sovereignty over a piece of property they considered theirs. The invasion went well to begin with, but the canal was blocked with scuppered ships and both the Americans and the Russians disapproved. It turned out to have been a mistake.

This took time, of course, but in the early days of the war the British press was full of stirring accounts of the bravery of Our Boys. I was eleven, and very excited. The news fluctuated daily. I followed the events on a map, sticking pins in remarkably square Egypt and its remarkably triangular delta. My father instead looked mildly worried and anything but military.

That winter saw the last great Smog of London. It killed twenty thousand people. The Clean Air Act was passed so that it wouldn't happen again. The fog didn't shut the school. I remember how extraordinary it was to feel my way from the bus stop to the school gates, touching the wall on my right and projecting on to this grey gritty screen a memory of where I was.

The following term I won the poetry prize, with an ode called 'Autumn'. The prize was presented by Peggy Ashcroft, and when she read out the poem it indeed sounded good. As a result of this I was made a school prefect. I did not want the job. I hated the idea of reading the Lesson at prayers, those snippets from the Bible which required at least a minimal self-confidence and the capacity to 'project'. I persuaded a friend and co-prefect to read for me. He read very well. I thought it was a fine solution to the problem. Not so. The headmaster called me up at the end of prayers and chastised me in front of everyone. I was avoiding my responsibilities, he said. It was not for this that he'd made me a prefect.

The headmaster had a wart on the back of his neck which he fiddled with when angry, and an old war wound in his leg that made him occasionally stamp. I watched him fiddling and stamping and I took off my badge, a silver Maltese Cross, put it on the table in front of him and said I was resigning. He refused to accept it and I was irrevocably condemned to the rank of newly commissioned officer.

From mid-October, Natasha and Stephen were in America. He had some lectures to give and she had arranged a concert tour on the East Coast. They stayed with Sam Barber and Gian Carlo Menotti at Mount Kisko, and then for a few days with Muriel Gardiner (now Buttinger) on her farm in Pennington, New Jersey. Having given his lectures, Stephen then returned to London to take care of us while Natasha continued her concert tour alone.

A few days after my father left, Chandler learned that Natasha had suffered whiplash in a car accident outside Boston. The pain was placing her tour in doubt. He wanted her to come immediately to California and recuperate with him. It was his chance to repay the tenderness she had shown to him during the previous year.

By this time he was living with a woman called Louise, who was easy to be with, but as he wrote to Natasha, he was not in love. 'I'll never get anyone as kind and gentle [as Louise], and even if we do have occasional disagreements, they don't have to be catastrophic. After all, I shan't live very long anyhow and I am too tired to care. It has been given to me as to few men to love two of the most wonderful women it is possible to imagine, and to have them love me.' (He meant Cissy, and Natasha.)

Louise heard that Natasha was on her way, and she took the hint. She left for San Francisco, where she still had a husband. 'All I can say is that I loved having her here, that she is a charming and indulgent companion, although not a great lady like you, that it is awful for me to be alone, but that damn it all, no second best is good enough.'

Giving it one last try, Louise came back to La Jolla a few days later. Bad luck had it that on Sunday evening, 18 November, she picked up the telephone – and it was Natasha from the East Coast, wanting to discuss with Ray her imminent visit to California. He was on the other line. 'When I hear your wonderful voice I like to try to express some of the ecstasy I feel.' Poor eavesdropping Louise at last got the message. After the call ended, she started drinking. 'I couldn't say she was ever drunk in the usual sense but her whole nature changed.' In fact, 'she turned out to be something less than a lady'. It would have been all right, wrote Ray, if he'd been drinking too, then they could have had a nice old-fashioned fight! The sad thing was that he didn't care enough for her to take that route.

Next morning, Louise got on the plane back to San Francisco. A few days later he received a touching note written from the airport saying that their relationship was at an end.

Was Natasha really coming? Ray could hardly believe it. Where could he take her? How about the San Marcos Hotel in Chandler, Arizona, followed by Palm Springs? Three times in his letters Ray chides her for worrying him about the sleeping arrangements. Yes, they would have separate bedrooms. No need to drum it in. 'You should know that I am not going to embarrass you or make any demand on you that you don't feel like granting.' Mind you, he knows of a hotel in LA which has a 'bordello wing' with cottages for privacy, 'but it is hardly flattering to invite a lady there'.

To Ray, my mother was a 'lady'. At some point he even goes as far as to imagine the day when Stephen becomes Sir Stephen and she becomes Lady Spender. That would be 'tremendous fun', wrote Chandler in his best hate-the-British mode. Ironically, in another episode of the Chandler saga set in the distant future, my father said to me, 'The thing is, Natasha is not what used to be called a "Lady". The reaction of a real Lady to all this' – he was referring to a biography of Chandler which assumed that an affair had indeed taken place – 'would surely be to forget the whole thing.' He was right. A well-brought-up Englishwoman, trained from an early age at one of those stoical boarding schools and finding herself wrongly accused of having had an affair, would say, 'God, what a bore,' and leave it at that.

Between 18 November when Louise left and 6 December when Natasha arrived in Arizona, Ray started drinking again. On 23 November he wrote to her, 'I wish you were here. The weather is rather jolly, bright and warmish. You could lie in the big double bed and rest and I could feed you.'

Did she really want to come? His love for her was immense, her compassion also – but he wanted love. It had to be all or nothing on both sides. He wrote to her, 'The thinnest tie of social friendship was always more important [to you] than my feelings. And I rather think quite rightly so. I came so late into your life and was so intolerable. But you must search your soul. If I mean so little to you, I mean nothing at all, and for us to be together in Arizona is just another amour sans amour.'

14

THE KINDEST FACE

A T ONE POINT during the Venice meeting earlier that year, a young American noticed two distinguished men crossing a steep humped bridge near the Ducal Palace not far from the Bridge of Sighs. The short man with pebble glasses and a downturned mouth he knew was Jean-Paul Sartre. He did not recognize the second figure, tall and deferential, but decided he had to find out who he was.

The second man on the bridge was Stephen, and the young man looking up at him was Reynolds Price. Thus, entirely independently but in some way parallel, my father began a relationship as contorted but as powerful as my mother's with Raymond Chandler.

At the end of September, Reynolds wrote a letter to Stephen in which he described this moment on the bridge and said he thought he had 'the kindest face I have ever seen'. Could they meet? Stephen replied cautiously. He was very busy at the moment, and soon he'd have to go to the US to give some lectures. Reynolds took this reply as encouraging, and he sent him some stories he'd written. Stephen found them on his return from the US and wrote to say that he liked them. They arranged to meet.

On 13 December 1956, the day after Natasha arrived in Arizona to stay with Chandler, Stephen invited Reynolds to lunch at Loudoun Road. Three days later Stephen accepted Reynolds' story 'The

Anniversary' for publication in *Encounter*. Before Christmas, he invited him to spend the New Year with us. Reynolds was staying in a boarding-house in Brighton at the time and Stephen didn't want him to spend the New Year alone.

I remember when Reynolds came to live with us at Loudoun Road: neat, not much older than me (early twenties), somewhat pockmarked with acne, extremely polite but frequently laughing, interested in us children. Reynolds stayed in the house for about ten days over the New Year. He slept in the bed in the study where Auden stayed whenever he came to London.

After he'd left, Stephen wrote to him to say how grateful he was for the time they'd shared. 'I think of this room where I am writing as your room and of how you understood the children and my preoccupation with them.' It was wonderful to have spent these days together,

> which were beautiful in themselves and in which we discovered what a lot of things we liked in common: Fidelio for example. I think it is having values and the ability to share them and the wish to go on sharing them and creating the circumstances in which we go on doing so that our friendship will find its future. We discovered the things we could share in common, and now what we have to know is whether we shall want to go on doing so. This is not really a matter of straining and willing things, but of trust, and patience and discovery of ourselves as much as of one another. I do have trust and I don't want to force anything. And whatever happened I would still have an awful lot from this week. One day I shall be able to write a poem about what that is. But I can't even approach doing so now.

This is clearly a love letter. How had Reynolds replied to this instant crush on my father's part? More than fifty years later, Reynolds told me with a grin: 'I could see that Stephen wasn't living alone, because there were two children at Loudoun Road. But if there was a Mrs Spender, where was she? And why hadn't she been mentioned?'

My father had lost his head. He'd invited Reynolds to share his life in exactly the same way that he'd wanted Tony to move in, twenty-four years earlier; or proposed marriage to Inez after seeing her just twice. But Stephen was not alone in the world any more. He was not a free agent. And Reynolds, a much cleverer man than Tony, had no intention of alienating the offstage Mrs Spender and the half of London that would inevitably take her side if he'd really moved into Loudoun Road.

One day, we went for a walk on Hampstead Heath. The day was cold but sunny. The Whitestone Pond had a sheen on it, sky and water were the same bright element. Stephen and Reynolds talked while Lizzie and I romped around, half showing off, half wanting to be called back so that we could check up on this new relationship. Children depend on grown-ups and any alteration of the status quo must be closely observed. With the feral anxiety of animals at the vet, they quiver in anticipation of some nasty moment about to be experienced.

This afternoon is clear in my memory, not least because my father asked me to take photos of him standing next to Reynolds. 'We' on this occasion consisted of Dad, Reynolds, me, Lizzie and Dimitri, the son of Francesca. On this walk we discovered that our relationship in terms of age ran 48:24:12:6, and 3 for little Dimitri. My father thought this created a pact between us.

I remember that my father and Reynolds talked about Yeats. Reynolds asked a question and Stephen answered, 'Well, I think . . .', crinkling his forehead to indicate the subject was serious.

Mum had caught up with Raymond in California on 12 December, the second anniversary of his wife's death. Ostensibly he'd offered her a rest from her concert tour so that she could recover from her whiplash. Natasha got into the passenger seat of his car and the first thing he did was run into a fence. Then he backed out and promptly drove off the road. Her neck still hurt, she hadn't slept for days and she was in a highly anxious state. She wanted to get out of the car and fly right back east, but instead she stayed. They got to the hotel. She went to bed and slept through the rest of the day.

Next day they drove aimlessly towards the mountains, came to a dead end and drove back. On day three, they drove two hours through the Tonto National Forrest to the Roosevelt Dam and back over mountain roads of the kind that 'would have given Cissy the jitters unless she had been driving herself'. The trip got Ray back into the habit of driving. He thought she now had confidence in him. On Sunday, she ate and slept and sunbathed. On Monday, they went shopping in Phoenix . . .

Ray described all this in a long letter to Stephen, the point of which was that he wanted her to stay longer. 'If we can't get this girl well, and I mean well, her life is bound to be a succession of exhaustions, near breakdowns, vitality too low to resist infection, and so on.' Unless she regains perfect health, 'she cannot live the exacting life of a musician and a mother of two rather demanding children whom she adores, and be the manager of a household, and also have even a limited social life'. If she had to give up her life as a musician she would cease to be herself. 'You of all people should know that an artist deprived of his or her art is a defeated human being . . . a true professional can never become an amateur, but only become broken-hearted by giving up.' She had to stay with him longer, otherwise 'it's going to be like Tangier; she will return looking immensely better, but it won't go deep enough to last'.

There is a great deal of truth in all this. My mother lived on her nerves, the effort of will was huge and it affected her health, but she wasn't going to be satisfied with becoming a second-rank musician. Yet in her article on Chandler written twenty years later, the only thing she was willing to reveal was that she had wanted to save him from suicide. This implies that hers was the position of strength. She was the noble and magnanimous nurse. As things turned out, Chandler died as predicted and her description of her role in retrospect was honourable, but it is by no means the whole story.

Back in London my father accepted Ray's argument, passing over the implication that he and Ray were two men taking care of the same woman, equidistant from her and with equal rights. He sent messages to Natasha encouraging her to stay – not surprising, since he had Reynolds in the house. On 1 January 1957, Ray wrote to thank Stephen for having encouraged her to be with him. If Natasha tells him that he's been 'angelic', it was only the truth! He'd deferred to her in everything! 'We are both – she and I – highly strung and capricious people. We both have quick tempers which are soon over.' This is carrying the triangle of two men plus one woman a step further. It's as if Ray and Natasha are on one side while Stephen is drifting away into the distance.

As for her concert career, it seemed to Ray to require 'more egoism than she is capable of'. Maybe she should try the Women's Club circuit? And what's wrong with her agent? It was such a shame that she's being given 'cheap little concerts in museums'. She tells him he's wrong to talk about money, but it's just as well that he has some; and it is at her service, and at the service of the whole Spender family. 'I rather feel now that the Spender family is my family. And I need the Spender family far more than they need me.' If Stephen needs money, he's ready.

However, behind his cunning use of money as a theme of their relationship, there lay a mundane reality. While Natasha was in Phoenix, whenever she ran out of places to drive to, she went shopping; and he'd picked up the tab. He hadn't earned anything in two years, he'd just scrapped the first draft of his new novel, and if he went on living off his capital like this, he would soon run out.

My mother's train of thought at this point went like this: Raymond wants me to leave Stephen and join him, but I won't. What can I invent that will keep this relationship alive, help him, and isn't just a hollow deception on my part? The answer was: a house. If Chandler wanted her, he could buy her a house, live in it, and she would come down and be there as often as she could. If it were hers, she would. The financial and emotional tensions of living with Stephen, compounded by her insecure childhood, needed to be balanced by a place she could call her own.

Chandler recognized an impossible fantasy based on a real need. It was similar to his own, of having Natasha replace his dead wife Cissy. He played through her wish-fulfilment to the bitter end. Where would this cottage be? In France? He spoke French and that would be no problem, but he wasn't sure if he wanted to live in France. In Wales? In Ireland? And what would happen if one day she invited some guests to come and visit her? As they sat over tea, they'd hear a curious tapping noise coming from the next room. What was that, they'd ask? She'd have to say airily, 'Oh, that's just Chandler at work on his new book.'

On Christmas Eve, she phoned London to wish us Happy Christmas. Then she left Ray in Palm Springs while she drove off on 'a round of visits'. She spent New Year's Eve in the house of Edward and Evelyn Hooker, two psychologists who lived in Los Angeles. In Natasha's absence, Ray started drinking again, and when he joined them for supper on 6 January 1957, they were appalled. He needed psychiatric help, they said. Natasha wasn't trained to deal with him. Her own health was precarious and she had more concerts to perform.

Through Natasha, Chandler invited Christopher Isherwood and his companion Don Bachardy out to lunch, followed by a drive around 'his' Hollywood. In the evening the Hookers invited Gerald Heard to dinner. Heard was a very English intellectual, interested in scientific and also in mystical ideas, a friend of Aldous Huxley and, like him, an early influence on the Californian counter-culture. The conversation was high-minded in the extreme and Chandler felt excluded. 'Very learned, but much too pontifical,' he wrote later. 'Americans generally seem to be quite content to be lectured at for a whole evening.' Isherwood and Bachardy came in after supper and brought the conversation back to the afternoon's drive, for which they thanked him; but he refused to cheer up.

Next day he drove Natasha back to Palm Springs to continue their vacation. With her in the house, Ray managed to settle down to work at his new novel, swim, eat regularly and go to the movies in the evening. This continued for five days. Then, unexpectedly, Edward Hooker died in LA of a heart attack. Natasha's instinct was to go back and join Evelyn so as to be supportive, but Evelyn overruled her. She should stay with Chandler and perhaps come up three days later for the funeral.

When the time came, Natasha went up alone and came back with Evelyn a few days later. Christopher and Don joined them on the following day.

Decades later, I was sitting gloomily zapping the TV and thinking of my mother and there she was, in her thirties, in a swimsuit, on the screen in front of me. She turned and gave me a cheerful wave. It was also a somewhat sexy wave – and at that point I assumed I was having a nervous breakdown, of the kind when number-plates in the street start sending you secret messages. I sat there rigidly, and it turned out that the programme was a French documentary on Chandler. Indeed, he was in the background doing somersaults from the diving board, looking froglike and cheerful.

I rang Mum and told her this story. The joke was that you can't always have a nervous breakdown just because the TV sends you messages. Sometimes it's coincidence! She brooded about this for a few days then rang back to explain all the circumstances: Evelyn's recent loss, Chandler's state of mind, the presence of Christopher and Don. Who had made this programme, she asked coldly? She didn't think my joke was funny.

In that motel after Edward's death, after the swim, the conversation turned to religion. Isherwood was involved with mysticism, and my mother was interested in religious experience, regarding which Chandler in his letters is sometimes catty. On deckchairs around that pool, Chandler told them that he knew that Cissy was gone for ever. He would not see her again. This was not the most tactful thing to say in front of Evelyn Hooker, who had just lost her husband – and here an element of competition crept in. Just because she'd lost her husband more recently than he'd lost Cissy, it didn't mean that Natasha had to give all her attention to Evelyn.

My mother in Palm Springs, playing patience when she should have been practising the piano, but keeping an eye on Raymond Chandler . . .

They began to talk about going back to Los Angeles, and at this point Chandler began to panic. Natasha wasn't thinking of leaving him, was she? She had a concert to perform and the Hookers had a piano on which she could practise. The motel didn't. She remained alone with him for another fortnight. He worked, she played patience. She was wined and dined one last time at the Starlite Room of the Riviera Hotel, then she flew from Palm Springs to LA. She spent the weekend with Evelyn and flew to Washington on Monday 28 January to resume her concert tour.

Crazy though Raymond Chandler's love for my mother may have been, it worked for him. When he was with her he could write and settle down to a ritual existence where everything was in place. When

. . . who was visibly falling to pieces. He labelled this photo 'Before the Autopsy'.

she wasn't, he immediately fell to pieces. But for my mother the visit to Palm Springs was equally decisive. Ray's competitive grief had shocked her. Since much of her attention was dedicated to helping people who were desperate, she assumed that among them there existed a hierarchy of need, and that Ray should have recognized that Evelyn's was greater than his own. The fact that he hadn't was a big point against him.

Clearly she wouldn't be coming back. The cottage in the country was Ray's last chance, and it had gone. He tried to marshal his thoughts in a letter to his lawyer, who was also a friend.

Stephen is a loving father and in many ways a very lovable man. His good manners and consideration for others rather hide the fact that he is really a ferocious egotist and egoist, who, fundamentally, thinks only of himself. The unforgivable crime, and Auden feels as strongly about this as I do, is for a homo to marry and thereby to destroy a woman's right to the love of a husband, above all a woman whose sense of duty will never allow her to inflict a divorce on her children.

It's a goddamned mess and it just so happens that I can do a little, not very much, to restore her to her pride in being desired.

He then went on to describe how to get the best service from waiters at the Starlite Room.

As a comment on homosexuality and marriage, it seems to me that Chandler makes a fair point (and Auden, supposing he really did think this). If there is no physical desire in the marriage, what has the wife got? But the dogmatism involved is surely wrong, for if two people live together, what business is it of outsiders to question the moral standards of the relationship? In this respect, and in spite of the emotional contortion of the Chandler episode, Natasha and Stephen were confident in each other in ways that were not at risk. In one of her letters to Stephen she promises him, 'no more lame ducks!' Which surely means that my parents were in agreement about the situation: Raymond Chandler was a sinking ship, and Mum had devoted too much time to him, and she blamed herself for having allowed herself to be distracted.

She wrote a thank-you letter (now lost) to Ray for her visit to California, in which she mentioned his having 'entertained' her. Was that the right word for what he felt about her, he wrote back? 'The most I really wanted was to take care of you.' But, 'forget it', let's discuss the future when she planned to 'entertain' him in privacy. 'You know damn well that Stephen won't be the one to buy or help you buy the little cottage.' But supposing he did, how could Ray fit in? 'I am not a friend asking you to lunch.'

She'd 'tried to give him everything he wanted': what did she mean by that? He didn't want to hear anything about giving. What they had together, they shared. She'd mentioned prayer in her letter: he had his difficulties with God. 'To me Cissy is utterly gone; to God perhaps not. To me prayer is not an asking; it is a communion, or an attempt at a communion.' And via three pages on prayer, back to Natasha. 'It takes great strength for a man like me to live alone. I think I have it now, but I did not have it then. I thought too much of myself and not enough of my dedicated love for you.'

It sounds as if he was going to try living alone. But wait. While writing this letter a woman had answered his advertisement for a secretary. He told Natasha that she'd described herself as a 'small, inoffensive person with no nasty habits'. His fingers were giving him trouble, the typewriter was unfamiliar.

This letter was followed by a telephone call in the middle of which Natasha hung up on him. He'd mentioned Helga Greene, to whom he'd told various things. 'After all, in my Will, I am making Helga my Literary Executor, and I have to trust her.' Natasha was never going to dedicate her life to Ray, but the idea that there were other women out there who would nevertheless made her jealous.

Early in February, with Natasha still in Phoenix with Chandler, Reynolds received another letter from Stephen. He wasn't going to write about Reynolds in his diary, he wrote, 'though I will do one day. But I shall not put anything you've told me even into that. Occasionally I note something of more or less historic interest like J. Hayworth's [he means John Hayward's] version of T. S. Eliot's marriage, and I write about affairs of people when these are fairly public anyway – in fact I note the Secret History of Our Time which is what everybody knows but which the Establishment keep to themselves. What I do not note is my [rare?] attachments to people and their confidences to me.' (If only my father *had* written the secret history of the British Establishment. This present book about my parents is partly an attempt to do just that, but he would have done it so much better.)

Stephen's letter implies that the moment when this relationship might have become physical was already over. Years later, Reynolds went out of his way to tell me that he and Stephen were never lovers, and I believe him. The letters suggest that as soon as this had been ruled out, my father set about creating a different basis for their friendship.

In his next letter he wrote to Reynolds about Rimbaud, who was:

not at all like Dylan Thomas, as I am sure all the dumbells suppose. He didn't so much systematically derange his senses (his slogan) as systematically undermine his own happiness. And I have always felt there is a great deal to be said for doing this. Happiness of a rather low-grade kind is the real bourgeois materialist trait of all our societies all over the world. Directly the note of authentic unhappiness – or refusal to be comfortable – is struck one recognizes something that does not exist elsewhere.

Stephen was forty-eight, Reynolds twenty-four. The identification with Verlaine and Rimbaud was tempting. 'I wonder whether you would have liked Rimbaud. If you were R and I were Verlaine, we would go to the furthest possible degree of every kind of exploration and exploitation of one another.' Stephen was fascinated by the idea of a reciprocal predatory relationship that produced quantities of poems. 'I think Rimbaud was aware of a problem which he learned about as the result of sleeping under bridges in the frost, being raped by soldiers in the Caserne . . . That is that although one knows things, one's desire for complacency or comfort is so great that until one becomes an object, an instrument, on which to inflict themselves, one remains "literary", that is, comfortable.'

Is this is about sex? No, I don't think it means that Stephen and Reynolds should emulate this aspect of the lives of Verlaine and Rimbaud. It's a sketch for a hypothetical future of unease that would charge the writings of Reynolds and Stephen with a new energy.

Reynolds was sympathetic, but being a much younger man his view of precariousness was different. He'd seen nothing of his own writing published, his B.Litt. on Milton was going very slowly, he had no partner and he wasn't sure what kind of a future he sought. He could understand the argument that a writer must avoid complacency and he could sympathize with Stephen's predicament as an established writer caught in a web of obligations, but a total derangement of the senses in order to become creative wasn't what he needed at this stage of his life.

15

A STRONG INVISIBLE
RELATIONSHIP

NATASHA CAME BACK from America in the second week of
February 1957.

Stephen was faced with the problem of how to present Reynolds
to her. He had no intention of keeping this relationship secret.
Reynolds was living in Oxford in digs at Headington, not far from
where Isaiah Berlin lived. Stephen wondered if he and Natasha could
visit Isaiah and then just casually drop in on Reynolds afterwards. If
this happened, Reynolds should put away the photograph of Stephen
that he had given him, 'because I took it out of Natasha's frame. I
have the negative in the office & will make another one for her.'

He warned Reynolds that his first meeting with Natasha might
be difficult. 'The point simply is that I want Natasha to like you so
much. I am sure that if we don't rush her that this will happen as
something we share between us all. But as you & I met when she
was away, our friendship is much longer & further gone than she
would anticipate.' Stephen thought that he and Reynolds could
somehow form a pair. 'I want us, besides meeting as often as we can,
to have a very strong invisible relationship in which we can, as we
do at present, share our thoughts.'

As I read it, in that first week after they met, Dad fell so madly in love that for a moment he contemplated dropping everything and running off with Reynolds. Where to? God knows. But as this incandescent moment took place right at home, in the study of Loudoun Road where they listened to *Fidelio* together in front of the hearth – where the gramophone lurked – it was compromised from the start. Reynolds sensibly decided that he was receiving two different messages. There was Stephen, the Verlaine to his Rimbaud, and there was Stephen, the happy family man with two bouncy children to whom he was genuinely attached.

I never felt that Reynolds was a threat, because it was clear to me that he had doubts about the *amour fou* which Stephen dangled in front of him as if it was an irresistible temptation. Dad was chasing the impossible: *amour fou* in a family niche.

Reynolds was very good about all this. If at lunch Dad fixed his eyes upon a serious subject and spoke only to him, to the exclusion of his wife and children, who could busy themselves changing the plates as far as he was concerned, then Reynolds would give us a short meaningful glance as if to say, 'Here we go again.' My poor mother's tolerance was surely tested to its limit on these occasions. If indeed she got up and changed the plates, there would be emphatic noises from the kitchen to indicate that yes, she was changing the fucking plates. But a look from Reynolds did much to support the idea that we were one big happy family – that he posed no threat.

It was done tactfully. It's not as if he rolled his eyes and winked.

Reynolds at this point was still a virgin, though gaining confidence in the fact that he was homosexual. At Oxford he was beginning to form a strong relationship with a young man called Michael, but it was friendship only. My father was fascinated by the idea of Reynolds and Michael living together and forming a couple – which they weren't, but probably this wasn't made clear to Stephen. When, a month or so after Natasha had come back from Phoenix, she decided to go away to Gstaad as the guest of Hansi Lambert, Stephen initially thought he'd go with her; and Reynolds and Michael could house-sit

15 Loudoun Road. Reynolds would sleep in the study, as usual; and Michael could have Lizzie's room, if we were all away for Easter.

In the end he stayed behind, so this scheme fell through.

Somewhere in my father's persona there was a wild need to create a male partnership apparent to all the world. In the same way that *The Temple* was a polemical book, a declaration of openness between men, he wanted his love for Reynolds to be accepted socially. That's fine. It's even noble. But it required the cooperation of Natasha, his wife. And he seems not to have given the slightest thought to how this would make her feel in public, at parties, at dinners, within the world.

Meanwhile she continued her secret life with Raymond Chandler.

Fresh from a stressful visit to Phoenix, my mother can't seriously have thought of Ray as a viable alternative. Let me state my opinion clearly: there was never the slightest chance that she'd leave Stephen and run off with Ray. But as a fantasy, a counterweight to my father's yearning for a public display of love between two men, at least it offered a distraction.

There remains a remote possibility that she would have gone off with Ray, if he'd been twenty years younger and irresistibly handsome instead of visibly falling to pieces. This is one reason why, when Chandler's biographer mistook the boasts about Ray's love for Natasha as if an affair had happened, Mum went berserk. The Bodleian archive has files a foot high documenting my mother's struggle with this unfortunate scholar, Frank MacShane. In the end he not only gave in, he allowed her to tinker with his prose. She insisted that she'd been disinterested, compassionate, positively saintly throughout, yet the very ferocity with which she fought MacShane suggests that deep down, she must have felt guilty.

Ray, writing from California where he did not expect Natasha to return, began to have doubts about that cottage in the country. Would they be sufficiently alone? She seems to have replied to him – he quotes her – 'we should only know the people we like and who like us'. It sounds as if Natasha was still dreaming of a secret hideaway. Then from Gstaad she wrote to him 'the most depressed and lonely letters you have ever written to me'. She was also trying to learn Beethoven's *Hammerklavier* Sonata – and at this point I have to abandon my persona as an objective historian and say, Mum, are you out of your mind? Beaches are littered with the bones of pianists who've tried to master that piece, and you've just had an operation, you're worried about your marriage and your future, and for peace and quiet you've had to abandon the family nest. The *Hammerklavier*?! But another characteristic of my mother was always to choose the hardest challenge, on the grounds that if she mastered that, easy pieces would become even easier.

By the middle of April she was back in London, where she'd been to 'two frantic parties', an expression that disgusted Ray. If she wanted to continue as an artist, he wrote, then she must give up her social life. But it wasn't working. She didn't want to marry him and he didn't really want to marry her, 'unless it was to protect you'. As for the piano, 'the more success you have, the less I should see of you. You are a strange woman in some ways. You loathe talk of money, but at times you accept it very readily.' And later, 'we have very different sorts of pride. Yours is to accept a duty and to fulfil it, no matter how humiliating or painful it might be. Mine is to declare that where one's deepest emotions are involved, there is no choice or half-way or quarter-way. Either there is fulfilment or there is nothing.' This was all very fine, but both sides knew and perhaps had always known that the choice of all or nothing had never existed. 'You are a noble woman. To say goodbye to you would cut my heart in half. But I may have to, and you may want me to.'

He couldn't resist continuing to undermine Stephen as an inferior being.

I'm sorry he has to work so hard at so many different things. The truth, as it appears to my feeble brain, is that he doesn't know how to work in any productive way, but fritters his energies on all sorts of things, none of which bring in much. English writers are very much handicapped by the poverty of their markets. One can't say much except that if a man can't learn the way to find how to achieve success, he is not going to have it dropped into his lap.

From Majorca, where she and Stephen were visiting Robert Graves, she wrote a letter containing the phrase, 'why don't you carry what you have in your heart and leave your mind open until we next meet?' She was playing for time. It was increasingly clear that the cottage in Oxfordshire was unlikely to happen.

On 30 May, Ray wrote her the first of several severance letters. 'There is really nothing to do but stop pretending that something exists that does not exist at all.' And: 'I am also too proud to say anything other than good-bye and God bless you.' And – evidently he was beginning to enjoy this – 'perhaps the best I can do is to cover you with all the lovely thoughts and memories of you which I have had, and then steal quietly out into the night'.

There followed a scene straight from a comic opera. Ray sent Natasha a long telegram of doom and gloom, followed by a special-delivery letter even more serious. Stephen happened to be alone in the house when it arrived. He signed the receipt and read it, assuming it was an engagement for a concert for Natasha. He then wrote to Ray explaining he'd sent it on to her, but he also discussed some of the points raised in the letter. Ray sent Stephen a letter of apology for having written privately to Natasha, adding some acid comments about the morality of opening other people's mail. Meanwhile he sent yet another letter to Natasha, this time via his London lawyer Michael Gilbert, who was supposed to sneak round to Loudoun Road in the hopes of slipping it to her without Stephen noticing.

Ray wrote a covering letter to Gilbert blaming Natasha for having married 'a handsome nothing'. If one touches something corrupt, he wrote, one risks becoming corrupted. 'I cannot any longer respect her acceptance of something which to me is detestable and obscene.' He meant a homosexual husband. Gilbert wrote a very English reply, handwritten to show he hadn't dictated it to his secretary. 'With regard to what you say about pansies I'm not so sure,' he wrote. 'I know dozens of them, of course, and they are of a type – sui generis, to use another piece of law latin – artistic, artistically creative in fact, self-centred, emotionally hard, easy to get on with at surface level, ultimately untrustworthy. But to dislike them as a class seems as illogical as disliking Jews, diabetics, or somatotonics.'

If Stephen had quickly abandoned the idea of pursuing a physical relationship with Reynolds, what alternative did he have in mind? 'I want what Rimbaud called "the new love" – which perhaps isn't what he knew even. Did he succumb to the expected, do you think, or was he getting something quite different from their relationship than that which Verlaine got?' This was close to asking Reynolds for his opinion, but it was up to Stephen to define what he wanted. 'Every relationship with a man in which I felt intense love has broken down: and I think it did so because it failed by the standard which makes each of us afraid in a letter to the other to write slovenly things, or a bad sentence.' He expected a great deal from Reynolds, but the world in which this would blossom was that of words on paper. 'Do let us keep going this miraculous communication between us. It has quite changed me.'

'Perhaps we are both to some extent people who look into others to discover an image of ourselves . . . If the image that each holds of the other is that which he wishes himself most to be, this means that we live in our relationship what we potentially are in our work. We are each other's poems for one another.'

This is extremely intense, but luckily Reynolds knew how to cut things down to size. One of their private jokes derived from an article by Leslie Fiedler published in Partisan Review in June 1948, 'Come Back to the Raft Ag'in, Huck Honey!' This argued that Mark Twain's Huckleberry Finn is full of disguised homosexual messages, and that the famous raft on which Huck and Jim floated down the

Mississippi in flight from the real world seethed with homoerotic implications. It was one of those ideas that were initially laughed at but wouldn't go away. So, whenever Stephen and Reynolds wanted to lighten the mood, they threw 'honey' or 'raft' into the context.

> I feel I'd sell everything I have and never go abroad again and mortgage myself for life and let the children just run wild in the hedges, if I could move to Westwell and stay there the next 30 years. Maybe at the end I'd have one of those real rocky impressive-looking faces like R. Frost blown up 20 times on the American embassy stairs . . . I might be persuaded to go to Oxford now and then and drawl out my poems in a voice natural and meandering as a river with rafts on it.

Westwell was a village not far from Oxford where my parents rented a house for six months. Natasha's search for a house in the country had not ceased, though she'd abandoned the idea of a secret cottage bought by Chandler. She was certain that a country haven would provide a solution to her anxiety.

Unfortunately, Westwell lay less than an hour from Headington, where Reynolds lived. Shortly before they'd travelled to Majorca in June to see Graves, Natasha had found out that Stephen had been quietly driving up to Oxford to see Reynolds. Stephen wrote to him that she was 'deeply disturbed and upset . . . I think therefore I had better not make any special effort for us to meet this weekend, as I don't want to give the impression (which would be false anyway) that Westwell is for me just a diving board to Headington.'

The house in Westwell used to belong to the scholar and poet Rex Warner and his wife Barbara Hutchinson, who was Peggy Ashcroft's sister-in-law. It had a handsome eighteenth-century front and a big central room with good acoustics. Rex and Barbara had separated, and my parents took over the lease. The front windows looked out on to the village pond and the woods behind the house were beautifully untidy. The Bechstein had come down from London and Mum was working. She thought the move away from the city had solved some of her problems, so the idea that Stephen was sneaking off to join Reynolds was a bitter blow.

In writing to Reynolds that they'd be seeing each other less often in the future, Stephen tried to explain that Natasha knew their relationship was only one of words, but this didn't make it any better. 'What also counts is that for Natasha there is a history in which in the past I have been bad – and inevitably she feels this is the same pattern.'

For some reason the Westwell phase did not last long, but luckily my parents were offered the loan of a Queen Anne cottage in the grounds of Bruern Abbey, an eighteenth-century Palladian house built on the site of a religious building destroyed in the Reformation. The house belonged to Michael Astor, whom they'd met recently. The Bechstein was carried across from Westwell to Bruern towards the end of August.

That summer *Engaged in Writing*, the novel about the Venice symposium on which he'd been working for months, with frequent advice from Reynolds, was rejected by his American publisher, Harcourt Brace. This unexpected humiliation 'seemed like a final God-inspired kick in the pants saying: "honey, you just have to chose between being a writer, and a writer who turns up at Congresses".'

He decided to cancel an engagement to travel to Japan for a PEN Club meeting. But as the tensions about Reynolds rose to unbearable heights, he changed his mind. He flew off on 23 August.

16

BARRENNESS AND DESOLATION

THE JAPANESE PEN Club had existed since before the war, and several Japanese writers, among them the great novelist Kawabata, wanted to improve contacts between Western and Japanese writers. The theme of the meeting was a discussion of the effects of one culture upon the other. Though there may have been some political implications in the background, the main point was that Japanese writers felt they were cut off from the rest of the world.

Almost two hundred speakers from abroad had been invited, and there were as many delegates from Japan, so the meeting was anything but intimate. Unfortunately, even though it turned out to be so poignant, Stephen kept no record at the time. There's just a later reference to an occasion when he, Alberto Moravia and Angus Wilson, hiding behind the pines in one of the Zen gardens at Kyoto, tried to escape from the clutches of the Duchesse de la Rochefoucauld. Eventually the three writers abandoned the meeting and slipped away for a few days' tour of the country by train, accompanied by Shozo Tokunaga, Stephen's translator.

My father told me a story about this episode, which he described later in his diary after Moravia died. It illustrates his idea that Italians, though outwardly cheerful, are by nature depressed. The scene is a railway carriage. Perhaps in pain because of his bad leg, Moravia 'always seemed poised over some abyss of boredom'. For hours, they'd been travelling in silence through the most wonderful scenery. Then Moravia gave a weary sigh and said, 'After all, it is a beautiful world.' For some reason Dad thought this was killingly funny.

During this trip, Stephen fell in love with another man whose surname also was Tokunaga, though he wasn't a relative of Stephen's translator. In a later diary he calls him Masao. This affair was instantaneous and passionate. The emotions of Masao, his beauty, his incapacity to take any practical decision about his life, were expanded by Stephen into a mood which gave to the whole of Japan a kind of irresponsible dreamy freedom that reminded him of his youth in Weimar Germany. Stephen would resign from *Encounter*, discard his family – which surely could get on without him – and resume the life he'd had in Hamburg when he was young. Masao and the 'floating world' he inhabited were the perfect embodiment of that state of living 'without guilt' which, to Stephen, represented a calling, a vocation, a quest.

When he came back, he wrote to Reynolds:

for a week I seemed to have in Japan something I had always been looking for and never found before, with the consequence that I know now what it is I was looking for. This sounds awfully sinister, but really it was a matter of feeling – far more than I realised at the time. This has the effect that I feel I couldn't possibly expect to find it again, and that all my previous attempts, as I say, seem in retrospect, humiliating or foolish or disgusting or importunate.

I clearly remember my father's return from Japan. In the front hall of Loudoun Road, he gave Lizzie and me our presents. Mine was a set of woodcutting tools and three perfect blocks of fine-grained balsa wood. Lizzie received a large Japanese doll; or perhaps it was a samurai. Then we were sent up to our rooms. This was odd, but as we had presents, we obeyed.

Through the floorboards I could hear our parents passionately discussing something in Dad's study. It seemed more of a fight than a reunion. Though I couldn't hear what they were saying, Stephen was telling Natasha about Masao and his plan to leave us and live in Japan. The atmosphere was tense but it was hard to tell what was happening. My father seldom shouted, and as far as I can remember my parents never quarrelled about their relationship in front of us children.

Thirty years later, when this tense period of their lives was long gone, my mother was faced with a situation that brought it all vividly back.

In 1985, my father wanted to travel to America in order to see Bryan Obst, the young ornithologist with whom he was in love. It was at the beginning of the AIDS epidemic and he was worried about Bryan's health – justifiably, as it turned out. Dad at this point was seventy-five years old and he had a heart condition, so Mum offered to come too. My father agreed, then almost immediately regretted it. So did she. But she couldn't back down, because of the health factor.

She foresaw that the trip would land her in endless awful predicaments. She wrote in her diary: 'I'm in despair over the California trip – I don't want to meet B – and to be an onlooker at the immense animation of the queer scene, although Chris & Donny will be nice. But one is bound to feel excluded.' What was she supposed to do? Sit quietly in a corner over on one side in that exclusive male atmosphere with a supportive smile on her face? Either she would be ignored, or she would be humiliated. Perhaps both.

She recalled the previous occasion when Dad had been infatuated with Masao. 'I remember when the feeling of barrenness and desolation first descended – walking round the garden at Bruern, when S wanted to emigrate to Japan, my pleading for the family – and saying why didn't he consult a friend who was devoted to his creative life? Why not consult Henry?' She meant Henry Moore. Dad must have been arguing that he had to place his creative life before anything else. '"Henry" – said S – almost contemptuously – yet with pity for H. "Henry has no life of his own at all." At that moment I knew that I would always have a place only on the perimeter.'

The state of being 'on the perimeter' raised in my mother an emotion even worse than the feeling that she was neglected. It was a sense of inadequacy. Had Stephen held true to this side of his nature because she'd failed to provide an alternative? It wasn't only a lack of physical attraction. She felt that nothing she said would ever amuse him. No opinion of hers on art, on books, not even on music, would distract him from his interior soliloquy. Indeed, she did not have the right to contribute to that soliloquy because if she did so, it might be interrupted.

> I would always have a place only on the perimeter – 'a life of one's own' being central – yet [I] would never be able to opt for any 'life of my own' – it's against my temperament. (– How absurd that sounds when one remembers my piano-playing years). But my temperament was to wish for a strong, vital, central, relationship – that wish now humbled to a desire to break through – out of my continual fear of saying the wrong thing, which strikes me dumb at home – knowing all the time that I cannot evoke the animation which B, or Xstopher, or Reynolds *e tutti quanti* [and all of them] are always able to, because they are at the centre. I am a shadow that hovers at the edge of vision – 'perimeter vision'. To become substantial would require some posi-tive act of mine, and that is not possible – because it would destroy the fragile, low-key, affection to which all must be dedicated, in order to help S's work.

Mum could have argued that she'd known about the situation ever since the Wittersham Interlude, when they'd first met. He'd always been open about his emotions. That's what she'd found so attractive about him. If Stephen needed this part of his life to continue, needed it for his work, she should not try to stop it. This is what my father wanted her to say. In an unusually blunt moment he once said to me, 'She knew what she was letting herself in for. She has no right to complain.' She knew what to expect, because he'd told her; and she'd accepted.

If he felt he was being attacked, my father could be tough; and that toughness included losing all sympathy for the other person's point of view. He challenged her: stand on your own two feet. I shall not budge. It's not quite the same as rejection, but it assumes that her grip on Beethoven, for example, was as strong and obsessive as his grip on Wordsworth.

Put like this, my parents' relationship turns into a kind of duel, one in which my mother was at an obvious practical disadvantage. She believed passionately in his writing, he was ambivalent about her music. She didn't necessarily feel that his writing was of a higher value than her music, because a love of art, any art, is yours; it can't be compared with anyone else's. But love of music is interiorized; and, because the concert comes and goes, ephemeral. The written page lasts longer.

Unable to balance my father's obsession with a corresponding obsession of her own, she provided herself with an alternative self-image: that of a self-sacrificing nun. She would dedicate herself to contemplation and good works.

I suppose that 'to thine own self be true' isn't possible because my temperament was never suited to the life I've had to lead. Over and above the natural dislike of the invasion of privacy, is the fact that I have never come to terms with the situation – it's not in tune with my beliefs about the way one should live one's life . . . In my heart, (whilst it is possible to *try* and accept that one is a bystander) I don't believe that human relationships should be like that. So the prospect of standing up for it, when it goes on public show, is the prospect of not being true to oneself.

In spite of her misgivings, the visit to Bryan came and went without mishap. My father, realizing the risks, warned Bryan (and Christopher and Don), and they behaved towards her with great consideration.

She as usual did well, though it required an effort on her part to present herself in such circumstances. Deep down, she was a nun in retreat living on a rugged peak in the middle of nowhere.

Returning to the late summer of 1957: how did Reynolds cope with the new Stephen after he'd come back from Japan?

Stephen argued that he desperately needed to create 'a kind of space around myself'. The things he was writing – a book of lectures, a libretto for Nicky Nabokov, editorials for *Encounter*, book reviews – they were nothing but distractions. 'I'm sure I can only really start writing poetry again if I get away for an interval.' The phrase is clear, almost objective. And probably true.

A photo of Reynolds Price taken by my father in May 1959.

Reynolds was interested and supportive, but at the same time he was anxious how Masao was going to affect their friendship. Stephen tried to reassure him. 'If you ask about our relationship, I think the answer is that we love one another but we are not lovers – and that is as it should be, surely. I should hope there is something in the love that is generous and forgiving, as well as believing and exciting.'

Reynolds insisted on knowing more. After all, if Stephen went off to live in Japan, Reynolds would be left behind along with everyone else. Stephen remained firm. 'That we won't be able to see so much of one another, has to do with my home, my finances, my work etc, and not at all to do with my having gone or my going to Japan.'

But meanwhile Stephen was being as helpful as possible to Reynolds' career.

'You have no idea how powerful your father was,' Reynolds told me when I saw him for the last time. 'All he had to do was pick up the phone to a publisher and a contract appeared in the post the next day.' In return, Stephen needed Reynolds as someone to whom he could show any piece of writing and receive back a comment that was both honest and supportive. For instance, my father at this time wrote an article on the sonnets of Shakespeare – a tremendously mined quarry, from the academic point of view. He sent it to Reynolds, who gave a detailed criticism, ending with a hint that he should abandon the piece. Stephen did so, and without hurt feelings. No one else subsequently earned such a degree of trust.

According to Reynolds' autobiography, his first sexual experience took place when he was twenty-five years old, on the island of Tresco off the coast of Cornwall, with a young man of his own age, during the Easter vacation of 1958. Thanks to Stephen, he had just published his first short story 'A Chain of Love' in the March number of *Encounter*. He was beginning to realize that he possessed the qualities of a novelist and his academic ambitions were receding.

Reynolds discovered that sex had an effect on his creative work, at the same time that non-sex was having an effect on Stephen's.

What I knew by the spring of my third year in England was the vital relevance for me of intimate union, not only for its powers of simple invigoration through the heights of physical pleasure . . . but also for my own adult self-respect and the ongoing growth of my work. That pleasure affected deeply the rhythmic vigour of sentences on a page as they attended closely to the precise moral implications of my subject at any given moment in my story.

As soon as Reynolds began to have lovers of his own, his relationship with Stephen became fixed. The touching thing is that it never faded. Throughout the remaining forty years of their friendship, my father would turn up at Reynolds' house in North Carolina, not far from Duke University, where Reynolds taught for many years. What he liked best was to sit outside on a deckchair and make drawings of the pond, or work on a long poem about his family which was never finished. Reynolds told me that it was puzzling how little Stephen wanted. He seemed perfectly happy just to be there.

After Reynolds left England in 1960, I did not see him again until several years after my father's death. In fact it was our daughter Saskia who met him in New York. He was coming out of a taxi and she recognized him from his book on suffering, which she'd read. They made friends. I happened to arrive in New York three days later and we had supper together.

He was being given a prize and the occasion was full of distinguished people, but Reynolds made me sit at his right hand, and throughout the meal he talked to me intensely about Stephen. He wanted me to come down to Durham and continue the conversation, but I refused. I wrote to him a few days later to say that as long as my mother was alive, I would feel disloyal to her if I started examining the distant past. This letter is the last item in the Price Archive in Duke University. I'd forgotten I'd written it. It was clear and true, and it took for granted that Reynolds and I understood each other even though the last time I'd seen him, I'd been only fifteen years old.

I couldn't start researching this book until after Mum died. She would have guessed, and it would have upset her. In Loudoun Road on the evening of the day that she died, I saw her body off the premises (a horrible moment; they used a sack with leather straps), and then I took up the telephone and rang Reynolds. The number was in her address book. I told him she was dead and that now I could finally respond to his frequent, generous invitations to speak to me about my father. He said succinctly: 'I'm sorry to hear about Natasha. Come as soon as you can, and stay as long as you can.'

So I went to Durham, North Carolina. I read Stephen's letters to Reynolds during the day and talked to him about them at night, after the library had closed. He said, 'Matt, you're the first person to read those things in fifty years.' It was a good week. On Saturday, I kissed him on the forehead and said goodbye and drove my rented car back to the airport. It was about three in the afternoon. He ate an early supper with his brother Bill, said how much he'd enjoyed my visit and how much I looked like Stephen. He went to sleep, and the next morning he was found in a coma. He died four days later.

17

TOO AMBIVALENT

BRUERN ABBEY WAS undoubtedly a beautiful property, and after Dad bought Mum a 2.8-litre Jaguar that she'd set her heart on, driving down from London to this country seat almost satisfied her craving for security. It was a 'cheap Jag' with constant health problems, but she loved it.

We'd drive out on Friday nights, through thinning lights as we left the outside parishes of London, and on, past Newbury and Hungerford. The last big towns would be left behind, with no more than a single dot now, of light from a house in the darkness, but with the silhouette of a hillside felt as a crest, a wave. Myself with my nose on the leather seats of the Jag looking at the back of my mother's neck as she concentrated on the driving. The sudden gush of air as we took our cramped limbs from the cocoon of leathery space and stepped from the car into the overwhelming breathiness of the countryside, with crackly sounds in the emptiness, the movement of some living thing against the background of utter silence that London never has.

Michael Astor, the owner of Bruern Abbey, was David Astor's younger brother. David was the owner of the *Observer*, so he belonged to Stephen's world of serious journalism. Michael however was a restless personality. He'd tried painting. He'd tried serving as a

Member of Parliament. At the time when we first borrowed the Red Brick Cottage, he was still married to Barbara McNeill, but the marriage was foundering.

The first thing Barbara asked me when I went to introduce myself was, 'Do you hunt?' I said politely that I was afraid I didn't. 'Oh. So can you ride?' No – but I would very much like to try. She said with an easy laugh, 'Well, we can't have any of *that.*' Meaning that she wasn't in the business of teaching stray juveniles how to ride. And that was as far as I ever got with Barbara Astor.

My sister Lizzie's passion for horses pulled her through this test. It brought her the friendship of Barbara's two daughters, Jane and Georgina. (I had no luck with their sons.) Barbara smoked and rode and drank gin-and-whatsits before lunch and avoided for the most part the new inhabitants of the Red Brick Cottage. But Lizzie was able to join in.

Mum did everything she could to encourage Lizzie's friendship with Jane, which indeed lasted for the rest of Jane's short and unlucky life. And whenever Mum looked at Lizzie playing with the Astor girls, an ecstatic look would come over her face. It was a complex expression, because confusion was mixed in there somewhere, along with the feeling of achievement. I've been reticent about including Lizzie in this book because I want her to tell her own version of the same events, but when Mum looked with such pride at Lizzie playing with the Astor girls, did it signify a lack of confidence? Did she remember her own adulation of the Booths when she was a child? Did she enjoy the fact that Lizzie was acquiring a similar role among the Astors?

My mother loved her children and her husband, but she did not think we had succeeded in becoming the strong, self-assured family she'd always dreamed of. I think she was wrong to believe this, but my childhood was secure and hers was not. I can see that when she remembered her own childhood, to her its finest moments had occurred when she'd been tucked away at Funtington in the tree house with the Booth children, protected from the outside world by branches and leaves. By delegating Lizzie to the families of Michael

Astor and John Huston, she was retrospectively handing herself over to the Booths, which was something she'd yearned for – and it had almost happened, but not quite.

She would not have seen this choice as failing her maternal obligations. On the contrary, she was sacrificing herself. She wanted Lizzie to enjoy the best opportunities. Today, having accumulated the roles of father and grandfather, I find this hesitancy touching, but at the time that ecstatic look she gave to families she assumed were in possession of the secret – a secret dependent on money – merely suggested that none of us was quite worthy of the family she had in mind. That we'd disappointed her by failing to attain her own high standards.

Of Michael Astor, she used to say as she picked up a house-guest from the train station, pointing at a row of plane trees that he'd planted in a long avenue up to the Big House, and shrouded with barbed wire so that the teeth of nibbling deer wouldn't damage them – waiflike as new trees are before they get a grip – 'I think it shows great faith in the future, don't you?' The word 'future' coming out as 'few-char', as she'd be using her 'grand' voice. Then one day she said, 'I think it shows great faith in the ffff—' and her voice tailed off. She'd remembered at the last minute that Michael was getting divorced from Barbara the following week.

In those early years at Bruern, Dad would occasionally invite me out for a drive. I always said yes, but nothing happened on these occasions. Silence in the car, a familiar route to the village, a trivial purchase and then back. It was companionable, but my father was so tightly locked up in his own thoughts, there didn't seem much point in my being there. He was a bad driver, so he wasn't showing off that particular skill. Maybe he just needed to get out of the house. Or maybe he wanted to confide something to me and never dared.

He also spent many hours drawing the heavy yews around the pond where ancestral carp floated languidly. His drawings had a soothing rhythm to them, the same line made again and again, like waves on a beach. It was hypnotic. He'd explain: that bit of the landscape echoes the other shape over there – which was a good idea, but he was unable to bring it forward in the marks he made.

From the beginning of 1958, Chandler planned to come to Europe. He wanted to interview the Mafia boss Lucky Luciano in Naples – of all the odd ideas! And he had one or two chores to do in London.

The only letters from Natasha to Raymond to survive are from this period, when Ray was due back in England. He destroyed all the others. Here, she replies to several letters from Ray filled with the usual derogatory remarks about Stephen:

> I couldn't despise Stephen as you do – you are right there. I see that he does the best he can, even with his failings – just as you do the best with yours. You simply have different outlooks & different failings, each of you. He talks sympathetically and respectingly of you – you don't do so well about him. In fact you judge and condemn others rather too freely sometimes . . .
>
> I still am in no position to condemn him, and above all whatever lack of love and harmony there may be in the family must somehow be made good by me. All other solutions would be a retreat from love – and I am certainly not going to teach my children to despise or judge their father. When they are grown, they will naturally perceive in an adult way; but I will not be the instrument of dissension, bewilderment – lack of security in my children. Where I have failed deeply – is in having brought you into it at all.
>
> For years I had schooled myself to the loneliness and although I was (how can I say it?) much pursued, my discipline was intact. I began to know what the religious mean by detachment. It is a cold word for the warmest feeling. The sense of communion through love – but love only through God. And in all those years I never lost a friend – only gained them in a real and deep way. With you I failed because what you so generously offered me in warmth and devotion tempted me

– it seemed like the most wonderful liberation and solace and I also had the illusion that my devotion saved you from a despair, which had been the most potent element in your having called upon me. You may remember that our first evening at the Connaught you played a trick. [He'd started crying and she'd had to comfort him.] You asked me for a sign of compassion, and immediately translated into something, almost I might say to use against me. I was determined not to desert you because you were about to sink beneath the wave – but I failed you and muddled myself by not, at that moment, sticking to my discipline. It just seemed too cruel – but I should have done it . . .

I think she means that she'd made a mistake in allowing Ray to believe that she was in love with him, as her 'discipline' included chastity.

When a gentle and kind letter arrives from you I feel an overwhelming happiness & solace – and I believe that what has always been the relationship in tenderness and devotion can't be killed – whatever is done to bash it on the head. The moment I read one such phrase (as above) in a letter from you – it is as if none of the dissensions had ever existed – That is the pure you – and all the other nonsense is dross.

If he came to London, couldn't she pick him up at the airport and bring him directly to the Red Brick Cottage? They could go through all their explanations in private. 'This place is peace – I live here alone whenever I can, like a Trappist, playing Beethoven, reading – meditating . . . I believe that something of the aura of the old Abbey exists in the garden (though the Abbey was destroyed in the Dissolution) and at all events the benign stillness of the place is therapeutic and feeds the spirit. And I would like to share this with you without a lot of foreign bodies about.'

Then arrangements. He should come before the children's holidays began so they wouldn't be disturbed. Stephen would be in Tokyo. It was annoying that Ray couldn't come before 5 April because of his tax problems.

I do 'care for you in a serious way' – probably far too serious for you – but it is for you to decide about that – but my seriousness is always welded into my discipline. I know that the fundamental loneliness that can be the lot of each of us, can only for me be redeemed by prayer – and by love within prayer (that sounds too grandiose a way of describing anything so simple and direct) . . . For a time I was tempted to believe that the 'human' way was open to me – and you certainly made me feel cherished for the only time in my life and I can never forget it. But nag, nag, nag was always the feeling inside me that this was a confusion of my deepest understanding of life. This was all terribly unfair on you – who were looking for something much simpler.

In the West last year I really behaved atrociously because I never could get near making clear to you what was bothering me. And I snatched at the opportunity to live on a hedonistic plane because I was on the run from facing this truth. When I look back after a year – and after having been honest with myself – I do quite literally blush with shame. You can quite understandably feel that I 'used' you. But you mistake my feelings utterly although it was just as hard for you as if I had set out to use you. I'm not trying to make it sound better than it is – but don't you see that my feelings about you are 'serious' enough? God knows I suffered quite atrocious behaviour from you too (which equally was not wilfully disgusting but had the same effect on me at the time as if it had been. Now I understand that it was a symptom of the underlying struggle) and I did my best to help you there – only my own inner conflict made me worse than useless.

It seems that in a lost letter he'd been bragging about his sex life, perhaps to underline the fact that with Natasha that aspect had been non-existent. 'I loved your saying that you are a "tiger with the right woman in the right situation". I am happy to think of you as you say, "—ing endlessly day and night" you old tiger you! It's right and proper for you and it's important to you. *Beata lei!* [Lucky her!]'

Can we imagine Ray fucking the right woman like a tiger when the mood was on him? No, we can't. He was too old and ill and alcoholic. Yet if there was an element of wish-fulfilment on his part, a parallel fantasy was being carefully nursed by Natasha. She accepted his self-image as a demon lover because she wanted him to accept hers, which was that of a pious woman wedded to her 'discipline', but brimming with spiritual generosity. Thus their relationship was bound together by reciprocal make-believe.

Darling Ray – don't you understand I carry you in my heart as much as I ever did, but I can't any longer run away from loneliness, when in so doing I involve other people in my predicament. You had enough frustration trying as you thought to help me. Well we can help each other by never denying the deep feeling we have for each other – always being kind to each other and respecting each others view of life. If your view precludes you from enjoying our relationship – then I respect it and you; and you must go in peace . . .

In the spring of 1958, while Natasha was writing these letters, Stephen flew back to Japan. It wasn't the free, careless flight from responsibility he'd initially dreamed of. It was measured, almost valedictory. He had one or two tasks to do for the Congress for Cultural Freedom, but as these weren't enough to keep him in the country for long, he'd arranged a lecture tour to pay for some extra days.

As soon as he arrived in Tokyo on 20 April, he was told that Masao had lost his job and been rejected by his current lover, an American; and, in despair, he'd tried to commit suicide.

Stephen met him as soon as he could and heard the whole story. The attempt had been serious, but Masao had also trusted to luck. Having taken a massive dose of sleeping pills, he'd visited his American lover, in front of whom he'd promptly collapsed. Thus he'd been saved. He'd now recovered and was working in a new job as a waiter.

Masao, having related this story, saw Stephen's schedule on his desk and asked if he could read it. For a moment, Stephen had doubts. Was he going to be possessive? But no. He merely wanted to see when both men would next be free to meet. This turned out to be in eight days' time, and Stephen felt relieved. He wrote in his diary, 'I really am concerned about him. He was very nice when he came, but very tired I thought, as if he would sleep for about two days if I just allowed him to do so in my room.' This strikes me as typical of my father's relationships. He loved Masao, and he'd travelled halfway across the world to see him, but in his presence he suddenly felt anxious about his privacy.

By 12 May, after endless lectures delivered over the heads of unbending Japanese professors, he joined Masao for their few moments alone. Masao, at those quiet hotels with hot baths in the gardens, became Stephen's protector, shooing off the female attendants and seeing Stephen through the ritual that was both a pleasure and an ordeal.

> Our happiest moments were when he cooled the water till it was of bearable temperature, took my Kimono off, then soaped me all over my body, then ladelled water out of the bath, in little tubs provided in the bath room for this purpose, and poured it over me. Once it was so hot that it caused me to give a violent jerk and rick my neck. This revealed Masao's indefatigable gifts as a masseur. Afterwards, he massaged me first thing in the morning and last thing at night, and often several times during the day as well. One day Masao said that he would ring up my next guide Shozo, when he got back to Tokyo, and give him instructions how to look after me. 'What will you tell him?' 'Well I'll tell him that he may take a bath with you and wash your back.'

Though Masao liked Shozo, he felt awkward among Stephen's other friends. Perhaps he should go back to Tokyo, said Stephen? After all, the expenses were piling up. First Masao said he would, then he said he'd like to come to Hokkaido with Stephen and Shozo, then he apologized profusely for having dared to suggest such a thing. 'This kind of moral scrupulousness surprised me after all the talk about the Japanese having no sense of guilt or sin. But perhaps it is something different.'

Back in Tokyo, Stephen made an effort to obtain a place for Masao in a university. Surely, given the opportunity, he would improve himself? The officials he dealt with were scrupulously polite, but they suggested that even if he were given a place, Masao would find the work difficult. Trying another possibility, Stephen wondered whether Masao couldn't go to the International Christian University. He'd write some articles and transfer the money directly to the British Council so that Masao would receive a 'scholarship'.

In the background, Masao was more interested in telling Shozo how to behave when he and Stephen went off for a week of lectures. 'You don't just have to be his interpreter, you can also enjoy yourself and be a friend to him. Sometimes he will want to think or read, in which case just be quiet and don't talk to him. You can take a shower with him and scrub his back. In the morning he does not like Japanese breakfast, but should have a fried egg & ham done Western style. The coffee may be bad in the country, so take a tin of Nescafe so you can make him nicer coffee for him.'

Stephen and Shozo went, leaving Masao behind. But after a few days alone with Shozo, Stephen began to feel besieged. Shozo wanted to translate the lectures Stephen had been giving; wanted to translate more poems. A different kind of demand was being made on Stephen, but he felt equally reluctant to part with these elements of himself. He felt some sympathy for Shozo, however. 'Perhaps the fact that he wants to get on and do things is less of a weight than Masao's real lack of concern about anything but personal relations.' Nevertheless, the idea that he might be exploited by Shozo was unbearable. 'The slightest degree of self-interest seems monstrous and introduces an element of the incalculable into a relationship.'

Outside Tokyo, Stephen finally visited the International Christian University and spoke to its President about Masao. This man seems to have been less polite, and Stephen began to falter. 'In this institution Masao and his "case" seemed strangely improbable. I remembered how Polynesian Masao looks, how unacademic, and thought there is really something about him that anyone in authority would immediately distrust. He is really designed to be Man Friday, I thought.' And: 'I was the Robinson Crusoe who saw his naked footprint in the sand.'

When he came back, he found he had to answer several questions from Reynolds. First of all, did Stephen love his wife?

I think the answer to your question about Natasha is that I do love her, but that our relationship is extremely frustrated for fairly obvious reasons: that I am too ambivalent and she is too repressed. If she were a different person she might have changed me, and if I were a different person I might have changed her. We probably chose each other because one side of each realized that the other would not change it; but at the same time without such change, real happiness is scarcely possible. Of course, by change I mean a lot more than might appear. I mean, for instance my being ready to give up my 'freedom', her being ready to give up concerts. But neither is quite willing to give up these things, for fear that he, or she, would not get anything but loneliness in return. It seems difficult in a way to see where the love comes in. I think it is that under everything else we recognise and respect one another's needs and problems and don't just dismiss them as 'selfish'.

I don't understand this. Why does Stephen equate his 'freedom' with Natasha's concerts? Surely they are different kinds of experience? Would he have given up his 'freedom' if she'd told him she'd give up the piano in exchange?

Really, I think Natasha and I live on a kind of deep down mutual respect, and perhaps also on hope – apart, of course, from the children.

Sometimes – as happened just before I went away – we draw very close together, which means more than something just momentary, because it involves the realisation that we are close together. We are also certainly married in the sense that we are for life and death totally involved, and would never get [each] other out of our systems. Unless, indeed she fell spectacularly in love, in which case – if with the right person – she might exorcise me . . .

About cruelty. Certainly Natasha has suffered a great deal in our relationship through my actions. But then I have suffered also. I am not made happy through causing her unhappiness. Not to be cruel would involve changing things in me which I do not know whether I could change (though I always accuse myself that I could change them).

One can become cruel through a kind of inverted unselfishness. Other people's misfortunes can seem so much worse to you than anything you might have to bear alone, that you simply cannot bear to hear or think about them. Fundamentally I feel that I can solve my own problems. But others all too often appear to me unsolvable, just because the other person lacks some-quality-or-other, and therefore I cannot bear to hear about it. Natasha arrive[d] on the scene with a more or less insoluble problem – her music (really a compulsion projected on her in her appalling childhood) which at once drew me to her and made me desperately afraid.

Imagining other people's problems is such a strain that you'd prefer to do anything else but that – this is an idea I can understand. What I don't understand is this curious duel concerning my mother's career as a musician. I don't believe that Mum's music was a compulsion imposed by her childhood experiences; and even if it was, it existed today in the present tense. It was a strain but it could function.

Was Dad trying to redefine her career as a neurosis in order to make her give it up, because he found it too hard to think of her and her problems? This is what it looked like as I read these letters in the archive of Duke University. All I can say is that when I was a teenager, I thought exactly the opposite. I thought my father wrote in one room and my mother played the piano in the other, and the two endeavours were balanced. I even thought it was an example to emulate somewhere in my own future.

That summer, my father was working hard to finish a translation of *Maria Stuart*, the play by Schiller. It had been commissioned by the Edinburgh Festival, and in September he and I drove up there in the Jag for the opening night, leaving Mum behind in the Red Brick Cottage to work on a concert programme and to see Raymond Chandler alone.

The trip took several days. Somewhere deep in the countryside I climbed a hill and became so overexcited, I couldn't sleep. Dad gave me an adult sleeping pill. It did the trick, but next day when we were having lunch at Chatsworth with the Devonshires I fell on my knees and vomited all over a valuable carpet. They were very good about it. They said if I hadn't been so busy apologizing, I would have made it to the loo.

I was the map-reader, and next day I drew a straight line from Chatsworth to Edinburgh. It led us through the Yorkshire Dales past a tiny hamlet called Muker. Empty, beautiful landscape. Dad didn't talk much. In a car he went into a dream – of what, I have no idea. Along a stretch with nothing but bleak heath on either side, we saw a blackbird in the middle of the road. We approached. The bird didn't move. It tried to fly away just as we were on top of it. My father gave a cry of agony as he crushed it, and I had nothing but the echo of that cry in my mind for many miles. It was touching – but was he over-reacting? After all, we ate chicken for supper every week. Was his sensitivity tuned too high?

His anxiety increased as we approached Edinburgh. I said, 'Don't worry, Dad. Whatever happens it can't be as boring as *Hamlet*.' We'd seen a lot of *Hamlet* that year. Once, it was supposed to have been *Cymbeline* but he'd picked the wrong day.

When we came back, we found that Mum had acquired a new household appliance by which she was evidently obsessed: a knitting machine. It was probably a present from Raymond Chandler, though she implied she'd bought it herself. It would pay its way when she'd completed a mere twelve jumpers, she said. She'd installed it on top of the piano, and whenever she got stuck in a passage of her Beethoven, she'd run an arpeggio on the knitting machine without getting up. Unfortunately this thing kept jamming, and her music would have to be ignored while she unravelled the disorder caused by the machine's wicked little teeth.

I was due to go to Westminster School that autumn.

At the time, the boys had to wear a made-to-measure suit, complete with waistcoat. It was expensive and wasteful and they grew out of them within a year. I remember I wore mine for the first time when Mum and I visited the Tower of London. Raymond Chandler, by that time in London, came with us.

The Tower of London has green spaces that require walking, and at a certain point Chandler stopped dead in his tracks and refused to budge. Mum went on a few paces, turned round and pouted. She mimed: Come on, you can do it. With a mad smile on his face, Ray trundled on towards her.

At supper with my parents and Ray at the Red Brick Cottage a few weeks later, we were eating soup. Ray was making a hideous slurping noise and I, a dear little English public-school boy, was disgusted. My parents began to make faces at me. Be polite! At a certain point, aware of the tension in our silence, Ray gave us each a sidelong glance: at Mum and Dad on his right, at me on his left. His neck was stiff, his cheeks were crinkled, his jacket was much too large for him. He looked like a decaying tortoise. Staring down at his plate, he started chuckling. He'd grasped both sides of this silent drama: the snooty schoolboy disgusted at his slobbery noises and the fearsome looks of two parents miming good behaviour at their son. He knew about England. He'd been to school here – Dulwich College, to be precise, along with P. G. Wodehouse. He knew what it took to make an English boy polite and it amused him.

What were the feelings of my twelve-year-old self?

I'd understood that Raymond Chandler and Reynolds Price were part of my family mechanism, but I'd never felt that the underlying relationship between my parents was at risk. I knew there were tensions, but I did not see how powerful they were. Probably Mum and Dad had made an agreement to keep us children out of it. This meant that they had to keep up appearances even in front of us – a noble thought, but it left a great deal unexplained.

My mother's position was that Dad's infatuations with young men had been a phase of his youth that had been discarded. His earlier self, as it were. Dad subscribed to this myth for her sake, even in front of us, but it meant that both of them were in conflict with the record. Their lives were well documented. There were no inaccessible secrets, even if a clue was no stronger than a photo of a sultry young man glimpsed in the back of Dad's desk as I raided it for stationery.

With regard to my father's relationship with men, I'd already detected something odd at the age of eight with Tony Hyndman. It didn't seem a threat, because Tony had charm and he was good at making things with his hands, which fascinated me. Reynolds, as I've explained, was an intelligent man who moved cautiously within the strange predicament in which my father placed him. Besides, he had a bad case of acne. Who could possibly find him attractive?

In my early adolescence, I was disturbed by the feeling that a struggle was going on between my parents, but I didn't feel that sex came into it. I was too young to understand what a powerful mechanism sex is. I thought they were both working hard, and if there were tensions, it was inevitable in a house in which every week there was a deadline for finishing an article or mastering a piece of music for a concert. I saw no competition between them other than that.

My father wanted to be free. It was a necessary condition that enabled him to write. I took his friendship with Reynolds as a by-product of this desire. Reynolds wasn't a threat but a symptom. There was no reason to feel resentment towards him as a person. And my mother wasn't in a position to complain, for she'd always made clear even to us children that she wanted my father to tackle his 'real' work, which was writing poetry.

Mum was strong. If Dad buggered off, it would be upsetting but we'd survive. We'd gather round the piano and give her our support. But was he ruthless enough to do it? My father was the least ruthless person one could imagine – or so I thought at the time. If you had a different view from his, you didn't have to worry that you might be squashed by force. If someone said something that he disagreed with, he'd either laugh or change the subject. He hardly ever lost his temper.

His lack of confrontation seemed to me a beautiful thing. Whenever I looked at my mother on the other hand, I saw someone who was needy and ambitious, with no generosity of intent. With her it was win or lose, all or nothing. Life was a series of hurdles, the higher the better. She valued the people at the top and she took for granted that this is where she and her husband belonged.

I remember that when I started to play the clarinet, I didn't tell her for several months. I knew she'd say something levelling – and she did. 'Well, you've left it too late to become a professional, but that doesn't mean you can't have a lot of fun.' I was fourteen years old. It's not easy to start the clarinet at a younger age, as the muscles aren't up to it. Even though I knew this and could discount her remark, I felt daunted. She'd meant to be supportive in her own weird way but dammit, she was discouraging.

I thought her values of success and failure were crude; but my father had also been explicit about his own desire to belong to the category of the 'truly great'. I saw that they were both equally ambitious people, and that their differences were merely those of style. However, when it came to the emotions, it was clear that my mother was neglected. Dad's attention lay elsewhere. He was an absent husband. If it came to that, he was an absent father. Behind his good manners there lay a detachment indistinguishable from boredom.

For six months I sided with my father, then for the next six months with my mother. Then one day I decided: this contest is not mine. It's entirely theirs. I have no say in this matter. I must keep out of it. After all, for better or worse, the family works. Odd decision for someone so young but I never went back on it. The family would be OK; that was enough.

My decision denied our emotions, mine and theirs. I never realized until they were both dead, with their ashes next to each other in the same wooden casket that I'd made for them with my own hands, how much their physical discontent had left them lonely. At the time, the most I could deduce was that neither was at ease. My father was restless. My mother was stressed. But – such is the conventionality of children, always more interested in family cohesion than anything else – so what?

18

YOU'RE UNIQUE

'We are having a hell of a time owing to Dwight – or at least I think we are going to,' wrote Stephen to Reynolds late in 1958. 'It is too long a story to write now, but he really is a damned cracklepotty vain goat-bearded stupid nuisance. I wish Trotsky had finished him off.'

Those who'd known him from New York had warned that Macdonald was too maverick to make a dependable co-editor for *Encounter*. For several months he'd acted as 'roving editor', and following this trial run, he'd filled Irving Kristol's post in London. Then, however, he wrote an attack on the United States which he wanted to publish in *Encounter*, and this led to a crisis that lost him his job.

Read today, 'America! America!' is more of a curiosity than a piece of criticism. It analyses the civilization of the United States and finds it vulgar. 'We are an unhappy people . . . a people without style, without a sense of what is humanly satisfying. Our values are not anchored securely, not in the past (tradition) and not in the present (community).' In the late Fifties, many members of the former New York Left underwent what in retrospect looks like a crisis of confidence. It wasn't so much a political crisis as a feeling of frustration with the culture of popular music, cheap food and expensive movies,

221

with which they felt no connection. The left felt removed from what he calls the 'community', and now it was time to appeal to 'tradition'.

The moment when Macdonald was given the sack and replaced by Melvin Lasky was one of the few occasions when the fact that *Encounter* was a front magazine for a United States agency might have emerged. According to Macdonald, the rejection of his article 'reflected the attitude of *Encounter*'s front office, the Congress of Cultural Freedom in Paris, which publishes the magazine with funds supplied by several American foundations. The people in Paris . . . feared it might cause American foundations to cut off supplies.' Was Stephen aware that, in the background, the decision-making process had gone up the line from London to Paris to the headquarters in America of the CIA? No, not according to the correspondence. Stephen thought the article was ridiculous and its political agenda outmoded, and he supported the decision of Josselson and Nabokov to reject it.

Dwight found another publisher in New York, and the fact that the article had been 'censored' permitted him to launch a few well-aimed barbs at the Paris CCF.

Cracklepot is delivering fiery attacks because we refused an article he wrote on America which appears in *Dissent*. He says we refused it because of the extraneous influence of the Congress for Cultural Freedom which cannot tolerate fearless anti-American honesty like Cracklepot's. What is really annoying about Cracklepots is that they drag one down in their polemics and controversies, so that you end up washing each others dirty linen in public and raking round the ashes of bygone schismatic days.

'Cracklepot' was a term that Stephen used only in his letters to Reynolds. It's a mixture of the English 'crackpot', meaning crazy, and the American 'cracker-barrel', that symbol of homely wisdom. From my father's point of view, Macdonald deserved to be sacked not because he was anti-American, but because he was out of date.

A family photo taken a few months before our semester in California in 1959.

At the beginning of 1959 we moved for a term to California, where my father had been offered a job as a visiting professor at Berkeley. This period of my life holds a warm place in my memory, because I was living at home and I had a schedule of work from Westminster which my parents had to go through with me.

I remember going to the edge of a lawn at a party in a professor's house in order to pee. Below me lay a wide valley filled with scraggly trees and I thought: over these hills there will be walks that people have never taken. Nowhere in Europe would I feel what I'm feeling now. There, every tree has been climbed, every blade of grass has been touched by friendly feet.

I was with Mum two hours a day with my homework. Maths, for instance, which she was good at and I hated. She straightened my fractions and corrected my grammar – which Dad never did, preferring to concentrate on style and meaning rather than the actual words. And now and again as she taught me, she became the schoolgirl she used to be, trying to earn that scholarship and find the way out, while assimilating the accents of her friends who'd tried less hard and never left Maidenhead. I liked that side of my mother. It was later obliterated by Lady Spender, a different persona, just as firm because she believed in it but, to me, less convincing.

In her Maidenhead schoolgirl voice she'd recite a little ditty that went like this: 'So 'arry went to 'arrygate, and 'arry lost 'is 'at. And when he got back 'ome, 'is Mum said 'arry, where's yer 'at? 'E said, 'anging on the 'anger in the 'all.' The last bit came out fast: ang-ing-ong-th'rang-ing-th'rawl. But whereas the usual upper-crustie who imitates a cockney accent makes it mysteriously condescending, Mum's cockney was the real thing. It was cheery and optimistic and it was evidently part of her real self.

My father's fiftieth birthday party took place at the end of February. He came into my bedroom, lay on my bed and gave a heart-rending sigh. I was trying to learn *The Rime of the Ancient Mariner* by heart. Outside various academics made polite conversation. But he didn't want academics. He wanted young poets and Beatniks. He'd met Thom Gunn and liked him. Ginsberg had promised to come but he hadn't turned up. I asked him if he was enjoying his birthday. He shut his eyes and shook his head.

Offstage, and far from well, there was Raymond Chandler. He'd written to my mother, 'I'll be delighted to see you over here, but I have regretfully to inform you that I can't give you the full treatment as before.' He discouraged her from driving down to LA to see him. He'd be going to London soon, anyway.

His biographers show that the last months of his life were absolute hell. He drove to exhaustion a nice male nurse who'd come back with him from London. A friend of Helga Greene's who'd replaced the nurse broke down after three weeks.

Ray's last letter to Natasha is dated 4 March. He sees no point in meeting her as he is about to go back to London with Helga. He encloses a cheque for seven hundred dollars.

How strange that you should want to live in America while I, despite the weather, much prefer England. I need hardly say that I am delighted that you are having a so long deserved success at the piano. Of course this is where the money is, and the California climate must mean a lot to you. I have had it so long that it has staled on me. Am I to infer that your staying here means more than appears on the surface? About time if it is, but too late in a way – if anything is ever too late.

Something in this letter made my mother tear it up, but she kept the fragments and stored them carefully in an envelope along with her other letters from Ray. She was maddened by Chandler's assumption that passionate love was still an element shimmering in the air between them, in spite of the fact that it was so self-evidently and so nostalgically 'too late'.

He flew to New York with Helga to accept the presidency of Mystery Writers of America. Helga flew on to London but he came back to California. Alone in the house and unable to take care of himself, he drank too much, collapsed in the garden and was taken to hospital. He died of pneumonia on 26 March.

Mum was not told immediately. I clearly remember the moment when she heard the news. It happened in a motel in a desert of Southern California, where we'd gone to see some adobe houses dating from the Spanish period. Outside, there was a lurid advert saying 'Learn About the Sex Life of the Date Palm'. Someone came up and told her Ray had died. An incredulous look came over her face and she sent me out to swim in the motel pool.

When I came back to where she was sitting on a deckchair, her eyes were red with tears. Why had nobody told her? Behind the tears of real grief I thought I detected rage that she hadn't been contacted by a lawyer to tell her she'd inherited everything.

In my second year at Westminster, I made the exciting discovery that I didn't belong to the male sex. In my passport there was neither an F nor an M, but a B. Class B, sexually speaking, was evidently a whole other thing. It probably occurred to me that B could stand for Boy, but the thought was discarded. It was much more exciting to be an unknown gender about which no information was available, and certainly none that could be discussed with friends.

Boarding school meant hot showers after rowing on the Thames, which meant facing the true hideousness of the male sex. So many organs, some of unusual colour, some evidently damaged, almost skinned. Though you'd been told that pricks were as noses, no amount of comparison could reconcile you to the fact that whereas a nose was familiar and visible, a prick was always a surprise and ugly.

Sex at Westminster was an offstage theme that never, at least for me, became real. There were two or three boys in the school who were self-declared homosexuals, but nobody seemed shocked. There was one in our house, a fat and unattractive boy. He tried to seduce me. I was in the sick room listening to my classical records when he joined me on the other bed in this otherwise tranquil room. After lights out he told me that he'd only pretended to be ill so that he and I could give each other hand-jobs. I told him if he left his bed and took a step towards mine, I'd scream for Matron.

For an adolescent boy whose sexual cravings were totally straight, there wasn't much in the library of Loudoun Road to catch my attention. There was a monograph on Titian's *The Andrians* which had a fabulous nude on the lower right. Her stout body was relaxed after a hard day working in the fields. I could fantasize about that. And there was a book given to Dad by Fosco Maraini, an Italian who'd spent much of his life in Japan. It showed the life of the Ama, bare-breasted fisher-girls who dived deep between the waves to prise out abalone from fluffy rocks using short bent chisels. I thought they were wonderful. Their bodies were robust like the girl in the painting by Titian, and as Maraini's caption put it under one of his photographs, they were splendid examples of womanhood.

I read Dad's autobiography in my second year at Westminster during this moment of curious changes in my body. I was about fourteen years old. Dad was thrilled, of course. 'And what did you think of *that*, I wonder?' Unembarrassed, he was curious about my response. Typical! He was far away in America and I must have written to him about it. Other boys in the same study at Liddell's House read it after me. Grins were exchanged, the occasional nudge. And there it was, as fresh as paint. At the time, homosexuality was illegal and you could go to jail for that kind of thing. That didn't worry us. But the story seemed so silly. Dad and Tony in the Spanish Civil War, wandering around the battlefields hand in hand.

Those who've read early drafts of this book about my parents have asked, But wasn't it a shock when you discovered that your father was homosexual? The answer is no, not that I can remember. Children are fine with just about anything as long as the situation is clear-cut, and such was my mother's determination to show that their marriage was perfect that I was prepared to believe her. Willpower on her part, good manners on his, papered over the cracks.

When it came to homosexuality, the thing that frightened me was the question of power. As far as I could tell from observing overt homosexual relationships, whether at Westminster or in the world of grown-ups, whenever two men were in love there was always a struggle to determine who led whom on what trajectory. This confused me, because I could not see where the limits of such a relationship would lie. Tony Hyndman had some emotive hold over my father. I could recognize this as 'sex', and I was OK with that, because it was none of my business; but I also saw that Tony despised Stephen, even though he depended on him. And his contempt somehow involved me. I was a symptom of something my father had done wrong. A betrayal.

I wasn't capable of thinking my way through this quagmire, but I didn't like it. Yet, in coming to terms with my father when I was an adolescent, the question of power seemed ludicrous. He was the least authoritarian person anyone could ever imagine. There was no question of him ordering anyone to do anything, let alone going in for obscure forms of psychological manipulation.

At this point in his career my father was middle-aged, restless in his work, not particularly happy in his emotional life, uneasy in London but lonely everywhere else. I picked up on his sense of solitude, though I was unable to attribute it to any cause.

> The other day I took Matthew to the Savile Club for dinner. Afterwards he said: 'Dad, I really don't know how you can talk to those people at that club. You have nothing in common with them. Of course, you're very awkward when you say anything, and I don't blame you. I would be myself.' I said 'Who can you imagine me talking with?' Matthew said: 'That puzzles me a lot. I really can't imagine you having a conversation with anyone. I often look at people and wonder, but I've never seen anyone the least bit like you. I'm afraid you're unique, dad.' I said 'What about Mummy?' He looked dubious and then said politely, 'Well, just.'

At Bruern, I lived outdoors, stomping through the brambles and crushing the primroses, or in the attic of the Red Brick Cottage, where I listened to Brahms on Chandler's portable gramophone. My parents worked downstairs. Meals seemed to hesitate up to the very last minute, not because my parents were working, though that too, but because secretly they were longing to be invited up to the Big House.

Conversation when it was just us at home was often full of gaps. If I said something good, my father would make a note of it – 'Ah, that's very interesting' – but then the subject would grind to a halt. He'd bring it up at the next Big House supper: 'Matthew says.' Well, it was flattering, and if challenged I could go on with whatever I'd intended to say. But what was so ephemeral about conversation at our dinner table that it could acquire substance only at Michael Astor's?

Over time, as I crept up the classes at Westminster and joined the

History Sixth, I learned how to argue at table. I remember one Sunday lunch at the Big House tackling an academic from Oxford about a controversy between A. J. P. Taylor and Hugh Trevor-Roper as to when Hitler had intended to start the Second World War. One said 1939 and the other said 1942, I can't remember which. I did well on this occasion, but the more the academic looked at me with respect, the more I despised myself. I was reading his mind as to where the argument was going, and giving it back to him just a moment sooner. I knew I was bluffing.

Selwyn Lloyd, the Foreign Secretary, was sitting next to Michael at the other end of the table. In a deferential moment when we'd all turned to him to listen, he said that when he'd been appointed minister, he had no idea where the Foreign Office was. He'd had to ask a policeman. The company laughed. The old Etonians at the table recognized the patrician quality of not caring about power in itself – though perfectly ready to wield it if it turned up.

Michael didn't know quite how to handle Lloyd. After lunch he said to him, 'I can't make up my mind whether I want to go upstairs and take a nap, or bring up a shotgun and give those pheasants on the lawn a bloody great shock.' Lloyd laughed politely and said he thought he'd just lie on the sofa and read a book. The muted public-school hint was that, actually, he'd be working.

On 15 June 1959, Selwyn Lloyd signed a Foreign Office circular summarizing the communist front organizations in the West, and also their 'free-world counterparts', which, as he points out matter-of-factly, 'are less familiar'. It's an extraordinary document because it says, in effect, that the Russians have their front organizations, and we have ours; and they are evenly balanced. This presupposes a major strategic decision going back many years.

Paragraph 9 discusses the work of the Congress for Cultural Freedom. It reports without comment: 'The organization is largely American-financed.'

The circular says that, with regard to the many international publications or organizations with which the FO is involved, it was necessary to remain discreet. Behind-the-scenes advice, without prodding, just a hint, no more than that. 'It is essential that any such assistance should be so given as to avoid the impression that these organizations are consciously used as "Western" fronts; their strength lies in their very independence of such political ties, in contrast with their rigidly controlled Communist counterparts.'

This circular was reissued by R. A. Butler, a later Foreign Secretary, in January 1964. It points out that with the increasing international interest in the fate of political prisoners, some of the work hitherto covered by the IRD was now beginning to be taken over by independent organizations, such as Amnesty International. There's a hint that the work of the IRD was now no longer necessary, in a world where information was increasingly accessible and awareness of injustice was increasing.

Over the summers of 1959 and 1960, my father sent me to Germany to learn German.

The first of these visits was to the family of his old friend Wolfgang Clemen, to whom he'd been introduced by Curtius in 1931. The Clemen family spent the summers in a huge house on the Chiemsee south of Munich. Wolfgang's son Harald is still a friend of mine. As a child Harald wore Lederhosen – than which nothing is more krautisch. You wear them with a swagger, hands in pockets, swinging the shoulders as well as the feet, and you walk in a lumbering gait that is unstoppable. He was learning English, and what I heard of the German language consisted of flaming rows between him and his siblings, accompanied by the scrapings of a string quartet where the professor behind closed doors played second violin with his friends. Beethoven, of course. But not the late ones. They were too emotionally challenging, he said.

The following year I was sent into the deepest woods, I know not where. My hosts were called Erpenbeck and the old lady of the house was an ex-Nazi. Had been to jail for it, someone in the village told me admiringly. She loved nature and hunting and she hated her son-in-law, who was a gamekeeper. The disputes in that house were muted but tense. I think the gamekeeper must have been a Social Democrat, so thoroughly did Frau Erpenbeck despise him. She was in charge of everything. The gamekeeper's wife was frightened of her mother and she chewed her food quickly in small blonde bites.

Frau Erpenbeck liked me, because I'm tall and blue-eyed. She took me hunting in the wood, screwing into the barrel of a hefty twelve-bore a short .22 rifle barrel with which I had no chance of hitting anything smaller than a house. We'd lie in wait for rabbits. Frau Erpenbeck panted behind me as cigarettes filthied the air in her lungs and alcohol pickled the food in her guts and then pop, another rabbit was missed. At the edge of the wood, under the oaks, the furry mounds that moved in the twilight would lie still for a moment then the ears would go up again and they'd go on feeding.

A young French boy joined us. Though only my age, he was in a bad way. His brother was off fighting in Algeria, and this boy knew all about the tortures going on in the name of Algérie Française. Wires were attached to your *zeb*, he pointed out this bit of anatomy on my body, and electricity was passed through you until you did whatever the army wanted you to do. Or alternatively you took a bedside lamp – like that one over there – and you stripped it down so that the prongs of positive and negative were visible and you shoved it against the *zizi* of a woman, if she was a woman. He was not old enough for military service but he would be soon.

The Erpenbecks kept a strange girl not much older than myself who worked in the stables. She was called Erika and we used to go riding together. She had mousy hair and no sense of humour and Frau Erpenbeck harassed her. One evening in the muddy courtyard of the farm I saw her carrying a goose. Its legs were tied. She put it on the ground and found a stick, then she picked it up by the legs and its neck curved up and it tried to look at her. Erika started tapping it on the head, not hard or viciously but with persistence. After about twenty taps the goose passed out. She put it on the ground, picked up its head and, using the same tapping movement and small knife, she made a hole in its skull. Then she held up the goose again and blood and brains seeped out gently on to the ground.

I thought it was the most erotic thing I'd ever seen. Erika wore a tight pleated dirndl like my mother's.

One morning I went off by myself. I found a cool stream and a bank of sand and I set up a high-jump with sticks I cut with my penknife. I was jumping and singing and enjoying myself and time was passing happily, then my foot got caught on one of the upright prongs and I came down with a bang, slap on my back.

I was winded and frightened and I thought I would be crippled for ever. I looked up at a lozenge of sky over the Schwarzwald framed by fluffy trees and wondered, Do my parents love me? What have I done to be exiled to this bleak place? What are they doing as I'm lying here? Flying around the world being grand, while all that's left to me is the sodden bank of a stream in the Land of the Nasties?

I knew my parents had had rotten childhoods. Maybe they just didn't know how to bring up children? It's not that children need much, I thought. A cuddle or two, a pat on the head as they're doing their homework, a cheerful remark as you pass through their room, a hunk of bread and jam on the lawn in the afternoon.

I missed my family. But missing them was pointless. I lay there quietly thinking: No, my back is not broken. I can get up. But I went on lying there for a while wondering what on earth my father had wanted me to learn from the Erpenbeck experience. And what was this thing about Germany?

Coming back to England I had to spend a couple of hours in Munich Hauptbahnhof waiting for a connection. I remember staring at several huge Bavarians drinking flagons of beer, standing by upturned barrels on top of which sat vast white radishes with their leaves still on, like green wigs. The men had greasy leathery Edelweiss sewn to their braces, felt hats with a pheasant tail-feather sticking out, and their knees were bare and they were fat. I thought, Cor! This is a country with muscle.

A major fight with my father took place after I'd come back.

We were looking at a TV documentary on the death camps in Germany. I said that if I'd been a fifteen-year-old when Hitler came to power, with no family background and no education, I probably would have listened to him and become a prison-camp guard and enjoyed murdering people, like anybody else. I was thinking partly of the matter-of-factness of Erika and the goose, partly of the insanity of expecting people to behave well in war. Homer was a glamorous cloak sitting on top of terrible things; yet sometimes these terrible things were also marvellous. I wasn't 100 per cent sure that I would have become a death-camp guard, but I thought I could see an area where Hitler and Homer met. I wanted to argue that we are all of us receptacles of good and evil. Glory and horror are indivisible.

My father took it as a rejection of everything he'd ever stood for. This was not the reason why I'd been sent to Germany, to come back with a soft spot for the Nazis. He went wild with rage – which I suppose was my punitive intention, after having nearly killed myself high-jumping by a Bavarian stream. But I didn't have the words to articulate my thoughts. The evening ended with violent emotions and slammed doors.

19

WITHOUT BANQUETS

Dwight Macdonald was replaced by Melvin Lasky, who became the American co-editor of *Encounter* halfway through 1959. I don't remember meeting the other editors of *Encounter* but I have a strong memory of Lasky.

The offices of *Encounter* consisted of a few rooms at the top of Panton House, a building on a side street between Piccadilly Circus and Trafalgar Square. From the window of my father's office one could see Horatio Nelson on top of his column, larger than life and vaguely inhuman in the weathered darkness that lay beneath his wedge-shaped hat. He stood on roofs of slate that glittered like the sea. I could stare at him for a long time from inside this cluttered room before turning back to the tin filing cabinets and the overloaded desk.

On the wall hung a lithograph given to Stephen by Jean Cocteau. It showed Baudelaire looking longingly at a sack of money. The sack had wings and was flying away and the piercing look of Baudelaire was unable to stop it.

Across a corridor the office organizer, Margot Walmsley, kept charge of a much neater room. She was ash-blonde and fluffy and when she became flustered, she stammered. When years later Mum and I learned that she worked for British Intelligence, all we could do was laugh. It was so unexpected, yet so obvious. If the CIA was running something in England, British Intelligence would have had to participate.

Melvin Lasky's office lay between Margot's and Dad's. Lasky was short, with a hard belly held in check by a waistcoat. His nostrils were large and he, like Kristol and Macdonald, wore a goatee. Behind him on the wall hung a dozen photos of himself next to various important people, and they also had goatees. Some of these photos were plausible: Lasky with Sidney Hook, for instance. I didn't know anything about Hook other than that he was as near to being a communist as it was possible to be while simultaneously loathing all communist regimes. But Lasky with Leon Trotsky? Lasky with Sigmund Freud? The cumulative impression was that they were all fake. I think Dad and I laughed about this over lunch at the Asiatique, a cheap Chinese restaurant off Trafalgar Square. It was surely childish to hang these things on the wall, we thought.

The duel between Lasky and Spender had elements of snobbery on my father's part. At one point he told a colleague that the trouble with Lasky, as with Macdonald and Kristol, is that they all came out of 'the Bronx Box'. He was referring to the common background of Trostkyite radicalism which, in England, counted for nothing. But there's also the suggestion that Lasky wasn't altogether a gentleman.

Lasky was certainly no fool, but he and my father were playing to a different set of rules. Mel had no use for Stephen's wishy-washy liberalism. He knew more about contemporary history, he was a fast and shrewd journalist and he paid attention to every piece of information that came out of the Soviet world. He could be arrogant and hard to work with and he made no secret of the fact that he thought the 'creative' side of *Encounter* was nothing but window-dressing for the serious business of writing articles on politics. 'Elizabeth Bowen and all that crap' was what he thought about the uses of literacy.

Yet the differences between Spender and Lasky only strengthened the total effect of *Encounter*. If a short story set in London's bohemia appeared next to an article by the young Labour policy-maker Tony

Crosland on the need for Labour to set itself new goals, the effect was to consolidate the Englishness of *Encounter*. London's brand of socialism wasn't as far to the left as that of the north of England, but it had a powerful tradition of its own. (Think of Charles Dickens.) But, come to that, British socialism had nothing to do with the United States. The mood of *Encounter* was British, which meant that the American political influence was left in the background.

Both Irving Kristol and Mel Lasky later boasted that they'd helped to push the British Labour Party towards the centre. But it takes two to tango. The Gaitskell wing of the Labour Party knew that Labour would never win elections if its radical base was not toned down. *Encounter* was the perfect magazine for Tony Crosland's articles.

Lasky, trained in the 'box' or boxing-ring of City College, used the same ruthless tactics that the old American communists had used to infiltrate left-wing organizations in New York before the war: the interminable meeting, the overruled decision and the suppressed minute. Perhaps he expected Stephen to recognize this elaborate game and join in. The fact that he didn't merely proved to Lasky that Spender was a weakling.

In a letter to Reynolds written in 1960, Stephen described how Mel worked.

What Melvin Lasky does is quite simply to accept so much material that there is no room in which to print most of it and I am reduced to having to write to people saying we cannot take anything. He also does not tell me what he accepts, and usually I learn about it weeks later. I am protesting as hard as I can, but conversations with him are almost impossible. He simply filibusters if you protest about anything, wastes hours going over every small point, and refuses ever to admit that he knows what you are talking about. He is the most wriggly person I have ever met.

A year later he wrote again to Reynolds:

I am getting to the stage of really detesting Lasky, who is the kind of person, clever, devious, philistine, whom I find it almost impossible to deal with . . . There is his endless commissioning of things without my knowledge, and the difficulty I therefore have ever to get things I have chosen or suggested (and got him to agree to) with the magazine. If ever I complain to the Congress they pretend to sympathise and perhaps do say something to Lasky. But he is in fact their man, being on their committees for deciding the projects of the Congress, and that sort of thing. Added to all this Josselson, the key man and father figure of the Congress has had two strokes, adores Lasky, and would probably have another stroke if I said what I really think. Above all, of course, they worship success. To them to say that we have a duty not to accept things and then not use them, or not to keep writers waiting 18 months before something is published – that we really have a responsibility to literature, which is writers – is pious cant.

In June 1962, Stephen wrote to Auden saying that unfortunately he'd lost Wystan's recent translations from Brecht. I can imagine Lasky finding these on Dad's desk at the *Encounter* office and just dumping them in the bin. Lasky hated Brecht. One of his greatest journalistic scoops on *Der Monat* had been to challenge Brecht to write an article critical of the Soviet Union, in answer to an article by Lasky criticizing the United States. Lasky published his. Brecht didn't reply, and Lasky left the page empty with an editorial note saying they were still waiting for Brecht's article.

In October 1959, a few months after *Engaged in Writing* was published, Stephen received a letter from Boris Pasternak. It was handwritten, and in English – a careful letter. It was clearly an overture of some kind.

Ostensibly Pasternak was commenting on some *Encounter* articles about his novel *Dr Zhivago*. But he went out of his way to mention that certain lines from an early poem by Spender had always meant a great deal to him. It was wonderful for Stephen to hear this. 'The idea that Pasternak knew these lines, and had perhaps carried them round in his head for twenty five years, really thrilled me, more than any review I have ever read. I think the parrotlike way in which people say there is no "communication" nowadays is rubbish really; communication is having the faith that if you do your utmost someone somewhere does and will understand this and sometime somewhere you will know it.'

A correspondence ensued, though Stephen found it hard to keep things simple. He was besieged by Russian specialists advising him what to say. 'I have received so much advice from Pasternak experts that I almost wish I hadn't got into all this.'

Towards the end of the first letter, Pasternak had written: 'My situation is worse, more unbearable and endangered than I can say or you think of.' This wasn't rhetoric. It was the truth. Nobody in the West could imagine the claustrophobia of a society in which nothing could be discussed and the penalties for non-conformity, if expressed in public, were so severe.

Lasky wanted to rush this into print and create a 'stir', but Stephen hesitated. He did not want Pasternak to get into trouble. Indeed, the letters were only published after Pasternak's death in May 1960. Pasternak's heirs immediately disowned them, and Stephen was appalled, but just as he was about to publish an apology he received a message through the Russian grapevine that Pasternak had wanted them to be published. It was just that nobody could ever have said so, officially.

In January 1960, after he'd received the Pasternak letters but six months before they were published, Stephen travelled to Moscow in the company of Muriel Buttinger, who wanted to make contact with a sculptor she'd befriended in the 1920s.

Through the British Embassy in Moscow, Stephen arranged to visit the Union of Soviet Writers. It took a day or two, and when he arrived he was met by two women who explained in a friendly way that all the writers he wanted to meet were unavailable, and that not many 'specialists' had ever heard of his work. If he came back on Tuesday maybe they'd be able to arrange 'a small gathering'.

Undiscouraged, Stephen told them that he thought the present arrangement of official meetings between writers of the East and the West was too cumbersome. Perhaps something simpler could be arranged? 'I thought it would be a good idea if a dozen or so people could go away together for a week or two and exchange their views in a quieter and simpler atmosphere without banquets and publicity. They were amused at this suggestion and seemed to think that it would be asking an awful lot of the participants.' Their laughter covered their embarrassment. It was highly unlikely that the Soviet authorities would agree to such a proposal.

Word went round that Spender was in Moscow. Since he'd accompanied Muriel in a private capacity, he did not represent anyone but himself. A couple of days later, at one in the morning, he received an unexpected telephone call from an old friend: Guy Burgess. They arranged to see each other on the following day.

Stephen wrote a record of their meeting. He had not sought it, therefore the initiative was with Burgess. His predominant feeling was one of compassion: Burgess wanted to justify himself. He told Stephen that his flight from England did not mean he was guilty of anything. He'd only intended to accompany Maclean to Prague and then come back to London. Maclean had panicked because of the ferocious attentions of the American police when he'd been working in Washington.

Now and again Guy referred to Stephen as an 'American agent', and when Stephen protested, Burgess backed off saying it was 'only a tease'. He seemed to remember every single occasion when they'd met: a conversation before the war in a Paris bar about a tragi-comic episode in Stephen's life when he'd tried psychoanalysis. Once, Stephen had lent Guy his flat. And when John Cornford, the young communist poet who was killed in the Spanish Civil War, had as a schoolboy sent Stephen his poems, Stephen had written him a six-page letter of advice.

Burgess knew this, too. He was evoking a list of good works: to flatter his listener, or was this just nostalgia? These incidents, all of which Stephen had forgotten, gave an air of having been polished as lovingly as a jeweller polishes stones. Stephen didn't know what to make of it. Burgess was behaving 'like some ex-consular official you meet in a bar at Singapore and who puzzles you by his references to the days when he knew the great, and helped determine policy'.

There came the moment when Burgess tried to describe what he'd actually done: which, he said, was to hand over information about what people had discussed, in those high diplomatic and political circles he'd frequented. What was wrong with that, he asked defiantly? Burgess said that Churchill, when in opposition before the war, had often passed information to Maisky, the Russian Ambassador. During the war British and Russian intelligence officers had met regularly, and 'the rules of secrecy were more or less ignored or considered to be suspended'.

Stephen said cautiously that it wasn't clear to him 'what was the borderland dividing giving away information from giving away real secrets'. If Dave Springhall had ended up in prison for having given the Russians some plans for an aircraft, he said – well, that was one kind of betrayal. Perhaps just handing on information fell into a different category. The example came from personal knowledge. Springhall was one of the commissars whom he'd had to confront in Spain when he'd tried to save Tony Hyndman.

A few weeks later, at a party back in London, Stephen was approached by the Home Secretary R. A. Butler. He told Stephen that if Burgess wanted to come back to England, he personally would have no objection – though he supposed that the boys in MI5 might have other views. If Stephen were to write to him . . . ? Stephen didn't follow this up. It didn't seem to offer Burgess any guarantee against prosecution.

A second figure intruded into this strange predicament: Tom

Driberg. At this time, Driberg was a journalist, a former Labour MP and member of the National Executive Committee of the Labour Party. He urged Stephen not to encourage Burgess to come back. Driberg knew Burgess well and had published a respectful biography of him. Stephen deduced that Driberg did not want Burgess to reappear in London and start naming names.

I met Tom Driberg in the street with my father soon after these events. It was the only time I saw him. I thought that he was loud and invasive, and although Dad was friendly, I detected a certain hesitation on his part.

As he and I walked away he murmured, 'That man is supposed to have been Moscow's representative inside the British Parliament.' I said I didn't understand. He explained that Driberg came from the communist wing of the Labour Party, and if the government needed to communicate something urgently to Moscow, well, they could rely on Tom to deliver the message.

I was shocked. It went against the whole concept of 'us' against 'them': the capitalists against the commies. There was a war in progress, not a nearby war, a distant war, a domino-theory war, a 'cold' war – but still a war. What was this private-chat option?

He said, with all his usual mildness, 'I think it's good when people go on talking to each other, don't you?'

Nothing could bring out more forcibly the difference between English and American relations with Russia at that time. American intellectuals couldn't even meet 'real' communists, because the McCarran Act kept them out of the USA; and here was Tom Driberg who apparently could pick up a phone and call his friends in Moscow whenever he felt like it. Meanwhile in London, though many people were shocked by the defection of Burgess and Maclean, it was assumed they had valid reasons for whatever it was they were supposed to have done. None of their friends rejected them with outraged cries of 'traitor'.

Years later, the art historian John Pope-Hennessy told me that when Anthony Blunt first heard that he was under investigation, he put on his coat, walked down to the MI5 building off Whitehall, walked through the guards and up to the third floor, found his file, put it under his coat and walked out again, unchallenged. This slowed down the investigation considerably! Pope-Hennessy thought it was a wonderful scene: 'Anthony was a very arrogant man. I can just imagine him doing it.' And he laughed.

If I'd said, 'But he betrayed his country,' Pope-Hennessy would have just changed the subject. It would have been a remark in bad taste. So, as an Englishman brought up within the rules, I kept quiet.

In 1960 I gave up rowing, with all that yucky business of comparing cocks among the steam, and joined the tribe of fencers.

One result of the Hungarian revolution was that Westminster had acquired a fantastic fencing teacher, Bela Imregi. Up until then fencing had been the sport of the non-sporty, who'd hang around dressed in white duck canvas, gossiping. Imregi taught us how to use our reflexes. Don't think, move; and always move forward.

A friend among the fencers was Simon Baddeley. His speciality in épée was a flèche to the big toe of his opponent. Risky, because all the opponent needed to do was tuck back his toe and stretch forward and Simon would be hit in the head. But, because it was so unexpected, it worked well on away matches.

During one of these matches I happened to be talking about the British Museum. Simon said, 'It's in Bloomsbury, isn't it?' To which I said, 'Where is Bloomsbury?' Simon was the editor of a literary magazine, so he published a snippet somewhere in the back: 'Spender, son of Stephen, asks "where is Bloomsbury?"' Dad laughed when he saw it, but it made me wary of Simon.

One day Simon said, 'Your father is part of the Establishment by now, isn't he?' I wasn't going to ask, 'What is the Establishment?' and find another droll quote in Simon's magazine. I had to edge around the subject. I learned that the Establishment stood for the skill with which England makes room for its critics, gives them a title or some other indication of rank and requires them to stand up for the very institution which up until then they'd done their best to challenge.

I didn't like the implications of Simon's joke. It occurred to me: can I ask my father, 'Dad, are you a poet of the British Establishment?' I knew that if I did, he would be offended. And Dad when he was offended really was upset, as if something much larger than his own feelings had been hurt. Did I want to descend so low? Could I? The answer was obviously no, I could not hurt my father. He was too weak.

Being a member of the Establishment attached Stephen to a much wider circle of English life than the restricted enclave of poetry. The next generation of British writers chose to live far from the centres of power. Philip Larkin in his library at Hull, for instance, complaining about his boring job – in fact complaining bitterly about practically everything. In his obtuse way, Larkin represented post-imperial England sinking back into a peripheral role after having controlled a third of the world's surface. 'Little England' was a virtue born of necessity. My father hated it. I remember him reading Larkin's first poems with a grim frown. Was he going to publish them in *Encounter*, I asked? Yes, he said; and sighed with exasperation.

In his willingness to go anywhere in the world on behalf of the British Council or the PEN Club or whatever, patriotism of a peculiar kind was involved. This patriotism had been clear to his friends Auden and Isherwood from a long way back. ('Little England' regarded this patriotism with misgivings. It seemed connected with Britain's imperial past. The thought was wrong, but perhaps understandable for the times.)

Years before, in 1936, Stephen and Christopher had retreated to Sintra in Portugal, where they hoped to set up a small community of writers. There were tensions from the start, mainly between Tony and Christopher's boyfriend Heinz, and the experiment did not last beyond the middle of March. At one point Christopher noted in his diary, 'My days are all poisoned and I can no longer discuss things frankly with Stephen – because we are divided from each other by a secret mutual knowledge of our intentions: Stephen means to return to England if things get nasty – I don't.' The reference is to the imminent danger of war. Christopher had already made up his mind that if war broke out, he would not participate. His attachment to Heinz, and thence to Germany, precluded it.

Auden shared this feeling from about 1938, when he won the King's Medal for Poetry. He knew this was 'the end', as he put it, because the prize signified his credentials as a freshly elected member of the Establishment. He did not want to become a respected icon of British literature.

My father's credentials were confirmed in 1983, when he was given a knighthood. I was deeply upset at the time. I thought it cut him off from writing poetry. I wrote him a bitter letter hinting as much. He wrote an extraordinary reply. Life, he said, is very much like school. Sooner or later one has to join the Sixth Form. Most of his friends were in the Sixth Form already: Sir Isaiah, Sir Stuart, Sir Freddie. What's wrong with that? (And besides, he added cunningly, think of the pleasure it would give Natasha when she becomes Lady Spender.)

Yet, if patriotism lay somewhere inside Stephen's many trips abroad, there was also the pleasure of leaving Little England behind. One of his last interviews consisted of a questionnaire in which he was asked what gave him most pleasure in life. He wrote, 'Any voyage away from England.' I was standing beside him at the time. We were in the garden of a villa outside Florence. I said, 'You can't write that.' I added to what he'd written – it's in my handwriting, '– and any voyage back to England.' It was too late for him to opt out.

A month after Stephen came back from Moscow, Konstantin Fedin, Chairman of the Union of Soviet Writers, arrived in London together with Alexander Tvardovsky, the main editor of the literary magazine *Novy Mir*. They told their hosts at the British Council that the one person they wanted to see was Stephen Spender.

He assumed that they just wanted to apologize for the snub he'd received from the ladies of the Writers' Union in Moscow, but in fact they seemed genuinely interested in the idea of arranging private meetings of small groups of writers away from the eyes of officialdom, 'if it was not conducted in setting one side against the other, and with interested parties looking over shoulders'.

Fedin at the time was a somewhat despised cultural bureaucrat. Tvardovsky was a more courageous figure, who subsequently got into trouble by insisting that Solzhenitsyn's *Gulag Archipelago* should be published in Russia. (It wasn't.) It's possible that Tvardovsky saw himself as a figure corresponding to that of Spender, in search of the same thing: better communication between writers.

Stephen took them to lunch at the Garrick Club. At the end of the meal, Tvardovsky referred to the idea of the seminars and said that it would be appropriate if Spender were to direct them. Stephen refused – which is interesting. If his initiative had been set up by the British Council or some other official body, he would surely have accepted on the spot. 'I tried to make it clear that I did not wish them to feel they were committed to having me.'

This meal was followed by a private supper at Loudoun Road in April. Spender showed Fedin and Tvardovsky the guest list before-hand. They balked at one name: Hugh Gaitskell, Leader of the Opposition. No politicians, they said. Spender persuaded them that Gaitskell would not be present in any official capacity. He was a personal friend, and he was an intelligent man.

They must have been puzzled that Stephen, on the one hand so eager to take groups of writers away from politics, should want them to meet the head of the Labour Party. Unfortunately, he did not write a diary entry on this occasion but I vaguely remember it, as Gaitskell sat at the head of the table and, as usual, I'd passed the peanuts up to that moment.

A few years previously, Gaitskell himself had tried to tackle the question of improving cultural relations between the two countries. He'd spoken to Nikolai Mikhailov, a young assistant of Khrushchev's. 'The exchanges of culture in which he was so interested would only be of value if they were completely outside the propaganda sphere.' But 'he struck me as a young man who was desperately anxious to bring off more cultural interchanges because his job depended on it'. If he was only interested in plumping out his CV, it hardly seemed worth pursuing.

At Westminster it was still compulsory to take part in the Combined Cadet Force, an Officer's Training Corps which was supposed to teach us military virtues. Our equipment went back to the First World War and some of the masters felt dubious about our activities; on the other hand we were studying history, and history includes battles, so we might as well learn what large-scale fighting involves.

My best friend at the time was Tristan Platt, another boy in Liddell's House. He was a militant pacifist, if that's not a contradiction in terms. Following his lead, he and I began to challenge the OTC. During an exam in which we were asked to look at an Ordinance Survey map and describe how to get from A to B using 'dead ground', we invented a bus route which took us off the map to an imaginary pub. This did not go down well.

A few weeks later Major French, who was fanatical about the Corps, gave us a lecture about different weapons: the Sten gun which cost a mere five bob to build but was only effective at close quarters; and the Bren gun, 'a beautiful weapon', which was good up to a range of five hundred yards. Tristan raised his hand to ask a question. Yes? 'Would you mind explaining to us what you mean by a beautiful weapon, Sir, given that you are describing a piece of machinery that can only be used for killing people?' This also went down badly.

By this time our study at Liddell's, a large room with desks for six boys, was beginning to discuss whether we shouldn't take part in the Ban the Bomb protests that met now and again in Trafalgar Square. I had doubts about unilateral disarmament. The others were more committed. One boy was a fan of Bertrand Russell, but I had doubts about Russell too, because he'd advocated war against Russia in 1945, changing his mind immediately after the Russians had acquired the atom bomb. (It was logical but it was weird.) The fun of marching finally overtook our political arguments. Six of us went forth one Saturday afternoon clutching an umbrella with a message that read, 'Eating People Is Wrong'. This was the only cause we could agree on. It was written in toothpaste and it melted in the rain.

One day the Dean of Westminster, the Right Reverend Eric Abbott, delivered a sermon to us Westminster boys in the Abbey. He described a motor tour he'd made through Germany during a recent vacation. He gave us his thoughts on the Second World War and the necessity for patriotism and I dozed off. Suddenly he brought the sermon to a close with, 'God give us something to live for, and God give us something to die for.'

Tristan, who'd been listening with great attention, got up and booed. I stood up beside him to be supportive.

The Dean was an independent authority whose office predated the Norman Conquest. He was older than the school by six hundred years – and the school had been founded by Queen Elizabeth I. We were ordered to apologise; and off we went. But Tristan had no intention of abandoning his pacifism. He told the Dean he was wrong to have made a warlike speech, however justifiable, in the House of God, since Christ had preached that we must love our neighbour, not try to kill him. The Dean grew angry but Tristan stuck to his theme, with me at his side murmuring occasionally, 'I think he's right, Sir.'

As a result of this, and on the grounds that we were irredeemably anti-militarist, Tristan and I were excused from further service in the Corps. Instead of stripping down a Lee-Enfield rifle, I was given permission to go to the Slade School of Fine Art to learn how to draw the nude. I don't remember how the Slade came into the picture, but the head of it, Bill Coldstream, was an old friend of Dad's.

The Slade was tucked away in the corner of the main quadrangle of University College, London. When I arrived, I found at the door a uniformed beadle with a big brass buckle round his waist. I presented myself to Coldstream, not knowing at the time how closely he was connected with several members of my family, though aware that my father had studied in a much earlier art school he'd organized somewhere along the Euston Road. I was free to do what I wanted, said Bill kindly, since I wasn't officially on anyone's books.

I went downstairs to the Life Class, a large room full of students sitting on their 'donkeys', a strange trestle table that was also a stool. They were drawing intently, holding up their pencils at arm's length from time to time in order to measure something. No one spoke. I found a spare donkey, propped my sketchbook against the cross at one end and raised my eyes to the naked woman posing on a stand not far off. So far I hadn't dared look at her. There she was, and I didn't know what to do. Her back was towards me and she was leaning on one leg. She was fiftyish and stringy and, yes, she was absolutely and totally without clothes. I put the tip of my pencil against the paper and kept it there, wondering what to do next. Just then a spasm went up her left leg. I looked at my paper, and there was a nice fresh mark on it, made when I'd flinched in sympathy.

The Slade at the time was very keen on marks on paper. A drawing was often a succession of marks, the freshest one 'qualifying' those already in place. There was a distant echo of Cézanne, but crabbier. One teacher called these marks, 'statements'. Thus you could have the sincerity of the statement and the integrity of the statement, and so on. A negative word was 'arbitrary', which could lead to 'I feel this statement is a bit arbitrary.' Some sense of truth was involved, as if there were a parallel between getting your words right in an essay on logic, and turning your marks on paper into a convincing elbow. One thing your marks must not be was decorative. The negative word in this case was 'slick'. As in: 'I don't like Modigliani. He's much too slick.' Dexterity was a trap, because if you did something automatically, it couldn't be sincere.

'Slick' signified consigning your soul to a generic formula inherited from the previous centuries, without scrutinising the object in front of you. Art must strive for the new, a fresh adventure taking place every time the artist sits down in front of the easel. The true artist reinvents the language. Art must not repeat itself. Art must be pushed forward. I couldn't help thinking that if you did the same thing day after day for decades, it would become a habit, and at some point resistance to style would itself become a style.

Anyway, I wanted to be taught how to draw with skill.

A teacher came over to have a look at my drawing. He was so old he hadn't even made it to the revolution of Cézanne. He was a relic from the age of Tonks, who'd taught Augustus John. He told me that I should study anatomy. The spinal column, he said, grows out of the pelvic basin in the same way that a geranium grows out of a flowerpot. On the side of my drawing he drew a delicate flowerpot-pelvis from which leafy vertebrae crept upwards. I thought this drawing was strange, but I liked it. Afterwards some students came up to me, grinning. This dear old thing was a figure of fun in the Life Class, a fossil dating from the days before sincerity had won.

20

OVER-PRIVILEGED?

DAD HAD BROUGHT back from Moscow several gramophone records that weren't available in London at the time. One of these featured three piano sonatas by Sergei Prokofiev played by Sviatoslav Richter, including the 9th, which was dedicated to him. This was before Richter had created a reputation in the West, but we'd already heard about him through the grapevine of musicians.

In my last study at Liddell's House, shared with a nice Canadian boy who felt detached from Westminster, late at night I'd play Prokofiev in this unavailable recording on a gramophone given to my mother by Raymond Chandler while smoking a Soviet cigarette sold by only one shop in Pall Mall and I'd wonder, am I over-privileged, or what? The cigarette had no filter, just a long tube one was supposed to pinch twice in a special way, as recommended in Orwell's *Nineteen Eighty-four*. The 5th Sonata lasted exactly the length of one cigarette. At midnight, after the housemaster had gone to bed. With the window open to let the smoke out, so that the experience was even more Russian: the cold bare steppes of London.

I was interested in my father's life and I'd tried to catch up with it, starting from my schoolboy knowledge, which as I've said was late imperial. From Conan Doyle and John Buchan and Saki I'd reached the First World War, which meant *Goodbye to All That* by Robert

Graves, and *Memoirs of a Fox-hunting Man* by Siegfried Sassoon. Since we were at a famous public school, my friends and I had read Cyril Connolly's *Enemies of Promise*, which led us to Orwell's *Such, Such were the Joys*, and thus to the state of England of our own childhood. It was a curious way of catching up with one's own father, for it involved stacking up English history like overlapping playing-cards. On the other hand we were studying history, and the pleasure of understanding how events follow each other was growing.

Yet over-privilege often brought with it a sensation of claustrophobia.

I remember once when Dad was driving me back to school one cold damp winter's evening, we'd turned off Buckingham Palace Road, and an ominous cloud unexpectedly loomed up in front of us. I said: 'It's fog that comes up Victoria Street from the Thames.' My father said, 'That's a line as beautiful as anything in T. S. Eliot.' I was happy to have made him laugh, but I also felt hemmed in. Had I made this subliminal reference to 'The Love Song of J. Alfred Prufrock' on purpose, as a form of flattery? Or was a desire to crack literary jokes one of those vices bred by too much culture?

Looking down at the great sycamore of Little Dean's Yard from the window of my study in Liddell's House, the feeling grew on me: is it possible to do anything original in England? I felt the tremendous weight of everything that had been done before, the familiar predicaments so intelligently described: the agony of public school, the embarrassment of belonging to the upper-middle class. As themes, they'd come and gone. I wondered if I shouldn't just write twenty angry poems, and die. Motorbike crash at Hangar Lane. Matt in black leather with his head lolling over the kerb. Tragic! But then I thought of Dad at my funeral being so brave, so proud, at last bringing to the attention of his adoring public the performance he'd imagined about being brave at his own father's funeral, only at Matthew's graveside not Harold's. And I thought, Oh God, but *every*thing has been done before, including my own funeral.

One weekend I was sitting at Dad's desk at Loudoun Road writing an essay on the Crimean War. This was the war that had featured the Charge of the Light Brigade, one of the worst disasters of the British Army at its most unlucky. It fitted in with Russia, too, because Tolstoy and his generation had written about this war; and without hate, without clichés.

Behind me on the bed sat Auden. He'd arrived the night before and would be with us for another week.

The weather was dark and gloomy. So was the subject. I read about the mess of the Crimean War as the day got wetter and more horrible all around the house.

Suddenly I realized that Wystan on the bed behind me was just sitting there, doing absolutely nothing. He was not reading. He was not thinking. From time to time, he sighed. And outside the window, filthy water coming down from the sky in tons.

The phone rang. A journalist from the *Evening Standard*.

Wystan radiant over the telephone.

'But I *like* the rain,' he said. 'I *love* British weather.'

After this, his mood entirely changed. He put *Tristan und Isolde* on the gramophone, the recording with Kirsten Flagstad. Now and again he sang over her voice, those beautiful lines about love-in-death.

I was young enough to be shocked by the sudden improvement in his mood. Wystan, I knew, was one of the 'truly great'. Did he really need a phone call from the *Evening Standard* to cheer him up? Surely mere vanity could not be part of the make-up of a 'truly great' man?

Even as late as the 1960s, people were unable to forget that Auden had not come back to England during the war. The resentment lasted for a remarkably long time. I remember an occasion when Auden was in London to launch a book of his: I think his *Commonplace Book*. Dad, in the car driving me to school, said this volume would cause 'an absolute sensation'. We were at the corner where Baker Street almost meets Regent's Park. The spot still has for me a feeling of divine glory about to fall from a magnanimous heaven. But I was old enough to check the reviews later, and they did not resemble the dreams of glory we'd had in the car, driving between the Nash terraces on our right and the flowering Judas-trees behind the park railings on our left. In fact, the critics were unduly harsh. Certain remarks were only comprehensible in terms of some long-held rancour.

For Auden, Loudoun Road was a safe haven. There, at least, he'd be secure from recrimination. In the evenings, he'd sit in the piano room in a self-absorbed heap, benign but remote. Wystan smoking: a small quick puff, and 'tah', the cough a moment later, like a well-oiled piston letting off steam. Now and again he'd emerge from this somnolent state and give me a direct, blue-eyed stare. It would only last two seconds, then he'd pull back within his usual frontiers, as if he'd corroborated some long-held suspicion.

Dad often said happily, 'Doesn't he look like me?' Wystan would shake his head. 'I see a lot of Natasha in him.' A principle was involved. We are all children of two parents, and we have to come to terms with both.

I remember my sister, care-taking for Wystan one weekend, seething about it in the basement with me. 'Aaah, Lizzie,' came his voice from up above. 'Aaah', as in an organ-pipe clearing its throat, 'Lizzie' with three notes, two going up, one down. And my sister not listening as he called down the stairs to say what he wanted her to do for him that day. She hissed at me, 'He's so *spoilt*, so *spoilt*,' and refused to call back. Wystan, pausing on the landing, wondering if he'd been heard.

Lizzie was referring to Wystan's complete lack of domestic talents, multiplied by his confidence that these gifts belonged to others and were at his disposal. Once, my mother rang him from central London where she was running late. Would he please go downstairs and put the chicken in the oven? Wystan did exactly that – without lighting the oven.

Auden's other-worldliness permeated his poetry. Reading his work at that time, I also wrote a poem about him. I showed it to my father.

One of the lines went, 'and did he ignore the "I" of its making?' Dad said he didn't understand what this meant. I explained that, in my opinion, Auden's detached and 'objective' voice avoided any true engagement with the subject of a poem. Why no emotions? How could you write a poem and exclude your feelings? Dad frowned and gave a little nod, as if he knew exactly what I was talking about.

In 1962, Stephen wrote to Reynolds about a recent poem that Auden had given him for *Encounter*: 'It revealed to me something I had never quite thought about Wystan: that often he uses the subject of a poem simply as an occasion for producing an effect of verbal smartness instead of writing out of the living experience of the situation. An idea occurs: click! He sees how it will make a poem.'

He states this as if it were a fresh thought, but in fact Stephen had always known that he differed from Wystan in his idea of what a poem should be. In 1932, during the second summer holiday that Stephen and Christopher spent on Rügen Island off the Baltic coast, Stephen compared himself with Wystan in a letter to Isaiah Berlin. Auden, he said, was able to write poetry 'simply by presenting pictures of what that world is like'. Auden was interested in the form of a poem, the poem as an object. 'Auden is a much "purer" poet than I, because even where he uses far more modern phraseology than I would use, he uses it so that it all fits into a pattern.' For Stephen, a poem must bear witness to a specific experience. 'The integrity of my poetry is proved or disproved by the fact of its solving or not solving the problems of my life and life in general as I see it.'

My father resisted the idea that a poem is an artefact. He refused to learn poems by heart. As he writes in his autobiography, when he read a poem, he wanted to grasp 'not the words and the lines, but a line beyond the lines, a sensuous quality which went, as it were, into the lines before they were written by the poet and which remained after I, the reader, had forgotten them . . . The *feeling* of a poem which I did not completely remember seemed to put me in

255

touch with the poet's mind in a way which the exactly recollected poem itself could not do.'

At the age of seventy, he wrote: 'True poetry is the external truth transformed in the poetry. It's the truth which reaches outside the enclosed poetry to the outside of nature, the human condition. Why one admires poets like Frost and Edward Thomas is because one sees so clearly that lines and images have an inside which turns back into their interior darkness, an outside which turns out towards nature and human beings. One doesn't tire of seeing them do this. I don't have confidence that I do it.' Yes, that was the problem. If he'd always pinned his poetry to specific events, when the events could no longer provide the experience, he could no longer write the poem.

I'm not the right person to praise my father's achievement as a poet; and anyway any assessment of mine will be discounted as being dazzled by proximity. It seems to me, however, that his sense of the grittiness of life, and his desire to handle this grittiness truthfully, accounts for both the strength and weakness as a poet. His poems are strong when we feel this immediacy over and beyond the physicality of the poem itself. They are weak when the grip on his sense of immediacy falters. When this happens, we become aware that the natural attributes of a poem, in the sense of metaphor, syntax and rhythm, have been sacrificed; and we want them back.

In April 1961, Mum drove us to Italy for Easter.

We stayed in the Pensione Bencista in Fiesole, which had a decent piano. 'We' included Eliza Hutchinson, the daughter of Jeremy Hutchinson and Peggy Ashcroft. Mum and Peggy had performed dozens of concerts together. For my mother, the Hutchinson family was one of those solid families she admired unreservedly, as if she couldn't dream of emulating such constancy.

My mother was a fiendish tourist, so the days were filled with movement and appreciation. 'You must admit it's beautiful,' she'd say of something. I was an adolescent and I kept turning this phrase over in my head. Does one 'admit' something is beautiful? It seemed to me this sentence started out from the wrong place.

One morning we ran into Henry Moore in the Brancacci chapel. He made us look at Masaccio's *Tribute Money* as if it were three-dimensional. 'Look where the feet are placed,' he said. 'They show that the figures are standing in a circle.' He said that when he'd lived in Florence as a student, he'd come in to see the frescoes of Masaccio every morning, first thing, whatever else he did that day. We tried to do the same, but Fiesole is a long way from San Frediano and we soon gave up.

A provincial museum in Tuscany, full of cheerful ceramics two thousand years old, and moving from the cool room of the exhibition to the hot outdoors, birds screeching, the creak of insects blurred within an undulating background of sound, with warm cypress trees and the detritus of cigarette butts by the overflowing rubbish basket of the parking lot. The grocery store where we stopped for water, the perfume of white soap from Marseilles and salt cod, a perfect combination, furry and ancestral, the smell of a strong woman's armpit.

I knew that Peggy Ashcroft was Mum's closest friend and that I was supposed to fall in love with Eliza. She was nice, but hard to pin down. Her opinions on art sounded good, but they floated insubstantially. You weren't sure if she really liked what she was talking about. Well, I did my best. On the wall of the Bencista, sitting side by side in the twilight, the birds now silent and one lone bat circling among the freckled stars, I tried to kiss her. At the last minute however she turned her head. All I got was a mouthful of wiry hair.

For the summer of 1961, a Westminster boy invited me to spend a fortnight with him in a house on the old Venetian port of Chania, on the west side of Crete. Dad sent me up to Hampstead to ask John Craxton for a few tips, for Cracky had lived in Greece for many years. 'Thank you very much,' he said when I described where we were going. 'That's my house!' He'd offered it to a friend, who'd invited James, who'd invited me. As he wasn't using it, Craxton said it was OK. He even gave me a list of things we should see in Athens on our way down.

I showed John a small Auerbach etching of a nude that I planned to take with me to study. Frank had given it to Dad. It was dark and obsessed and I liked it very much, but I didn't understand it. Auerbach was teaching at the Slade and I'd had one short intense lesson with him. He was among those who thought that traditional skills got in the way of seeing things freshly. I thought I wanted what he had, but John told me I should look at the icons in Athens. 'At least they have technique. You can learn from them,' he said. 'You can't learn anything from this. You can't even tell which is her buttock and which is her breast.'

Two days before we left, James and I went to see *Les Noces* in the Albert Hall. Four pianos, plus chorus, plus that family connection with my grandfather. In that vast Victorian space, the tinkling of the pianos ceased to be notes and became a brilliant silvery texture, like chain mail. When we got home to Loudoun Road, I was so excited I drank half a bottle of vodka straight off. It should have killed me. Instead, next morning I found I'd thrown up all over the top floor. I had to spend a humble day scrubbing carpets.

Train to Venice, then boat to Athens.

Lying on the bulbous iron cover of a well behind the Accademia, I noticed that a star in the sky was slowly moving. I looked at it most carefully, and it wasn't my imagination. It was a Sputnik. I felt it was a good omen. The future had arrived. My life was about to change.

One afternoon we came back from the beach and found a beautiful girl lying on my bed. She was wearing a white Mexican shirt with large flowers embroidered with black thread, a big black patent-leather belt and a pink, knee-length cotton skirt faded by frequent washing. Her legs were brown. She was propped up on my pillows with her arms behind her head so that her beautiful breasts pointed towards the ceiling. Then she spoke.

This bed was now hers, she said, because her mother had given Craxton two hundred pounds with which to buy half of the house. She was taking over the room and the rest of us boys would have to go up on to the roof to sleep. (James and I had collected some other Westminster boys along the way, so the house was crowded.) She'd just been walking in the Peloponnese with Beatrice Rothschild and she was exhausted. Beatrice had been flown back to Paris on a chartered Caravelle, because she'd become dehydrated on their walk and she needed to go to hospital. Several very expensive doctors had already looked at her.

Before she and Beatrice had left Paris to begin their walk, Christian Zervos had taken her to meet Giacometti, and Giacometti had turned to Zervos and said, 'Que voudriez-vous que je fasse avec une poule comme ça?' The girl laughed. I thought it was confident of her to tell a story in which she had been snubbed. And note the appropriate use of the conditional tense: 'What would you expect me to do with a chick like that?'

I felt the boys behind me drift away. Some went up to the roof to smoke, the others went down to the port to drink. I knew by the way they shuffled, they thought this girl was just name-dropping, but I recognized a quality common to those who in early youth have handed out peanuts to their elders on literary lawns. It wasn't familiarity. It wasn't irreverence. It was humour. She hadn't been offended that Giacometti couldn't be bothered to talk to her on the grounds that she was 'une poule'. She merely implied: great painters can be silly, too. So my first thought about Maro Gorky, my future wife, was an odd one for a sixteen-year-old. I thought: this girl is going to be cheerful even when she's sixty.

It wasn't so much love at first sight as instant confidence in the long haul.

We all went out for supper, she and I and the boys, but already within our separate aura. Then we went for a walk just the two of us. As we left the table one of the Westminster boys said darkly, 'I think Matthew has been very clever.' On our walk, awkwardly clutched together, we were chased by two local Greeks on a Vespa, which was disturbing though also exciting; and we ended up sharing that bed. Not that anything sexual happened. We were too shy for anything more than a chaste kiss.

We must have been unbearable in our selfishness, because after a couple of days the Westminster boys disappeared. The house was much nicer empty. I could listen to the stories that lay behind the throwaway lines of her first speech. How had she managed to meet all these grand people? The Rothschilds, for instance?

She'd met the French Rothschilds because Jacob Rothschild, of the English Rothschilds, was the son of Barbara Hutchinson by her first marriage and Maro's mother knew her; and Jacob had introduced Maro to his cousin Beatrice when she, Maro, had gone to Paris to study.

Barbara was Peggy Ashcroft's sister-in-law and one of my mother's oldest friends. This was the first hint that Maro and I belonged to the same world.

One day, Wolfgang Reinhardt came for drinks at the Rothschild house on the Avenue Marigny. Wolfie was a film producer, said Maro. Her mother had had an affair with him when John Huston was shooting his movie on Freud. When Wolfgang appeared, Beatrice told Maro that unfortunately she couldn't stay for lunch, because she was wearing trousers. Her parents always insisted that women wear skirts at meals. Wolfgang told Maro: come with me and I'll give you lunch with Sartre instead.

Over lunch in a restaurant, Sartre sat Maro beside him. He was amused that the Rothschilds didn't allow women to wear trousers at lunch. The last of the 'Grands Bourgeois', he said. Then he and Wolfgang discussed the changes that had come over Paris since the war. During the war, everyone used to meet at the cafés, and they stayed there all day as it was a way of keeping warm. Ideas, gossip, even writing whole books took place in the cafés. After the war, there was a gradual retreat into private life. Meanwhile a few families tried to revive the *salons* of pre-war days, but it wasn't the same thing.

There was no general pattern to Maro's stories, and no ulterior motive. No 'I want to explain to you the upper levels of Paris society.' No 'I desperately need to belong, and I think I am doing all right.' On the contrary, there was an implication that although this recent Parisian phase of her life had been enjoyable, it had come and gone. Fantastic, but unlikely to lead to anything further. This made me feel – and nothing else could have carried such weight – that Maro was grounded in a remarkable way. For if she could create and leave behind such social conquests, surely it implied self-confidence?

I'd never come across anyone who knew my world better, or was so capable of cutting it down to size.

We continued to sleep together, knickers on, no sex, as Maro wanted to consult her gynaecologist in London first. Contraceptives were available only from the old man who sold bananas from a cart in the street, but we neither of us dared buy anything from him, not even bananas. So we just lay close in bed, within each other's frontier.

It didn't take long to set up a routine that we've kept ever since: paintings, books, conversation. With regard to painting, we disagreed all along the line, then and subsequently. Maro knew more about art than I did, she said firmly. And being two years younger than her, it's physically impossible for me to catch up.

21

MIGHT JUST AS WELL BE
MARRIED

FROM NOW ON, this account of my parents' relationship involves three other protagonists: myself as a person who was no longer on the same trajectory as the rest of my family; Maro, who was unable to come to terms with my mother; and Maro's mother Mougouch Phillips (as she was then), a feisty person in her own right, in search of a very different role in London from any that my mother could approve of.

Because an underlying trust in my relationship with Maro was there from the start, I underestimated the turmoil we caused among the older generation. I thought our affair was none of their business, so I did not take their views seriously. I was sixteen and Maro eighteen, and I did not understand that to accept publicly our identity as a couple was like removing a snail from its shell with a toothpick, where the shell stood for the conventions and the snail was us. The crazy thing was that these conventions were ostensibly liberal, freedom-loving and tolerant towards transgressions of any kind. So what was so hard to accept about our being together? When it came to affection between two people of the opposite sex, no couple ever kept things simpler than Maro and myself.

I remember meeting Mougouch for the first time as soon as we'd come back from Greece. For some reason I stayed the night at her house in Chapel Street instead of going back to Loudoun Road. As my pyjamas were dirty, I borrowed one of Maro's nightgowns. This caused a sensation when we came down to breakfast the next morning.

Mougouch was at this point in her early forties, a beautiful woman, self-confident and extremely social. She was born Agnes Clara Magruder, the elder daughter of a high-ranking officer in the US Navy. On her father's side she descended from some unruly MacGregors who'd come to America with Lord Baltimore in the 1640s. Her mother's maiden name was Hosmer. That branch of the family had emigrated even earlier. (There's a Farmer Hosmer who appears in the lives of Thoreau and Emerson on Walden Pond.)

Mougouch's childhood, spent in various naval stations all over the world, had given her an ease with travelling, even a certain restlessness. When hardly older than twenty, she'd married a penniless Armenian artist called Arshile Gorky, who'd committed suicide in 1948. They'd had two daughters: Maro, and her younger sister, Natasha. Mougouch's second husband, from whom at this point she was in the process of obtaining a divorce, was Jack Phillips, a Bostonian aristocrat (if America has aristocrats) by whom she'd had two more daughters, Antonia and Susannah.

Since Gorky's death, Mougouch's life had been one of adventure, partly driven by anger against her late husband for having left her so violently. Jack Phillips was everything that Gorky hadn't been: at ease, confident socially and relaxed about his work, which involved architectural projects with frequent meals out. Maro once described him as an 'interval' in her mother's life. She took down a photograph album of their travels through Europe after Gorky's death and there was Mougouch, washing pans by a stream, filling the car radiator from a watering can with her children huddled in a corner. She's by the seaside, stripping, and she doesn't look up. She comes back from the waves and puts on a shirt, and now she realizes that Jack is

taking a photograph. Then she looks at the camera and smiles brilliantly. 'There,' said Maro, 'she's ready for somebody else.'

On that morning in Chapel Street, the first thing I noticed at
breakfast was the scrubbed oak table beneath the cutlery. It had an
indented texture produced by washing with bleach every few days
– so they told me. I'd never seen anything like it. Outside the kitchen
where we ate (there was no dining room), the hall was freshly carpeted
and painted, for the family had only moved in a few months earlier.

Mougouch had a sense of irony, and seeing me sitting next to her
daughter dressed in a nightie certainly made her laugh. In a whispered aside, she checked with Maro about how far we'd 'gone', and
since the answer was 'not yet', she could settle down and watch the
development of our harmless friendship; or even participate in it.

I don't remember the reverse introduction when Maro met my
parents, but from the start it ran into trouble.

The first thing Maro told Mum was that she'd decided to go to
the Slade and study art, not to London University to study French
philosophy as she'd originally intended. Since places were usually
assigned in June and we were now in September, my mother thought
this was sheer arrogance. 'It's not so easy to get into the Slade,' she
said. 'I know that Eliza Hutchinson had to work frightfully hard.
You can't just present yourself expecting the doors to open for you,
just like that.'

But Maro had worked hard in Paris. She had two books filled
with drawings she'd made in the room of Tanagra miniatures in the
Louvre, plus a portfolio of nude studies made at the Académie Goetz,
plus a thirty-page illustrated fairy tale of delicately veiled sexuality.
Eduardo Paolozzi, a friend of Mougouch, looked them over and gave
her a letter of recommendation. She already had a generic letter of
approval from Christian Zervos, the editor of *Cahiers d'Art* and the
publisher of Picasso's catalogue raisonné, written to help her gain
admission to provincial museums when she'd gone to Greece with

Beatrice. Off she went and knocked on that door. She was immediately accepted.

My mother discounted what Maro had actually produced and saw only the machinations of Mougouch, whose progress she'd been following for a couple of years. Hadn't someone told her that Mougouch had had an affair with Eduardo? Mum should have suppressed this thought, but unfortunately she couldn't. Maro getting into the Slade soon became evidence of the intrigues of Chapel Street, in contrast to the integrity of Loudoun Road. If you'd told Mum, But your son has been at the Slade for the last two years because Bill Coldstream is an old friend of Stephen's, she would have said, 'That's different.'

Mum should have asked to see Maro's work. She couldn't, because she understood nothing about art. She wouldn't even have been able to bluff. 'That's a particularly fine one,' would have been beyond her. Besides, this would have encouraged Maro to take a step away from Chapel Street towards Loudoun Road; and, from the first, I think Mum instinctively felt that the two houses represented irreconcilable opposites. Loudoun Road, set in leafy and intellectual St John's Wood, full of writers and musicians, was serious. Chapel Street, in the lee of the great wall surrounding Her Majesty's garden at Buckingham Palace, was not.

St John's Wood signified intellectual creativity, whereas Belgravia stood for the pedantry of embassies. Once, Susannah and Antonia had a fight, at the end of which they threw each other's knickers out of the window. A gentle breeze took one pair over to the Embassy on the opposite side of the street, where they landed in front of a policeman. He collected them all and brought them back. 'Oh, *thank* you, officer,' said Mougouch. 'Can I offer you a slice of cake?'

Seeing that Maro and Eliza would be starting out at the Slade together, Mougouch gave a tea party at Chapel Street so they could meet. Mum came too. At a certain point she started to hold forth, mainly for the benefit of Eliza, about the virtues of a new pianist who was then all the rage. Mum said that one listened to him with curiosity because his dynamics were 'counter-intuitive'. He played loud when you expected soft, and vice versa. This was the wrong way of obtaining the attention of the audience, she said.

Mougouch wandered silently among the tea things and I saw that she was being left out. She had no knowledge of music and she didn't know what Mum was talking about. And my mother went on and on. Suddenly, Mum realized she'd been excluding Mougouch. This had not been her intention, but she didn't know how to get out of it. She faltered. When Mougouch changed the subject abruptly, Mum was left high and dry. Mougouch's choice of a new subject was crushing: the garbage situation in Russia.

Maro and me shortly after we'd met.

I thought about this ridiculous incident for ages. Mum was a more serious person than Mougouch, probably. The atmosphere of

Chapel Street was elegant rather than hardworking. Mum had been doing her best to be friendly – but there'd also been an element of bluff, of showing off in front of Eliza. And she hadn't been able to fall back on a joke. She should have said, 'What IS the garbage situation in Russia?'

My father couldn't exactly disapprove of our affair, since he believed that sexual freedom was the first of all freedoms. He took me out for a serious talk, which started by his saying that if he'd met an attractive girl when he was sixteen, his life might have turned out very differently. This was irrelevant, so I let him say whatever he wanted and just murmured, from time to time, 'Yes.' He also said, 'Don't lose touch with your generation,' which was a reasonable point to make.

To my mother, however, the question involved parental authority. I'd come back with a girl one day, and moved in with her – when I wasn't at school – without waiting for the permission of my parents. There was something wrong somewhere.

I remember driving down to Bruern with my parents about a month after coming back to England. I watched my mother's face in the driving mirror over many miles. She was wearing full make-up, including dark-red lipstick that made one side of her mouth curl higher than the other. My mother's smile was always higher on one side than the other, and to see it backwards in the mirror exaggerated its reproving quality. Evidently she was giving herself a speech, as from time to time she shook her head in tense little tremors. No doubt she thought she was being good, because she wasn't speaking, but her feelings were as obvious as if she'd shouted at me every inch of the way.

Michael Astor had heard obliquely that I was with Maro, and he was curious. That seemed odd. Then I remembered there'd been a moment when he'd wanted to marry Mougouch. The first I'd ever heard of Maro's family was a year before, in Mum's Jaguar driving to school one

Monday morning. When we were outside Caxton Hall, near Telfer's Hot Meat Pie stand that was always parked there for the cab-drivers, my mother said to Dad, 'We must do something about Mrs Phillips.' Mrs Phillips was a new friend of Michael's; and, one never knew, after his divorce from Barbara, she might end up as the new Mrs Astor.

On 26 September 1961, a mere month after we'd met, Dad wrote to Reynolds: 'Matthew and his girl keep on turning up. In a way I am a bit worried because although beautiful and perhaps intelligent, she is extremely pretentious.' He was worried that Maro was telling me too many home truths about my painting. On the other hand, 'I dare say he could be got out of his self-absorption by someone who attacked him violently and whose problems he had to make his own.' In the face of Maro's attacks, 'Matthew stands up for his views.' All this chaos was tiresome, however. 'In fact, they might just as well be married.'

I didn't see Maro's straightforward qualities as pretension. Wasn't it self-confidence? She spoke three languages and had read extensively in all of them. At the French Lycée, she'd earned her baccalauréat with a 'Prix d'Encouragement', which was not bad, considering she'd come from Italy speaking no French at all just three years previously. All this counted as naught, because from my parents' point of view Maro didn't treat the older generation with respect. But it was this very quality I most admired. She wasn't in awe of anyone and she didn't mind going out on a limb. She had no secrets, nothing was disguised and she always said what she felt.

If someone had compared the address books of Natasha and Mougouch at the time, 70 per cent of the names would have been common to both. For some reason this divided them rather than bringing them together.

Mougouch was a woman of style. In that respect, even though the competition was of a high level, Chapel Street won hands down over Loudoun Road. My mother's William Morris wallpaper couldn't compete with the crisp eggshell white, top to bottom, of Chapel

Street. Mougouch's bedroom had silk wallpaper, it's true, but only because Wolfgang Reinhardt had given it to her after their season of love. Apricot silk. Perfect, except for a fist-shaped dent where her husband Jack had punched it during one of their quarrels. Every other wall was white to bring out the paintings. Where Dad had prints from the cancelled plates of Picasso's etching for Ovid's *Metamorphoses* going up the staircase – fabulous, well worth looking at, as the cancellations added to the images – Mougouch had works by Matta and the two highly worked drawings that Giacometti had given her in 1949. And Gorky's paintings. And more drawings by Gorky, hundreds of them, in fat portfolios under the bed in the basement, with not even a sheet of tissue-paper between them.

Loudoun Road was crammed full of art, and my father looked at what he owned constantly and thoughtfully. His taste, however, was mainly British. He'd followed the early progress of several painters who'd gone on to have solid careers: Henry Moore, John Piper, John Craxton, Lucian Freud, Francis Bacon, Frank Auerbach; and in the Sixties, David Hockney and Ron Kitaj. What he said about them showed great shrewdness, of a kind that could never be used in a presentation of these artists, because these thoughts came from the inside. Of Auerbach he said: 'It's refugee art, isn't it? Frank will never get out of bombed Berlin.' Of Henry Moore: 'It's such a shame the Arts Council gave Henry all that bronze. He's much better when he carves stone, because it puts up a bit of a resistance.' (This implies that Dad understood the role of the Arts Council in making Moore into an official artist.) Of Bacon: 'I can see what Francis means when he says that abstract art risks becoming "decorative", and that figurative art risks becoming "illustration". But making decoration and illustration into opposites can only mean something to Francis himself.'

'It's such a relief that Francis has turned out to be a success,' he said when Bacon was taken up by the Marlborough Gallery. 'Because he'd make a truly terrible failure.' This was an extremely loaded observation. My father endowed the concepts of success and failure with almost mystical qualities.

All these remarks, made as we stood in front of the works of painters before they became famous, were treasured by me and added to a small cache of things I thought about constantly. And yet in spite of this, Chapel Street knocked me out in a way that Loudoun Road never did.

At Loudoun Road, there was a sunken fosse outside the dining room, and ferns grew out of the cracks of the stonework and the atmosphere was dense, as much as could be seen through the iron bars to keep out the burglars. Ferns, and in the spring white flowers that nodded like tender bells, utterly Victorian, the fluttering spirits of so many dead babies. Chapel Street instead was scrubbed oak, not polished mahogany with Mum in the background worrying about the scratches. Chapel Street was light and airy, and on top of the physical beauty of the house, there was life-style, and the two were separable, leaving the beauty like a powerful bass line underneath the daily squabbles of a female environment. Her house offered the perfection of its taste without worrying about whether or not Mougouch was a serious person. The one serious element was the collection of *Cahiers d'Art* that Gorky had accumulated with such difficulty in New York in the Thirties, and many of the illustrations in these books had paint marks round them, and some had quick neat sketches in the margins, so that these were lessons, wordless and persistent, the example of dedication in poverty, even though all around us shimmered the one word that in Loudoun Road was always conspicuously absent: Money.

Most of all, Gorky's paintings. When I first saw them I had no idea what they were, but I knew they were *about* something. They were abstract, but they were not 'decoration', in the way that Francis meant it. They were lively and ambitious, and they came from an exceedingly remote place. Those canvases by Gorky added a weight that shattered all comparisons between Loudoun Road and Chapel Street. Mougouch was frivolous, so my mother thought. Well, maybe she was and maybe she wasn't. But those paintings were to me as serious and challenging as an unexplored continent.

'But what does Mougouch DO?' my mother shouted at me. I tried to explain how beautiful Chapel Street was. In my innocence, I wanted to make Mougouch sound attractive so that Mum would like her. But we were in the Jaguar driving too fast. (Driving that car brought out her demonic side.) 'Nonsense!' After a couple more traffic lights I told her that she was rapidly approaching the point when I'd have to tell her she was intruding. 'In that case we're rapidly approaching the point where I have to tell you you're a bloody fool.'

Tentatively, I reported this back to Mougouch. She sympathized, at least to the extent that she had no wish to turn my mother into an enemy. 'You should have told her that I bring up four daughters. That's quite enough!' She thought about it some more, took a few steps up and down. 'No, that's the wrong answer. Come to think of it, it's the wrong question! Tell your mother I do nothing, but it doesn't matter. In a hundred years nobody will care two hoots about any of us.'

For some reason this last remark stuck in my mind. It was undoubtedly true of Mougouch. Nobody I've ever met has lived more beautifully in the present tense. Society was everything for her. If nobody else was around, she'd dazzle the maid. (I once heard her say to the maid, 'Don't crawl away, you modest little thing, I want to give you some money.') For Mougouch, the past existed as a series of reminiscences, of which she was usually the centre. If she entered into the world of Diderot and Grimm – one summer was spent on whether there was a plot involving these two – somehow their gossip was today's. My father thought instead in terms of the centuries. He imagined that Byron and Wordsworth were colleagues working in other rooms; but the concept of the 'truly great' meant seeing himself as a third person acting within history, and this seemed to me crazy. Mougouch's view connected frivolity with immediacy. I loved her idea that only the present tense is real.

Mougouch and her four children were bound together in existences that were both immediate (what are we doing right now?) and also tremendously long-haul. Till death do us part. But Mougouch didn't care about the usual problems. School? Exams? Insurance? Chapel Street floated by indifferently. There was nothing to stop Mougouch pulling up those tent-pegs and moving on. The world was full of people she could charm. Italy's fun to live in, too. And Spain.

Mum, seeing the frivolity of all this, would have liked to dismiss Mougouch as a social climber of a particularly American kind: a Henry James heroine, perhaps. I'm sure she tried, but there were several difficulties with this interpretation. To begin with, Mougouch had turned down Michael Astor because she'd found him, and that Bruern Abbey of his, boring. This suggested that gold-digging was not a priority. Secondly, Mougouch's own background was sufficiently assured for her to sweep aside questions of status. There was even a real Henry James connection, come to think of it, proved by a first edition of a book by William James, Henry's brother, dedicated to Mougouch's great-aunt Marion Hosmer. It lived in the front hall on a shelf next to Max Ernst's *Une Semaine de bonté*.

Mougouch told me that when Henry James visited her great-aunt Marion, he found it so difficult to talk to her, he just sat there and drank nineteen cups of tea.

She resembled the heroines of Henry James and Edith Wharton in one respect. In fiction of the Edwardian period, the American woman who sets out to conquer England is at first fascinated. She longs to penetrate the mysteries of social behaviour, not just in terms of rank but also in terms of books read, grand houses visited, poems quoted, languages spoken. But there always comes a time – in fiction and in life – when a gale of irritation sweeps through the truly American heroine. She remembers she's a child of the Revolution. With a wilful gesture she shakes off the fusty cobwebs of our windswept isle.

Many of my mother's oldest friends were gathering at Chapel Street, fascinated by the immediacy of her days. It was not a plot. It was life-style. But Mum continued to view Mougouch's conquest of London with the deepest suspicion.

Mougouch herself was flattered by my mother's sense of rivalry, which she took as a compliment to her gifts. She couldn't resist playing up to the idea that I was in love with her, not with Maro – my just punishment for having raved about Mougouch's virtues. She was always prepared to occupy centre stage, and in this case a deliciously wicked role had been conjured up for her by Natasha Spender. 'You can't have him this weekend,' she'd tell Mum, 'I need him for a dinner on Saturday night.' She wasn't above saying this, even when Maro and I hadn't been invited to the said dinner party. My poor mother brooded for decades over social slights such as this.

Back at Liddell's, I volunteered to paint the study I shared with my Canadian room-mate. The housemaster Stephen Lushington had been pleading for years for someone to take on this chore, and he'd been dropping hints that I, with my Slade experience, would be the perfect man for the job. I chose a very small paintbrush, so that what usually would have taken me two hours took two weeks. I also said I'd have to sleep out, because the smell of paint would be bad for my tender lungs. I told him that the nearest house I knew was in Chapel Street, less than half an hour away. OK, he said.

After an afternoon painting a couple of square feet, I'd walk twenty minutes up Victoria Street, buy a bag of chestnuts for sixpence outside Victoria Station and anemones (the cheapest flowers) for a shilling, walk another two hundred yards to Mougouch's front door. It would open. I'd go upstairs and hand her the flowers and she'd say 'Oh, thank you, dear.' A cup of tea and perhaps cinnamon toast in the kitchen and gossip (in Italian) with Franca, the maid. Then Maro and I would sneak downstairs for an hour of love before supper. And more love again afterwards. I don't know where Prep fitted in to the existence of this decadent schoolboy, and sometimes it was an effort to get up in time for prayers in Westminster Abbey next morning at nine.

My mother was furious. She may even have thought of phoning Mr Lushington to complain. He was a nephew of Susan Lushington of

Ockham Hall where she'd retreated in 1940, so she felt he was part of an extended family. If she had, he would have told her with Sufic brevity, 'He's painting my walls.' He knew about Maro already, because she'd come to Liddell's unexpectedly one afternoon bearing a chocolate cake for tea, tied up in white cardboard and dangling from a bow. She'd worn an olive-green suede skirt of her mother's and an original Emilio Pucci shirt and an American Indian turquoise necklace. Liddell's was just coming out of lunch and the boys reeled at the sight of her. A woman! Help! They drew back in two lines on either side, through which she marched without hesitation. 'Who was THAT?' Mr Lushington asked. 'Oh Sir, don't you know?' So our affair had his tacit approval.

Early in May 1962, Dad invited Maro and me to a poetry reading by the young Russian poet Yevgeni Yevtushenko, some of whose poems had recently been published in *Encounter*. We sat in the front row. Yevtushenko's style of recitation was very passionate and he came forward on stage to communicate as directly as possible: the Mayakovsky in-your-face mode. Thus Maro received on the tip of her nose a small bubble of 'poetic spit', as she called it.

After he'd finished, there were questions. This part of the performance rapidly turned sour. Yevtushenko was challenged by several Russians in the audience; and he hesitated. He only recovered later when we all went out to supper at the Café Royal. I remember that for dessert Yevtushenko pointed to a big red jelly wobbling on the trolley of sweets. The colour of my ideology, he said.

'He's a car salesman,' said Maro in the tube going home. 'He has a wide face and bright blue eyes. Anything he says will be believable for a bit.'

Would Yevtushenko have been familiar with *Encounter*? It's unlikely. It was banned from distribution in Russia. Copies may have appeared in the Ministry of Foreign Affairs or the KGB or any other bureaucracy that employed foreign experts, but in the nature of things these bureaucrats would not have spoken to writers.

In conversation with Isaiah and others, my father said that Yevtushenko's position was a difficult one. Isaiah – I hope I'm remembering this correctly – called him 'an operator'. The remark wasn't necessarily critical, although Berlin held a low view of his talents as a poet. He wrote to Stephen, 'as a man of letters Ye. does not exist it seems to me', and my father would have accepted this estimation as Isaiah spoke Russian and he didn't. For all that, Yevtushenko was an interesting phenomenon. The background of these discussions was the constant attempt of Stephen and Isaiah to understand how Russian writers lived their impossible lives. The mere fact that Yevtushenko was in London was hopeful, and the compromises he'd had to make in order to get there, insofar as they were understood, were forgivable.

One of the compromises would have been to file a report for the KGB. Everyone who left Russia was obliged to do so. Care needed to be taken so as not to write anything substantial. Nobody knew if these reports would ever be read. Whereas in the West, writers may have been given a surreptitious push now and again, in Russia, a wrong word could send someone to jail.

From the British point of view, communication was improving, but February 1956, Khrushchev's speech denouncing the crimes of Stalin, to October 1962, when this phase of East–West relations withered as a result of the Cuban Missile Crisis, is more than six years. That's too long. Improvement in the cultural world took place too slowly, and it was always vulnerable to confrontations taking place in the world of 'real' politics.

On 21 May 1962, Maro and I left the Slade early to go to the opening of the first one-man show in London of the American painter Larry Rivers. He'd been teaching at the Slade for almost a term, where Maro had met him. We walked in, and the first thing we saw was a painting about 70 × 50cm, showing an amateurish copy of a packet of Camel cigarettes. We looked at it for perhaps fifteen seconds, then I turned around and asked for a drink. It seemed the best way of avoiding any negative comments. But I was still at school, Maro was at the Slade, and we were juveniles who shouldn't be pretending to be grown-ups.

Behind us stood my parents looking like thunder, Larry Rivers himself and Bill Coldstream. Before anything worse could happen, Bill said, 'We'll go to a pub,' and led us away. Bill knew everything about the Spenders. He'd been married to Nancy, my cousin Philip's mother, before she'd married Michael, Stephen's elder brother. He was one of Wystan's oldest friends and he was an even closer friend of Louis MacNeice. I can't remember what happened at the pub, but we'd been shaken by the grim parental faces and, in an avuncular way, he did his best to lighten our anxiety.

Next day, my father wrote a reproving letter, not to me but to Maro.

I want you to consider whether it is really right or fair to Matthew's school and parents that you and he should behave on his school work days in the way you were doing yesterday . . . If it gets back to the school that you & he spend time when he should be either at the Slade or at school floating round London saying you want drinks, not only will his privileges be taken away, but his housemaster will be made to feel that he has been foolish trusting Matthew . . . We don't want to do anything to interfere with Matthew & you in your relationship but this is not to do with that, but with rather public behaviour which is embarrassing.

The situation was confused. Maro was being taught by Larry Rivers and she had every reason to come to his opening. If I happened to be present, it was incidental, drinks or no drinks. But I detected my mother's anger in all this. When he said, We don't want to interfere with your relationship, he/she meant exactly the opposite. I didn't know about my father's theory of having no will of his own and always doing what his friends told him to do, but I did think: Why is Dad such a weakling?

With Larry Rivers himself, things turned out OK. At that point I'd become the head of a literary society at school, so I could invite people to speak to the pupils. I apologized and invited him to Westminster. He came ten days later, playing a tenor saxophone. Behind him was Gregory Corso. Their performance was intended to shock, and it succeeded. The last straw was when our religious instructor asked Corso what it was like to be a poet in the United States. He replied, 'That's a really creepy question,' and stomped out, followed by Rivers tootling his sax. I could see by their backs that they'd had a good time. They went down the stairwell laughing, and the portrait busts within their marble ruffs did their best to look offended.

That summer, Maro and I went back to John Craxton's house in Chania.

Opposite us lived Kyria Sultana, Craxton's charlady. My first introduction to Maro's view of life took place when we went through Sultana's small wooden door into a walled courtyard filled with old olive oil tins painted blue, filled with herbs and flowers. Her chickens lived on the flat-topped roof of her bungalow where they roosted in boxes or shat on the old and cracked cement. Inside, a vaulted ceiling shielded a long plant that grew from a hole in the floor, bottom left, and curled round and round the room to leave for the open air, top right. It was beautiful. All you had to do to acquire such an object was plant it and wait.

Kyria Sultana served her family, the hopeless but ambitious young nephew and the failing grandparents. Her husband was a customs official but, incontinent and half blind, he wandered among the pots as we sat there chatting and peed in a corner near a verbena, of which she was particularly proud. Kyria Sultana and Maro shared the same archaic convictions. Each and every one of us in life goes through the same trajectory. Through the centuries, the cards are equal. Only some have better luck than others, that's all: some individuals have better luck, some cities, some nations.

She was thrilled to hear that Maro was Armenian. They shared those Turkish centuries in the background. Crete only broke free in 1905 – which at the time was living memory. She and Maro laughed at the harshness of experience and I felt that a whole other room had been opened in my life, without famous names, without success, without careers or social stratifications.

My first attempt to enter their world involved washing the sheets. I put them in a marble tank in the basement of Craxton's house and stamped on them in bare feet, in my knickers, while Maro said 'Hut, hut,' like an Arab herdsman encouraging his camels. Kyria Sultana stood beside her holding a broom, an ecstatic smile on her face.

On 14 October 1962, in the classic pose of a public-school boy after lunch, legs straight out from a leathery armchair, I picked up a newspaper and saw on the front page that Kennedy had threatened Khrushchev with atomic war unless he recalled some ships carrying Russian missiles to Cuba.

I was horrified. I'd paid no attention to the Bay of Pigs fiasco, I had little interest in unilateral disarmament, I'd gone on only one 'ban the bomb' march and I disliked Bertrand Russell. I'd dismissed the subject from my head, for the simple reason that it would never happen. Politicians would never dare take such a risk. Yet here we were, on the brink of the smouldering pit.

For me this was the beginning of the Sixties. I was never an 'easy rider' or a counter-culture protester, but when Kennedy gave his ultimatum I thought: Gambling with the end of the world is dumb, this man should not be in charge of a government. The hero of that dreadful confrontation was never, for me, Kennedy. The hero was plump, occasionally foolish, even though ruthless, Nikita Khrushchev.

This did not mean I automatically supported Russia from that moment on, but it did mean I was an early convert to one of the great illusions of the Sixties: where power is involved, there's nothing to chose between one side and the other. There is just one System, and it incorporates all of them – all the leaders, all the manipulators of manifold destinies. But, for my father and everyone around him, Kennedy was the great white hope of liberal democracy. I could not say to him: Politicians like Kennedy are not fit to wield power. It wasn't serious. Yet the thought refused to fade. It inhibited me from talking to him thereafter about politics.

Decades later, I received confirmation that my gut reaction hadn't been as foolish as I'd assumed. In Venice, I happened to sit next to a diamond merchant who'd formerly worked in the Kennedy administration. I mentioned my reaction to the Cuban missile crisis; and he said Yes, I was right to have been terrified. His job at that time had been to establish an alternate chain of command for all the key government positions, down to forty levels below the President. He told me that Kennedy had prepared his country for a first-strike loss of a hundred million people.

I thought of what Dad had told me about Tom Driberg and asked my stranger in a Venetian restaurant: 'Wasn't there anybody in Washington who could phone Moscow and head things off?' He said, 'No, there wasn't. You'd be amazed how little communication there was at government level. We've been meeting secretly ever since. We need to go through the whole thing again and again and see what went wrong. People on both sides still break into a cold sweat', said the diamond merchant casually, 'at how close we came to ending the world.'

22

A NICE LITTLE NICHE

THE WINTER TERM of 1962 meant getting into Oxford. It was harder for me than for most of my friends in the Upper Sixth because at this point I was confused. My love-life was ahead of those of my friends but my ability to concentrate was shot to pieces as a result.

In those days each college set its own exam. First was Christ Church, which reserved a number of scholarships for Westminster boys. Instead of letting me read up to the last minute, the day before the exams Maro insisted we go to not one but two films, afternoon and evening, in order to make me 'relax'. And I had to smoke a cigar after dinner. Next day, I sat the exam in the gym at Westminster feeling sick. The silence and the race against the clock just seemed silly.

A fortnight later in the interview at Christ Church, they asked me if I'd accept a place instead of a scholarship. One of the dons was yawning. He'd probably been up all night glossing Euripides. Another seemed to have been felled by a catatonic depression. I looked round and decided I didn't like any of them, so I said, 'No.'

Stephen wrote in his diary:

Suddenly I realised that I wanted him very much to go to Oxford, that it is an élite, that his friends Conrad Asquith and Philip Watson are going there, and that if he doesn't he will be left behind by the best members of his own generation. I felt this specially driving into Chipping Norton to get the Sunday papers. It is a thought that runs contrary to my principles and even my sympathies, but I realised that I thought of my Oxford contemporaries as in some way superior beings. Going there makes one enjoy such conversation and exchange of ideas in circumstances of easy companionship and comparative leisure with the best contemporaries of one's generation, during their most formative years.

Next stop was Merton, where we had to stay for three days while we wrote our papers. Oxford was cold and bells rang all around us every fifteen minutes. It was a bad winter and heaps of snow turned black with diesel fumes stood endlessly on the pavements, like the grotty graves of scholars. A neurotic boy kept me up all night saying how miserable he was in Scotland. In the interview, I said that I wanted to become a painter and they said, 'Why not start now?' The Scottish lad got a scholarship, I flunked.

In the car driving down the Haymarket, Dad told us that I had to concentrate on getting into Oxford. I said I wanted to become a painter. He lost his temper. We got out of the car and Maro tried to quench my hot tears as I blinked up at the billboards of Albert Finney starring as Martin Luther in John Osborne's play.

Third stop, New College. By this time my father was in a turmoil. I was not to say that I wanted to paint. I was to say I was very interested in English Literature. 'You have to show them that you'd be a nice person to teach.' Freddie Ayer was asked to coach me in how to take an interview. He was kind. He was also having an affair with Mougouch at the time, which meant he was interested in the situation. He told me to keep eye contact and answer clearly – it really wasn't all that difficult.

At my New College interview I was asked by John Bayley what I thought of Walter Pater, and I could manage an answer. I could 'burn with a hard and gem-like flame', at least on that occasion. Finally, I was offered a place.

By this time it was mid-January 1963. I felt humiliated. My mother had obviously arranged what she used to call 'a three-line whip of friends'. What was the point of proving oneself on these terms? Maybe I should have failed five straight exams from December until May by waving my paintbrush in front of those carbuncular professors?

The offer of a place came with a proviso: Matthew must do something about his languages. My mother devised a plan to send me to France to improve my French. I avoided taking a decision and hid with Maro in a flat near Barons Court that she'd just moved into, sharing with Bimba MacNeice and Eliza Hutchinson. Bimba was the daughter of Louis MacNeice, so she was part of the brigade of poetic offspring. It was a great flat. Bimba's room was wedge-shaped, like the prow of the ship about to sail out of London towards the West Country. Food, conversation, books, sex. Unfortunately, I didn't bother to tell my mother that's where I was. I'd assumed she knew. It wasn't hard to guess. I made a wooden bed for the Pirelli mattress Maro had just bought and painted a small canvas of the roofs of the Queen's Tennis Club outside the window.

At the end of January, my father wrote a savage letter to Mougouch.

'I feel I simply must consult you about money. Since Matthew left school I have left his income exactly as it was, namely one pound per week.' He was prepared to subsidize my stay in France as soon as it materialized. But 'as far as I can make out he is living as before in the flat of Maro . . . We have never been told by him that he intended living there, or living separately from us. If he had wanted a room alone we would have been understanding about it and helped him to get one. But I don't see how we could have financed this arrangement.'

If they intended to live together, he wrote, then Matthew and Maro should pay their own way. 'It might be quite good for them if they are going to cohabit to realize what the responsibilities of doing this are – that they should support themselves.' Matthew ought to be in the South of France by now. 'I am just not going to pay for situations which are presented to me as faits accomplis.'

Here again I hear my mother's voice speaking through my father. Left to himself he would have realized he was being absurd – an Uncle Alfred complaining about the youth of today. But if my mother complained enough, he'd give in and become a funnel for her anger.

Twice, my father wrote that Mougouch was not to show this letter to us, but she ignored these instructions and handed it over to Maro with one of her grand gestures: make of this what you can. Maro merely read it and put it away. She took it as a straightforward message from Natasha: my mother didn't want us to live together.

I wondered if I hadn't hit upon the one thing that would irritate my parents: domestic bliss. If I'd run away to Buenos Aires with a sailor, my father would have understood. If I'd begun to hang out at the Colony Room with Francis Bacon and drink all night, he'd have sympathized, because this was the 'lower depths', and therefore creative. If I'd starred in a porno movie shot in a cellar in Soho, he would have been secretly amused, because it would have reminded him of his experiences around the docks of Hamburg when he was young. But happy straight coupledom? No, not that!

At the time I didn't know about Dad's obsession with Rimbaud's 'derangement of the senses', but I knew that he hated property and was helpless domestically. The difference between us wasn't trivial. There was some world-view involved. He thought that art needed a state of permanent unsettlement. I thought – we thought – that houses had their own needs and virtues, so did the streets, and also and more serenely the beaches. Art was in there somewhere, not an inevitable by-product of tidiness but as the flowering of analogy among objects that felt happy with their own weight.

In 1962, the *World Marxist Review* published an article by Ernst Henri entitled 'Who Financed Anti-Communism?' He revealed that the financial backers of the Congress for Cultural Freedom were the Ford Foundation and the United States government. This first article prompted the Irish diplomat Conor Cruise O'Brien to write a hostile review of the 100th number of *Encounter*. From this moment on, my father's relationship with *Encounter* became increasingly equivocal.

On one of my father's visits to New York at that time, Jason Epstein warned him about the rumours that were floating around in the wake of these articles. The CIA is involved in your life, he said, as tactfully as possible. As Epstein told me recently: 'All your father said was, "Oh," in that way of his.'

They were having lunch at the Périgord restaurant, just a couple of blocks from the office of the Farfield Foundation. This entity, owned by Julius Fleischman – his friends called him Junkie – was one of the official backers of the Congress for Cultural Freedom. Many New York intellectuals were sceptical. 'We strongly suspected that the Farfield Foundation, which we were told supported the Congress, was a filter for State Department or CIA money,' as Diana Trilling later put it. The title of a book of her essays, *We Must March My Darlings*, suggests that Diana was cheerfully cynical about left-wing politics.

After lunch, Stephen walked uptown to the Farfield office and talked to Jack Thompson, the man in charge. He was told that there was no truth whatsoever in the rumours. Then Stephen strolled back down to Epstein's offices and told him what Thompson had said. And that, Epstein told me, was the end of the story.

Epstein liked Spender. 'A sweet man, and very bright.' All the same: 'I always thought that he couldn't have been *that* innocent.'

Jack Thompson had been an instructor at Columbia University. He was an expert on prosody and a friend of Robert Lowell. Then Lionel Trilling, Diana's husband, obtained a job for him at the Farfield Foundation. It's confusing – if I may cut a long story short. Trilling was supposed to be the great liberal critic of his time, yet many of the neo-cons of the future came from his circle.

I am not a conspiracy theorist and my book can do nothing to calculate the damage done by the CIA's plot to turn world culture into an instrument of American foreign policy. I am very interested, on the other hand, in the question of who knew what at any given time, because this is a social question. In the USA, the plot involved the universities, the literary journals, the directors of foundations and congresses, the theatre world and the art world. How much was known, or at least guessed, in New York at that time? At those cocktail parties, did everyone know what position his neighbour represented? Was there some overlap between the intellectuals and the intelligence services, as there was in London?

When the American Committee for Cultural Freedom was in one of its perpetual crises about money, its Chairman Norman Thomas was overheard to say, 'Don't worry, I'll ring up Allen.' Meaning Allen Dulles, head of the CIA. A thousand dollars arrived in the post soon afterwards – perhaps not from CIA funds, for Dulles was a rich man and a personal friend of Thomas since their university days. Diana Trilling thought the money came from the CIA, 'but none of us, myself included, protested'.

I asked Jason Epstein whether anyone in New York knew Cord Meyer, the man within the CIA who was in charge of cultural affairs. Meyer had begun his career admirably, working for three years with the United World Federalists to consolidate world peace by creating an agreement between the United States and Russia. Only when he realized, at the San Francisco Conference of 1948, that the Russians were using these meetings for the purpose of propaganda did he change his mind. (It was a trajectory similar to that of Christopher Mayhew in England at the same time.)

Epstein spoke to me as if Meyer was someone he'd occasionally talked to, but I had the impression that they did not share the same common ground as existed among a similar circle of people in London. All power in England, political cultural and financial, is concentrated in the capital, but in the United States there's New York and there's Washington and the usual social overlap is not so frequent. However sympathetic Meyer may have been, he was not accessible. Yet, although Epstein's sense of outrage at the manipulation of culture has, if anything, increased over the years, his sense of recrimination for those personally involved has diminished. The problems of government are huge. Those in charge do the best they can. 'He himself I am sure was a well-meaning, rather simple-minded guy, as I understand it. He must have thought he was doing something useful, the CIA . . . I can see why he might have done it innocently, without thinking it through.'

Back in London, my father wondered whether he shouldn't resign from *Encounter*. The 100th issue would provide the perfect occasion – with a cover made for it by Henry Moore, obtained by Stephen. Instead, an alternative financing was arranged through Cecil King, the newspaper magnate. Both editors stayed in place; and King got on well with Lasky. Meanwhile Stephen encouraged his friend Frank Kermode to take over his own role.

I remember that at one Sunday lunch in London at this time Richard Wollheim asked my father who actually paid for *Encounter*. 'Well, that's the mysterious thing,' was Dad's answer. The backing had been found by Malcolm Muggeridge. 'Of all people,' said Dad. Muggeridge was an eccentric author who'd become passionately anti-Soviet during a trip to Russia in the Thirties, where he'd witnessed an artificial famine in the Ukraine created to force peasants into collective farms. 'Malcolm just said, "Leave it to me," and in a matter of days, there the money was.' My father told this as a funny story of no consequence.

Richard Wollheim was a man of powerful but unpredictable opinions. For instance he loathed Parma and adored Padova – or perhaps it was the other way round. He was head of the Philosophy Department at London University, his political views were usually to the left, he'd worked in Field Intelligence in the war and he was fascinated by the *Encounter* story. At this dramatic moment, he also was asked if he'd like to become a co-editor with Stephen. He looked through the accounts and turned the job down. Years later, I tried to ask him about it. He just smiled. We were out of England by then. He looked around our garden surrounded by olive trees and said, 'It makes a lot of sense.' When I asked him what he meant, he just nodded and smiled and said, 'Just take it from me, it makes a lot of sense.'

Painting a landscape in the style of Cézanne at the
Château Noir, 1961.

In the middle of February 1963, I went off to the South of France with Conrad Asquith, who'd landed a place at Christ Church in hurdle one. We planned to live in Marseilles.

At lunch at Chapel Street shortly before we left, Paddy Leigh Fermor asked whether we knew what we were letting ourselves in for in choosing Marseilles. What if we were accosted by some 'Apaches'? I said I didn't know what an Apache was. 'Come on, Mougouch, let's show Matthew how an Apache gets his girl.' They stood up, Mougouch perhaps reluctantly. Paddy tipped out the bread from a wickerwork basket and put it on his head, tilting it forward so that it covered his eyes. Then he stuck a fag on his lower lip and turned to Mougouch: 'Viens, môme!' He started pulling her this way and that. 'Gently, Paddy,' said Mougouch laughing. 'You're going to break me.' I thought: An Apache routine would be unthinkable at Loudoun Road, and yet Mum thinks of Paddy as one of her oldest friends.

Marseilles turned out to be cold and hard, so we found a room outside Aix-en-Provence at the Château Noir, a big house once used as a studio by Paul Cézanne. The surrounding landscape still held many reminders of paintings by Cézanne: the pine outside my bedroom window, the shimmering trees going up the hill to the quarry of Bibémus, where he'd also painted. I tried to emulate Cézanne: green on green with short sharp strokes, sitting in a path among the pines where the sunlight never kept still. I'd be joined by our landlord, who pretended he was Cézanne's illegitimate son. Once he looked over my shoulder and said, 'Ouai, les Anglais sont toujours bon à faire les épinards.' The English have always been good at painting spinach.

Maro came out for Easter. I abandoned Cézanne and painted two large cheerful images of her in the style of Matisse. We moved to another room in the same Château Noir, where the tachiste master Tal-Coat had worked two years previously. His paint-marks were still visible on the walls. And M. Tessier, the landlord, brought to our attention the fact that André Masson lived down the road towards Le Tholonet.

One afternoon we walked down to see Masson. A maid opened the garden gate and we saw Masson on a deckchair in the sunlight, reading *Le Figaro*. He got up briskly and came over to greet us. He knew all about Gorky, had met him once, and he looked at Maro with curiosity. I knew nothing about Surrealism at that time. I only wanted to talk to him about Matisse. A shame. Masson was a key figure in Gorky's life, and we hardly knew it.

———————

At Easter my parents appeared.

If at first sight my mother was displeased to see Maro with me, she didn't show it. However, a couple of days later, she said that they'd be driving over to see her old friend Anne Dunn at Saint-Estève. They wanted me to come, but Mum said there wouldn't be room in the car for Maro as well. Maro said: 'But I know Anne very well. We used to go to lesbian night-clubs together in Paris.' Mum smiled as if someone had made a bad joke and ignored her.

This left me with the choice of staying with Maro or going with my parents. Reluctantly, under pressure from my father, I went with them. When we got to Saint-Estève, the first thing Anne said was, 'Where's Maro?' I mumbled that she'd been left behind, because Mum didn't believe they knew each other. Anne said, 'Is this true, Natasha?' My mother just smiled and blinked.

Maro went back to London in my absence. She was upset.

After she'd gone, my parents drove to Maussane near Saint-Rémy, where someone had found a Provençal ruin for sale. They took me with them. Mum fell in love with the house and everything was fine, except I was in a foul mood because I felt she'd made me dump my girlfriend rudely and, for all I knew, definitively. My mother just wanted to talk about her plans for her ruin. She sketched on bits of paper while I tried to get her to admit that she'd behaved badly to Maro. A fight broke out. I remember saying, 'I'll help you build your house, but don't expect me to ever live in it.' Dad just sat there looking embarrassed.

Next morning, Mum behaved as if nothing had happened. My father could afford the asking price of five hundred pounds, so that was that. He called it 'Mum's ruin', as if it was entirely her responsibility. Thus Mum finally acquired the house she'd always wanted – not a honeysuckle-entwined cottage in Oxfordshire with Raymond Chandler in the attic, but an abandoned sheep farm that had once been used for target practice by the Germans.

It was called Fengas, a Provençal word signifying mud. My mother didn't like this, so she called it Mas Saint-Jérôme, and told the postman and the local tax office. She admired St Jérôme, who in paintings is always depicted as working quietly in his study, sometimes with a lion curled up at his feet.

My mother stuck to that house for the rest of her life. In the autumn she'd drive out from London her oldest friends with whom she gathered her olives. Peggy Ashcroft was one. When the property burned down in a fire about ten years after Dad's death, she rebuilt it. I kept telling her that she was too old, she couldn't live alone there anyway, and therefore she should sell it. She paid no attention.

The garden, about which she wrote a book that sold well, measured about seventy yards by thirty. She worked for more hours than I care to imagine on this garden, though the soil was barren and the water source feeble. Into this small space she lavished her love for the gardens of Sissinghurst and Chatsworth and all those other stately homes that she admired so much. She planned an elaborate pathway, and I can hear her voice saying 'and then you turn the corner and you are in the White Walk'. This was five yards of white flowers. And when Dad said, 'What will happen if a pink butterfly perches on a white blossom?', she said without a smile, 'Oh I don't think that will matter, do you?'

She called her shrubs by their Latin names, and they cowered. My father said that whenever shrubs in the local nursery heard they'd been chosen for Lady Spender's garden, they'd start trembling, as if they knew they were destined for a concentration camp. He did not love that house, but he never told her. In summer it was so hot he couldn't work, and it was bad for his heart, but he never refused to go and he pretended he was happy there. That house was his penance, his cure.

When Lizzie and I sold it after her death, a strange thing emerged. The caretaker, a sweet Provençale woman, said that Mum had told her that she'd suffered very much as a child, because her mother had been a gambler who'd lost all her money at the Casino; thus they'd been miserably poor. This was exactly the story of the caretaker's mother. It was a case of Mum trying to show sympathy by telling a lie. When I said, But our grandmother never gambled, the caretaker just gave a little nod. She hadn't believed my mother, because the story was a mirror of her own. She did not hold it against Mum, for she knew she'd lied in order to be friendly. It was a moving example of Mum's capacity to use those different voices that she'd learned in her childhood. Reality could be reassembled to fit the other reality of people's feelings.

After my parents had gone back to London, one evening as I rode my motorbike back up the hill from the bar at Le Tholonet, looking up at the full moon and thinking how beautiful life was, I ran slap-bang into a telephone pole. I was chipped and churned and the bike refused to go up hills after that.

It was a seven-mile walk into Aix for the groceries and seven miles back. Once I was so hungry that when I got home I cooked and ate the entire week's provisions.

The market lay beyond the barracks. The French Foreign Legion had recently been recalled from Algiers. The war was over at last. Tough-looking soldiers stood outside in the street with their hands on their hips, glowering at the citizens of France who'd betrayed them.

Missing Maro, I hitchhiked back to London.

Chapel Street had remained the centre of Maro's existence for some time after she'd moved into St Andrew's Mansions. Then one day Mougouch had said, 'Off you go, dear, back to your little world of Barons Court.' This so annoyed Maro that, indeed, her psychological base switched from her mother's kitchen to St Andrew's Mansions, where a huge map of Europe was hung as a curtain over the window in the kitchen, with 'Greater Armenia' on it, taking over most of eastern Turkey, northern Iraq and western Iran.

I was in London secretly, so I went to a theatrical store and bought myself a big moustache, larger than Hitler's but smaller than Stalin's. I thought it would provide anonymity. One evening we all went to a play. I knew my parents were in the audience, so I hid behind a pillar. Bimba's father Louis MacNeice was also present. When she brought him over to show me in my splendiferous mustachios, he murmured, 'It's nice to see a Spender with a sense of humour.'

For some reason this remark got to me. It was the first time I had an inkling that among my father's generation, among his immediate peers, there were those who did not see him as an eminent figure.

I went back to France a few days later. As I left, Maro took all my cash off me as rent. This was the result of the secret letter that Stephen had written to Mougouch saying we ought to be serious about money. I told Maro that I couldn't exactly swim the English Channel, so she gave back just enough for the boat ticket.

In France, I slept for the first night under the marquee of a wedding in Calais, which I found by mooching about aimlessly in the suburbs; and the second night in an orphanage in Clermont-Ferrand, which I found by asking a gendarme. I was very hungry by the time I got back to Aix.

I went up to New College that autumn.

There's not much to be said about my Oxford career except that it was squalid. I was not depressed, in fact away from Oxford I was very happy, but I knew I wasn't doing my best with the opportunities the university provided. I did not want them. On the other hand I could not do without them. Westminster had given me the appetite. I was in a bad way, because I felt that the opportunity to go to art school had come and gone and that every step I took towards Oxford took me away from art.

From the rooms in the Old Quad that I shared with another student, we looked down on the Mound, an incongruous heap of vegetation surrounded by an immaculately razored lawn. I got into the habit of climbing out of college at dawn to paint a cypress tree in the local cemetery. Over time, the tree withered under my gaze. Back for a quick lunch of beer and a pork pie, a snooze, then at three in the afternoon my academic life would start. I knew how to write an essay. I should have been finding ways to feed this skill imaginatively, but I simply turned it into a vice. I gutted books and wrote my lines and that was that.

I did not join any societies, I did not go to lectures and I did not eat in Hall. Instead, I joined the Ruskin School of Drawing and drew nudes. I read catalogues raisonnés in the library of the Ashmolean Museum, vast tomes with no colour reproductions, but the black and white photogravures had a solidity of their own. The Ashmolean owns the beautiful Piero di Cosimo of a fire in a wood, hung not far from *The Hunt* by Paolo Uccello, among whose dark trees the strident riders reminded me that in Italy nostalgia is not ornamental, it is an attribute of nature.

I studied Japanese prints. I went to the Victoria and Albert Museum and arranged to guide tourists, but the Proctors heard about it and politely told me that I couldn't study at Oxford and earn money in London at the same time. While in the V&A, the Keeper of the Print Room took me to one side and said that I should change from Modern History to Japanese at Oxford and come back to him in three years' time. 'You could carve out a nice little niche for yourself here at the V&A.'

At the end of my first year, I earned an Honorary Exhibition. My essay on Bishop Anselm had apparently made an impression. No money, just a fluttering gown. My friends heard the word 'exhibition' and thought it was a show of my paintings, but these were getting smaller and tighter and more antique by the minute. Meanwhile the cypress tree tilted over on one side and was fenced in by ropes.

In the interest of making us all get on better, I asked Maro to turn off her natural instinct for contradiction whenever we went to Loudoun Road. Couldn't she just sit there and listen, for once? 'I can't,' she said. 'Conversation is supposed to be a ping-pong. But with your parents, it's all ping and no pong.'

One supper during my first year at Oxford, we went there for supper. The other guests were Auden and Freddie Ayer, who'd written a brilliant book on Logical Positivism that neither of us had read.

Auden at table wasn't the easiest of guests. His presence was benign, but he smoked between courses, wasn't interested in the food, and when he spoke he was oracular rather than conversational. On this occasion, he announced that often one pretended to have read a book, even though in fact one hadn't managed to get through it. The worst was to have written a review of a book before reaching the last page. That was 'naughty'. He liked the idea of rules and morality, and this occupational hazard, which must face all book reviewers – and there were two others at the table – obviously broke an important rule.

'For instance,' he added, 'I never got to the end of *The Alexandria Quartet*, even though I gave Durrell a good write-up.'

Before Freddie or Stephen could say anything, Maro said that the great thing about Lawrence Durrell's novels set in Egypt was the descriptions of the city and the feeling of being a European exile in Alexandria – though he wasn't so good on the subject of the Egyptians themselves.

Then it was Dad's turn. He said he'd never seen the point of Rabelais. 'But have you read him in French?' said Maro quickly. 'The way Rabelais describes food is marvellous, but it doesn't come out so well in English. And anyway, the English aren't interested in food.'

No, said Dad heavily, he had not read Rabelais in French.

Finally it was Freddie's turn. Freddie said that he'd never managed to get to the end of *Don Quixote*. Maro started saying something about the emptiness of the Estremadura and Dad turned to her and said, 'SHUT. UP.' It was so emphatic, the full stop was audible between the two monosyllables.

So Maro shut up. She didn't seem discouraged, though. She'd read the books. The others hadn't. Why shouldn't she have chipped in?

Not long after this, we were having supper at Loudoun Road when the subject of the origins of language came up. Before anyone else could say anything, Maro said that the origins of language were obviously onomatopoeic. 'The Chinese word for strawberry will be like the noise of a Chinaman eating a strawberry.'

Unfortunately, one of the guests at table was a professor of philology. He tried arguing. She persisted. He lost his temper. Nothing was more simplistic or inaccurate than what she'd said. The origin of language couldn't be reduced to the imitation of natural sounds.

Maro backed down, but she happened to be sitting next to my mother. In a kindly but persistent way, Natasha whispered to Maro that if one were sitting at table with a distinguished professor, one really had to pay respect to his superior knowledge. I saw Maro's face begin to crumble. Next minute, she was going to start crying.

Before this could happen, I rose from the table and said I really had to get back to Oxford. I had a train to catch. She and I got up. The professor started to apologize, but I said Never mind I really do have a train to catch, I'm sorry to break up the dinner party, please don't mind us.

In the street, I tried to take my mother's side. Couldn't Maro just keep quiet whenever we went to supper at Loudoun Road? She said, No. Well, couldn't she at least think before she spoke, I said bitterly? 'No,' she said. 'How can I tell what I think until I've said it?'

If that was her attitude, why had she become so upset? If she'd ignored the social customs, she had to take her chances. She said, 'But under the table your mother was pinching me!'

There was no answer to this.

'I can't stand your mother's respect for academics. That professor,' said Maro. 'He was just arguing with the argument. That's what professors do. They squibble. But let's not talk about it any more. I'm so tired, I can feel my eyelids creaking.'

It was a long way back to Barons Court.

'Oh, your mother,' said Maro as we went to bed. 'I refuse to be figged and I refuse to be tossed by her.'

We stayed away from Loudoun Road. It was for the grown-ups to defuse the situation. No incoming calls came through, however. I brooded. Still the telephone kept silent. Was Maro right? Was there something remorseless about my parents?

Many years later, on one of our 'honeymoons', when Dad and I went off together in order to bond in the absence of our wives, I mentioned the strawberry incident. Dad remembered it, and he added a detail which made me posthumously furious, as it were. He said that next day the remorseful professor had sent to Loudoun Road a big bunch of flowers with a letter of apology addressed to Maro.

'Why didn't Mum sent them on?'

'Natasha thought that it would spoil Maro.'

I looked at Dad, dumbfounded. If Mum had stuck to the rules, the flowers would have been received, Maro would have written a note to the professor, and the incident would have been closed. Why hadn't he insisted that Mum send them on? He whose manners were so perfect?

'Yes, I feel very badly about it,' he said, trying to disengage.

These incidents carried a weight out of all proportion to what had actually happened, because my mother always insisted that Maro had to learn from her mistakes. I'm sure that in the eyes of almost anyone, we were behaving badly. We were over-privileged and familiar and casual – I plead guilty to almost any reproof regarding my earlier self. But my mother took the view that we were all of these in relation to standards cast in bronze. It was this faith in her own rightness that made it so hard to talk to her.

Dad came round to Maro in the end.

It happened that one day he complained because someone had sent for publication in *Encounter* several poems written by an Eskimo. What could he possibly know about Eskimo poetry? Maro said, 'But Stephen, surely you know that marvellous Eskimo poem that goes, "Granny, you are too old. It's time we put you on to an ice floe and pushed you out to sea."' Dad almost broke a chair laughing. Maybe it's what he'd always wanted to do with his mother-in-law, Ray.

While I was in Oxford keeping my head down, Bimba took Maro up to Hampstead to meet Bill and Hetta Empson.

My father probably met William Empson in the mid-Thirties through the Mass Observation project, where Stephen's younger brother Humphrey worked – as did the second husband of Inez Pearn, Stephen's divorced wife. Then Empson left England to teach in China, whence he returned shortly before the war. He went back to China to teach at Peking University after the war, and when he returned to London he gave the impression that he'd become a sympathiser of the Chinese Communist Party. Stephen admired and liked him, but there'd been an estrangement that had taken place soon after *Encounter* was founded.

In 1954, at a party given by Louis MacNeice, Bill had cornered Stephen and accused him of having 'taken sides' in the conflict between America and the communist bloc. Stephen explained that he considered that *Encounter* was 'a platform in which American points of view confronted and were confronted by opposite attitudes in other parts of the world'. Bill told him briskly that, if this was his intention, he'd failed. Others at the party tried to defuse the situation. Someone said that Empson was on such good terms with the leaders of the Chinese Communist Party that the wisps of his beard communicated with them directly by radio. The confrontation got worse, and in the end Stephen threw a glass of wine over Empson. Bill was good about it. He said there were so many stains on his suit, one more wouldn't matter. Since then, however, the two distinguished authors had been on 'non-speaks', as the expression of the time had it.

Bill Empson lived in a nimbus of his own, but he didn't insist on deference if he threw out fragments of his thoughts. I remember one afternoon when he tried to convince his son Mogador that what the Chinese really needed was cheap timber for coffins, and he should buy lumber in Canada and set up a carpentry shop. Wearily, Mog waved his hand.

Meals at the Empson house in Hampstead were cheerful mayhem. There was none of the respectful hush that my mother cultivated at Loudoun Road. If what Bill was arguing became too arcane, he spoke to the ceiling and the rest of the table went on rowdily saying whatever came into their heads. Once, Hetta leaned across me and said something particularly intense to Mogador, in Chinese. I asked for a translation. Mog said calmly, 'She's just told me that I'm an unspeakable mountain of shit.'

Hetta was what used to be called 'a free spirit', but the scale of her freedom was so grand it made most other bohemians look shifty. I remember dancing with Hetta once, and soon she was clasping me in a tight clinch. I think this must have been at the Round House at one of those dance-and-poetry readings. I didn't know how to cope, so I said, 'Hetta, not in front of *them*.' She looked over to where a neatly dressed couple was watching us curiously. 'What's the matter?' said Hetta. 'You owe 'em money or something?' I said, No. 'Well then, fuck them.'

With what contempt Hetta cornered one of Bimba's boyfriends and said, 'Don't tell me you're a *Trot*.' In London at the time, to be a follower of Trotsky signified an intelligent approach to communism – but not to Hetta.

I think it was driving in a taxi to another gig at the Round House that Bill leaned across Hetta and tapped me on the knee. Does Stephen know he's working for the Americans? Flustered, I said I wasn't sure. Bill started to expand on this warning, but Hetta interrupted saying he shouldn't interfere. What have Matthew and Maro got to do with it?

I told Mougouch about this strange remark. She said, 'He probably means that *Encounter* is paid for by the CIA.'

'Is that so? You seem to take it for granted.'

'Everybody's known about it for years.'

'Everybody? My father doesn't,' I said. 'So, if I may ask, how do *you* know?'

She puffed at her cigarette. 'Maybe John Gunther told me.' This was a famous journalist of his time, whose 'Inside' books had provided American readers with intelligent observations of countries in Africa and Europe. His wife Jane had known Gorky since the mid-Thirties. 'I can't remember who told me. How funny that Stephen says he doesn't know! I can hardly believe it.' Another puff. 'And Junkie's an old friend of ours.'

'Ours? Junkie Fleischmann is a friend of the Magruders?'

'A friend of my uncle Sidney's,' she said. 'I saw him as a child when I went to Ohio. He's a very friendly person. Everybody liked him out there. And it wasn't a secret, what he was doing. They all said how sweet it was that he enjoyed working for the State Department.'

'What! Your uncle Sidney was a friend of Junkie Fleischmann?'

She told me that her uncle Sidney Hosmer, her mother's brother, came to a sad end in about 1942. He ran away from Ohio to New York and she and Gorky had had to take care of him. He was an alcoholic, 'Wouldn't you know?' And one day he was mugged and ended up in Bellevue among the loonies. She took him a pair of Gorky's pyjamas, for he had nothing – and there was nothing to be done. He died a short time later, still in Gorky's pyjamas.

'Please! So you knew Junkie Fleischman as a child?'

Her father Captain Magruder had resigned from his club at Newport, Rhode Island, because they'd refused to serve his friend Junkie Fleischmann, on account of him being a Jew.

'We all got up in a flurry of dignity and my father said that if Mr Fleischmann was barred, they could do without the Magruder family, too. And so we left. I remember, because I was hungry and I didn't understand why we couldn't eat first.'

I felt dizzy. This was what Maro and I used to call a 'short circuit', meaning one of those moments when her world and my world turned out to be too intimately connected. It always made me uncomfortable. I didn't want us to be all riding along in the same machine.

Maro and I were beginning to feel that our lives were much too dominated by the previous generation, whose mixture of approval or disapproval seemed to have no connection with the high-minded world they were supposed to represent.

A literary party in the early Sixties.

Upstairs, Louis MacNeice chatting to W. H. Auden, who'd asked especially to see him – had telephoned from New York to arrange this supper at Loudoun Road. Wystan had been ready for hours in the piano room before Louis, tall and pale, arrived.

Leaving them to it, we could hear the boom of Wystan's voice from up above, while in the kitchen my mother was being helped with the supper by Chester Kallman, Auden's companion, and Sonia Orwell. Sonia and Chester were both sweet people but they brought out the worst in each other.

'I mean it's become absolutely imp*oss*ible to talk to Louis,' said Sonia, stirring a pot. 'He's comp*lete*ly sold his soul to the BBC.'

And Chester egged her on. He disliked London, where he could appear only as second fiddle to Auden, a role that understandably he detested.

At that moment Louis walked in. He asked for an ashtray.

Of the occupants of that tiny kitchen, was I the only one to feel shame? Was this the dark side of having a reputation? If so, it did not seem worth it.

My father disapproved of Chester. He thought he treated Wystan badly. Indeed, Chester was chronically unfaithful. A story Dad told several times was of sitting in a square with Chester and Wystan, then Chester saw a handsome boy pass by, got up and followed him. Wystan went on talking in a completely normal way, but my father noticed that he was weeping.

Chester knew more about opera than Wystan, at least at the beginning. Chester's advice was essential when Wystan came to write the libretto for *The Rake's Progress*. Thus we have one of the strangest stories of twentieth-century creativity: one genius, Stravinsky, leaning on another genius, Auden, leaning on Chester Kallman – who, loveable though he may have been in many ways, would surely qualify for a World Prize as Broken Reed. Chester didn't believe in heterosexual love. As a result it's absent from *The Rake's Progress*, which is in all other respects a masterpiece.

Dad disliked this opera, and he took it as evidence of Chester's underlying frivolity. In a moment of irritation he said to Wystan, 'You could leave him, you know. There must be plenty of other people who'd love to live with you.' Wystan just shut his eyes and murmured, 'Schluss.' Meaning, the argument is closed.

Yet Chester always got on well with Maro and me. Perhaps we felt a similar unease with London life. We once met him outside a grand cocktail party. 'Hello Maro, hello Matthew,' he said – and we were pleased he'd recognized us, for we didn't see him that often. 'My first instinct in these kind of things is to flee.' For us, the perfect remark.

About a year after I'd been living with Maro, I showed Wystan a poem. It was about the images that went through my head when I was fucking. Since my only love at the time was Maro, showing him the poem was also a provocation.

If I'd expected a comment on our relationship, I was disappointed. He read it through fast, once, and handed it back saying, 'It's a good poem. Ah – perhaps too many hyphenated words; but no, it's a good poem.'

Anyone else would have been thrilled to receive praise from W. H. Auden but for some reason, I wasn't. I'd wanted to hear what was wrong with it, followed by a lecture about what a poem should aim for. To have written a poem that was merely 'good' deflated the whole thing.

Towards the end of the Sixties, Auden began to withdraw into himself. Many forms of social behaviour became harder for him. He could foresee the end of a story long before it arrived, and would start saying 'ya, ya' halfway through. It required persistence to talk through this barrier. You thought that what you were saying was banal, or that he was bored, or both.

My parents did their best to force him to participate. There was one joke which I must have heard Auden tell half a dozen times at the dinner table, encouraged by Dad. It was about Wystan and the sadomasochist. The punchline was, 'I'm no boy scout, my dear. I can't tie knots.'

My mother told me that when they were alone in the house he'd start breakfast with a list of the things he was grateful for. It was a litany he had to recite, she said, before he could face the day. It was almost a prayer.

Wystan's aura of solitude was tempered by his love-thy-neighbourliness, which nearly overcame it, but this was expressed in flashes that were thrown out briefly before he subsided again. Pills and alcohol had worn him out. Uppers in the mornings, downers at night and alcohol in between. He thought of his mind as an engine that needed an engineer. He switched himself on in the mornings and off again at night. The pills were the switches.

His huge mouth gobbling pills, lower lip flapping, elephantine, washing it down quickly, with an air of There, that's that. Now I'm ready. Now I'm done.

'Wystan thinks he's going to live till he's eighty,' said Dad, who'd spoken to Auden's doctor in New York. 'The trouble is, he IS eighty.' In fact, Auden was not much older than sixty at the time.

Among themselves they talked about death as if it was another prize they were all aiming for. I remember Wystan telling Dad, 'My dear, you're the one who'll have the last word. You're going to bury us all.'

23

TRUST

AFTER I'D SPENT six months in France and about a year in Oxford, it became clear that my relationship with Maro wasn't going to evaporate, so my mother decided she had to make friends with her. This was a hard decision, as by that time Maro had accumulated several black marks against herself, socially speaking.

In order to offer Maro her friendship, my mother had to assemble everything she knew about Maro's childhood: her mother's East Coast background; her father Gorky, the famous suicide. This was dangerous territory, as Maro felt very possessive about her past, even though she loved bringing out at the dinner table casual horror stories about her earliest experiences. These were presented with such a flourish, however, that it was impossible to believe this voluble young woman had been in any way traumatized. Or at least not traumatized enough to render her speechless.

One day, at supper when there was just the three of us, my mother said to Maro, 'It must have been a dreadful experience for you to lose your father at such a tender age.' This didn't immediately produce the desired reaction. 'I mean,' she said, leaning towards her, 'poor Maro.'

She stretched out her hand.

'I'm nobody's poor Maro,' said my future wife coldly.

It was a terrible rejection, and it had happened so fast I hadn't been able to stop it.

My mother was coaxing Maro into a role where she, Natasha, could bring out the best in herself. She wanted to show compassion. But compassion is a gift, and if it is offered, it has also to be received. Quick as a flash, Maro had grasped that compassion requires the giver to occupy a higher moral position than the receiver. She was not prepared for that kind of a relationship with Natasha Spender. From her point of view, there wasn't much to choose between my mother, the instructor in table manners who pinched, and my mother, the compassionate prop of the downtrodden.

No, this is unfair.

My mother's patience with those who were in real need was infinite. I can think of at least three people who owe her such a debt for her help that they'll reject with outrage the point of view of my eighteen-year-old self, even allowing for the fact that I feel retrospectively protective about Maro. It's hard for me to be fair to both aspects of Mum's character: my mother as a saver of desperate people, and my mother who had such inexplicable difficulties in forming equal relationships. Except with a few people with whom she worked professionally, like Peggy Ashcroft, she wasn't at ease with the idea of equality. There were those whom she admired unconditionally: the 'absolutely alpha' kind of person, as she'd put it. And there were those whom she could help.

After Maro had refused so bluntly the role of victim, my mother was placed in a quandary. It was very hard for her to think of a role which did not involve compassion. Sacrifice, especially self-sacrifice, stood at the very centre of her values, not just as a gift from her to another but also as a spiritual aim for herself.

After several months spent brooding about this rejection, my mother found the victim she needed in this story. Unfortunately, it was herself. She decided that Maro and 'her crowd' were against her. Though occasionally there were better moments thereafter, my mother was never able to revise this interpretation. Maro was against

Maro and me in our student years.

her – and it wasn't just a question of personal incompatibility. Maro had rejected the underlying Christian ethics on which the principle of compassion rests. There must be something 'unspiritual' about her. Maro's mother was also against her. I, her son, was against her. I had been corrupted by the conspiracy whose one aim was directed against her.

This predicament was solidified for all time two years later, when my mother told Maro that Mougouch, her mother, was responsible for the death of her father. Maro could say such a thing – and often did, directly to her mother's face – but it wasn't for other people to intervene.

'Natasha,' said Maro ominously, 'what do you know about it?'

'And what do *you* know about it?' said Mum, implying that Maro was floating frivolously on a cushion of lies.

There was something mad about it. My mother wanted to be compassionate, and this led her to say the one thing that was the absolute negation of compassion. The extraordinary thing is that whenever my mother delivered one of these supposedly 'objective facts', she felt much better for it afterwards. Next morning she'd have forgotten that she'd said anything wrong. The rest of us would just have to bleed and pass the breakfast cereal.

I never was able to find a way out of this predicament. If I'd been tremendously wise, I suppose I might have fixed things. But in the back of my mind there was always my father's remark – quoting Anna Freud, no less – that any attempt to unravel Natasha Litvin could end up disastrously.

And decades later, Maro's daughters were against their grandmother.

A few years before my mother died, at a lunch I gave, the guest of honour asked Mum politely, 'And do you see your grandchildren often?' Mum said: 'Well, as they were brought up in Italy, the answer is no, not very often.' At this point our daughters had been living in London for more than half their lives. Fifteen years had passed during which Mum could have made friends with them. But I bit my tongue and said nothing.

In the summer of 1964, Maro, Mougouch and I set off to drive down through Yugoslavia to Athens and take the ferry to Crete.

Things began well. In Calais we picked up a brand-new Volkswagen Beetle with export number-plates, and off we went. Gripping the wheel, Mougouch said happily, 'This is such a *tight* little car.' Running away always brought out the best in her.

In Dubrovnik Maro and her mother had a flaming row, of an intensity I'd never seen before. They were accusing each other of the most horrendous crimes. I thought that I must be involved, as both parties kept appealing to me – for what? I was out of my depth.

I told them next morning that I would take the boat to Athens, and they could get on with their whatever-it-was without me. It was an irresponsible decision, but meekly they took me to the docks

308

and waved me off. They drove on through Albania, subdued, and with no more fights; and luckily they were not molested on the way.

I met them in Crete in a village twenty miles west of Chania. We found a hutch on the beach of Platanias, two villages further along. After Mougouch left, Maro and I bought paint and painted our hutch inside and out and the whole village watched in awe, knowing that we'd only be living in it for a month.

In the local café, Maro and I had a conversation which changed my life. She said that I treated her as if deep down I believed that men were superior to women, and that my thoughts on history were more important than her female concerns with day-to-day living. The accusation was true. That's exactly what I did think. I vowed to reform. The big trees with whitewashed trunks fluttered all around us as the clients of the restaurant came and went, and the bottles of retsina piled up between us, and the more the bottles accumulated the righter she became.

This change in my personality was partly a tribute to my parents. I'd seen from their example that a pianist could work in one room and a writer could write next door; and they were equals. Years later I realized that if I'd been thinking of Stephen and Natasha, nothing could have been further from the truth. My father, deep down, put performing musicians in the same category as actors: however good they were, they did not dwell in the world of the imagination. They just dressed up in other people's clothes. I understood that, to my father, Mum had never been his equal, because what she did was interpretative, not creative.

My father placed a very high value on the creative act. He believed in the 'vision' – the supreme moment when something wonderful is revealed. This initial spark could dart sideways in several directions: into a poem or a painting or a sculpture or a piece of music. It was the moment of revelation that mattered. The reader or the listener or the onlooker had to search for this kernel in the work of art. Everything that got in the way, including errors of the artist

309

himself (ungainly sentences or 'filling-in' painting or banal har-monies), could be ignored as long as the 'vision' was understood.

In many ways I still admire this point of view, because it does away with questions of taste. It's the opposite of the aesthete who lingers over some particularly fine detail hidden away in the bottom left-hand corner of a painting. But was he right or was he wrong? The idea that all artistic disciplines spring from the same initial spark has become an obsession that has lasted all my life. I've tested it personally: the language of sculpture, of painting, of writing a book, even of composing – or at least of arranging – a piece of music. Without saying that Dad got it wrong, I can only say that in my experience each discipline is different, and the body responds accordingly as the thing is made.

The fight in Dubrovnik was the first time that I'd come up against the constant drama that existed between Maro and her mother regarding Gorky's death. I had no idea how to handle it at the time, which is why I'd run away. Indeed, I didn't even know the story. It was only later, patiently over many years, that I became a kind of shock-absorber between two women who otherwise often looked as if they were going to tear each other to pieces.

Maro took up her father's cause with a constancy that never wavered. It didn't stop her from loving her mother, but, as she frequently put it, even to Mougouch herself, 'I love her, but I don't like her.' She wasn't motivated by revenge, and it wasn't neurosis, and it wasn't really an unresolved trauma. It was ideological. Maro thought Mougouch was responsible for Gorky's death, and that she should admit it and say she was sorry.

Losing her father when she was only five years old had had the effect of turning Maro into an adult even at that early age. She'd been rejected; for suicide is also rejection. She disapproved of her father's rejection. He should not have taken that step. That closed the subject. (Perhaps, having grown up so young, she kept alive some part of her five-year-old self. It would explain her lack of awe and the absence of censorship between what she thought and what she said.)

Yet if her father was dead, her mother was still alive. Mougouch also was responsible. As Maro put it brilliantly to me one evening, 'There are two sides to Van Gogh's ear.' She meant that Gorky was wrong to have hanged himself, but that Mougouch was also wrong to have pushed him into taking that step.

Her mother was damned if she'd ever apologize to anyone about anything, least of all about *that*. When Mougouch was feeling confident, she was actually proud of what had happened. She'd found a penniless artist stuck in a rut, a middle-aged follower of Picasso, and she'd inspired him to take a great leap forward in his art and 'flower' into a genius – greater than anyone in the generation that followed, because his love of paint was greater. But he'd betrayed her trust and, as a result, she'd abandoned him. And then he'd killed himself.

Trust was a key word in this interpretation: 'I couldn't trust him.' The question of 'trust' revolved around a key incident that had happened a few weeks before Gorky died. Mougouch, stressed beyond endurance by her husband's state of depression, escaped for a brief weekend of love with the great Surrealist painter Matta. When she came back, Gorky was ominously silent about her escapade. She could not 'trust' him to think she had been forgiven.

There were moments when she felt crushed by guilt. She'd created, with the help of Gorky, an edifice of beautiful paintings, and then she'd destroyed the creator. In the fifty-two years I knew her, she could reveal this face, the face of a guilty woman, but always with a certain bravado. For coequal with her sense of guilt lay her pride, her idea of herself as 'muse'. She possessed the ability to take a man and inspire him to do great things. The power was hers. She, Mougouch, was the prime mover. She herself had always been in charge, from the moment she met Gorky until the day he died. Those paintings were hers. She'd made them. The only difference was that some days she felt proud, some days she felt shame. But she resisted that shame with tremendous energy.

Mougouch believed so strongly in the 'muse' idea that, for her, children were a gift the mother made to her man as a tribute to his masculinity; a peculiar idea, possibly Surrealist. (Matta, for instance, left his wife Ann Alpert when she gave him twins, on the grounds that they were an insult to his testicles. They constituted over-production.) Mougouch's daughters picked up on the fact that they were tender little gifts with no autonomous virtues, and there was a feeling in Maro that went: What was the point of Mougouch giving Natasha and me to Gorky as a tribute to his maleness if then she'd turned around and killed him?

Maro refused to accept her mother's idea that Mougouch was responsible for Gorky's paintings, because it left Gorky in a subordinate role. Her mother had never been in charge. She was not a creative person. She had no idea how to assemble a consecutive thought or draw a line on a piece of paper, let alone paint. Her gifts were entirely to do with taste. She was neither Kali the creator nor Kali the destroyer. She was just a housewife who'd made a mistake.

Maro disapproved of women who sought power through men. This was a matter of principle rather than a critique aimed at her mother. She thought all women suffered from a slave mentality brought about by the simple fact that men were stronger and could, if necessary, beat up their spouses to make them toe the imaginary line. It was not angry enough to become a political ideology. It was merely an observation she made whenever she saw a woman steal a man or manipulate a husband. She shouldn't do it – was her line – but she can't help it. She's a woman, therefore a slave. She has to manipulate the world if she wants to fit in.

The 'muse' idea, as Mougouch presented it, always placed the woman in front. Maro thought that if the 'muse' existed, she was stuck somewhere at the back. She'd inspired the man, then the man had actually gone out there and done it, while the 'muse' went back indoors to wash dishes. Not good enough. Maro wanted to do the doing herself.

———————

Mougouch knew she was fun. Fun was how she'd stolen that address book which she and Natasha Spender had in common. This gift was connected to her rootlessness, for she could exercise it anywhere: in an Albanian café, in a villa off Bellosguardo above Florence, in high society or among gnarled Cretan shepherds. In any given room there was always someone to conquer. My mother instead never felt confident about taking social risks and Loudoun Road was stiff with artifice.

Mougouch was sympathetic regarding my difficulties with Loudoun Road. 'You have to be patient with your parents,' she'd say. 'After all, they have careers.' She said this neutrally. She wasn't implying that careers were things to be avoided. On the other hand, she *did* imply that a certain heaviness on their part was due to the fact that their social life was connected to their work; and consequently, it was not free.

There was also the question of sex. In this area Mougouch joined in, my mother did not. Mougouch met Mum's women friends, and they swapped notes in delicious intimate lunches of plovers' eggs and champagne, with toast on the side kept warm in a linen napkin poised in a basket. There was a bed nicknamed 'the Battlefield' in the background of one of these friends. But Mum's 'discipline' kept her out of this aspect of the world they shared.

Mougouch could be very funny about her love life.

In the interest of straightening out a footnote for this present book, I asked her when she was very old whether she'd ever had an affair with the great Hungarian writer Arthur Koestler. I'd seen them together once in about 1964, but I wasn't sure.

'Oh yes,' she said, 'but it didn't last long. He asked me to go canoeing with him along the canals of the Loire. I knew what *that* meant, so I called it off.'

I was aware that Koestler had had a reputation for being a brute, sex-wise, but canoeing sounded like a gentle occupation.

'Ah,' she said. 'But, as you know, I have a weak back. If you go canoeing with a gentleman along the canals of the Loire, there always comes a point when you have to lift up half a canoe!'

Was she interested in sex, or was she interested in power? I do not know. But it was always important for her to be out in front.

'Madame Cinq à Sept', Mougouch occasionally called herself in Chapel Street in the Sixties when she felt despondent. It was true that several powerful men had tea with her after their office hours and before they went back to their wives, but there were also moments when 'Madam Five to Seven' didn't have enough hours in the day to keep everyone happy. She had to invent an aunt in the country to justify her occasional flights from Chapel Street.

When a friend of mine from Westminster saw her on a station platform with Freddie Ayer 'looking as if she was about to elope', I passed it on to her; and she was furious. No, she was *not* going to elope with Freddie. What a ridiculous idea! Fifty years later she added, 'and anyway, it didn't count if you had an affair with Freddie. Everybody did.'

Philip Larkin's famous poem about sex being invented in 1963 just before the Beatles' first LP but rather late for him, is nonsense; and to say he's being ironic doesn't make the thought more real. Sex in the Thirties was just as free, and with some interesting rules that faded later, such as that jealousy was socially unacceptable. Sex in the Sixties wasn't more free. It was merely out in the open.

Maro took a dim view of her mother's pursuit of love, and Mougouch responded by being condescending about Maro's. Meaning me. According to Mougouch, Maro just wasn't trying. And I'd say: You are absolutely right. Maro ought to make more of an effort in that area. Why only me? Let's face it, the world was full of men, and certainly sooner or later she'd find someone who did it better than my humble self.

Though my mother was wrong to say I was in love with Mougouch, it was true that I enjoyed forming a team with her against Maro. This was peculiar, but we all enjoyed it. Maro always relied on her mother, always loved her, so to see me and Mougouch united gave her a sense of security, even if she was on the receiving end of jokes that could go wrong.

Maro's position was that, as far as sex was concerned, she preferred tenderness. She wasn't interested in sex, she said. This wasn't repression. It was history. She said her refusal derived from her Armenian background. 'Centuries of rape by Kurds and Turks means we have to stay numb, in order to pull ourselves together next morning and tidy up.' Rape destroys Eros, but it could not eradicate the state of loving, because love depended on other sources of emotion. That was her position, half comic, half sincere. She saw sex and tenderness as natural opposites.

Rape is about power rather than sex, and Maro's rejection of sex-as-rape was surely a rejection of power. Perhaps, in view of her mother's dedication to its pursuit, to reject sex-as-power was also to reject Mougouch. Anyway, Maro took a vow to remain anorgasmic for the duration of our sex life, which was otherwise perfectly happy and lasted for forty-five years. She had no hesitation in announcing at supper, surrounded by her mother's guests, that if she ever sank to the level of an orgasm, she would join her mother in Hell. She would have become complicit in the death of her father. And whenever Mougouch tried to use her sexuality as a form of snobbery – and she did: Your orgasms aren't a patch on mine – Maro would say, 'Ha! I knew it. You killed my father!'

Mougouch usually retaliated by telling Maro that Gorky had always been no good as a lover, and a woman has every right to feel sexually satisfied. She insisted that her affair with Matta had only lasted for that one weekend, and her 'betrayal' was a justifiable gesture signifying freedom, so that Gorky wouldn't treat her 'like a garage'. But Maro knew that the affair had been more serious than her mother pretended, because she could remember Matta with Mougouch at the time, even though she was only five years old.

At this point everyone would be shouting.

I found this mayhem riveting, because at Loudoun Road the last subject that could be discussed in any shape or form was sex. This was the foremost question that could not be asked, but since this subject was closed, so were many others. Politics, for example. In retrospect I do not understand why this was so, but it may be that I accepted my father's passionate conviction that sex and politics were part of the same condition.

Maro's duel with her mother went on for years. Neither would abandon her position and their reciprocal front lines became fossilized. Before she died, one of the last things Mougouch said to me was that the only thing she regretted in her life was having killed her first husband. It was said casually, truthfully – the ultimate throwaway line.

In my second year at New College I belonged even less to the university. On days when I had a tutorial I would get up at three in the morning, read five books by breakfast, write the essay by ten, read it to the tutor at eleven and by lunch the whole experience had come and gone like a car crash glimpsed in a newspaper.

I'd learned from my mother how to procrastinate. It had something to do with her sense of timing, which was part of her musicianship. I could feel her postponing the time when she absolutely had to learn a passage by heart, and she'd approach the moment, and then she would do it, and that would be that. I could work in the same way myself: set myself the hour for the essay, steal a moment halfway through to enjoy the view outside the window with the detachment of a goldfish floating in its bowl, go back and catch up with myself, overtake a paragraph, linger on the curve and finish with a sprint to coincide with the second hand ticking up the clock-face to the hour.

The rest of the time I painted offal. A sheep's head cost a shilling in the market and it fitted a square canvas nicely. Or interlocking fish. Or, in the style of Giorgio Morandi, I painted the slanting rain against the slanting slate of the New Buildings.

One of the rare lectures I went to was the last given by a gnarled man who had spent his life reading archives relating to the Wars of the Roses. He gave few tutorials and fewer lectures and he was not accessible to mere conversation. He never wrote, but now he was dying of cancer and he had to give the results of his researches to the world. In some blackened Oxford hall he spoke slowly over a silent sea of students and professors, who took down his words as dictation, this being before the days of the portable tape recorder. A feeling of awe came over us as we absorbed small details concerning the lateral branches of the Poles and de la Mares. How on earth could this be useful? The larger themes of the fifteenth century were reduced to the fact that certain families had became extinct, right down to a third cousin twice removed. A tireless researcher, this wonderful man was beyond synthesis.

Beryl Smalley, my tutor in my second year, was tiny, and so thin that when she crossed her legs under her old tweed skirt, they became one. She also sought precision. At one point she interrupted me as I was reading my weekly essay. The subject was Berengar's options during the Second Crusade. 'Excuse me, Mr Spender, but are you identifying with the person under discussion?' I replied, 'Of course. How else can I understand what he was trying to do?' There was an ominous silence. I asked her tentatively, 'Don't you identify with the people you research?' The silence became longer. I'd said something that had disturbed Miss Smalley. 'I think', she said at last, 'I would have known what to say to Innocent the Third.' I was speechless. She'd spent thirty years editing the correspondence of Pope Innocent III, in Latin, in untold volumes.

I did not have the right to waste the time of such valuable people.

But by this time the restlessness that overtook the Sixties was beginning to emerge, like bamboo growing through the debris of a forest. I remember at the cinema, on Pathé News, there appeared a 'mini-gun' mounted on a helicopter in Vietnam. The word 'mini' was fashionable. Girls in London were wearing mini-skirts, and here was a mini-gun. It was appropriate to the age in which we were living. A voice-over on screen said how many rounds this gun could fire per minute, and the camera looked down on a Vietnamese fisherman as he dived from his boat into a froth of bullets. Someone behind me said in a languid Oxford accent, 'A mini-gun – for mini-life.'

In the newspapers every article on Vietnam ended with a body count. What did it mean? That when a certain number of Vietnamese were declared dead, we could all pack up and go home?

24

KILLING THE WOMEN WE LOVE

IN SEPTEMBER 1964, my mother was diagnosed as having cancer. She had to have an operation immediately.

I heard this news at the Marlborough Gallery during the opening of an exhibition of recent work by Francis Bacon. I was standing in front of *Man on a Bicycle*. Sonia Orwell was just this minute saying intently, 'At last Francis has managed to paint a cheerful painting.' Then I was called outside. My father was in tears. He did not use the word 'cancer'. He just kept repeating, 'Afterwards the doctors say she'll be able to lead an absolutely normal life.' I couldn't understand what he was talking about. I assumed that Mum was about to die. My only reaction (I'm ashamed to say) was selfish: She's done what she was put on the planet to do, give birth to me.

We now know from her letters to Raymond Chandler that she'd been suffering from a physical ailment for years. Whether this had any connection with the cancer, I do not know. My mother was incredibly secretive about her illnesses. She didn't want any of us to know, and she insisted then and for several years afterwards that Lizzie and I weren't to be told that she'd been operated on for cancer.

Though Dad knew that my mother had problems with Mougouch, he came to Chapel Street to talk about it. Mougouch offered to help. He said, 'Well, if you could do something about the garden.'

Mougouch's only garden was a bay tree in a wooden tub on the roof outside the kitchen at Chapel Street, but she telephoned for some professional gardeners and she paid the bill.

My mother had always neglected the garden at Loudoun Road, because the house was rented and she didn't think of it as being hers. She lived in that house for nearly seventy years and she never spoke of her potentially beautiful garden as being anything but a 'problem'. Seeing from the piano room window how nicely it was coming along, with three gardeners turning it into a little gem, my father telephoned Mougouch and asked her (and Maro and me) not to mention to Natasha, when she came back from the hospital, that Mougouch was paying the bill. It would upset her, he said.

I said thank you awkwardly to Mougouch several times. I felt ashamed. She thought it was rough, but she pushed Mum's garden on to one side and told me briskly, Don't worry, Natasha will recover. 'Most women have to go through that kind of an operation,' she said. She herself had been told that her womb was a 'leathery old thing' which would have to come out sooner or later. This reassured me, because it was so matter-of-fact.

During this visit, Dad told Mougouch something so strange that she didn't pass it on to me for several weeks. 'We Spenders have always succeeded in killing the women we love.' To her it was meaningless but maybe I could make something of it. She raised her eyebrows and looked at me full in the face, her eyes particularly green. I said that I thought it might have something to do with the death of his own mother; but he'd also placed himself in the forefront of what was surely my mother's problem, not his. She nodded. 'We can forget about it,' she said decisively.

On the day after the operation, in bed and presumably still under the influence of morphine, my mother had an experience that she treasured for a long time.

The magic of that day in the hospital – trussed up to machines – one of which made a noise like a motor boat going round a Greek island, and absolved from all duties, guilts and exertions. Peacefully listening to the sounds – suddenly from the pretty little Victorian garden below my window, with its little drinking fountain with tin cups attached on chains – a sound of many rapid pattering feet – scuffles rattles of the tin cups on their chains – a multitudinous sound like a flock of chattering birds – more pattering of feet departing, and then a clear solitary silver voice of a young child – saying 'You fucking bastards – why can't you wait for me?' I thought I had never in my life heard anything so beautiful as that little voice.

She decided there and then that she should treat every subsequent day as a gift, to be treasured as if it were time acquired in the face of death. She wrote this entry in a moment of depression, when she'd let herself in for the trip to California to meet Bryan Obst, my father's last lover. She was counting up the moments in her life that she valued, and this was one of them. She noted that in the South of France where she was brooding, sometimes the days came and went without anything happening at all. 'Yesterday's accidie [laziness] therefore is inexcusable, according to my "every day is a gift".'

Sonia was ready for her when she came back from the hospital. She'd primed my father on what he had to do. When Mum came in, Sonia hissed: 'The flowers, Stephen, the flowers.' Dad produced a big bunch of flowers and offered them – to Sonia. 'Not to me, you fool! To her!' Mum staggered through this scene and went straight upstairs to bed.

My mother was told that she'd never be able to perform a concert again.

She didn't touch the piano for two years. Not only that, but she refused to go to concerts, or to the opera, or even listen to music on the gramophone. My father was shocked. This made me feel that either he didn't know about music, or he didn't know his wife. It seemed to me utterly reasonable to dump the whole thing. No second best! No tinkling the ivories between cooking his meals! That's what she'd always said. Did Dad think she didn't mean it? Or had he never taken her music seriously to begin with?

Not being able to perform meant that Mum had to give up the camaraderie of the musical world, with its feeling of 'let's row this boat ashore' that performance entails. She never said that she missed it. On the contrary, she always implied that the world of music, except at the very highest level, was limited. But, without her career, she had to face the reduction of her sense of self to that of housewife and helpmeet. Silence was never so precise as in Loudoun Road thereafter.

Over the winter, my mother did her best to pull herself together after the operation.

In Dad's study I overheard her tell him: 'One has to be so careful in this second chance sort of life. One can't risk making any mistakes.' A touching remark. But I brooded about it. Wasn't there a kernel of ambition in there somewhere? Didn't it mean that she wanted to recover, catch up, overtake, succeed?

Over the winter, she decided that she'd go back to university and start again. Richard Wollheim at London University was encouraging. She started learning Latin from scratch for an O level; and she'd certainly manage music A level, even though it meant studying a symphony by Sibelius that she hated. A group of Auden's poems was set for her English exam. The next time he turned up at Loudoun Road, she handed them to him for the latest corrections. I remember seeing 'Spain' with a vertical line crossing out the whole thing.

The second interesting remark that I overheard occurred during a private conversation between my mother and Sonia. After one's body had been so martyred, Mum said, there's no question of taking on a new lover. It's hard enough to retain the lover one has, and then only because he recognizes what he used to love.

To me, this was a very unexpected remark. I'd assumed that the big difference between Mougouch and my mother was that Mougouch was inside the world of love affairs, Mum wasn't. It suggested that, however faithfully my mother remained loyal to her 'discipline', the idea of a new love had survived until then, ticking away somewhere in the back of her mind.

In the early summer of 1965, when he was fifty-six years old, Stephen met and instantly fell in love with Nikos Stangos, a young Greek poet working as a press attaché in the Greek Embassy in London. Twenty-eight years old, Nikos was slim, curly-haired, well read and brilliantly intelligent, but touchy. It's a quality I'm grateful for. In Stephen's love letters to him, time and again he has to explain what he expects from love.

They'd hardly met before they were separated by the summer holidays. From 23 July, Stephen and Natasha were in the South of France, where my mother struggled with her Provençal house. Maro and I joined them there for a week. Mougouch had told Maro that she mustn't mention the word cancer to me, as Natasha wanted to keep her operation secret. Mum wanted to seal the floor of the kitchen with a polish called Starwax that she'd brought out from England. She became fanatical about spots on her kitchen floor. Maro layered that floor daily with Starwax, but she wasn't pleased that Mum persistently called her by the name of her Portuguese maid back in London.

As part of me was still a sulky adolescent, I thought the tensions in the house were normal, so I hid in the bedroom. But there was one evening when my mother went wild and escaped across the hillside. Perhaps she'd guessed something about the still invisible Nikos. We all went out to look for her, Dad included. We'd never have found her if she hadn't said, from beneath a Provençal rock, 'Go away.' My father told us gently but firmly that he'd deal with the situation now. So Maro and I wandered back to the house. As usual, my parents kept their problems to themselves.

Stephen tried to nurture his relationship with Nikos with letters. Fantasy fuelled his patience during a long, difficult summer. 'Now what I would like is that we always – or for a long long time – regard one another with the same affection and consideration. Which means that during the next year or so, we must accept intervals in which we write to and think of one another.'

Maro, my mother and me at Saint-Jérôme in the summer after her operation.

He longed to see Nikos again, but between the end of the summer and his departure for Washington in October, there wouldn't be much time. He arranged for them to spend two days alone and built fantasies around this expectation as my mother struggled with her garden – that barren patch of land desperately needing to be fed. And the water problem. And the builders. But she was determined to make that house work – because, unlike Loudoun Road, it was hers.

In England, over the weekend of Friday 3 and Saturday 4 September 1965, Stephen joined Nikos somewhere in Sussex.

They drove back to London on the Sunday, stopping off for a walk along the Sussex downs, where they sat and talked under some trees on a low hill. Stephen asked Nikos about his relationship with a friend. 'That is a pornographic thought,' said Nikos sharply. Later, Nikos rolled down the hill, which Stephen thought was a magnificent gesture. It was a curious two days. At one point Stephen had to make a detour and speak to Malcolm Muggeridge. He left Nikos outside in the car. The weather was also strange, glowering as if to send them back to the city, then brightening up.

Driving towards London, Nikos told Stephen of a recent dream that had disturbed him. Stephen kept thinking about it.

When you are relating a dream as you did on our drive home, or when you explain your attitude to poetry, or when you write a letter then I think you are a writer, as Proust was, perhaps. Now I know I'm taking terrible risks saying this, but it is said out of my love for you: which means that I am not pressing you in any way with my opinion, but giving it because you want to know what I think, giving it so you may reject it instantly.

Less than a week later, Stephen flew to Washington to take up his job as Poetry Consultant at the Library of Congress. He was required to be in an office from nine to five, preferably writing poems. 'There is something too creepy about the idea of the official poet sitting in his office really writing poetry. The idea of "behaving" exactly to fit an allotted role is a bit mad really, like a depressive maniac really looking depressed.'

His fantasies about Nikos balanced the absurdity of his official duties. And so, back again to that meeting in Sussex: 'I must try and think about that day we had on the downs in a way that makes it not just a recollected happiness but a present one, which it is.' In his mind, he went over everything he'd said to Nikos, regretting that he hadn't been clearer on some points, continuing the discussion of others. 'I thought always that if we were alone for two days every minute would count as an hour and there would be moments we would keep for the rest of our lives. This really is so, and I thank you more than I can say.'

Nikos had a distinctive voice: precise, with a faint touch of bitterness. Stephen's imaginary conversations were real to him because he could hear that voice in his mind. Sleepless in Washington: 'During the night I was trying to explain to you that when I asked you about you and Nickyphoros and you said "that is a pornographic thought", somehow I adored your saying so in that way too much to explain that really I meant something quite different which was: "is what we really want more than anything with each other a passionate conversation?"'

Nikos often responded sharply to Stephen's interpretation of his personality. He was good at reading between the lines and detecting hidden drops of poison. It was maddening for Stephen to have to keep apologizing for having insulted Nikos, but Stephen longed to forgive him. 'You always relate everything to some standard which is marvellously clear and pure in your mind. When you say things which seem severely critical I can recognize the truth in them and feel that I was longing for them to be said. That is partly of course in the way in which you say them.'

Because so much had been left unsaid, that one memory could become a creative fuel. 'I found what you said in the car very convincing. You think of me as judging or as untouched. The position really is that I am anxious to learn . . . I would like to say to you "please write more poems so that I can learn from an act of writing of a kind which has been blank for so long in me".'

This, I think, is the key. The afternoon with Nikos on the Sussex downs was elevated by Stephen so that it became a kernel of intense experience, of the kind that his poems came from. Over and above whatever he loved or expected from Nikos, Stephen hoped that he himself was still capable of the intense feelings from which a poem springs.

Let me try to sum up my father's expectations from love.

There are many clues in this book that Stephen had doubts about the reality of his own feelings. He always insisted that he was the victim of his friends; had no will of his own; had doubts about the condition of love. Auden had said, early on, that this was all untrue: Stephen needed love as much as anyone else, but he didn't want to reveal the fact, because it would make him vulnerable to others.

In the earliest phase, when at Oxford he was in love with a young man he calls Marston in his first book of poems, the love object was untouchable. Wystan blasted Stephen out of his hesitation. The second phase, the boys from around the port of Hamburg and from the *Lokalen* of Berlin, was complicated. There was sex, and there was an attachment of sorts, although this love was linked to *The Temple*, the polemical book that Stephen wanted to write about the experience, and to his need to prove something to himself and to his friends.

When he met Tony in 1933, Stephen recognized an amalgamation of sex plus intelligence and he chose it instantly. It was a courageous attempt, but unfortunately Tony lived only for the moment. He had no other dimension, clever though he might have been. It was impossible to live with Tony, because he required constant attention of the kind that would drive anyone insane. And so Stephen counted out for ever the possibility of living with another man. Two men in one apartment would always disagree, because each to the other was, as he'd once put it, 'a substitute for something else'.

There followed the relationships with Muriel, Inez and my mother.

In his relationships with women, I think my father's sense of pity predominated. He could empathize with a woman's unhappiness, but it also made him panic. This reaction perhaps went back to the lack of sympathy he'd shown to his mother when she was about to die a miserable death, a rejection of unhappiness as a rejection of death – but this is to drift into psychological areas where I'm not qualified to have an opinion. Suffice it to say that he could offer sympathy to a woman if she were unhappy, he could tune into that unhappiness to a remarkable degree, but to help her do something about it was beyond him. The most he could feel was helpless, because he had no will of his own.

Sympathy and good manners are excellent virtues for a long and solid marriage, but they lack the vital element of desire. Inez, recognizing this, left. She reclaimed her initiative. My mother was tempted to leave, but a) the tempter (Raymond Chandler) was physically unattractive (and off his head), and b) she truly enjoyed the creation of a home, plus status, which marriage to my father brought with it.

When Nikos came into my father's life, Stephen opted as soon as possible for the solution he'd already found by trial and error with Reynolds Price: the young man as a source of inspiration, the creator of events that might crystallize into a poem. However physical his relationship with Nikos may have been (and I have no information about this), Stephen wasn't going to run away from Loudoun Road and live with him.

Meanwhile, because these feelings were so heavily imbued with fantasies that were not his, Nikos resisted any of the attributes that Stephen wished on him. Nikos insisted he was a real person, not a pretext for a poem.

In spite of my dislike of Oxford and my waste of its benefits, my academic interests refused to die. I took Dante as a special paper, on the grounds that I'd never read him otherwise. It was hard work, made harder when Maro came down for the day and read the whole of the *Inferno* in one go, sitting in the Radcliffe Camera in a ray of sunshine. She said she liked it. I felt helpless. Liking it wasn't part of what I needed to do with it.

I took a special paper with Edgar Wind, whose lectures on the Sistine Chapel I'd admired. 'Here vee see zee dagger sretning zee örthh.' Was that supposed to be, 'threatening the earth'? He thought that Michelangelo was a follower of Savonarola. (I've since been told that he fudged the evidence.) He wore his spectacles on the tip of his nose and he had a long stick to point with, and I thought he was a kindly man. I knocked on his door and asked to join a class he was giving to postgraduates. I wasn't eligible, but he let me come anyway.

The class was on the *Discourses* of Sir Joshua Reynolds. This was the attempt by Reynolds to create an art-loving public in England in the 1770s. He argued that art beautified a gentleman's country seat and conveyed to the owner a mysterious halo of superiority. 'Is he rrright in zaying zis?' Just for the heck of it I said, 'Yes.' 'No,' said Dr Wind. 'You are abzolutely wrong.' Art sprang from the innermost feelings of the unbound spontaneous liberation of the human spirit. Dr Wind was everything one wanted in a German professor: opinionated, and a firm disciplinarian.

I had been heavily reproved – and I brooded. Reynolds had tried to make the Brits love art. Why didn't they love art anyway? Why in France and Italy does the picture fit the frame, the frame fits the room, the room fits the house, the house fits the square and the square fits the city and in England, it doesn't? Art in England was as Reynolds described it: a sprinkling of sugar on top.

I began to think of art as an interior *need*. It wasn't a question of an ornament or an expression of taste or a means to a reputation. You had to *need* it. This need was an interior craving that required no visible manifestation to make it real, though obviously a work of art ought to appear at some point, too. In Europe, the need for art was part of the culture of several countries. The same had not happened in England. The period from Henry VIII to Oliver Cromwell, so formative politically, had had the side-effect of destroying art as an integrated part of society.

I persisted nevertheless with Wind, and he took me under his wing. As my Finals approached, he said that he wanted me to take a doctorate and go to Moscow to study the works of Matisse in the Shchukin collection. I said thank you, but I want to paint. Ach, he said, looking puzzled. A week later he told his secretary, Well it will serve Stephen Spender right if his son does becomes a painter. It will be the judgement of heaven for that bad book he wrote on Botticelli. Wind's secretary passed on his remark and I grinned. Wind was right. Dad's book on Botticelli was bad.

I was doing fine with Dante, too. Dons gave me hints about my academic future. 'This is the Keeper of Western Manuscripts. You'll find he'll come in useful when you go on to do research.' I shook hands with a large lugubrious man and left the room as soon as possible. Panic was setting in. Did I want it, or didn't I?

Via Dante, I came across the great Italian historian Gaetano Salvemini. His book on Florence in the late thirteenth century put forward a Marxist theory of class struggle that I thought was wrong. A second idea for a doctorate was that I'd go to Italy and research the Florentine archives to see if the guilds of the period could be described as 'class', in a Marxist sense. I suggested this to one of my tutors and he said Yes, this is a good subject for a PhD.

Whenever I talked about Marxism with my father, I said the problem was that I couldn't think of people as being representatives of a class. He didn't understand. Couldn't I see that there was some-thing called the Working Class, he asked? No, I said. I could meet a man in a pub and he might come from a different background from mine, but to me he would be just someone to talk to, or not, as the case might be. He would not be a 'representative of the Working Class'. Dad thought this was very funny. Fancy that! Matthew can't understand the meaning of Class War!

There was something awkward about this exchange. I suddenly thought: is he listening to me, or to a 'representative of the Youth of Today'?

I ended my miserable Oxford career stuck in the library with books I loathed reading and no brain to make sense of them. But I was there, in the Upper Bodleian, and my father was disturbed by what he took to be my academic ambition. One day he asked Maro: 'Is Matthew really going to become a Donny-wonny?'

Oxford is anti-creative. It wants to turn people into nice people not embarrassing boars [bores?] who do things. Scholarship is tolerated, because it shuts people up and prevents them being social nuisances: unless they are clever enough to be both scholarly and excellent after dinner conversationalists. But the arts when actually practised and not seen in museums are like muddy boots on the carpet. However, even they are allowed if you can convert them into social currency.

This isn't a wild adolescent reproof of mine against my father. It's a letter from Dad to me, giving what he thinks is supportive advice. He may have intended it to calm me down, but it was the exact opposite of the advice he'd given me when I'd started out at New College, which was that artists need to cultivate their brains. He'd have done better to say nothing at all. And part of my being at Oxford, so I thought, was to obtain the degree he'd failed to win himself. To please him! What was he doing casting doubt on the whole process?

My father's Oxford career was in its way spectacularly successful, even though he went for a bicycle ride instead of taking his Finals and so failed to obtain any degree at all. He'd written and published the Marston poems, which many critics say are his finest achievement. He'd drafted two novels, though the first had to be abandoned and the second, *The Temple*, didn't find a publisher for fifty years. As head of the Oxford English Society he'd been able to talk to many distinguished authors, who always seemed happy to come up to Oxford from London in order to meet the students. He'd published his first book of poems in a small edition, half of which was subscribed before publication by his friends, 'most of whom got Firsts', as he put it blandly in a letter to his grandmother. Above all, he'd made friends with Auden and Isherwood so that the three of them, if not exactly forming a gang, certainly added up to one of the strongest literary movements of the decade. All of which my father presented as 'Don't worry about Finals. I've never passed an exam in my life.'

As for failure, the clincher came decades later when he was stopped by a policeman driving his car around Trafalgar Square when drunk. He was asked to blow into the famous compromising balloon, but it failed to react. 'I'm so sorry, officer,' he said. 'It's just that I've never been able to pass a test.'

At some point during that autumn my father took me to one side and asked if he could dedicate a poem to me. It was called 'The Generous Days'. I read it several times over a period of a week and rang him up to say No, I'd prefer it if he didn't.

I disliked this poem, partly because I thought he was trying to send me a message in public of the kind that he would never dare to give me in private. The poem was about love, and I could glimpse Maro and myself in the background. But 'Mindless of soul, so their two bodies meet.' The couple in the poem wandered about, hopelessly kicking the leaves. And wasn't there something masochistic in their relationship? 'Soul fly up from body's sacrifice, / Immolated in the summons.' Also: 'After, of course, will come a time not this / When he'll be taken, stripped, strapped to a wheel.' The 'of course' was especially offensive, because it seemed to take my fate for granted. I had no desire to be strapped to a wheel of daily life by my father, not even in a metaphor.

Deep down, I felt that Dad disapproved of my relationship with Maro because it was happy. At the time, I knew nothing about his comments to Reynolds Price on Rimbaud and the 'derangement of the senses'. I just felt that he disapproved of happiness in the same way that he disapproved of academic studies, because both seemed to him complacent.

On my desk in front of me there's the copy of *The Temple* which he gave us when the book finally came out in the Eighties. The dedication reads: 'to Maro and Matthew, these youthful indiscretions, love dad'. I can't help feeling there's a gleeful note in there somewhere, a mild reproof.

———————

The lease on St Andrew's Mansions ran out and Maro began looking around for somewhere else to live. By chance, Sonia Orwell was leaving her old flat in Percy Street off the Tottenham Court Road in order to live in a house she'd bought in Kensington; so Maro took over from her.

Three rooms, a tiny kitchen, and a bathroom remarkably full of plumbing. One of the rooms was known as the 'divorce' room, because halves of estranged couples would squat there while their relationships irretrievably crumbled. Sonia was a good woman, but she loved taking sides in marital disputes.

We redecorated the whole flat in our usual double-quick time. The 'divorce' room was so small Maro could only paint gouaches in it. The living room had a wonderful Gorky in it, on loan from Mougouch. When I left Oxford, the bookshelves filled up with my academic books, plus a collection of old *Horizons* which we'd found in the attic that Sonia said we could keep.

This had been George Orwell's last flat, though I don't think he lived there long. It was also haunted. Several times Maro woke up and found a sandy-haired young man staring down at her. She said he had a very 1930-ish atmosphere. I never saw him.

Percy Street was within walking distance of the Slade, but Maro had finished her four years of study there. She began working in interior decoration. An early job was to decorate a bathtub for Ricky Huston, ex-wife of the film director John Huston (and mother of Anjelica). Ricky and Mougouch did gym together, writhing their elegant limbs on an antique kilim and swapping gossip about various friends they had in common. Painting that bathtub took Maro a long time. She was a quick worker, but Ricky thought the price she'd quoted was high in relation to the hours she'd spent on it, so she made Maro repaint it three times.

Opposite the British Museum, I discovered the communist book shop where Tony Hyndman used to hang out in the Thirties. I was fascinated by this shop. On a table in front of the entrance lay *The Little Red Book* we were supposed to wave on protest marches. Tucked away at the back were volumes by Mao Zedong on the tactics of guerrilla warfare, which were down to earth, and horrible. How to shoot class enemies. There was also a shelf of books by the victims of the Russian totalitarian state: Victor Serge and Ivanov-Razumnik. These were later overshadowed by the works of Solzhenitsyn, but even before his books came out, there was plenty of information on how badly things had gone wrong.

I wasn't political. Just wishy-washy left-wing. It was the Kronstadt Rebellion that kept me from sympathizing with the Trots. The followers of Trotsky thought that if he'd taken power instead of Stalin, the revolution would never have gone bad, but it seemed to me that Trotsky had been perfectly capable of acting ruthlessly, because ruthlessness was part of the predicament.

I remember having a conversation about this with a friend after a party. We were both drunk. The question was: where is the morality in being communist? We both knew about the persecution of the kulaks and the Purges of the 1930s and both of us, therefore, hesitated in our left-wingery. Underneath a lamp-post, we talked it over. Surely there's *some* moral high ground in communism?

He said: Everything to do with Russian history leaves one too dazed to form an opinion. For instance, one of the reasons why they won the war is because Stalin moved their heavy industries behind the Urals where the Germans couldn't get at them. The cost of this operation was staggering. Thousands of people shot, incredible disruption pushed forward with brutality. He said that nobody in the West dared to argue that it was worth it, because it enabled Russia to win the war, even though it was probably true. 'We just aren't capable of calculating the morality of decisions made on such a scale.'

My Finals crept up with historical inevitability in June 1966.

During those dreadful eleven days, I kept clear of both Maro and my father, as neither of them believed in what I was doing. Instead,

I phoned my mother each evening and she steered me through. She knew about performing on a particular hour of a particular day.

And six weeks later, my Viva came and went in a flash. I was asked to define the English Gentleman, as I'd said something iffy on that subject. The result was a decent Second, with a touch of alpha in four papers and gammas in three others. You can't really be an academic with a gamma double-minus in the background, so whatever temptation there was, withdrew.

Maro and I spent that summer in Majorca, where I started painting again.

I wrote to my father saying that I was trying to unlearn the habit of thinking in words. It was similar to something he'd said before my Finals: 'Maybe you will be able to shed some of Oxford in the next two years.' But he'd also said that artists in England were stupid. 'The great ones of course are clever and don't need educating much, but the majority even of quite good ones are such inchoate oafs.'

I must have written him a letter saying I wanted to join the oafs. In midsummer he wrote back, to both of us: 'When Matthew writes about having to learn not to think I see what he means but wonder whether he is right. Obviously a painter has to work from his senses and a certain kind of thinking is bad for this. On the other hand the idea that a painter has to be a dumb instinctive animal seems very Anglo-American and accounts for the limitations of Anglo-American painting . . . Painters don't think enough. Nowadays the best of them seem to have one-track minds, which make them arrive at a formula – Motherwell, Rothko, Rauschenberg and even Francis Bacon – and then they stick to this out of an inability to think of anything else.' There was one exception: Picasso. 'The point is to be one thing one doesn't have to jettison one's other gifts. One somehow has to do the one thing out of the development of all of them.'

Just as I was wondering what to reply, he sent us a crushing letter written from a hotel halfway up France. We'd been planning to visit them, but Majorca to Arles wasn't an easy journey and I must have asked him for some money. 'Even if you don't feel things you might consider other people to the extent of trying to enter into, imagine their reactions. Not to do so is just embarrassing, like Melvin Lasky.'

Dad's harsh letter was the result of three stresses. We'd delayed telling them what our plans were, and 'what are your plans' figured highly in my mother's sense of order. Then André Malraux had invited him to Paris, and he wanted to go, and so did Mum (because she wanted Malraux to force the phone company to give her a telephone, which he did). If we'd told them earlier that we were coming, Dad might have cancelled Malraux: but on the other hand, maybe not. (The argument was hard to follow.) Last but not least, an article had just appeared in *Time* magazine about the machinations of *Encounter*.

Even at this late date, my father tried to laugh it off. He wrote to Nikos that the article 'enraged Natasha so much (partly because I treated it as a joke) that it was really quite appalling. In a funny way I don't think we'll ever quite recover.' Lasky was involved, and my mother honed in on him as the root of the evil. But Stephen wasn't about to assign all the blame to him. He added mildly, 'Lasky does seem to have this gift for making the wives of his colleagues hate him, while his colleagues merely despise him.'

I arranged for Maro and me to sail back to England as the crew of a tiny yacht. There was room for just the three people: us two, plus the skipper who at least knew how to sail. I looked at this lopsided sloop tucked away in the harbour and thought, With any luck we'll be drowned, so I won't have to face any more of this.

25

YOUR FATHER WILL SURVIVE

W E DIDN'T DROWN as we sailed across the Bay of Biscay, but the trip was grotesquely uncomfortable. There was a leak in the exhaust of the diesel engine and the yacht staggered along, full of fumes. I must have vomited on every nautical mile of the sea between Vigo Bay and Portsmouth, spattering on the heaving asphalt of the Atlantic confetti-like fragments of my insides. Good. It had the effect of placing a full stop, new chapter, underneath my Oxford days.

I found a studio on the top floor of a house in Holloway near the Nag's Head. The building was owned by a racketeer who couldn't evict his tenants and the place was a mess. Underneath me, a veteran of the First World War thought I was dropping grenades on him every time I walked across the room. Underneath him lived a bus driver with a young wife and baby daughter. As Mr Puttock, the war veteran, was off his head, I made friends with the wife and baby, especially the baby. I made a portrait of her. It was a fat baby on a fat pillow, pink on pink.

In my attic, I went back to the former themes of New College: rooftops, slabs of meat and self-portraits. I hated what I was doing and my head was full of words. I'd paint for an hour and then have an interesting thought about Titian or Frans Hals; stop to write it down, then tear it up impatiently, as 'words on paper' was not the medium I wanted to create in.

Walking back from a pub one day, I heard a voice in my head say, 'And he was using up his pencils at the rate of one a week.' Where did this voice come from and whose was it? It was ridiculous to claim that using up one pencil per week meant anything, for what 'he' was drawing might be completely worthless. But who was 'he'? Well, obviously, 'he' was me.

I protested. But I don't want a 'he' in my head pretending to be me. It's crazy. And there are too many people up in my head anyway – the ultimate attic, far above Mr Puttock who can't forget the trenches. Twenty-two years old, free of education, free of exams, out in the big wide world, no problems with my love life, yet here a worm-like voice still dug its way through the churned suburban burden of my mind.

I decided: this voice isn't mine. It's my father's.

Through the clutter of trying to make decisions about my life shone this interior commentator I'd inherited from him, from Stephen. For it was Stephen Spender, the poet with the alliterative name, who carried with him the eternal commentator, the divine recording angel of his own success. Wasn't 'success' behind 'him'? Yes, because otherwise the commentator wouldn't have been impressed – and he shouldn't be impressed – by the fact that I was using up one pencil every week.

In June 1966, Nikos Stangos met David Plante, a young American writer who'd recently arrived in London. They became lovers, and after a week Nikos invited David to come and live with him. Even though the gesture was generous, Nikos warned David not to come too close; or, as David wrote in his diary, 'I must not think that this meant I should feel I had to return the feelings Nikos had for me.'

Stephen at this point was an absent 'older Englishman', who'd have to be told about the new relationship when he came back to London. Luckily, when they all met a few weeks later, Stephen was thrilled. For him it solved an increasingly difficult situation. The tendency of Nikos to reject any compliment, however mild, had begun to exasperate Stephen to the point where he thought he'd have to bring the relationship to an end.

Nikos Stangos and David Plante.

Nikos didn't want to be tied down. When he complained about his rooms and wondered if he shouldn't redecorate them, Stephen said he liked them as they were; but even this was a risky thing to say. 'I suddenly realized the reason is that I had never seen your rooms apart from you. They are, in my mind, irradiated by you, and somehow miraculous. Probably you'll consider this subtly insulting and write an angry protest.'

As the memory of that first weekend in September began to fade, Stephen turned to trying to help Nikos find his way as a writer, both with advice concerning the writing itself and with recommendations to various people for jobs. At one point he wanted Nikos to help him turn his inaugural lecture at the Library of Congress into a book. They'd split the profits, fifty–fifty. He accepted a poem by Nikos for *Encounter*, then hesitated, partly because Frank Kermode was now in charge of the literary side of the magazine, partly because he could not be sure that the poem would ever come out, given Lasky's delaying tactics. Finally, after about a year, Stephen agreed to revise some translations of Cavafy that Nikos had started years before. These were eventually published in a special edition, with illustrations by David Hockney.

Two weeks after David arrived in London, Stephen was sent by Natasha to plant some trees in her garden in Provence. She was swotting for her exams and couldn't go herself. At Nikos' suggestion, Stephen took David with him. Nikos evidently thought this was the quickest way of integrating David into the relationship that he'd awkwardly shared with Stephen: or maybe he thought David could become a part of it.

On the train to Paris, Stephen caught sight of Francis Bacon, about to attend an important exhibition of his work at the Galerie Maeght. They joined forces, and for a few days David was introduced to a glamorous side of English and French life that hitherto he'd never even imagined. Mary McCarthy, Philippe de Rothschild, Louis Aragon. Jokes were made about having to plant plants with Plante. And when Stephen and David continued down to the South of France to plant those trees, Francis Bacon came with them.

David had not yet met Natasha. Indeed, for several months an elaborate charade was performed by Stephen as to when she should be told, how she should be told, and whether or not she would be upset when finally she *was* told. David formed the impression that Stephen wanted 'to keep Natasha alerted to his sexuality without admitting it to her, to make her wonder'. It isn't correct, for my mother of course was acutely aware of my father's sexuality, but it was a nice game to play within the world of men-against-women. It continued for some time. When finally Nikos and David had lunch with Natasha at Loudoun Road, they had to pretend they'd never been to the house before.

Years later, my mother integrated the tree-planting episode into a book about her garden in Provence. And retrospectively, she took charge of the whole thing. 'I had managed to design the walk on a large roll of cartridge paper, and Stephen took a holiday break between books and went with Francis Bacon and David Plante to translate my plan into action.' And they'd all had an improving time down there. 'Stephen's autumn expedition had been felt by all three friends to be not only a horticultural adventure but also a golden interlude of inspiration with which Provence endowed them. While Francis was wandering the sites of Van Gogh's years of painting in Arles and Saint-Rémy, Stephen and David applied themselves to deciphering and fulfilling my plan.'

She hadn't met David at that point, and there's no mention that Bacon was in Paris for the opening of his show at Maeght. It's hard to imagine a man like Francis Bacon going in for 'a golden interlude of inspiration', let alone a 'horticultural adventure'. Her version underlines the tenacity with which my mother controlled the marriage that she, even more than my father, had created. However hurt she was by the dramas that resulted from my father's insistence on his 'freedom', she always managed to present everything as if it had happened on purpose, with the noblest of motives and completely under her control. Once she'd invented such an interpretation, she firmly believed that the past had actually happened that way.

It may have seemed a slight step from Stephen loving Nikos to Stephen supporting Nikos and David as a couple, but it was huge. The first relationship was individual, with elements of secrecy, the second was shared and in the full light of day. My father needed to be in love, because he always hoped that it would bring him the feelings that could be turned into a poem. In greeting Nikos and David as a couple, however, Stephen was saying goodbye to intimacy and substituting for it social recognition. Love was poetry, social recognition was politics.

Stephen told David: 'I wish that when I was your age I had had what you have now with Nikos.' David replied, 'But Stephen, you are giving us both what you didn't have at our age.' This was true. By treating him and Nikos as a couple, Stephen helped them to become a couple. 'I feel he has given Nikos and me a world in which our relationship can expand and expand, so that in discovering the world he has opened to us we are discovering one another.'

There remained the vicarious fantasy of young men all together, facing the world in order to conquer it. And within the confines of this fantasy, Stephen could remain the same age he'd always been: a boy of seventeen, 'without guilt'.

Nineteen-sixty-six was the year when the *Encounter* scandal finally broke.

In May, my father was still in America teaching at Northwestern University in Evanston, Illinois. In his absence, Maro and I were heavily involved in keeping my mother calm in the face of Lasky's perfidy. As my father put it in a letter to Nikos, 'Natasha is hysterical on the subject of Lasky & *Encounter* and the children are having hell trying to cope with her rage.'

A fortnight or so before he arrived back in London, Maro and I invited Mum to supper at Percy Street. After supper the three of us sat down to summon a spirit through the Ouija board. We thought it would be a distraction for her. Mum addressed the room in a serious voice: 'Who is behind the financing of *Encounter*?'

The upturned glass started moving, slowly at first, then faster. I looked at Maro, and her eyes were jumping to the appropriate letter a fraction of a second before we got there. The Ouija board told us, 'Malcolm Muggeridge.'

Afterwards, when we were alone, Maro hotly denied that she'd cheated. But we knew the name of Muggeridge was in the forefront of Natasha's suspicions. He'd worked in British Intelligence during the war and had kept up his contacts ever since. Years later, it turned out that Mum's suspicions had been justified.

I've probably given too much weight in this book to the *Encounter* affair in relation to other aspects of my father's life: for example, his genuine and generous concern for young writers, his intuitive understanding of art, his great capacity for producing unusual books of criticism and his own considerable achievement as a poet. But he'd also aimed at editing a magazine for at least ten years before *Encounter* materialized, so I cannot argue that it was an accidental distraction. Life did not impose this task on him. He'd sought it. Thus *Encounter*, for me, stands for the parts of my father's life that are the real enemies of literary promise: the contamination of art by power, the ambiguous role of the intellectual in society and the political relationship of England with the United States. *Encounter* in my mind stands for Temptation.

I need answers to the following questions: Was he aware of what he was doing? In what way did *Encounter* represent the CIA? And how did my father manage to emerge relatively unharmed, whereas most of the others who had been involved with the Congress for Cultural Freedom were tainted for the rest of their lives?

First, a quick run through the facts.

On 27 April 1966, the *New York Times* published an article discussing American support of anti-communist liberal organizations, such as the Congress for Cultural Freedom and its magazine, *Encounter*. The next day Arthur Schlesinger, in a TV interview with the left-wing scholar and politician Conor Cruise O'Brien, admitted that support of the non-communist left was a part of American foreign policy. Five days later, Stephen wrote to Mike Josselson asking whether the Congress for Cultural Freedom was a CIA front organization. This letter was not answered, but it seems that it was read and discussed in the CIA headquarters at Langley, Virginia.

In the background of these events lay President Johnson's irritation with those Democrat left-wingers who were coming out against the war in Vietnam. His anger at what he saw as their betrayal was swiftly becoming paranoid. The previous June, he'd told one of his assistants: 'I am not going to have anything more to do with the liberals. They won't have anything to do with me. They all just follow the communist line – liberals, intellectuals, communists. They're all the same . . . I'm not going in the liberal direction. There's no future with them. They're just out to get me. Always have been.' So it's possible that the whole 'international non-communist left' was dumped as a result of a peremptory order from President Johnson.

On 19 May, Conor Cruise O'Brien read a lecture at New York University suggesting that *Encounter* was part of the 'power structure' of Washington. (A personal dig, seeing that Stephen, while working at the Library of Congress, had recently been living in Washington.) O'Brien's piece was immediately published in *Book Week* and distributed by the US branch of the PEN Club. In response Goronwy Rees, for the August number of *Encounter*, wrote an attack on O'Brien. Over the summer, O'Brien wanted to publish a reply in the *New Statesman*, but Frank Kermode persuaded the editor not to print it.

For a while things hung fire. In the background Spender and Kermode tried frequently and unsuccessfully to obtain a straight answer about the CIA background. From September to October, Stephen was in India on behalf of UNESCO. In January 1967, he took up a teaching job at Wesleyan University in Connecticut. Then in February, O'Brien sued *Encounter* for libel contained in the personal attack by Rees, cleverly choosing to present his case in Ireland, where he was something of a hero. *Encounter* lost. Which implied that his thesis, that *Encounter* was subsidized by the CIA, was true.

From then on the situation deteriorated. At Wesleyan, Stephen was contacted by *Ramparts* magazine saying they were about to reveal the connection between the CIA and *Encounter*, and what did he think about that?

Ramparts was more interested in the CIA's use of infiltrators within the international students' unions. Having read this in a newspaper report, and not noticing the implications regarding *Encounter*, I wrote to Dad asking whether infiltrating student unions with secret agents constituted Fascism.

Out to dinner that evening at Wesleyan, my father put this question to an 'Admiral type' who happened to be sitting next to him. 'The effect was electrifying. He shot about 2 feet into the air and said: "I'd have you know I'm the greatest friend of Allen Dulles (head of the CIA) and we planned this thing together. Tell your son, that it is like your BBC or British Council. You Europeans will never understand how we Americans do things."'

I'm thrilled my letter produced this indirect confirmation that there was a difference between Britain and the United States when it came to fighting communism. But to go on with my father's letter:

America is *not* a fascist country. It is much more complicated than that. A thing like the CIA affair is more like the conspiracies of big business than like the police state. It is really more a form of cornering a market, the commodity cornered being power rather than money, though lots of money made it possible. Paradoxically it arose originally as a move by Central Intelligence to get round McCarthyism. In 1949 the great Foundations had not got going properly, and all arrangements for travel, culture etc were subject to attack by the UnAmerican Activities Committee for being Red. This meant in practice that the fare of a student to an international conference could not be openly paid unless the student was approved by McCarthy or not likely to be attacked by him. So some rather bright and even liberal people in Central Intelligence used secret funds to sponsor indirectly through respectable seeming channels (like the Congress for Cultural Freedom, the Asian Foundation etc) people who presented a 'liberal' though anti-communist image of America. The people, of course, were not told about this and mixed among them were CIA agents and very skilful amoral operators gifted in deviousness concealment and not so much lying as never telling the truth, of whom a prime example is Melvin Lasky. Above all these operators have a limpet-like tenacity and once they have got into a position it is almost impossible to remove them, because you can never obtain evidence to prove they are agents because the Intelligence agencies are the only people who could supply the proofs.

For the first time my father heard that the man in charge was Cord Meyer. Again, coincidence gave him clues. A colleague of his at Wesleyan happened to be Richard Goodwin, a former adviser to both Kennedy and Johnson. In his letter Dad writes: 'I asked him the other day "Who is Cord Meyer?" He said: "He's one of the top CIA directors, responsible for culture." I said: "He seems to have played quite a role in my life the past twelve years." Dick Goodwin said: "Don't I know it!"'

Back in London, a new British representative was appointed to the board of *Encounter*: William Hayter, the Principal of New College (where I met him several times), a former ambassador to the Soviet Union with experience in secret matters.

Everyone wanted to damp down the scandal. Nobody wanted Spender to leave and start writing articles criticizing the way *Encounter* had been managed over the last decade. By this time it was widely suspected that Lasky was employed by the CIA. I remember Stuart Hampshire telling my mother, 'He's a blown agent,' which immersed the matter into the murky world of spy stories. In London it was taken for granted that Lasky would resign and *Encounter* would return to what it was supposed to be: an English magazine run by English editors. But Lasky was a fighter and he refused to give in.

At this point the difference between Spender and Kermode on one side and Lasky on the other becomes clear. Lasky was a Cold Warrior. They were intellectuals. They believed in telling the truth, he was prepared to do whatever he felt was necessary to win. If they assumed that having been publically unmasked, he would withdraw in confusion, they were mistaken.

Lasky had Cecil King, the newspaper magnate, on his side. King had ostensibly taken over the financing of *Encounter* from the CCF in 1963, when questions about the CIA had first been aired. He hadn't interfered in the running of the magazine; nor (it seems) had he looked at its accounts. He was the perfect owner.

King's political agenda was as tough as Lasky's, and he preferred Lasky to Spender as *Encounter*'s editor. At a later date, King was involved in a bizarre plot to overturn the Labour Prime Minister, Harold Wilson, in a coup d'état. (King thought that Wilson was a Russian spy. He tried to replace him with an emergency government headed by Lord Mountbatten.) Since King owned *Encounter*, there wasn't much to be done. There was, however, an Encounter Trust that oversaw the running of the magazine. A meeting was scheduled for 20 April 1966, so that King and the Trust could come to an agreement.

Arthur Schlesinger flew to London for this meeting.

My father had arrived back from Wesleyan the day before. Even at this late date he could still feel bored by the whole thing. As he wrote to Nikos, 'The trouble with this *Encounter* row is it is all about trivial things to do with quite trivial people – and yet at the same time it has to be fought.'

Egged on by my mother, the first thing he did on arrival was to telephone Malcolm Muggeridge. Hadn't Malcolm always told him that the money for *Encounter* came from private donors with impeccable credentials? According to my mother, Malcolm told my father: 'So I did, dear boy, so I did. But I wouldn't bet your bottom dollar that's where it really came from.'

Next day, Maro and I were invited to Loudoun Road for supper, during which Schlesinger was supposed to be won over to Stephen's side.

We arrived early. Dad opened the door. He was tense and jet-lagged. Along with everything else, he'd lost his voice. He hissed at us in the front hall, 'Whatever else you do, be polite. Everyone says Arthur's going to be the next Secretary of State.'

When Schlesinger arrived, we were left alone with him in the piano room. Mum was downstairs cooking, Dad was so nervous he stayed in his study. He was probably thinking that Arthur must have known about *Encounter*'s financing from the very beginning. How would he get through the evening without betraying his anger?

In the piano room we were polite to Schlesinger as requested, but we were not over-awed by the future Secretary of State, because Maro had a family connection with him. Schlesinger, like several other members of the East Coast liberal left, was a regular summer visitor on Cape Cod. Mary McCarthy and her then husband Boden Broadwater also summered on the Cape, her former husband Edmund Wilson lived in Wellfleet, Dwight and Nancy Macdonald had been there for years. Some of the properties owned by members of this group had been sold to them by Jack Phillips, Maro's ex-stepfather. There were Slough Pond and Horseleech Pond and Slag Pond – lots of pond life among those drab, moth-eaten pines. And cocktail parties. Maro as a child had often passed the literary peanuts on several distinguished lawns. One evening, instead of passing the peanuts, with her Phillips half-sisters she'd gathered up baskets of frogs and thrown them at the feet of the grown-ups.

So Arthur knew Maro from Cape Cod, and for a while we talked about that. Then, of all things, the subject of the Marx Brothers came up. Arthur gave us a seminar on their movies: the early ones with a muted social context and the later ones that gradually reached total anarchy. Their hatred of war, for example. He said the Marx Brothers came from a tradition of Jewish radical socialism that went right back to the Russia of the 1880s.

Dad still did not appear. Finally I asked Schlesinger: could he please tell us something about the CIA and *Encounter*? He was embarrassed, but the explanation that followed had the same friendly but didactic tone with which he'd just compared Groucho's political rage with Harpo's gentler one. And it corroborated what my father had just told me in his letter. The CIA, he said, is a large institution employing many people. Most of the personnel come from the military. It's divided into sections that are often in competition with one another.

The group in charge of ideas – and we wouldn't deny that *Encounter* was an 'ideas' proposition – is extremely small and beleaguered and despised by everyone else. The military prefers to support right-wing governments, in Europe and elsewhere, because direct confrontation is instinctive to them. They distrust the subtle, long-term calculation of using the centre-left to win over votes from the communists. In spite of this, the CIA is the only American institution that could ever have supported such a plan. 'You'd never have convinced Congress to back anything that had the word "socialist" in it,' he said. 'For a liberal magazine like *Encounter* to exist at all, it's almost a miracle.'

My main reaction at the time was disgust that my father, an English poet, should have become a cog in machinery so complicated, and so utterly bound up with the United States.

I don't remember what happened at supper, but afterwards Maro and I drove Arthur back to Claridge's Hotel in my cramped Morris Minor. It was raining. There was more talk about Cape Cod as the windscreen steamed up and we felt our way towards Mayfair. (What was Mougouch up to now? Does she like living in London?) We got out of the car to say goodbye and stood under the hotel's wet awning. Arthur said we shouldn't worry about Stephen. All this would blow over. It wouldn't affect him. 'He'll survive.'

As for the *Encounter* crisis, it was hardly worth having crossed the Atlantic for. 'It's really not that important.' Then, feeling that our silence was not entirely on his side, he added defensively, 'Except of course people's feelings are always important.'

My father went back to Wesleyan without attending a second meeting of the Trust on 5 May. At this meeting Cecil King made it clear that he supported Lasky. On 7 May, Kermode and Spender resigned as editors, and on the following day Stephen gave an interview with the *New York Times* stating his position, which was that he could not continue to work as an editor of a magazine that had been financed by the CIA.

The Trustees thought they'd also better resign, and they did so as quietly as they could so that *Encounter* could survive. Spender, threatened by Lasky, resigned from the Trust on 11 May. Lasky had told him he'd tell the press that, as Stephen had been Chairman of the British CCF back in the early days, he must know more about the financing of the Congress than Lasky did!

On 20 May, the *Saturday Evening Post* published an article by Tom Braden, one of the founders of the 'non-communist left' strategy. He was proud that the CIA had been immoral, he wrote. This is taken by scholars as the moment when the CIA washed its hands of a discarded policy. Braden would never have published his piece without the CIA's approval.

Now to the three questions that interest me. Did my father know? Was *Encounter* run from Langley? How did his reputation survive?

With regard to the first question, let me play the devil's advocate and summarize the case against him. He'd wanted to edit a magazine from the late Thirties onwards, and he'd become the co-editor of *Horizon* at the beginning of the war. Towards the end of the war, he'd worked for the Political Information Department, which was the public face of the Political Warfare Executive, in charge of all propaganda directed at Europe. In 1945, he'd wanted to start an Anglo-German magazine with Ernst Robert Curtius. In 1946, he'd been asked by Information Services Control to provide a plan for an international magazine, and he'd done so, complete with the suggestion that the British government should pay for it. Meanwhile the bureaucratic successor of the Political Information Department was the Information Research Department, the subsequent British backer of *Encounter*. While it lasted, he was Chairman of the British Committee for Cultural Freedom. He made numerous trips outside England on behalf of the Paris CCF, the British Council, the International PEN Club, UNESCO, the BBC and occasionally, in a very nebulous way, the Foreign Office. (I am guessing that his contacts with Guy Burgess had some FO connotations.) On the other hand, he was never an employee of the British Civil Service, and he never signed the Official Secrets Act. His engagement by the above bodies was always fee-earning, which meant he could accept a task or not, as he felt like it.

I am sure that most readers of this book will say: It's impossible that he did not know what he was doing. That he didn't depends on understanding the power of his 'ambivalence'. Whether vice or virtue, my father's 'ambivalence' kept him open where to others the choice would seem either/or. 'Ambivalence' in fact means not choosing, not selecting, not dismissing new experiences, not concluding, not – and I cannot stress this strongly enough – being pinned down.

Stephen always claimed that he never knew about the CIA connection and that from 1962 until 1966 he had been consistently deceived by his employers. His anger was sincere, but righteous anger of an uncontrollable kind often overcame him whenever his 'innocence' was placed in doubt. For example: his anger with the political commissars during the Spanish Civil War when they didn't see why they should release Tony Hyndman from his duties, or his anger with Inez when she'd left him after she decided she couldn't accept his continued relationship with Tony.

The mere fact that he was sincerely angry does not convince me of his innocence. Yet one aspect does strike me as curious. Whenever he writes to his friends or in his journal about Irving Kristol, or Dwight Macdonald, but most of all Melvin Lasky, politics do not feature in his complaints. He held against them their hatred of literature, their self-serving manner and, in Lasky's case, the habit of lying to cover his tracks. He thinks that the ruthlessness of Lasky, like that of Michael Goodwin before him, is due to their pursuit of personal 'success', not that they were working to a secret agenda. He gives no hint that he himself was involved with power, influence, propaganda or cultural manipulation, or that he was aware that his colleagues were.

Against this plea for his innocence there is one small incident.

David Plante tells me that twenty years later, in the period of Gorbachev's *glasnost*, he and Nikos invited Stephen to tea to meet a young Russian friend of theirs, Sergei Belov, recently arrived from Moscow. The subject of *Encounter* came up. 'The whole story had been prominent in the Soviet news; blinking, as if wondering if he should speak or not and finally giving way to the presence of this young Russian, Stephen said, "I knew, somehow I knew," and we were all then silent.'

David comments: 'He knew, but only "somehow", and don't you think that this "somehow" was a constant helpless doubt he had about everything he did, "somehow" never sure of anything?' No, I don't believe he was unsure about what he did, though it's a plausible argument. On the contrary, within the cloud of ambivalence that surrounded him, Stephen was remarkably persistent in pushing forward his ideas over a long period of time. In that respect, to admit to a Russian what he'd never admitted to anyone else seems to me significant, because there was a Russian side to the whole story that did not die when my father left *Encounter*.

My verdict: he did not know about the IRD, or the CIA's financial involvement, or the serpentine chain of command going back to Cord Meyer. But he knew what *Encounter* was *for*, even though his *for* was absolutely not the same as Mel Lasky's.

I often thought of saying to my father, 'Dad, you think you're a poet but in fact you're a politician, and a brilliant one,' but I never did.

Auden wrote a tolerant and understanding letter to my mother when she wrote to ask his help against Lasky's attempt to subvert Stephen's reputation. 'You and I may think he has been a little naïf, and even, perhaps, once he had got *Encounter* really on its feet, a little negligent. But his artistic, political and financial integrity are so obvious that I can't imagine what they could possibly accuse him of.'

With regard to the second question, how much propaganda was involved in *Encounter*, much work has been done by specialist scholars and more still remains to be done.

From 1954, the man in charge was Cord Meyer, who within the CIA occupied a precarious position. He'd once been investigated by the FBI for 'communist tendencies', and it took him a year to clear his name. This corroborates Arthur Schlesinger's impression that the cultural department of the CIA was a beleaguered minority, with rival departments constantly intriguing against it. The chain of command travelled from Cord Meyer to Mike Josselson to Melvin Lasky – all under the strain of having to keep things secret. Plus, in the background, the British IRD, which constantly resisted any attempt by the CIA to move 'their' magazines towards overt propaganda.

In my opinion, the chain of command was too convoluted for the story of *Encounter* to be interpreted as a successful CIA plot. Money passed hands. Nothing more. No instructions.

This assessment does not alter the fact that, if you are a writer who has been selected because you represent an undisclosed government programme, your writing is loaded with messages that you didn't intend. It's one thing if a ballerina dances because she's ambitious and loves dancing, and entirely another if she's been chosen without her knowledge to represent the West's idea of political freedom.

Meanwhile my father's participation in *Encounter* reveals many differences between England and America regarding how the Soviet bloc should be confronted, and the ways in which their respective intelligence services fitted into society. In my view these aspects have not been sufficiently discussed – but at this point I have to give way to feelings that cannot be so detached. The fact is, I absolutely loathe the mixing of politics and culture. Although I think I've managed to create a life that is generally free from stress, on this subject I am unable to think coherently.

I know that there have been periods when art has been used politically, and that sometimes the results are marvellous. The baroque churches of the Counter-Reformation, for instance. And what about the Parthenon? And the great paintings that Jacques-Louis David dedicated to Napoleon? I even like moments when political rhetoric goes mad, such as in the portrait busts of late

Roman emperors, when the vulgarity of different coloured stones unconsciously mocks the nobility of their demeanour. But all such cases involve the transparent use of art. It's politics by visual means, and we can judge it accordingly. With CIA involvement, the US covert programme mocks the art it's designed to support.

In the 1970s, articles were written to suggest that the American Abstract Expressionist movement was a vast CIA plot. To put it briefly: Jackson Pollock was pushed to the front because his manner of painting epitomized the freedom of the West. And it was a success. The Soviet East was unable to offer a counter-offensive. Italian painters such as Afro, Scialoja and Vedova abandoned Social Realism to follow the lead of the Abstract Expressionists, and the Italian Communist Party embraced them, thereby moving Italian culture into a fluid role somewhere between America and Russia. Social Realism was so out of fashion by the Seventies that figurative painters had a hard time finding exhibition space.

Some left-wing critics viewed this American influence on Italian art with misgiving, and the idea that it might all be a CIA plot went straight to the heart of conspiracy theorists. And, inevitably, one day I came across an article that mentioned Maro's father and my father in the same breath as tools of American imperialism. This dark thought had lurked in the back of my mind for a long time, but I was unprepared for my own reaction when it appeared in the press. I was overwhelmed by physical revulsion. It was a 'short circuit' between my father and Maro's of the worst possible kind.

I should have recovered by now but I don't think I have. The fact that our fathers were involved means that, for me, this particular punch goes way below the belt.

Third question: how did my father emerge unscathed?

When Arthur Schlesinger told Maro and me under the awning of Claridge's, Your father will survive, I was irritated because I assumed that of course he'd survive. What was he talking about? But it was a good point. Mike Josselson and Nicky Nabokov saw their lives damaged by exposure. 'Your father is still famous,' Josselson's daughter told me recently, 'my father is just slightly infamous.' Stephen was saved by the fact that *Encounter* was only one part of a complex life. 'Ambivalence' also meant being interested in more things than *Encounter*.

Stephen never held it against Nabokov that he'd been involved in the deception. On the contrary, he felt sorry for him. Far in the future, when Nicky was long dead, a rumour surfaced that he'd been paid half a million dollars for *not* writing his memoirs about the Congress for Cultural Freedom. Because he did not care about money, my father thought this was merely amusing; but my mother, who was as careful as Dad was frivolous when it came to money, felt that the person who ought to have been paid a fat sum was Stephen, not Nicky. As the editor of *Encounter*, Stephen had been far more influential. And he'd also been the Agency's dupe.

Stephen took for granted that he'd succeeded in keeping his political life separate from his creative life. Literary London accepted this, as it accepted with unexpected calm the revelation of yet more American interference in English politics. It was only to be expected. 'Too much politics' was not the accusation levelled against my father by literary London in his later years. Critics attacked him because he'd been too 'social'; and the idea that to his peers he'd become a 'parlour poet' hurt him deeply. The sense of failure that often came over him in his old age had more to do with wasted time and a feeling that he had not used his gifts properly. The novels he'd written didn't really work and too many poems had failed to materialize because he'd been busy with other things. He tried not to let his sense of failure, which was sometimes strong, overwhelm him. My father was, after all, an optimistic man.

26

ROMANTIC FRIENDSHIPS
BEFORE ALL

W E SPENT THE summer of 1967 on Patmos, where Mougouch
had rented a small house on the unfashionable side of the
bay: Maro and me, her sister Natasha, Mougouch and her two other
daughters, plus various guests who appeared expectantly on the
veranda at mealtimes.

Mougouch was unhappy because a man she loved had refused to
marry her. It was the first time in her life that she had ever been
rejected and she took it very badly. She'd left England for a year
delegating the mothering role to Maro – which was tough, as Antonia
was rebelling against her boarding school and Chapel Street had
been leased to a madwoman. 'I can always count on you, dear,' said
Mougouch cheerfully when Maro asked for help. 'You are my Little
Meg. Maro Efficiency Gorky.' This as an alternative to coming back
from Athens and taking charge.

That summer on Patmos, Mougouch was dazzling in her unhappiness, but all of us were a bit mixed up. I was making horrible paintings
that I threw away at the end of the summer. Susannah was an adolescent, and beautiful, and yet she didn't want to say goodbye to her
childhood. Maro was broody for babies, though it wasn't yet apparent.

She found a half-drowned kitten on the beach and nursed it back to life. In the early hours of the morning she'd latch it on to my breast, because she said that although she fed it well with an eye-drop pipette, it needed to suckle, otherwise it would be psychologically deprived. My tit was more like a cat's than hers, she said. So I lay there patiently every morning as this wild thing kneaded my breast with adamantine claws and chewed my nipple with needle-sharp teeth. After a week, I began to lactate. Everyone thought this was very funny, but later, on the laborious trip back to London, my breast became infected. In the end I had to have a mastectomy. Our domestic solidarity was thus confirmed by losing my right breast to a kitten.

Barbara Hutchinson joined us. She and Mougouch decided that if Maro and I got married, Mougouch would be able to come back to London with a flourish. Her feeling of rejection would be forgotten and social life in Chapel Street could start up again. I distinctly remember the two of them watching the Patmos boat drift across the bay and pick up steam before chugging off towards Athens. There was only one boat every three days. I couldn't escape! Then they turned to me smiling and started work.

Maro and I thought of ourselves as being married already. What was this bourgeois convention they were insisting on? Why make promises of permanence when permanence was already there? And hadn't Barbara been married three times?

'Yes,' she said passionately, 'and every time I've always believed it was absolutely the right thing for me to do, and even when a marriage failed, I still believed it to be right. Every time! Absolutely right! It's a gesture, you see – a protest against time. Time always wins, but in the meantime you've said, I defy you! Here I am! Here we are! We are facing the challenge of the future, side by side, through thick and thin.'

I thought this was terrific; so I said Fine, we'll do it. I sank to my knees and proposed. Maro, who always refuses any gift, didn't say yes and didn't say no, but over the next few days it was obvious that the answer was yes; and that deep down, she'd been longing for this moment.

Mougouch on Patmos, wearing a broken umbrella as a sun hat.

I set off by the next boat two days later to join my parents in the South of France and tell them the news. Piraeus to Brindisi through the Corinth Canal, deck class on a sleeping bag, the rhythm of the boat aggravating my swollen breast. Train up Italy, the council houses around Bologna glowing in the afternoon sun. In Milan, I sat in the station offering mugs of wine to anyone who'd come near, and thus I missed the connection to Marseilles. I was scared. I didn't want to get there.

No news was received more despondently by any parents. 'We thought you must have something up your sleeve,' said my mother wearily.

I sneaked down to the post office and sent Maro an enthusiastic telegram in their names. It hadn't occurred to either of them to send a message welcoming her into the family.

I think we met David Plante that autumn. Dad brought him to tea with us at Percy Street. David sat on the edge of his chair and was very polite.

In the car travelling down Gower Street a few days later, Dad asked Maro and me what we thought of him. I said, making a joke, 'I think he must be one of those creeping plants.' The result was scary. Dad slammed on the brakes – luckily there was no one behind us – and said tragically, 'How CAN you treat ANY human being with such contempt?'

I thought about this for a long time. Was he overreacting? Yes! To make a joke about Plante's name was corny, perhaps even in bad taste, but surely no more than that? However, thinking it over, I decided that Dad's anger was justified. My casual remark was a form of rejection, not so much of David Plante himself as of this whole arcane world that my father valued, which I felt I couldn't enter.

He always spoke about David and Nikos in intense, hushed tones. Perhaps he just wanted to introduce us to them as one young couple to another, but at the time I misread his signals as being connected with a certain kind of glamour. When it came to glamour, I could see what Dad desired. When glamour struck, being alive bound him to the way the whole world moved. His hair rose in a halo, his face turned pink. His sense of self suddenly fused with the greed of the planet. Success is hyper-awareness of time, a prickling of the skin. Fun – as I've learned for myself in the few spasms when it's come up in my life. But at the time I rejected it as a form of madness, for pleasure so intense could only mean something to the person it touches. And glamour spurns everyone outside its magic circle.

Dad enveloped Nikos and David in a part of London life where creativity and glamour overlapped and, by doing so, he gave them something they wouldn't otherwise have had. It made me uneasy then, and I'm awkward as I write about it now, for I can't quite pin down the problem. After reading an early draft of this book, a friend told me, 'You're making it too complicated. You were just jealous of your father's lovers!' It's almost true. I was wary of Nikos, whose purity combined with intelligence often seemed poised to produce razorblades out of thin air.

But there was something else. Two men living together seemed alien to me, not because I took some moral position about homosexual relationships, but because of the atmosphere. The choice of objects to look at, the special meals to cook, the tidiness of the mantelpiece, the absence of children, the social striving, all seemed to me set to a different rhythm from anything I thought was domestic. It made me feel claustrophobic.

I told myself that I was suffering from a rejection of the homosexual world, a resurgence of my ancient prejudice regarding homosexuality and power, only this time with pining infants shimmering offstage. I told myself I was wrong; and I was certainly confused. To simplify things, I reverted to a decision that I'd made years previously when I'd decided that the tensions between my parents were not my business. I vowed that I'd never again comment on my father's sexuality.

Over time, however, I discovered that keeping this vow was in itself a form of rejection. My silence was accusatory. The Creeping Plante episode, slight though it was, became a key moment when I began to cut myself off from my father.

Years later, Dad tried to talk to me about his love for Bryan Obst. The words he used to introduce this offstage young man, whom I never met, were these: 'I have a friend, and he is kind and intelligent and – well, everything, really. And he tells me that he can't listen to the music of Mozart because it reminds him of a toothpaste advertisement.'

I greeted this with absolute silence. I didn't laugh, though I thought the remark was ridiculous. The pathos of 'well, everything, really'. I'd like to give myself credit for not laughing, but it's not good enough. I should have said politely, 'How awful,' as if Mozart really could be devalued by a toothpaste jingle. I could even have said, 'When did you meet him?' And quietly listened to the rest of the story. Instead, I said nothing at all. But I knew my silence signified rejection. And so did he.

We did not broach this subject again.

Years later, after Bryan had died, my father told me bitterly that

AIDS was the worst thing that had ever happened in his lifetime. I said, 'Worse than the concentration camps? Worse than the Second World War?' 'Yes,' he said. 'Because AIDS stops people from doing what they like with their bodies, and that freedom is the first of all freedoms.'

There was another point in cutting myself off from this aspect of my father's life: loyalty to my mother.

It was tiresome that Mum didn't see the attraction of the woman with whom, at the time of the Creeping Plante episode, I'd been living for the past six years, and was now about to marry. But I was damned if then or later I was going to join my father in a conspiracy of men against women. Whatever the difficulties I had with my mother – and there were plenty – I could see that my father's frequent infatuations with young men were painful to her. Why should I become a part of them?

My mother at that point had finished her exams and had started a course in Psychology at London University. She was planning a dissertation on Aural Perception, to find out if musicians could hear a barely perceptible bleep, if it occurred in time to an imaginary beat in a bar. She tested Maro and me by wiring us up to headphones and pressing a button on a recording machine. I scored halfway between the musicians and the non-musicians. Natasha was thrilled to discover that Maro failed to score anything at all.

Stephen took no interest in this new life of Natasha's, either then or later. Thus she'd sacrificed a musical career in which he felt little interest in favour of a new quest in which he felt none at all. It hurt. She wrote in her 1985 diary, 'it makes no difference to S whether I read psychology or trash – I don't talk about either'.

Though she subsequently made a new career for herself and was able to teach Visual Perception at the Royal College of Art for several years, it never raised a flicker of interest in her husband. She felt that, as far as he was concerned, her only role was that of wife. 'The feeling is strong upon me that I have *wasted* my life – The policy of the last 20 years, progressively giving in from the point of view of asserting or even respecting my talents, culminating now in their complete surrender (in the hope of some felicity yet to be discovered to help S) seems to have led to barrenness, though a moderate atmosphere of affection *is* a little reward.' But moderate affection could be ascribed to Stephen's immaculate manners, with nothing behind it.

> I have resigned all ambitions which have annoyed Stephen – I have blotted all commitment to anything but wifemanship from my life. S likes my helpfulness, and it is a surprise to me that he's more often appreciative & less scolding, so it is rewarding. Perhaps if I had always been only a wife he would have been happier – but no – there would always have been long absences, and I would have been totally without resources.

The absences were justified by work, for Loudoun Road needed money just like any other household. However, when the house was empty, there was always the suspicion that Stephen, even if he said he missed home, was also seeing his friends in that 'animated queer scene' that did not include her.

She bravely put forward the 'work' argument, quelling her secret doubts. 'S always thinks in terms of himself & justifies putting his work before his personal relationships (at least his central personal relationships)' – but this brought on worse thoughts so she immediately adds – 'although of course he *hasn't* really devoted himself to his work which has always taken second place to going to conferences or social life.'

A day later, this thought becomes harsher: 'S would always put everything else before his closest personal relationship – work before wife but also conferences & social life before work and intense romantic friendships before all.'

The role of wife had to be rewarded with something more than mere politeness. How to win more? All she had to offer was her wifely skill. 'The truth is, if one is not loved, it avails nothing to offer devotion.' This is what Raymond Chandler had told her so often and so relentlessly: without desire, there can be no love.

Her diary is the only remaining evidence about what she really felt; for her usual rule was that, to the outside world, appearances must take precedence over feelings. I think she would have burned this document in her final years if she'd remembered its existence. I found it after her death in the bottom of a cupboard as I rummaged around in the empty house and waited for my sister to come back from Australia so we could bury her.

Of her case against my father – if I can put it like that – I knew nothing from her personally; and I resent it. If in this book I've sounded hard on her, there's a reason. I could not stand her sense of privacy. Her reticence grew from pride, and it had a certain dignity, a desire to keep her children out of it. Her own childhood was dreadful; I knew that. She wanted to limit the range of suffering. It wasn't hard to understand. But it was also a form of rejection. It left me with two options: either to accept the edifice she presented of a family that functioned, with firm walls and solid furniture, or move out and try for an alternative myself.

In 1967, in the background of what must have been a difficult period of my mother's life, the laws against homosexuality were at last repealed. The celebrations, if any, were muted. David and Nikos just laughed. Criminals? That's what the newspapers said they'd been, one morning when they'd woken up in bed together side by side. They'd been criminals all this time and hadn't even noticed? Well, they'd never *felt* criminal.

The repeal of those laws produced a subtle change in my mother. It was as if a great weight had been lifted from her mind. It made me realize that, up until then, the idea of a public accusation aimed at my father, or still worse a court case brought by the police, had always lurked in the back of her mind. I did not notice this anxiety until it had disappeared, but then I thought: Social shame would destroy her. It would not have had the same effect on my father, or even on myself; but my childhood had been secure, hers had been filled with stress.

I don't believe my father had ever worried about being arrested. When he was young, he may even have nursed a fantasy of himself in the dock behaving magnificently during the trial for obscenity of *The Temple*. After the war, with a wife and two children, the risk of his arrest was almost non-existent, provided he did not provoke the police by importuning in public.

If as an adolescent I'd raised with Mum the question of my father's sexual orientation, she would have denied it. His homosexuality was in the past and all evidence to the contrary was brushed aside. With the homosexual law reform bill, she began to move cautiously away from her position that this part of Stephen's life was over, because public embarrassment was no longer a threat.

Patiently and skilfully she began to make friends with Nikos and David, moving from a state of polite hostility to one of wise understanding. This did not mean that she'd accepted her role as 'peripheral' to Stephen's inner life. It was more of a question of gaining confidence in public. Other women could look at her at parties and guess how much it cost her. Occasionally I could see someone thinking: Natasha's doing a fantastic job of keeping up appearances.

My father's strength was his weakness. My mother's weakness was that she always had to appear strong.

As Nikos and David slowly became integrated into the lives of both Spenders, there were times when they felt they were becoming part of an elaborate game. David, on the phone to Dad, would hear heavy breathing on the upstairs line as Mum listened in. And if the conversation between the two men became facetious, there'd be an audible click as Mum rang off. That click was as effective as a slamming door. The game was simple. Stephen was saying to Natasha as she eavesdropped: 'I can always run away and join the boys.' The ominous click was Mum saying, 'No you can't.'

Over time, David became her friend, and when thirty years later

Nikos became terminally ill with cancer, she was extremely supportive to them both. Even before that she was always civil, but she'd never allowed either of these young men to occupy the role in Stephen's life that he himself wanted. Verlaine was not allowed to run away with Rimbaud. After Dad died, David told Natasha that he thought Stephen had loved him. 'No,' said my mother with assurance, 'but he was very fond of you.' This meant: Even though Stephen is dead, I am still in control.

Back in London after Patmos, before we got married, I arranged for all Gorky's work in Chapel Street to be photographed. It was the first step towards a catalogue raisonné – which incidentally is still unfinished. It took a long time and it wasn't done particularly well, but it was a beginning. Those portfolios of drawings under the bed in the basement, the massive safe that had been installed in the house by Charlie Chaplin when he came to England, which used to contain all his films and now was stuffed with Gorkys – it was time they were documented.

Once the photos had been numbered I started going through them with Mougouch.

'He had to begin somewhere,' she said as we looked at a straight copy of a work painted by Picasso in 1923. 'Everybody does. Sometimes he was still adding the final coat when I was around. He never seemed in a hurry to let go of anything.'

'But even the railings are French! Those are not New York railings. I've seen them near the Place Ravignan where Picasso used to live.'

'He didn't care about that,' she said. 'And anyway, I didn't know it.'

Gorky's devotion to the old masters fascinated me. Quotations from Ingres and Bruegel were tucked away in strange corners of his own work, like ghosts from other paintings.

'Yes,' she said. 'He wasn't interested in breaking with the past and doing something new. Gorky thought he could carry the past along with him. I suppose he'd lost so much, he didn't feel like "killing the father" or whatever it is a man is supposed to do. He'd tell me: you just have to give it a personal twist. It doesn't have to be much, he'd say, but it has to be yours.'

She'd translated for André Breton when he came to the studio. And Breton was marvellous. 'He understood everything immediately, whereas those New York critics always thought Gorky was just a follower. All that business of doing something first, which is so typically American. It's just as well I spoke French!'

After the paintings we started on the drawings.

'Ah,' she said. 'That's a walnut tree in the valley. He did a whole stack of drawings from that tree when we were in Virginia, then back in New York he did more, to unravel them.'

'I just see the unravelling. Where's the tree?'

'You'll get used to them. I cannot *not* see the landscape. And this one', she pulled out a drawing, 'goes with that one.'

I looked at the two side by side. 'I'm sorry, Mougouch, I just don't see it.'

'Oh. Well, maybe the wind's coming from the other direction.'

The work was fascinating. It involved history, chronology, sorting, New York gossip, her views on the Surrealists. Her life with Gorky had been wonderful, frightening, funny, serious, ridiculous, and some days all of the above.

I told her she should write everything down. 'No,' she said.

My parents saw this as a distraction, and they were right. 'You're becoming the bailiff of the Gorky Estate,' my mother said. I wasn't a historian or even a trained curator, she added. True enough. 'Maybe you should join the Courtauld and take a course in curating? If you are serious, that is.' My attention wasn't professional. But – this was deeply buried but I felt it was there – my mother also thought that the attention I gave to Gorky was a distraction from the attention I ought to be giving to my father. It was another manifestation of the competition between Chapel Street and Loudoun Road.

Mindful of my mother's warning, even though it contained an element of bile, I tried to remain detached from the Gorky story and merely act, as it were, as a long stop near the boundary. Every five years or so, for the next twenty-five years, I encouraged Mougouch to write her own version of her life before someone else produced a hostile biography. She always said no.

Twenty years later when she married the writer Xan Fielding, far away in a new house in a new country, I asked her one last time. If she didn't want *me* to help her, surely she could tell Xan the story and he'd write it down? She said, 'You've asked me before and I'll tell you one last time: I am through with Gorky! I am happy now! May Gorky rot in his grave!'

Mougouch would never have said something so harsh to a stranger, but by that time I knew her extremely well. She felt that she had every reason to be defiant, because Gorky had lied to her. He'd never told her he was Armenian, he'd adopted a pseudonym that had already been used, his love letters had been copied from Gaudier-Brzeska. His relatives – including his father – had been kept secret from her. How was it possible that she'd shared her life with such a secretive personality? She'd been open with him. She'd given him everything she could. What level of intimacy had she received in return?

I'd been there when the article on the copied love letters was published. Mougouch's shame was painful to see. Something as intimate as the letters that had seduced her had been copied from a book. I took her side. It was awful. Yet Maro, who in all other things told the truth (whatever the price), defended her father's lies. He was an artist, she said. Artists' lives are themselves works of art.

Gorky was a man who'd reinvented himself in the wake of a genocide, and that was understandable; and yes, life as a work of art was surely an admirable thing. But at this point he'd been dead for decades, and here Maro and her mother were fighting over differing loyalties to – what?

The 'rot in his grave' moment occurred in Mougouch's new garden outside Ronda, in Spain. Xan was watering the roses. I looked up at

Maro standing on the veranda. She wasn't upset, thank heavens. 'Mummy,' she said, 'if you find a bucket filled with muddy water, you wait until the mud settles, then you pour off the water into a glass and drink it and you make a tile out of the mud at the bottom. But instead you just keep stirring that bucket and it's always cloudy!'

When we were alone I told Maro: This is all very well, but you and your mother can't go on fighting for the rest of your lives over your father's life. We know too little about it. One day we must set the record straight. If Mougouch won't do it, we'll have to.

One day, my mother appeared at Chapel Street to tell Mougouch that she wanted me to take a job. This in itself this was straightforward, but as she spoke she became distracted. Here, in Chapel Street, it seemed to her as if she'd come instead to reclaim the soul of her son from the coven of witches that had appropriated it.

She told Mougouch that when I was sixteen I'd 'accused' Stephen of not writing poems. 'But poor Stephen couldn't just write poems. Doesn't Matthew realize the sacrifices he's had to make for him?'

This was a complex subject. In this precarious moment after he'd resigned from *Encounter*, my father's only source of income consisted of lecture tours or visiting professorships, so the prospect of prolonged absences was in the air. Money, plus me, plus absence, often confused my mother's train of thought. In adolescence, these sessions with my mother about money always ended in a spasm of guilt on her part, in which I felt obliged to join her. But as tears rolled down my cheeks, I'd wonder: Is this money being earned for me, for her, for us? Whose anxiety is it?

What should have been a practical conversation between two experienced women ended with my mother weeping and Mougouch completely at a loss. As much as she'd understood of Natasha's diatribe, it seemed an accusation aimed at herself. My mother didn't approve of me spending time with those portfolios is how she'd interpreted it. And beyond those portfolios, my mother didn't approve of Mougouch.

369

'It just seems to me that somehow she's reached – we've reached – a dead end,' Mougouch told me afterwards. 'She tries too hard – and I don't see why. She doesn't have to emulate and she doesn't have to compete.' My mother must have tried to enlist Mougouch's support for her values. 'I'm not going to be converted – and anyway, there's nothing to be converted to. There's no one good way of doing life. Doesn't she realize that when it comes to the direction of your life, it's only the things you throw away that hit the mark?'

This last observation made a big impression on me. I loved the idea that my entire existence could be won or lost like rolling dice.

To her own parents, Mougouch had 'thrown herself away' when she'd married Gorky. Her father had never ceased to believe this, in spite of liking Gorky himself and acknowledging that over the years he'd won a great reputation. He'd wanted something simpler and more wholesome for his beloved daughter – as fathers often do. When he lay dying a few years later he told her, 'Aggie, you've always been a rotten picker in the garden of love.' She was in tears when she came back from his bedside and told us this. She couldn't see that the remark wasn't a reproof, but an expression of love.

I don't remember having 'accused' my father of not writing poems, but probably some adolescent confrontation of this kind had indeed occurred. Looking back on it, however, I wonder if the real target of my forgotten reproach wasn't her, not him. I wanted to challenge her idea of what Dad's 'work' entailed, because I thought her interpretation was wrong.

My mother's idea was that Dad would sit quietly in his study writing magnificent poems, which she herself would be the first to admire. She would be practising, and he'd come stumbling into the piano room holding a piece of paper and he'd say, excitedly, 'Read this.' It was a good fantasy, and I am sure that in certain moods my father shared it; or maybe once or twice it even happened. But my father's sense of what a poem should be included the spark of an original event that had to be captured, and this was always built around an adventure. I never discussed this with Mum, because it was forbidden territory. But she couldn't have it both ways. She couldn't have Dad quietly in the study doing his 'real' work, as she often defined it, without accepting the existence of Reynolds, and Nikos, and later on Bryan, because they were essential to the one activity about which she was entirely supportive.

My father always knew that, to him, creativity was linked to sex. When he was very old and at last impotent, he felt his perception of the world had been destroyed by a form of blindness. A month or two before he died, the realization that his sexuality no longer existed sent him into a kind of panic. 'I do not believe that writing or any other activity I am capable of can exist without sex.'

For my mother, once the poem was finished and published, it was transformed into the bricks and mortar of the author's reputation. This was another paradox. Mum may have believed that creativity was an interior process similar to prayer – the quiet hush of St Jérôme in his study – but everything to do with cultivating a reputation went in the other direction. Publicity. Fame. The world. And she enjoyed being famous. When the time came, she enjoyed being Lady Spender. Yet I could never tell her, all this involves ambition. It would have meant attacking her conviction that a poet is innocent. ·

My mother's 'innocence' was not the same as my father's. To him, the fact that he was *unschuldig* meant he could do anything without feeling guilty. It was part of his concept of freedom. Perhaps I should say, without *being* guilty. Such was the strength of his conviction that he was free from guile, deceit, ambition etc., that the mere fact *he'd* done something automatically conferred on it the virtue of his innocence.

My mother avoided thinking about her husband's ambition by convincing herself that his reputation had been awarded to him incidentally. The creative act was solitary – the monastic moment – and its worldly recompense was unsolicited. Success was not evidence that he'd ever sought it. The world had rewarded this unworldly man because what he wrote was good, not because he was ambitious.

Strangely enough, Mougouch believed in a similar fantasy. To her, Gorky had rejected the temptations of the art world and the machinations of the New York critics, like Harold Rosenberg or Clement Greenberg and 'all those other Bergs', as she once put it, with a smidge of snobbery. His paintings, however much they acquired the spirit of New York, always projected the feeling of that intense bucolic mountainside hidden away in – where was it? She couldn't quite remember. He'd never explained where.

I didn't believe Mum on the subject of Stephen's innocence, and Maro didn't believe Mougouch on the subject of Gorky's. I felt that my father was an ambitious man, whose life had been complicated by the distraction of politics, and these had slowed down his capacity to write poems. Nevertheless, I'd subscribed to his theory that sex and freedom and poems went together and I'd always, since I was twelve, thought he had a right to pursue all three. If self-deception came into it – fine, we are all guilty of that vice. Just as long as he didn't try to involve me in the process.

The fact that my mother insisted on Dad's 'unworldliness' meant it was yet another subject I could not broach with her. Indeed, I accepted the theory for far too long. The only clue I'd received so far that art isn't pure was Auden's unexpected joy at having been given a pat on the back by the *Evening Standard*. For shame! And the silly old *Evening Standard*! My obsession with that moment merely underlined how subservient I'd become to the theory that talent is rewarded in proportion to its innocence.

The pain, for me, of the *Encounter* business was that I absolutely *had* to decide how much my father had known about it. If he'd known even a teeny-weeny bit, wouldn't that destroy Natasha's theory that poets are innocent?

I could even reverse this thought. My mother's hatred of Lasky and the CIA was necessary to her, to allow her to continue to believe in my father's innocence.

Maro's view of Gorky's failure in New York was simpler. She thought, in a rough-and-ready way, that he'd done his best. It was just that he hadn't had much luck. New York was tough, that was all. But he'd been successful in the end. Gorky had won his gamble posthumously.

Maro and I were both children of artists of talent, and we shared an intuitive idea of what was involved. There was the talent, and there was the world, and the two were connected in a mysterious way. If an artist says, I shall pitch my fantasy of the world against the reality of that world and see if I can win, it's a magnificent spectacle. But if the challenge is rewarded, if for a while the taste of the world and the idea thrown at it combine, then the person of talent finds himself caught within his idea and the world into which it now fits. Nothing can penetrate the hard shell where these two elements intertwine. This is why the lives of successful artists are often so sparse. In time the taste of the world inevitably ebbs away, leaving the carapace of this drama as the only thing still visible.

One last time I went up to Loudoun Road to go through my fervent marital ambitions and rejection of all worldly ones. 'Mougouch didn't understand what you were getting at, last week,' I said. 'Can we keep it simple? What kind of job do you imagine would suit me?'

The answer was unexpected. It wasn't too late for me to sit the Foreign Office exam, was it? I'd studied history, hadn't I? The exam wasn't *that* hard, and we could probably find someone to 'recommend' me. I'd enjoy working in the Foreign Office. 'It might be rather fun to end up as an ambassador, don't you think?'

I just laughed. Maro was hardly cut out to be an ambassador's wife. I pointed out that she had no sense of tact, and her habit of treating a secret as if it were a delicious substance to be spread over a large area, like anchovy paste on toast, would hardly go down well in the Foreign Office.

Mum couldn't resist saying: 'Well, quite!'

There was something odd about this comment. I asked her what she meant. My mother, with a careless air as if she might as well be hung for a sheep as for a lamb, said that Maro's lack of tact might be a very good reason for me to choose someone else to marry.

I thought this was very funny, and so did Maro, but all the same it somehow represented the end of the line. We were getting married in about a fortnight, and here was Mum making a last-ditch defence of what was right by saying we shouldn't.

It was frustrating. Mougouch was a much tougher personality than my mother, and at this point my prospective mother-in-law was revealing occasional rough edges by showing pleasure in having defeated Mum. But why, for heaven's sake, had it always been such a battle? Mum was a vulnerable woman held together by rules. Mougouch was a buccaneer. Mum's rules had never stood a chance. She shouldn't have stuck to them.

My father, sent by my mother a fortnight later to try to achieve some understanding with Mougouch, took her out for a drink. We joined them and kept quietly in the background. Stephen explained that he and Natasha wanted to contribute to the expenses of the wedding; not perhaps all of it, because their finances were in such a bad state. Mougouch told him firmly that it was the duty of the bride's parents to pay for the wedding, so he needn't worry.

'I want at least to pay something,' said Stephen. He laughed. 'Maybe we could take on the cube root of whatever it'll cost?'

After he left, Maro asked her mother why she hadn't even let him pay for the drinks. 'Oh well, you've heard of something called pride, haven't you? Pride! Sometimes when you get up, you can see it still stuck to the chair.'

I had the impression I'd heard this gag before. Never mind. It suited her.

At St Pancras Town Hall, the man behind the desk said something discouraging along the lines of, British law recognizes one wife per one husband at a time. We were asked to say yes, so we said yes. Afterwards Maro said loudly, before we'd even left the room, 'I didn't believe a word of it.' She was right. It was the meanest of marital vows. We'd wanted 'with this body I thee worship'. Something transcendental, but it was beyond anyone's appetite in those days.

The party was chaotic. Mougouch had to make conversation with Sir George Schuster, my father's great-uncle, who talked about Stephen's wedding to Inez in 1936. Cyril Connolly talked to Moura Budberg, in whose arms the other Gorky, Maxim, was supposed to have expired. There were lots of children who, encouraged by Maro, danced all over the room like imps. My father, who'd looked gloomy throughout, sought a telephone towards the end and rang Nikos and David to say how pleased he was that they were together – those two, not us two. 'Stephen, sentimental about how Nikos and I love each other, sounded drunk, and Nikos and I were embarrassed for him.'

For our honeymoon we went to Amsterdam. I wanted to compare and contrast Rembrandt with Frans Hals. The bath in our hotel was as small and square as a Japanese coffin, and I got stuck in it with my knees under my chin. Maro had to pull me out. There was a sullen squelch and we ended up on top of each other with water everywhere. She said, 'This is the last time I get married to *you*.'

After walking through the museums, Maro wanted to see some movies as light relief. We saw five different episodes of *Angélique*, about an uptight Frenchwoman who survives every indignity in order to end up with the deeply unattractive Robert Hossein. She was raped constantly, though the camera always shied away at the last minute to concentrate on the floorboards. Then we'd drink young gin and eat rollmops.

One bar near the hotel had an aquarium with some very sick fish. My diary of the time has Maro saying: 'I wouldn't eat that scrawny old fish if they paid me, with his eyes going round in their saucers. Do you see him, Matt? He's on his last legs. But it's nice how they rest on the sand. One feels immediately protective towards the little darlings.'

It was December and the weather was foul. She said, 'Can't we go away? I'm not a fir tree. I'm a lemon tree or an orange tree. My leaves fall off if it gets too cold. Every time I want to laugh, shivers run up my legs. I'm an ice bucket with the cubes tinkling in my belly.'

I wondered, and not for the first time, if we couldn't just leave England. Perhaps we could keep on going, beyond Amsterdam and down towards the sun, and never come back?

27

THE RIGHT TO SPEAK

THE EXPOSURE OF *Encounter* as a weapon of the CIA caused my father a great deal of anguish, especially in the United States, where both in public and in private he had to face some very direct questions. At Mount Holyoke College in Massachusetts, where he'd been invited to speak to the English Department, a student got up and asked him how he felt about the *Encounter* scandal. His reply was emotional and confused. The student was the daughter of Mike Josselson, but she did not feel like introducing herself afterwards to ask for a clearer answer.

It would have been the perfect moment for him to give up politics and retreat into a life of writing poetry and books and book reviews. His wife's fantasy. As it was, within a year he'd taken up a cause that in its way was even more important than *Encounter*.

On 12 January 1968, *The Times* in London and *Le Monde* in Paris published a letter from the Russian scientist Pavel Litvinov, asking for help on behalf of two dissidents who'd just received heavy sentences in Moscow. My father instantly telephoned Isaiah Berlin, saying that an appeal such as this could not be ignored. A telegram signed by as many distinguished people as possible must be sent to Moscow before the weekend was over.

Among those who responded immediately were Freddie Ayer and

Stuart Hampshire. If over one weekend Stephen was able to raise such support with just a few telephone calls, it was because a wide sympathy existed among his friends for what he'd just been through. Freddie and Stuart might even have had a twinge of guilty conscience. They'd been called in to advise how MI5 could be reorganized after the defection of Burgess and Maclean – Dad told me this in a typically indiscreet moment – so they must have known about *Encounter*'s financing and the ghostly presence of British Intelligence.

On the Monday morning, the telegram was duly sent, with a copy published in a newspaper. A few weeks later Litvinov replied by sending a long letter to Spender in which he proposed the formation of an international committee to defend the freedom of expression of all writers everywhere, not just in the Soviet Union, but across the world, as a matter of principle.

This was a big step forward from the kind of non-governmental connection that for several years Stephen had been trying to establish between Britain and Russia. In the background, many things were changing. Samizdat literature was being circulated, communications between Russia and the outside world had improved, the Russian government was increasingly unsure how it should deal with its dissidents. Repression was still the natural response, but the bad publicity it provoked worldwide was hardly creditable to the cause of Soviet freedom.

Following the letter he'd received from Litvinov, Spender was able to set in motion the creation of Writers and Scholars International and the magazine *Index on Censorship*, whose first issue appeared in 1972. Whereas *Encounter* had had a tiny circulation in Russia, *Index* went on to create a strong impact. It was circulated as samizdat to a much wider audience and it helped Russian writers to feel they had contact with an audience abroad.

At this point all my objections to my father's political involvement give way to admiration. He may have been ambivalent and evasive and a whole host of other adjectives signifying hard to pin down. He was always sure of his integrity, even when what he'd actually done seemed equivocal to everyone else. In relation to myself and my wife and my eventual family, he was bored – I think that's the simplest explanation – because we insisted on living far from the centres of cultural power. But beneath all the charm of his manners, which never ceased to be courteous and non-confrontational, he was persistent. He was always, and in subtle ways, a man of action.

Initially, my father had tried to raise money in order to found a new magazine that would drive *Encounter* out of business. Revenge, through literature. Several times he had to endure the obvious joke, 'To be called Under the Counter, eh?' My father would give a polite laugh, but my mother always rose to this heavily: 'On the contrary, it should be called Over the Counter, as it's *Encounter* which is suspect.'

He decided to bring out an advertisement asking for support for this new idea: a declaration signed by his friends. This had come to nothing. Although they initially said yes, they mysteriously changed their minds. I think Julian Huxley was one. Another was Henry Moore, who telephoned a week after he'd agreed to lend his name, saying, 'Stephen, I've been nobbled.' My father understood. He didn't ask for an explanation and he didn't hold it against Moore. In fact he liked Henry's frankness so much he turned it into a funny after-dinner story. And it was obvious to him who'd done the nobbling: Kenneth Clark, who besides being a strong supporter of Moore, was also a key member of the Establishment.

My father's new magazine never materialized, and then his energies were taken up by *Index on Censorship*, on behalf of which he made several trips to America to raise funds. The Ford Foundation was helpful, but there were frequent and recurring difficulties with the State Department, which was worried that *Index* would come to the rescue of anti-American writers imprisoned in South America.

In 1974 I was in Paris, where I was holding my first one-man show of paintings in a tiny gallery on the Île Saint-Louis. My father appeared and was supportive; and then he took me off to have lunch with Mary McCarthy.

We met at her flat. At some point during the usual introductory conversation she said, with reference to his recent fund-raising activities on behalf of *Index*, 'Stephen, tell me what's been happening about your new magazine.' Before he could reply, she turned to me and, so that he didn't see, she gave me a grossly exaggerated wink. I was stunned. It wasn't a wink that said, 'He's got a tough job ahead of him.' It was a wink that said, 'Poor sap! He hasn't a hope in Hell!'

Mary McCarthy's relationship with power was particularly clear-headed. She knew every single permutation of left- and right-wingery, both in the United States and in Europe. She also had a deep understanding of how governments and bureaucracies respond to pressure from outside. There was something about her tough childhood that had made her highly observant without becoming cynical. She'd obviously heard a thing or two about *Index* and she knew it was never going to receive the support of the State Department or any other government institution. Meanwhile my poor father continued to explain in all innocence how curious it was that he could only get so far with the American authorities, and then suddenly everything would collapse.

On 1 February 1968, coming back from Holloway to Percy Street on the 29 bus, I saw on the floor a crumpled newspaper with a photo of one man shooting another man in the head. The photographer had managed to click his camera at the very moment when the killer was squeezing the trigger.

I picked it up and smoothed it out. We were in Vietnam. The horrific thing was that neither the killer nor his victim seemed monsters. The victim looked like the usual untidy student, the man with a gun seemed to be an intellectual. It was the predicament that was awful, not the people involved. Which made it worse. Why should we have anything to do with two citizens of a remote country murdering each other?

Up until that moment, Maro and I hadn't taken part in any political protests. My only feeling about Vietnam was that it was bad for Americans. Half a million young men had been given guns and told to shoot Vietnamese soldiers indistinguishable from the peasants they were supposed to save. According to Mao's book on guerrilla tactics, which I'd read, the guerrillas were allowed to hide behind the peasants, and the Americans would shoot the unfortunate non-combatants and feel horrible about it afterwards. It wasn't too hard to imagine this happening. It would surely drive the American soldiers insane with guilt.

In retrospect, it seems peculiar to have taken part in a protest against the Vietnam War out of sympathy for the United States, but at least it was an idea. Those gulags inside the Arctic Circle where they sent unruly intellectuals had frozen my communist sympathies, and I had no opinions as to whether the regime in Vietnam was good or bad. With regard to Chairman Mao's China, Mog Empson had taken us out of earshot of Hetta one afternoon and told us that there were large areas in the western districts where something very bad had happened, though nobody could say what. It's odd that so much of that country is completely invisible, he said cheerfully.

Talking about Vietnam with my father, however, toughened my position. His view of the war was even feebler than mine. A worried look would come over his face and he'd hedge: 'Well, I think the position of the Americans is very difficult.'

Our conversations became increasingly polarized. Was he for or against the American intervention in Vietnam? Surely he couldn't be in favour? This made him lose his temper. 'Either one knows something—' he shouted; then he hesitated, not knowing how to get out of this sentence: 'or else one doesn't have the right to speak.'

I took this very badly. He was denying my right to hold an opinion. The US Air Force was by this time bombing civilians in Hanoi. Was this something I was too dumb to know? Or were we supposed just to look at the ceiling and say how worrying it all was?

His views altered after he'd resigned from *Encounter*. In a letter to Nikos, he wrote: 'I am beginning to feel an immense relief at having left Encounter: as though being there was like some inhibition in my life which prevented me thinking freely about certain things, like Vietnam.' It's an honest admission, but it's also frightening. He's saying that while he was editor of *Encounter* he could not allow himself to deviate from supporting the United States government. Which in turn implies that he knew more about *Encounter*'s politics than he ever admitted to me; or perhaps even to himself.

On 28 March 1968, Maro and I joined the big protest in front of the American Embassy in Grosvenor Square. This was an important turning-point in the so-called revolution of 1968, as it showed that a wide and potentially chaotic gap separated the government from the governed.

We arrived at the march with three little girls in tow: Maro's half-sisters Antonia and Susannah, plus Lucy Warner, the daughter of Barbara Hutchinson and Rex Warner. We greeted friends who stood on the pavement. Mogador Empson said hello but he told us cautiously he'd prefer not to join the march.

Lucy took up the slogan 'Ho, Ho, Ho Chi Minh', which she robustly sang with the best of them. The other two joined in. Ho Chi Minh was the pale, almost saintly leader of the Vietnamese liberation movement. It was impossible to have any suspicions about a face as beautiful as his. But I ticked her off. We have no idea who Ho Chi Minh is, or what the communists are doing in Vietnam, or anything about China, or anything else in South-East Asia. We are here to say that we think that the war in Vietnam is a bad idea, and it's especially bad for America. The girls went right on singing 'Ho, Ho, Ho Chi Minh,' with cheerful rosy expressions on their faces.

We approached Grosvenor Square. In front of us marched a group of disciplined German students. They put their left arms round their neighbour's waist, raised their right arms to the shoulder of the man in front, and suddenly we were no longer walking with human beings so much as following a truck made of men. They didn't make any noise, but they knew what they were doing. We stuck to this group. Maro took one side of our girls, I took the other.

Five minutes later I found myself pressed against a young policeman, who'd locked arms with other policemen along the base of North Audley Street, barring our way into the square. A very English conversation took place. 'I want you to know, officer, that there's nothing personal in my squashing against you like this.' The policeman said that he quite understood, sir. I said I was worried about my girls (they were squealing with delight at being squashed); and he said perhaps I should have left them at home. I said, 'I had no idea that things were going to turn out as rough as this.' The policeman said, 'No, sir. Nor did we.'

Then he said: 'I think we are going to break.' And break they did, letting this flush of excited humanity flow its sudden way into the big bare square opposite the American Embassy.

We caught up with the German contingent. They were still in one hard pack and they were about to attack the horses of the police. They had prepared a plan. Word went round that they were throwing ball-bearings under the hooves of the horses. This sounded bad, so I hustled my group over to one side. The protest began to lack the usual light-hearted quality of Brits showing displeasure with their government.

Then a horse went down. It screamed as it fell. A perceptible gasp went through all of us. It was magnificent and frightening, the animal so obviously not a part of our predicament, yet frightened and hurt.

Afterwards things turned nasty. From the violence at the front, it was obvious that both sides had lost control. We wandered off, secretly hoping that the German contingent would get clobbered. If any of us Brits were arrested, hopefully they'd be released by the magistrates in the morning with nothing worse than a reprimand.

We left England to go and live in Italy about a fortnight after the Grosvenor Square march. There was something hysterical about it. We sent forward via the train service of Passenger Luggage Advance three ancestral trunks full of stretchers, paint rags, a used bar of soap with some good still in it – all the necessities for a new life off the map of responsibility.

When I broke the news to Mum she said, 'But you can't leave England now. What about Granny's flat?'

That winter, I'd painted a portrait of Granny, who still lived at the top of the house in Rothwell Street where my mother had lived as an adolescent. At the end of the morning I'd absent-mindedly thrown my turpentine into the fire, thinking this was the easiest way of getting rid of it. A great black cloud rose up and moved along the ceiling in a wave, reached the far wall, tipped over and rolled back. Scars of soot were left on the walls and dust lay everywhere.

It was a bizarre way for Mum to tell me that I couldn't leave England, but I took her at her word. 'I'll paint it,' I told her. 'I'll paint Granny's flat. I admit it, I fucked up her walls.' So, with only one day to go before taking that train, I turned up at 13 Rothwell Street with a suitcase full of rollers in one hand and a gallon of white in the other. I pressed the doorbell and waited.

There was no distant tinkle. Granny was deaf. Her bell was a flashing light, and it was only luck if she ever noticed it.

I put down my equipment, leaned on the bell and lit a cigarette. I gave that bell one whole cigarette and stared up at Primrose Hill. Immense sycamores unfurled their first tender leaves and the grass was darkening on the bare hill where the anti-aircraft guns had been mounted in the years before I was born. Below the hill, I heard the sound of animals yearning for each other in the zoo. I pressed and pressed Granny's bell, and still there was no answer.

Goodbye, Primrose Hill, goodbye, the shelf of books on guerrilla warfare written by Chairman Mao, and St Bernard of Clairvaux on monasticism, and the beautifully wrong-headed Gaetano Salvemini. Goodbye, the sandy-haired ghost of Percy Street and the bent pillars of Loudoun Road. Goodbye to my other selves: the Foreign Office mandarin, the art historian, the crabby keeper of Japanese prints.

I felt that if I abandoned the things I didn't want, I could start afresh. I knew I was throwing away a helluva lot of privileges, but I felt these were just pinned on to my backside, like the tail on the donkey at a children's party. What was left over may not have amounted to much, but it would at least provide a kernel of simplicity.

The night before we left, we happened to run into Eduardo Paolozzi. We told him we were leaving England and he nodded. To leave the city and pursue wisdom in the countryside, he said, was one of the options artists could take. 'But let me give you a bit of advice,' he added. 'You will find that the world won't beat a path to your door. If anyone does, if anyone finds their way to you and offers either of you a show or a commission, whatever it is, say yes. Otherwise living just the two of you in a bucolic retreat will send you mad.'

When we reached Italy we stayed for a fortnight in a villa above Florence. Mougouch and Maro knew it well, as they'd lived in this beautiful corner of the city for several years before coming to London ten years earlier. They could chat to the pessimistic gardener Ugo about old roses and the diseases of cypress trees.

I went to bed. I needed to brood on Eduardo's last-minute advice. I accepted the underlying message: in this world, you have to compete or else go insane. But when it came to making works of art, what was the competition? Or playing a piece of music or writing a poem? Where lay the connection between preoccupations so interiorized and the voracious needs of the city?

I do not remember reaching any conclusions at that time, but thereafter I accepted Eduardo's advice as a talisman: always say yes to those who beat a path to your door. It's remained 'house rule number one' from that day to this. If it has meant agreeing to mount exhibitions in impossible places with impossible people, so be it!

I stayed in bed for ten days. From time to time my wife or my

mother-in-law would come in and look at me without comment.
They thought I was scared – and they were right. Moving to Italy
was no big deal for them. They had no nation, no fixed abode – no
''Tis-of-Thee' as Maro put it, perhaps too light-heartedly. I was
abandoning everything I possessed, except what I'd created with
them. The effort was like wrestling with an illness, but I knew I'd
never go back.

My father and one of my cabbages at the time of Saskia's birth.

28

GUILELESS AND YET OBSESSED

M Y FATHER CAME out twice in order to persuade us to return. He was present at the birth of our first child, Saskia, in Florence in 1970. Next day, he and I went to the Uffizi together because I wanted to look at paintings of babies. He was amused to be rushing from one painted baby to another ignoring all other aspects of Renaissance art; and he wrote a 'diary' poem about it the next day. I thought all these babies were hideous. None was as beautiful as ours. In fact they looked like lunatic dwarves, not babies. Then, as we drank a cup of coffee at Rivoire's, my father said that all the same, babies or no babies, Maro and I shouldn't allow ourselves to become cut off. I couldn't just grow cabbages. To punish him, back in the countryside near Siena where we now lived, I took a photo of him clutching one of my cabbages, which for some reason that year were spectacular. He saw the joke and laughed.

A few months later my father told me that Auden would soon be coming to Florence and he wanted to speak to us.

We learned that Wystan's first words as he got off the plane at the airport in Pisa were, 'When am I to meet the Spenders?' We heard this over the telephone and looked at each other like two soldiers who'd been told of an unscheduled inspection by the general. It will be OK, we said nervously. We'd spent the previous fortnight painting the entire house and making it perfect, for although Auden lived in a mess himself, he liked families that led clean and cosy lives.

Before lunch, I took him down to my studio and showed him a huge painting on which I was working: a life-size copy of *The Battle of San Romano* by Paolo Uccello. After one brief look he said, 'That's great fun.' I wasn't sure if I wanted it to be 'fun', but at least the comment was positive.

We presented our new baby and he glanced at her. 'I've always got on well with babies,' he said. 'I was pleased to see the other day in someone's letters that I was known to be good with babies. That was nice.'

'Do you think she looks like me?'

'No,' he said decisively. 'Babies only look like other babies. The question of looks is much exaggerated. You don't look at all like your father, for instance. Your nose is completely different.'

This raised one of his favourite themes: if you'd happened to be present at the moment when your parents decided to marry and you'd had a vote in the matter, would you have voted yes or no? I thought about this for a moment and said, 'No'. 'Exactly,' said Wystan. 'And thereby you are denying your own existence.' He looked triumphant.

'Can't I have been the product of some other couple?' I suggested. He wouldn't accept this. 'You are the product of your father and mother and nobody else.'

I felt uneasy. Was this one of his abstract theories, or was he referring to Stephen and Natasha? I'd just voted no: did he want me to disapprove of my parents' relationship? I didn't disapprove, but I'd often wondered if they might not have been happier with two other people. Wystan picked up on my anxiety. He put a hand on my arm. 'Your parents love you very much,' he said. I realised that Auden was just as much on duty as we were, trying to live up to his role as a mender of fences.

Towards the end of lunch he talked about a recent meeting of scientists he'd attended in Sweden, organized by the Nobel Committee. Auden always held a great respect for scientists, whom he treated with a deference he rarely gave to his fellow authors. In his speech at Stockholm he said that he was extremely worried about the state of the world. 'I told them that I thought that we have been placed here for a purpose, and we are neglecting that purpose. I'm glad to say that most of the scientists agreed with me, even those who said they were atheists.'

'A purpose given to us by God?' I asked doubtfully.

'Yes. We have a duty towards the molecules, and we are neglecting that duty.'

This was Auden at his most peremptory. He did not care if what he said sounded strange.

'I'm sorry Wystan, but I don't understand,' I said. 'Do you mean that the molecules which are in the marble of a sculpture by Michelangelo are happier and better molecules than the ones that are still in the marble up in the quarry?'

He shut his eyes and smiled ecstatically. 'Yes,' he said.

Mougouch was very supportive of our withdrawn existence. She taught us how to hold our daughter and chat to her, for initially we looked at this wee thing with dumb respect. So that was one baby. And two years later, when Maro was heavily pregnant with our second daughter, Mougouch took us out on a picnic which opened a new door in our lives.

I'd accompanied my village band in a march through the gloomy Tuscan town of San Gimignano. Though it was 1972 the revolution of 1968 was still current, and we clarinettists had been drowned out by students yelling that they had a right to receive university degrees without taking exams. An hour later, sitting among olive trees, we ate our boiled eggs and admired the towers from a distance. 'When I die,' Mougouch said, 'I expect to be remembered for a few picnics. The rest doesn't matter.'

Then she started talking about Arshile Gorky's relationship with Willem de Kooning. Without Bill, she said, Gorky would have been left behind. He was too delicate, too non-political, too 'foreign' for those New York critics, who were desperately looking for an American hero. They'd found him in Jackson Pollock, she said. Gorky couldn't stand Pollock. They'd very nearly had a fight, once, right there on the sidewalk near Union Square. Friends had had to intervene and separate them.

She was now giving us something more than those glamorous stories of which she was always the epicentre. Here was turmoil, here was intrigue, here lay the edge where politics and creativity over-lapped. This was my world. I recognized its frontiers. I had to make an effort and build upon what I already knew.

'Tackle your Parent-Complex Year' took over most of 1975.

It's not that Maro or I felt we were any more neurotic than the average bus-driver who, as long as he can drive from A to B, is doing all right. It wasn't complexes we felt we suffered from but lack of information.

It started with a trip during which my father and I went alone to Venice. 'If this turns out to be a failure,' he said first thing when we met, 'we can always blame our wives.' This pre-empted any thoughts I may have had of reproaching him.

Dad kept a journal, but it's mainly full of his thoughts about art. Like so much in his journals, he wrote down his observations half thinking about their eventual publication. He seldom discussed personal matters in his diaries and on this highly charged occasion, the key conversation isn't even mentioned.

We were sitting at a restaurant not far from St Mark's Square. Dad had just described being in Venice with Stravinsky after the first night of *The Rake's Progress*, the opera he'd written with Auden. Afterwards, the Venetians had come out from their bars and restau-rants and applauded as the Maestro walked through their city, and he was touched. Then the subject turned to my sister Lizzie. She was studying to become an actress, but her teacher hadn't inspired any confidence in him. In fact Dad thought he was crazy. He said that, nevertheless, sooner or later Lizzie would become a 'success'. He was sure of it.

My father and me in Venice in 1975, discussing the question of success.

This was the very subject I wished to broach. He'd told me several times that growing cabbages in Tuscany was inadequate. I wanted to know what alternative he had in mind. What career, what success?

I'd always felt that my father possessed a mystical reverence for 'success' as something palpable. A rock, rather than a mirage. A substance that was somehow independent of the objects created in order to achieve it. I asked him what he meant by 'success' – but the conversation immediately went wrong. Dad thought I was accusing him of trying to 'pursue' success. In other words, of promoting himself. 'Most of the successful people I know would never dream of promoting themselves. Wystan for instance. And I have never in my life done anything in any way in order solely to promote my career.'

This was the first time I'd come up against my father's toughness when he thought he was being attacked. I could not go on. In my diary I wrote: 'This last sentence of his, about his own lack of promotion, stuns me, and strikes me as being blindingly true. His own success came so early and was so total that he was never required to make an intellectual analysis of the way of the world, and so tempt it towards cynicism.' I was trying ineffectually to reconcile my parents' idea of my father's 'innocence' with how I saw him actually behave. 'He is guileless, and yet obsessed,' I wrote; but my use of the word 'cynicism' means that subconsciously I thought he'd made a pact with the Devil.

If he denied his interest in power – what then? Would I have to confront him with his relationship with the Establishment and turn my love for him into a fight? I'd never felt like fighting with him before and it was too late to start now.

At the time I was unaware that both Wystan and Cyril, two friends who'd known him extremely well, had viewed my father's self-proclaimed lack of worldliness with scepticism, but I certainly felt there was something odd about his self-image. How could anyone so tremendously involved with power think of himself as an innocent? But all I thought at the time, in a rough-and-ready way, was that there wasn't much difference between my father's idea of success and that of his own father, except the metaphorical Mendip Hills of Harold were now the towering Himalayas of Stephen. Success was such a reality to him that those who were successful occupied pre-cut niches in a cave where a multitude of deities were worshipped. Even the unsuccessful had roles to play, as acolytes looking ever upward, believers in the inviolable status of success.

At that Venetian restaurant in this key conversation I dropped the subject; but I brooded in my diary: 'At the same time, there is no doubt that Dad has a fascination for the whole idea of success and spends a great deal of time if not thinking about it at least talking about it, and using the word in a way that's odd, even obsessional.' I remembered the moment when my father had told me in hushed tones that our family physician, Dr Berkeley Way, had defined me as a more 'successful' baby than he, Stephen, had been. Dr Way had seen us both as babies so he was in a position to know.

I saw Dad three times alone in Italy in later years. Our 'honeymoons' involved touring the villas of Palladio or visiting the dusty studio of Canova at Possagno. We ate and talked, but I never again revived the question of 'success', or *Encounter*, or politics as it had intruded in our lives – though occasionally I tried.

Living in Italy meant I'd had to accept the fact that cultural life was dominated by the Italian Communist Party. (This continued until the PCI withered away into social democracy.) I hated the way that to be intelligent and creative in Italy presupposed allegiance to the Party and I was willing to discuss this with Dad, but he was unresponsive. I decided that although he liked talking about political ideas, political tactics made him nervous.

The equivalent to *Encounter* in Italy in the Fifties was *Tempo Presente*, one of whose directors, Ignazio Silone, was an old friend of Dad's. This magazine sought a cultural 'Third Way' somewhere between the doctrinaire bias of the PCI and the solid conformity of the Christian Democrats. It failed, because the big political parties controlled the apparatus by which culture is distributed. Over the years I'd heard rumours that the 'Third Way' had received American backing, and on my last 'honeymoon' with Dad I wanted to talk with him about this. Again, he didn't respond. I'd learned that *Tempo Presente* had received its money in the simplest way possible: Mel Lasky used to arrive on a regular flight from Paris bearing a little suitcase of cash. I didn't dare tell him, not even as a joke.

In November 1975 we went to New York to talk to as many friends of Gorky as were still alive. This was Maro's half of 'Tackle your Parent-Complex Year'. I kept a diary, and the trip was fascinating.

I couldn't help noticing that some of the people we interviewed seemed amused at the thought that Matthew, son of Stephen Spender, had ended up with Maro, daughter of Arshile Gorky. Several New Yorkers were aware that American art was the invention of American art critics, and that the Congress of Cultural Freedom was in the mixture somewhere. It was seen as one of life's little jokes that we'd ended up married to each other.

Our progress was complicated by the fact that Dad was also in New York at that time. He didn't like the fact that our trajectory through Manhattan had nothing to do with our own careers. When he heard that we were planning to go to Philadelphia to visit the Barnes Collection, he said that he wanted to arrange a lunch for us with Henry McIlhenny, a key figure in that city. We said no. He took us down to South Houston to see the studio of Jasper Johns, which was in a vast former bank. That also led nowhere. When I told him I'd met Leo Castelli – at that time the most important dealer in New York – and he'd asked to see my work, Dad wanted me to go back next day with photos and a catalogue. He said he'd come with me. I said that I didn't feel confident enough to do so. He insisted. I laughed, not believing him. 'He'll certainly be more interested in you than he is in Gorky,' he said. 'Because you are alive and Gorky is dead.'

This disturbed me. It was touching, in its way – but we also had a job to do.

On Wednesday 19 November, we went to a cocktail party given for Maro by Jane Gunther. The company was so distinguished it was hard to believe that certain people were actually real: for instance Mr Jones, of the Dow Jones Index. Or Charles Addams, to whom later in the evening when I was full of liquor I tried to give an idea for a cartoon: Adam and Eve as in the fresco of Masaccio, stark naked on a beach, being asked by a heavily dressed policeman to identify themselves. (Charles Addams smiled grimly.) It was a year when people were being arrested for taking off their clothes.

Dad was also present. An edition of Raymond Chandler's letters was being assembled, and Dad was having a wonderful time telling Arthur Schlesinger how Mum had tried to stop the inclusion of several letters in which Chandler had boasted about their love affair. (My father would not have been so entertaining if Mum had been present, but she was in London.)

Dad turned round. 'He appealed to me across Arthur's cocktail glass,' says my diary. So I told Arthur about the occasion when Raymond Chandler and Mum and I had gone to the Tower of London together. I described Ray's frail state and said that I didn't think that anything sexual could have taken place between them. 'They did not give off that kind of atmosphere when they were together.'

Something about my know-all-ness irritated Dad. He asked me what I could possibly have known about 'that kind of atmosphere' since I was only about twelve years old at the time.

Before I had time to reply, he turned to Arthur. 'My children are going to curse me with their total recall,' he said. 'They remember everything! I can just see Matthew now, in front of some court, saying to the judge, "Oh yes, Your Honour, I remember exactly the moment when Dad signed his contract with the CIA. I was under the table at the time – aged two!"'

Arthur looked tremendously embarrassed. 'Dad, of course, thought it was hilarious,' says my diary. 'Everyone else looked around for a hiding place.'

At the end of the cocktail party I came across Dad curled up in a corner of the room in a foetal position, trembling. He was red in the face and I thought he'd had a heart attack. But no. He was merely imitating the pose of our second daughter, aged three, who was asleep behind the sofa on a heap of coats. 'Doesn't she look like me?' he said as he got up, laughing, and dusted himself off.

A few days later, Maro and I went to have supper with Jeanne Reynal, a mosaicist and an old and trusted friend of Gorky and Mougouch. We arrived early, because Maro wanted me to see the house.

Jeanne was Maro's godmother and this extraordinary house was a key part of her childhood. Above the mantelpiece hung a Gorky, yellow with smoke from the fire. A fabulous Pollock of about 1938 hung above the drinks tray, thickly painted and darkly sinister. One whole wall of the next room was taken over by a birdcage, and on the opposite wall hung numerous Hopi dolls. When the French Surrealists arrived in New York during the war, they'd snubbed the US artists and concentrated on Hopi dolls and Eskimo masks, so Jeanne's taste was a reminder of their passage through the city. Between the Hopi dolls hung exotic ear-rings and Navaho jewellery: great bear claws on a thick red string separated by bright blue beads.

Jeanne had invited the art critic Harold Rosenberg and his wife Mae, because she wanted Harold to arrange a meeting between Maro and Bill de Kooning. This took place at the end of the following week. De Kooning talked to Maro about Gorky without interruption for ten solid hours. It changed her life, because de Kooning described Gorky's choices in the early days as if they were happening now. This allowed Maro to see her father as a painter, a person with problems similar to her own, without having to peer through the usual misty cloud of fame.

Also invited to that supper were the left-wing critic Nico Calas and his wife, for Elena Calas had something she wanted very much to tell Maro.

My father came too, as he'd met Jeanne at the Jane Gunther party and invited himself – which was tiresome, as it wouldn't be easy to talk about Gorky in his presence. He hissed to me in passing that he'd never been able to stand Nico Calas, not since they'd first met in Spain in 1937. I remembered that Calas and Rosenberg belonged to a brand of New York ex-Marxists with whom Dad had some distant bone to pick; and that *Partisan Review*, to which Calas and Rosenberg often contributed articles, had been for years the trans-Atlantic rival of *Encounter*. Sure enough, at supper, my father challenged Harold Rosenberg about *Partisan Review*. Should that magazine have been more partisan, or less? I had to block my ears. It ended with Calas shouting and Harold banging his stick angrily on the floor, so it must have been a powerful exchange.

Elena was at our end of the table. She came from Georgia, which is next door to Armenia, so she shared with Gorky a distant background. She was telling Maro about Gorky's last days. How Gorky had wandered through the woods of Sherman, Connecticut, with Maro and a rope, asking Elena to choose a good tree from which he could hang himself. And Elena, not contesting his right to die, but saying to Gorky: You must not speak of these things in front of your daughter.

Of all the short circuits between my father's life and Gorky's, this evening was certainly the most dramatic.

Next morning Maro and I went back to Jeanne, bringing her a case of champagne. As we chatted about our recent discoveries, she told us something that struck home like an axe felling a tree. 'The thing about Mougouch', she said, 'is that she thinks she's better than any man.'

We got on well with Jeanne. She made things with her hands, like us. We could talk to her about the glass-makers of Murano and the intense gold tesserae of Byzantine mosaics. This was the kind of conversation my father would have found maddening. To him, only the idea counted. The making of things was incidental. But for Maro and me, in our new-found life among craftsmen and peasants, we'd gone back to the myth of Heraclitus: 'There is harmony in the bending back, as in the bow and the lyre.' Seeing Jeanne with her back bent over a little anvil cutting tesserae in the basement of her brownstone on the edge of Greenwich Village was a moving experience. Fragments of cut glass had over the years worn out her lungs, yet she refused to give up.

In those last violent weeks of Gorky's life, Jeanne knew that he was going to die. She held it against him that he'd done it so badly. 'It would have been so nice if now and again he'd said something simple, like what a nice day it was. Don't you see?' She said this to Maro; and it was so harsh, so true, I felt I shouldn't be there. Women, who are in charge of life, often have a pragmatic attitude to death. Without being censorious, without taking into consideration the role of Mougouch in his death, Jeanne took the view that Gorky should have gone through that door with tact and dignity. And Maro, accepting from Jeanne what she wouldn't have accepted from anyone else, was comforted.

'Your father's last words to me were that he'd come back and haunt me. He stared at me through that very window. His mouth was open and his eyes were huge and he looked like a ghost already. I didn't even dare open the door.'

'And did he?'

'Haunt me?' said Jeanne. She smiled, with a curious air of being pleased with herself. 'Oh well, you know. There have been so many.'

Hesitantly, we told Jeanne the version that we'd heard in Chapel Street: Mougouch had been forced into infidelity by Gorky's cruelty to her during the last six months of his life.

There was a long pause. Jeanne patted her hair absent-mindedly.

'Yes,' she said. 'I noticed, last time we'd met, that Mougouch has been honing down those fine old stories.'

Maro insisted on knowing more. What was the truth about her mother's affair with Matta? Was it love? She had to know.

'She was very young,' said Jeanne, tactfully. 'And the situation was kind of extreme. Gorky wanted her to be submissive and respectful and assume that he was right about everything; and there were certain things – like sex, for instance, or the consequences of his cancer operation – which he passionately refused to discuss. Her task was to obey and listen and follow him at a distance, so to speak. Well, that's not our Mougouch! She did her best to live up to what he wanted in a wife, but she couldn't. Nor could you. Nor could anyone. It was an unfair thing to ask.'

Jeanne, though she was light-hearted, spoke with authority. 'You're grown up now, aren't you, dear?' she said to Maro. 'You surely must have enough experience to know that we can't do everything right.'

On our way back to Siena, we stopped off for a week in London. Mougouch was irritated with us. We'd started to gather new information about her and her late husband and it lay beyond her control. There was a suggestion of betrayal – though she made this point with her usual glorious indifference. Perhaps she was right. Maro now possessed a part of Gorky's life that had nothing to do with Mougouch. There was the Armenian genocide, which did not concern Mougouch – though it was a constant undeclared presence in Maro's imagination. And there was Gorky's relationship with the New York intellectuals, with whom we could talk, but Mougouch apparently could not.

Maro, at a simpler level, came back from New York much heartened by her renewed friendship with Jeanne. She insisted on building a huge birdcage on the loggia behind our bedroom at San Sano, and soon we had to live with the nattering of fretful finches and colourful canaries. When Mougouch turned up to stay with us, one day when we were out shopping, she opened the cage and shooed them all away. Or rather, she'd 'freed' them – said with a brilliant smile.

The weather was cold and Maro took her mother's destruction of the finches as a rejection of Jeanne Reynal. I wouldn't have thought of this myself but to Maro it was obvious. In the bathroom we all shared, she took down the photo of her mother and put up a photo of Jeanne in its place. This worked. For the next thirty years Mougouch looked at this photo moodily whenever she visited us. Then she'd turn to a blank patch of wall where she implied that her own photograph ought to be hanging.

By the 1990s, when I started writing my book on Gorky, my relationship with Maro had lasted five times as long as Mougouch's with any man. My impeccable constancy, plus Maro's desire that her husband should be entrusted with this book, did not put me into a strong position, however. Mougouch thought fidelity was pathetic. Sheer laziness. A coward's ploy. Not facing the challenge of Love with a capital ell. Thus, although she was flattered by the attention I offered in writing her story, she did not give me exclusive access. She told the same story to Nouritza Matossian, an Armenian who passionately took Gorky's side, and to Hayden Herrera, who accepted Mougouch's version of events but mixed them into her interpretation of Gorky's work. So I had two rivals who were also engaged in writing Gorky's life. Hayden, moreover, was the daughter of Jack Phillips by an earlier marriage, and this made things internecine.

I'd never felt upstaged by Mougouch on the subject of love or sex or the joys of existential mayhem, because I wasn't competing. But to write a book – and it took me seven years – while thinking all the time that Mougouch was giving my research to my rivals, was a painful experience. Occasionally, when my rivals appeared to be overtaking me, she was even pleased. In those moments, I really did feel I was her abject slave.

My mother observed these moments of tension from a distance. From time to time she was even sympathetic about the tortured path I'd chosen, but there was also an element of reproach. If I was so interested in ancestral stories, why wasn't I channelling all this energy into my father, instead of into my father-in-law?

I tried to explain the attraction of a man who'd invented a past in order to protect himself, for reality was unbearable. But Mum had no sympathy with this predicament. There is always the truth, she implied; and its opposite is a lie. I suddenly realized that my mother was constitutionally incapable of understanding my late father-in-law, for she was just as much a self-created personality as he had been.

As for our own lives, it's hardly surprising if we've played things straight. Maro's fidelity is based on a rejection of the confusion that her mother's love-life always involved. My fidelity derives from the fact that I cannot desire a woman without seeing her as a vessel containing our future children. The one-night stand for me is out. It's permanence or bust. I can see now, having written this book, that I possess at least one family characteristic: a version of my father's desire for instant domesticity, only in my case the first successful pounce was also my last.

Choosing to be faithful doesn't save you from the disaster of falling in love. Over the years, there have been four subjects of my impossible yearnings: Susannah (Maro's sister, and therefore an absolute no-no); Vittoria (the heroine of my book on Tuscany); Marta (who was in love with Maro, I think); and finally Fiamma, an opera singer with whom I became infatuated when we were on tour together – in Bari, of all places, and in the dead of winter. (It snowed.) In the evenings on stage I took the role of Noah in Stravinsky's *The Flood*, while in the daylight hours I wandered the backstreets of Bari pining for Fiamma. I'd look at her hopelessly in the bar we all frequented and think: what will our future be as we wait for our babies to burgeon? Will I be washing our knickers in the bidet of a remote hotel while she's five blocks away, singing brilliantly on stage?

My father thought that domesticity could be manipulated so that he could enjoy his freedom. My idea of domesticity is the opposite: total immersion. But in what? In the lateral thinking of women, so laced with impossible long-term vendettas, yet at the same time so immediately tied to the present?

This book started as an imaginary conversation with the ghosts of two parents whom I never challenged while they were alive. It was intended as a gesture of mourning and affection, an attempt to answer several unasked questions concerning their relationship. Revenge came into it, too – a rejection of my mother's idea that appearances must be kept up at all costs. But in these last pages I'm overtaken by the strangeness of all our choices. Do the lives of Stephen and Natasha hold insights about their time and the customs of their country? I hope so. It would be satisfying if clues about human behaviour lie in the background of these two distinguished twentieth-century individuals. But perhaps fidelity, and love, and work, and freedom and sex and self-sacrifice, twist themselves together in different ways for all of us.

There is no logic to my father's conviction that freedom and marriage can be made to fit together, or that a poet can immerse himself in power yet retain his innocence. There is no logic to my mother's idea that she could simultaneously be the formidable Lady Spender, and a compassionate woman whose life was entirely turned inwards. There is no logic to my feeling that to possess time in which to make a work of art is all the privilege I need, and all other privileges must be rejected. There is no logic to Maro's idea that her ancestors watch over her and stand invisibly in the corners of the kitchen garden, and that she at last has been given all the rewards that centuries of repression once kept from them.

This book is for our grandchildren, who will soon wonder how the predicament of inheritance affects their own lives. I look at them and ask: Is there a glimmer of Stephen's dreaminess in Aeneas? Does Ondina have Mougouch's craving to dazzle and dominate? Is my mother's brow visible in Cleopatra's clear features? Is Marlon the maker of things as manual as Gorky?

It takes us half our lives to discover who we are and where we come from, and the other half is spent thinking, But of course! There are two streams! The river above my head concentrates my ancestors in me, and the river that springs below me will dilute my genes in my grandchildren. And theirs. And in turn, theirs.

NOTES

In the notes that follow, the place of publication is London unless otherwise stated.

Previously unpublished letters and journal entries by W. H. Auden are quoted with the permission of the Estate of W. H. Auden.

Previously unpublished letters and diaries by Raymond Chandler are quoted with the permission of the Estate of Raymond Chandler.

Quotations from letters to Stephen Spender at the T. S. Eliot Archive, London © the Estate of T. S. Eliot and reprinted with the permission of the Estate and Faber and Faber Ltd.

Excerpts from Christopher Isherwood's letters and diaries, copyright © 2015 Don Bachardy, used by permission of The Wylie Agency LLC.

Previously unpublished writings by Lincoln Kirstein © 2015 the New York Public Library (Astor, Lenox and Tilden Foundations).

Locations

BL	British Library
Bod	Bodleian Library, Oxford
CDP	Collection David Plante, London
CMS	Collection Matthew Spender, Siena
Duke	Special Collections, Duke University Library
DUL	Durham University Library

KV 2/3215/6   Stephen Spender's MI5 files, The National Archives, Kew
NA   The National Archives, Kew
NSJ   Stephen Spender, *New Selected Journals*, Faber & Faber, 2012
NYPL   New York Public Library
RCAB   Raymond Chandler Archive, Bodleian Library, Oxford
SSAB   Stephen Spender Archive, Bodleian Library, Oxford
SSUJ   Stephen Spender unpublished journals, Bodleian Library, Oxford
Tam   Tamiment Library, New York University
TSEA   T. S. Eliot Archive, London
WWW   Stephen Spender, *World within World*, New York, The Modern Library, 2001

People

AMG   Agnes Magruder Gorky, 'Mougouch'
CI   Christopher Isherwood
ERC   Ernst Robert Curtius
IB   Isaiah Berlin
IK   Irving Kristol
JE   Jason Epstein
JH   Julian Huxley
LK   Lincoln Kirstein
MS   Matthew Spender
Nikos Nikos Stangos
NS   Natasha Spender
PT   Philip Toynbee
RC   Raymond Chandler
RP   Reynolds Price
SS   Stephen Spender
TH   Tony Hyndman
TSE   T. S. Eliot
VW   Virginia Woolf
WHA   W. H. Auden
WP   William Plomer

Natasha's last wishes

p.3 the biographer gave in: the scholar whom my mother challenged was Frank MacShane, for *The Life of Raymond Chandler* (1976).

One: A worldly failure

p.8 'God knows what kings': poem is dated 18 May 1957, CMS.

p.9 'a great way off': WWW, p. 8.

p.11 'When they are very young': SS, 'Miss Pangbourne', circa 1990, p. 70, SSAB.

p.11 'A thin match-boarding': Violet Schuster, Skelgill journal, 1917, Collection Philip Spender.

p.12 'Wordsworth was a man': SS, 'Miss Pangbourne', p. 195.

p.13 'It is no exaggeration': WWW, p. 10.

p.13 'He saw what he had never seen': SS, *The Backward Son*, Hogarth Press, 1940, p. 263.

p.15 'Until now, writing for him': 'Instead of Death' (1928), pp. 96–104, SSAB. This picnic is described more briefly in WWW, p. 69.

p.16 'Now dear, don't make a fuss': David Plante, *Becoming a Londoner*, Bloomsbury, 2013, p. 238.

Two: Without guilt

p.17 'ganged up and captured the decade': Evelyn Waugh, review of WWW in the *Tablet*, 5 May 1951, p. 356.

p.18 'from the sea': from Auden's poem '1929'. 'What is odd . . .' and all the quotations that follow are from Auden's 1929 diary, now in the Berg Collection, NYPL.

p.18 'My dominant faculties': WHA to SS, April/May 1940, in Katherine Bucknell and Nicholas Jenkins (eds), *The Map of All My Youth: Early Works, Friends and Influences*, Clarendon Press, 1990, p. 72.

p.18 but some of the boys: for the boys from the *Lokalen*, see John Henry Mackay, *Der Puppenjunge*, translated as *The Hustler*, Boston, MA, Alyson Publications, 1985.

p.19 'I have always regarded': SS, *The Temple*, Faber & Faber, 1988, p. 54.

p.20 'an exquisite example of Stephen's lust': Louis MacNeice, *The Strings are False: An Unfinished Autobiography*, Faber & Faber, 1965, p. 128.

p.21 'You are right down in the scrum': CI to SS, 'Tuesday', n.d., circa 14 March 1929, photocopy in SSAB.

p.21 'Christopher, so far from being': *WWW*, p. 135. See also CI, *Christopher and His Kind*, Eyre Methuen, 1977, pp. 46–8.

p.22 'The whole system was to him': ibid., p. 114. The scene is also in 'Instead of Death', pp. 193–202.

p.22 'He had grown to hate the gushings': CI, *Christopher and His Kind*, p. 55.

p.23 'It is a wonderful thing': ERC to SS, 13 Aug 1929, SSAB.

p.23 'Within this inner world': *WWW*, p. 131.

p.24 'Your politics are guided': ERC to SS, 6 Dec 1931, SSAB. The original German was 'Ihre Politik ist erotisch & ästhetisch determiniert.'

p.24 'He has introduced Order': SS to IB, n.d. [1931], IB Archive, Bod.

p.25 'He is bored': SS to Erich Alport, 8 May [1931], BL Add MS 74771B, folio 47.

p.25 'magical with the mystery': *WWW*, p. 129.

p.25 Georg 101: 'Georg 101' appears in letters from Stephen to William Plomer, in DUL. The teaching experience in Berlin is in Stephen's letters to his grandmother Hilda Schuster, in the Schuster Archive, Bod.

p.26 He solemnly told: Stephen and Christopher's quarrel is covered in *WWW*, p. 191. And in CI, *Christopher and His Kind*, p. 85.

p.26 'It's as though': SS, *Burning Cactus*, Freeport, NY, Books for Libraries Press, 1971, from edn of 1936, p. 173. SS spells his name 'Hellmut', whereas CI, in *Lost Years: A Memoir 1945–1951* (2000), spells it 'Hellmuth'. The former is closer to the idea of 'Light-strength'.

p.26 'I think that all he needs': SS to VW, 25 Oct 1932, SSAB.

p.26 'We were very affectionate': SS, 1931 diary *Root and Branch*, in SS, *Letters to Christopher*, ed. Lee Bartlett, Santa Barbara, CA, Black Sparrow Press, 1980, p. 155.

p.26 'I have the stupidity': ibid., p. 157.

p.27 'Hellmut is a nice person': SS to IB, 29 Dec [1932], IB Archive, Bod.

p.27 'Hellmut is a homosexual': SS, *Letters to Christopher*, p. 52.

p.28 'To me the book': SS to Hilda Schuster, 1 Aug 1931, Schuster Archive, Bod.

p.28 If he'd ever been arrested: Radclyffe Hall's letter, dated 4 Dec 1928, is in the SSAB.

Three: Suicide or romanticism

p.29 'the son whom I attempted': *WWW*, p. 200.

p.30 'To me, from the moment': TH to SS, 30 Oct 1974, SSAB.

p.30 'In Levanto' and 'What happened': from Tony's two drafts of his unfinished autobiography, SSAB.

p.30 'I want to go away': *WWW*, p. 192.

p.31 'When I was first here': SS to IB, 15 June 1933, IB Archive, Bod, folio 41.

p.32 'I feel more & more happy': SS to LK, 21 Sept 1933, photocopy in SSAB.

p.32 'It's horrid not having you': SS to TH, 5 Oct [1933], SSAB.

p.33 'He is one of those lucky people': SS to LK, 15 Oct 1933, photocopy in SSAB.

p.33 'I see being young is hellish': VW to Quentin Bell, 21 Dec 1933, in *The Letters of Virginia Woolf*, vol. 5: *The Sickle Side of the Moon*, ed. Nigel Nicolson, p.34 Hogarth Press, 1979, p. 262.

p.34 She could provide: SS, *Vienna*, Faber & Faber, 1934.

p.34 'I find the actual sex act': SS to CI, 14 Sept 1936, Henry E. Huntington Library, San Marino, CA. In John Sutherland, *Stephen Spender: The Authorized Biography*, Viking, 2004, p. 168.

p.34 'As a "character" I am no good': SS to WP, 19 June 1934, DUL.

p.35 'Tony has been terribly upset': SS to LK, after 19 Sept 1934, photocopy in SSAB.

p.35 'We had come up against' and 'The differences of class': *WWW*, pp. 201–2.

p.36 'I had your companionship in my mind': LK to SS, n.d., SSAB.

p.36 'As far as homosexuality goes': SS to LK, 5 Aug 1935.

p.36 'Its an uncontrollable unpolarized attraction': LK to SS, n.d., photocopy in SSAB.

p.38 "I have no character': *WWW*, p. 115.

p.38 "she had the kind of drive': Elizabeth Lake (pseudonym for Inez Pearn), *Marguerite Reilly*, New York, Pilot Press, 1947, p. 309.

p.40 "I'm just not capable any more of having "affairs"': SS to CI, 22 Nov 1936, in SS, *Letters to Christopher*, p. 125.

p.41 Harry Pollitt . . . invited Stephen: *WWW*, p. 230.

p.41 a missing Russian ship: For an account of the search for the *Komsomol*, see the first half of Cuthbert Worsley's *Behind the Battle*, Robert Hale, 1939.

p.41 'Stephen Spender was born on 28.2.1909': KV 2/3215, doc. 83.

p.41 'Up till now, as far as we know': ibid., doc. 82. It transpired that the

Komsomol had been sunk by the Italians, so the anxiety of the British authorities was understandable.

p.42 'Oh my darling, it all seems': TH to SS, circa 22 March 1937, SSAB.

p.42 'What with your family and your friends': TH in PT (ed.), *The Distant Drum: Reflections on the Spanish Civil War*, Sidgwick & Jackson, 1976, p. 128.

p.43 'certain methods which were used in Russia': SS, *Life and the Poet*, Secker & Warburg, 1942, p. 16.

p.43 'what is so nice': *WWW*, p. 269.

p.43 'an irritating idealist': Wendy Mulford, *This Narrow Place: Sylvia Townsend Warner*, Pandora Press, 1988, p. 98.

p.43 'She was concerned, she said': ibid., p. 66.

p.43 'When I was in Spain': SS to Harry Pollitt, 29 July 1937, KV 2/3215, doc. 68.

p.44 'Stephen, she said, was utterly thoughtless' and 'I leave the Communist Party': PT diary, vol. 10, 30 March 1937, Bod.

p.45 'I believe in communism': SS to WP, 6 Feb [1937], DUL.

Four: A sly Shelley

p.47 'We must, must do something': PT diary, vol. 9, 2 Jan 1937, p. 161, Bod.

p.48 but to say 'lying is wrong': *WWW*, p. 271.

p.48 'Stephen's affairs are in a fine old tangle': CI unpublished diary, 19 Nov 1937, p. 28, Henry E. Huntington Library, San Marino, CA.

p.48 'In China, I sometimes found myself': ibid., 20 August 1938, p. 41.

p.48 'If I was scared in China': ibid., p. 40.

p.49 'Wystan in tears': ibid., p. 42.

p.49 'the breaking up': *WWW*, p. 281.

p.50 'I believe I married': SS to WP, 6 Feb [1937], DUL.

p.50 'I feel that people can't exist': SS, *Letters to Christopher*, p. 124.

p.50 'If a human relationship': 10 Sept 1939, in SS, 'September Journal', in ibid., p. 174.

p.51 'although our affection': Inez Pearn to SS, n.d., Mary Elliot Collection, Hartford, CT.

p.51 'His movements like his voice were indolent': Julian Maclaren-Ross, *Memoirs of the Forties*, Penguin, 1965, pp. 63 and 74–80.

p.51 'periods of intense energy': *Horizon*, vol. 11, no. 12, Dec 1940, p. 279.

p.52 'below them come': *Horizon*, vol. 11, no. 9, Sept 1940, pp. 77–85.

p.52 'They are far-sighted and ambitious young men': *Horizon*, vol. 1, no. 2, Feb 1940, pp. 69–70.

p.53 'of course I wasn't offended': WHA to SS, late April/early May 1940, in Bucknell and Jenkins, *The Map of All My Youth*, p. 73.

p.53 'an artist ought either to live where he has live roots': *Horizon*, vol. 1, no. 7, July 1940, p. 464.

p.53 'I wonder how much of value can be created': *New Statesman and Nation*, 16 Nov 1940.

p.53 'Your passion for public criticism': WHA to SS, 13–[14] March 1941, in Bucknell and Jenkins, *The Map of All My Youth*, p. 74.

Five: Mutual renaissance

p.55 'Oh come on ducky, you'll enjoy it': from my mother's unpublished memoir, SSAB. All further quotations from my mother are from this text, as yet without dates or page numbers, unless otherwise stated.

p.56 Cyril Connolly: For a description of Cyril Connolly as editor of *Horizon*, see Maclaren-Ross, *Memoirs of the Forties*, pp. 63 and 74–80.

p.56 'Spender praised the representatives of culture': KV 2/3216 , docs 23–5. This MI5 file lists eight public meetings held between October 1936 and November 1938 in which SS took part.

p.59 Charles Booth: Charles Booth, author of *Life and Labour of the People in London* (1889–91), was an important philanthropist and early sociologist.

p.59 'I walked with Miss Litvinne': VW, Thursday 30 March 1924, in *The Diary of Virginia Woolf*, vol. 2: *1920–1924*, ed. Anne Olivier Bell, Hogarth Press, 1978, p. 174.

p.59 'Poor Ray Litvin': VW, Thursday 14 May 1925, in *Diary*, vol. 3: *1925–1930*, ed. Anne Olivier Bell, Hogarth Press, 1980, p. 20.

p.67 'He had lived his life in phases': NS memoir.

p.67 'His assuming total responsibility': NS memoir. See also *WWW*, p. 306.

p.68 '"Being married"': SS to JH, 2 April 1941, Julian Huxley Papers, Fondren Library, Rice University, Houston, Texas.

Six: Fires all over Europe

p.71 'No! He couldn't be that stupid!': NS memoir.

p.72 'You may notice that I wrote': SS to Michael Spender, 19 Feb [1940], Collection Philip Spender.

p.72 'I had to undergo an extra week': *WWW*, p. 352.

p.73 'Working-class people have a somewhat limited': SS in William Sansom, James Gordon and SS, *Jim Braidy: The Story of Britain's Firemen*, Lindsay Drummond, 1943.

p.75 'We have been': TSE, 'Portrait of a Lady'. See also Lucy Hoare, 'The Apollo Society', *Arts Council Bulletin*, April 1951.

p.77 'Stephen Spender, like several other': KV 2/3216, no doc. number, 28 Nov 1943.

p.77 'I don't think I shall ever go back': SS to TSE, 30 May 1943, TSEA.

p.79 'The interviewer at the end of the table': SS to JH, 4 Dec 1944, in Sutherland, *Stephen Spender*, p. 298.

p.79 'We can assure you, Mr. Spender': WWW, p. 333.

p.80 This resulted in: the secret report on Germany by SS is in FO 371/46935, paper C-6450.

p.82 he would have spoken differently: ERC to SS, 27 Dec 1945, and [undated] Jan 1946, SSAB.

p.82 'Most people here have taken': SS to ERC, 9 Feb 1946, SSAB.

p.83 'You discuss the reasons': TSE to SS, 12 Feb 1946, SSAB.

p.83 'who have my sympathy': SS to TSE, 11 Feb 1946, TSEA.

p.83 'It is very difficult': TSE to SS, 15 Feb 1946, SSAB.

p.83 an SS officer: Hermann Grimmrath, etc: I am grateful to Frank-Rutger Hausmann for these details about Curtius during the war.

p.84 'Against what damage': TSE to ERC, 16 Feb 1946, TSEA.

Seven: The purity was hers

p.85 'a role which I could not seriously': SS, *European Witness*, Hamish Hamilton, 1946, p. 96.

p.85 'impossible for anyone': ibid., p. 116.

p.86 'The important thing': TSE to SS, 26 March 1946, SSAB. The draft for a magazine is in both SSAB and TSEA.

p.88 UNESCO: Frank A. Ninkovich, *The Diplomacy of Ideas: US Foreign Policy and Cultural Relations 1938–1950*, Cambridge, Cambridge University Press, 1981, p. 149.

p.92 'I suppose you've never been really happy' and the other quotations are from 'The Fool and the Princess', in SS, *Engaged in Writing*, New York, Farrar, Straus & Cudahy, 1958, pp. 170–6.

p.93 'What makes separation so bad' etc.: SS to NS, circa 18 Aug 1947, SSAB.

Eight: America is not a cause

p.96 'sold out' etc.: Carol Brightman, *Writing Dangerously: Mary McCarthy and Her World*, New York, Lime Tree Press, 1993, pp. 325 and 661.

p.96 'doing the hatchet work' etc.: Mary McCarthy, 'My Confession', in *On the Contrary*, William Heinemann, 1962, p. 102.

p.99 'It is not surprising': SS, 3 April 1949, *NSJ*, p. 56.

p.99 'The cars as fertile as weeds': 4 April 1949, SSUJ.

p.100 'America is not a "cause"': 24 April 1949, *NSJ*, pp. 61–2.

p.100 The second was his essay: *The God That Failed*, ed. Richard Crossman, Bantam edn, 1965, p. 241.

Nine: Your sins of weakness

p.105 'The mere announcement of fact': Melvin Lasky to William Donovan, in Giles Scott-Smith, *The Politics of Apolitical Culture: The Congress for Cultural Freedom and the Political Economy of American Hegemony 1945–1955*, Routledge, 2001, p. 165.

p.106 'We had invited them here': Melvin Lasky, letter to the *Manchester Guardian*, 24 July 1950.

p.107 fabulous meals: Diana Trilling, *We Must March, My Darlings*, New York, Harcourt Brace Jovanovich, 1977, p. 60.

p.107 don't forget John Wayne: from a conversation with Betty Woodman, 30 Aug 2013.

p.107 The Russians were building: JE to MS, 23 May 2012.

p.108 'To many people, though' etc.: SS journal entry for 12 March 1952, SSUJ.

p.110 'He is, to me, a new type': ibid. To add a detail of which my father was unaware: Michael Goodwin was also the editor of the Bellman Books series, published by Ampersand, which recently was revealed to have been the cover publishing house for the branch of British Intelligence that subsequently lay behind *Encounter*. See Paul Lashmar and James Oliver, *Britain's Secret Propaganda War*, Stroud, Sutton Publishing, 1998, p. 100.

p.110 'Have read World within World several times': WHA to SS, 20 June 1951, in Bucknell and Jenkins, *The Map of All My Youth*, pp. 84–5.

p.111 'I believe that you are a very strong, ruthless character': WHA to SS, 12 April 1942, in ibid., p. 82.

p.111 'Mr Spender has always seemed to me': Cyril Connolly review of *WWW*, reprinted in *The Evening Colonnade*, David Bruce & Watson, 1973, p. 360.

p.115 'what on earth did he think': KV 2/3216, doc. 49.

p.115 'I still believe Guy to be a victim': WHA to SS, 14 June 1951, in Bucknell and Jenkins, *The Map of All My Youth*, p. 84 n. 3.

p.115 'I feel exactly as you do': WHA to SS, 20 June 1951, in ibid., p. 84.

p.116 'into a little pin-striped shoal': Cyril Connolly, *The Missing Diplomats*, Queen Anne Press, 1952, p. 31.

p.116 'It is very difficult to understand': KV 2/3215, doc. 19. The person in the US who would have been able to make such revelations was Michael Straight, who'd belonged to the ring of Cambridge spies. My parents knew the Straights. We stayed with them on our way to California in 1959. Michael's version of events is in his *After Long Silence*, New York, W. W. Norton, 1983.

p.117 'At one time it was thought': KV 2/3216, doc. 27, Minute sheet dated 1 Feb 1955. Also doc. 55, 10 and 11 July 1951. The biography of Kim Philby by Bruce Page, David Leitch and Phillip Knightley describes Skardon as 'perhaps the best operator MI5 ever had' (*Philby: The Spy Who Betrayed a Generation*, Penguin, 1969, p. 140).

Ten: Don't you ever tell a lie?

p.125 the Locrini family could not be called poor: *NSJ*, p. 127.

p.126 'all the old business': *NSJ*, p. 20, April 1949, p. 59. See also Allen Tate, 'Literature of Social Agitation', in *The Hovering Fly and Other Essays*, Cummington, MA, Cummington Press, 1949, p. 33.

p.127 'Brer Rabbit and the Tar Baby': Joel Chandler Harris, *The Tales of Uncle Remus: The Adventures of Brer Rabbit*, was first published in 1881. There are numerous editions.

p.127 'Perhaps you could': SS to IK, 22 Feb 1953; Kristol's reply: IK to SS, 26 Feb 1953, Tam 023, Papers of the ACCF.

p.127 'draw an adequate salary': TSE to SS, 9 April 1953, Tam 023, Papers of the ACCF.

p.127 'it looks as if': SS to IK, undated [early May 1953], Tam 023, Papers of the ACCF.

p.128 'Not my branch but you might like them': SS to IK, 26 April 1953, Tam 023, Papers of the ACCF.

p.129 'Irving Kristol fascinates me': *NSJ*, p. 147.

p.129 'There was always the possibility': IK, *Neoconservatism: The Autobiography of an Idea*, New York, Free Press, 1995, p. 23.

p.132 'Special Branch began compiling': *Sydney Morning Herald*, 25 Oct 1953, in Peter Wildeblood, *Against the Law*, Weidenfeld & Nicolson, 1999, p. 46.

p.132 'I asked him whether to be arrested': n.d. [1 July?] 1955, *NSJ*, p. 172.

p.133 'Why should they climb a tree?': Wildeblood, *Against the Law*, p. 176.

Eleven: Dreaming one's way through life

p.139 'an act "outside" historical materialism' and 'strongly attacked the Congress': 24 and 27 Oct 1954, SSUJ.

p.141 'And the frowning schoolgirl': W. H. Auden, 'The Model'.

p.142 'social-democratic Britain was better placed': Christopher Mayhew, *Time to Explain*, Hutchinson, 1987, pp. 62 and 106.

p.142 'We regard the Stalinist communists': FO 1110/533.

p.143 'has created an especial resentment': 6 Jan 1955, draft statement to the CCF in Paris, to be signed by US members of the CCF, Tam 023, Papers of the ACCF.

p.143 'I had assumed that we were writers': Arthur Schlesinger to James Burnham, 16 March 1955, Tam 023, Papers of the ACCF.

Twelve: Scandalous gossip

p.145 'yammered': RC to NS, 3 Sept 1957, SSAB. The publishing house was Hamish Hamilton, but Jamie never used Hamish as his Christian name.

p.146 'outmanoeuvred': RC to NS, 27 April 1955, SSAB.

p.146 'it would have been a comfort': RC to NS, 11 Nov 1956, SSAB.

p.146 'Stephen knows quite well': SSUJ, and partially in *NSJ*, 18 May 1955, pp. 153–4.

p.146 'Orch bad': Chandler's pocket diary for 1955, RCAB.

p.147 'he has the drunkard's': 20 May 1955, SSUJ.

p.147 When he was asked to leave: Chandler's biographers suggest he was asked to leave the Connaught for chronic alcoholism, but in fact the problem was incontinence.

p.147 'it's no good dreaming one's way through life': 10 June 1955, *NSJ*, p. 163.

p.148 'Stern Daughter of the V. of G.': Alison Hooper letter to Frank MacShane, 29 Nov 1975, photocopy in SSAB.

p.149 'for reasons I no longer recollect': IK, *Neoconservatism*, p. 461.

p.150 'if we are building a theatre': Jennifer Josselson to MS, 26 May 2012.

p.151 sixteen or seventeen magazines: John Hunt to MS, 24 June 2012.

p.151 'My colleagues': 28 July 1955, *NSJ*, p. 193.

p.151 'Dwight has spent a fruitful life': IK, *Neoconservatism*, p. 461.

p.154 'At Poros, I had a walk with Matthew': SS typescript headed '1955, 6–16 Aug, August holiday', p. 23, SSUJ.

p.155 'I think you should have left Stephen': RC to NS, 21 March 1957, SSAB.

p.156 'the fatal day': RC diary, 9 Sept 1955, RCAB.

p.157 'As nanny my greatest problem': RC to Jamie Hamilton, 25 Nov 1955, RCAB.

p.157 'the endless prowling of bazaars': RC to NS, 2 July 1956, SSAB.

p.158 'I think it is absolutely true' and 'In all these things': RC to SS, 22 Dec 1955, SSAB.

p.159 'rather nice': RC to NS, 1 Feb 1956, SSAB.

p.160 'You cannot be damaged' and 'The whole idea is a fake': RC to SS, 9 March 1956, SSAB.

p.160 'I regard financial failure': RC to Jamie Hamilton, 22 April 1949, in Frank MacShane (ed.), *The Selected Letters of Raymond Chandler*, Jonathan Cape, 1981, p. 170. See also, quoting himself, RC to SS, 1 Jan 1957, SSAB.

p.161 'when I left England': RC to NS, 13 Nov 1956, SSAB.

Thirteen: The irresistible historic mixed grill

p.165 American GIs walking around Red Square: my memories of Joseph Brodsky are in Valentina Polukhina (ed.), *Brodsky through the Eyes of His Contemporaries*, vol. 2, Brighton, MA, Academic Studies Press, 2010.

p.165 'They were mere embellishments': Zinovy Zinik to MS, 22 January 2014.

p.165 'The Writers' Union': Ilya Ehrenburg to Alexander Werth, in *Russia: Hopes and Fears*, Penguin, 1969, p. 205.

p.166 'In spite of everything': SS, *Engaged in Writing*, pp. 35 and 151–2.

p.168 'He dictated to me the entire action': 19 July typescript, re 8 July 1956, SSUJ.

p.169 'I think I was fooling myself': RC to NS, 7 June 1956, SSAB.

p.169 'Any time': RC to NS, 10 June 1956, SSAB.

p.169 'He is the sort of man who': RC to Michael Gilbert, 11 June 1956, RCAB.

p.169 'I like this fellow Spender very much': RC to Jamie Hamilton, in MacShane, *Selected Letters of Raymond Chandler*, p. 170.

p.170 'I don't know when I have been so unhappy': RC to NS, 29 June 1956, SSAB.

p.171 'It was hellish with the furniture': RC to NS, 29 June (bis) 1956, SSAB.

p.173 'I'll never get anyone as kind': RC to NS, 13 Nov 1956, SSAB.

p.173 'When I hear your wonderful voice': RC to NS, 19 Nov 1956, SSAB.

p.174 'You should know that I am not going to embarrass you': RC to NS, 30 Nov 1956, SSAB.

p.174 'Tremendous fun': RC to NS, 14 July 1956, SSAB.

p.174 'I wish you were here': RC to NS, 23 Nov 1956, SSAB.

p.174 'The thinnest tie of social friendship': RC to NS, 3 Dec 1956, SSAB.

Fourteen: The kindest face

p.175 'the kindest face': the phrase appears several times in the correspondence between RP and SS, now in the library at Duke University. The same scene is told retrospectively in RP's memoir, *Ardent Spirits: Leaving Home, Coming Back*, New York, Scribner, 2009, pp. 108 and 201–4, etc.

p.176 'I think of this room where I am writing': SS to RP, 10 Jan 1957, Duke.

p.178 'would have given Cissy the jitters': RC to SS, 12 Dec 1956, SSAB.

p.179 'We are both – she and I – highly strung' and 'cheap little concerts in museums': RC to SS, 1 Jan 1957, SSAB.

p.180 'Very learned, but much too pontifical': RC to Jessica Tyndale, 18 Jan 1957, in MacShane, *Selected Letters of Raymond Chandler*, p. 416.

p.183 'Stephen is a loving father': RC to Michael Gilbert, 26 Jan 1957, RCAB. The later paragraphs of this letter are in MacShane, *Selected Letters of Raymond Chandler*, p. 417.

p.184 'The most I really wanted was to take care of you': RC to NS, 'Saturday' [late Jan 1957], SSAB.

p.185 'small, inoffensive': RC to NS, 'Sunday night, Monday also' [late Jan 1957], SSAB.

p.185 'After all, in my Will, I am making Helga': RC to NS, 30 Jan 1957, SSAB.

p.185 'though I will do one day': SS to RP, 4 Feb 1957, Duke.

p.186 'not at all like Dylan Thomas': SS to RP, n.d. [Feb 1957], Duke.

Fifteen: A strong invisible relationship

p.187 'because I took it out of Natasha's frame': SS to RP, 25 Feb 1957, Duke.

p.189 'we should only know': RC to NS, but quoting NS, 15 March 1957, SSAB.

p.190 'two frantic parties': RC to NS, 22 April 1957, SSAB.

p.190 'I'm sorry he has to work so hard': RC to NS, 16 May 1957, SSAB.

p.191 'why don't you carry what you have': RC to NS, 14 Aug 1957, SSAB.

p.191 'There is really nothing to do': RC to NS, 30 May 1957, SSAB.

p.191 'I am also too proud': RC to NS, 30 May 1957, SSAB.

p.191 'perhaps the best I can do': RC to NS, 21 June 1957, SSAB.

p.191 'a handsome nothing': RC to Michael Gilbert, 5 July 1957, RCAB.

p.192 'With regard to what you say': Michael Gilbert to RC, 12 July 1957, RCAB.

p.192 'I want what Rimbaud': SS to RP, 13 April 1957, Duke.

p.193 'I feel I'd sell everything': SS to RP, 28 May 1957, Duke.

p.193 'deeply disturbed and upset': SS to RP, 20 June 1957, Duke.

p.194 'What also counts is that for Natasha': SS to RP, 21 June 1957, Duke.

p.194 'seemed like a final God-inspired kick': SS to RP, 27 June 1957, Duke.

Sixteen: Barrenness and desolation

p.196 'always seemed poised over some abyss': 28 Sept 1990, re Moravia's death on 26 Sept, SSUJ. Also *NSJ*, p. 671.

p.196 'for a week I seemed to have in Japan': SS to RP, 5 Oct 1957, Duke.

p.197 'I'm in despair over the California trip' and the following quotations are from NS unpublished diary for 1985, SSAB.

p.197 'I remember when the feeling of barrenness' etc.: ibid., 2 Feb, p. 14, SSAB.

p.200 'a kind of space around myself': SS to RP, 22 Oct 1957, Duke.

p.201 'That we won't be able to see so much': SS to RP, 27 Oct 1957, Duke.

p.201 'What I knew by the spring': RP, *Ardent Spirits*, p. 268.

Seventeen: Too ambivalent

p.208 'I couldn't despise Stephen as you do': NS to RC, 19 Feb 1958, RCAB. The surviving letters from Natasha to Raymond Chandler entered the Bodleian with the other Chandler papers in the 1970s. She made sure that access was restricted during her lifetime but they are now accessible.

p.212 'I really am concerned about him' and all subsequent quotations in these paragraphs are from Stephen's Japan diary. He sent this to Reynolds Price for safekeeping. Price typed it and returned the typescript to Stephen, who edited it for the *Selected Journals* of 1984. The manuscript was returned to me after the death of Reynolds by Bill Price, his brother.

p.214 'I think the answer to your question': SS to RP, 3 July 1957, Duke.

Eighteen: You're unique

p.221 'We are having a hell of a time': SS to RP, 13 Dec 1958, Duke.

p.221 'America! America!': Dwight Macdonald, 'America! America!', republished in *Discriminations*, New York, Grossman Publishers, 1974, p. 44.

p.222 'reflected the attitude of *Encounter*'s front office': ibid., pp. 57–9. It's possible that Josselson was trying to abandon the CIA backing and acquire funds from the Ford Foundation and the Rockefeller Foundation, which would never have tolerated criticism of this kind. See Sarah Miller, 'The Impresario: Michael Josselson, the CIA, and the Congress for Cultural Freedom', D.Phil. dissertation, University of Cambridge, 2013, p. 165.

p.224 'I'll be delighted to see you': RC to NS, 30 Sept 1958, SSAB.

p.225 'How strange that you': RC to NS, 4 March 1959, SSAB.

p.228 'The other day I took Matthew': 30 July 1959, SSUJ.

p.230 'It is essential': FO 1110/1726, FO Circular no. 37, NA.

Nineteen: Without banquets

p.235 Margot Walmsley: Frances Stonor Saunders, *Who Paid the Piper?: The CIA and the Cultural Cold War*, Granta Books, 1999, p. 176.

p.236 'the Bronx Box': Keith Botsford to MS, 12 January 2014.

p.236 'Elizabeth Bowen and all that crap': Stuart Hampshire to Frances Stonor Saunders, 1977, quoted in Stonor Saunders, *Who Paid the Piper?*, pp. 331 and 464 n. 10.

p.237 'What Melvin Lasky does': SS to RP, 30 March 1960, Duke.

p.238 'I am getting to the stage': SS to RP, 27 March 1961, Duke.

p.238 'The idea that Pasternak': SS to RP, 5 Sept 1959, Duke.

p.239 'I have received so much advice': SS to RP, 24 Sept 1959, Duke.

p.239 'My situation is worse': 'Three Letters', *Encounter*, vol. 15, no. 2, Aug 1960, pp. 3–6.

p.240 'a small gathering': *NSJ*, pp. 267–79.

p.240 'I thought it would be a good idea': 4 Feb 1960, SSUJ.

p.242 Stephen deduced that Driberg: Tom Driberg (1905–76), Labour politician and journalist, was an old friend of Burgess, of whom he wrote a memoir, *Guy Burgess: A Portrait with Background* (1956). See also Francis Wheen, *Tom Driberg*, Chatto & Windus, 1990, pp. 316–18.

p.244 'My days are all poisoned': CI, unpublished diary, 3 Jan 1936, Henry E. Huntington Library, San Marino, CA.

p.245 I wrote him a bitter letter: MS to SS, 17 June 1983, SS to MS, n.d., CMS.

p.245 'Any voyage away from England': 1994, CMS.

p.246 'if it was not conducted': 31 March 1960, in SS, *Journals 1939–1983*, ed. John Goldsmith, Faber & Faber, 1985, pp. 216–19, and *NSJ*, p. 280.

p.246 'The exchanges of culture': Friday 20 April 1956, in Philip Williams (ed.), *The Diary of Hugh Gaitskell 1945–1956*, Jonathan Cape, 1983, p. 500.

Twenty: Over-privileged?

p.255 'It revealed to me something': SS to RP, 6 March 1962, Duke.

p.255 'simply by presenting pictures': SS to IB, 11 July 1932, IB Archive, Bod.

p.255 'not the words and the lines': *WWW*, p. 65.

p.256 'True poetry is the external truth': 2 Oct 1980, *NSJ*, p. 564.

Twenty-one: Might just as well be married

p.269 'Matthew and his girl keep on turning up': SS to RP, 26 Sept 1961, Duke.

p.276 'as a man of letters': IB to SS, 17 Nov. 1966, IB Archive, Wolfson College, Oxford. Thanks to Henry Hardy for bringing this to my attention.

p.277 'I want you to consider': SS to MS, 22 May 1966, CMS. The address on the letter is approximate and I think Dad half hoped it wouldn't arrive.

Twenty-two: A nice little niche

p.281 'Suddenly I realised that I wanted': 3 Dec 1962, *NSJ*, p. 324.

p.283 'It might be quite good for them': SS to AMG, 22 Jan 1963, CMS.

p.285 'We strongly suspected': Trilling, *We Must March My Darlings*, p. 60.

p.285 the end of the story: JE to MS, 23 May 2012.

p.286 'Don't worry, I'll ring up Allen': Sidney Hook, *Out of Step*, New York, Harper & Row, 1987, p. 425.

p.286 'but none of us': Trilling, *We Must March My Darlings*, p. 61.

p.295 *The Alexandria Quartet*: Lawrence Durrell's *The Alexandria Quartet*, consisting of four interconnected novels, *Justine, Balthazar, Mountolive* and *Clea*, was published between 1957 and 1960.

p.298 'a platform in which American points of view': 14 July 1954, SSUJ.

Twenty-four: Killing the women we love

p.321 'The magic of that day': NS unpublished diary, 2 Feb 1985, SSAB.

p.323 'Now what I would like': SS to Nikos, 23 July 1965, CDP.

p.325 'When you are relating a dream': SS to Nikos, 20 Sept 1965, CDP.

p.325 'I must try and think about that day': SS to Nikos, 5 and 16 Sept 1965, CDP.

p.326 'During the night I was trying to explain': SS to Nikos, 20 Sept 1965, CDP.

p.326 'You always relate everything': SS to Nikos, 14 Sept 1965, CDP.

p.330 Dad's book on Botticelli: SS, *Botticelli*, Faber Gallery, 1945.

p.330 His book on Florence: Gaetano Salvemini, *Magnati e popolani in Firenze dal 1280 al 1295*, Florence, Carnesecchi, 1899.

p.331 'Oxford is anti-creative': SS to MS, 3 Dec 1965, CMS.

p.335 'Maybe you will be able': ibid.

p.335 'When Matthew writes': SS to MS, 22 Aug 1966, CMS.

p.335 'Even if you don't feel things': SS to MS, 20 Sept 1966, CMS.

p.336 'enraged Natasha so much': SS to Nikos, 15 Sept 1966, CDP.

Twenty-five: Your father will survive

p.338 'I must not think that this meant': Plante, *Becoming a Londoner*, p. 5.

p.339 'I suddenly realized the reason': SS to Nikos, 16 Sept 1965, CDP.

p.340 'to keep Natasha alerted to his sexuality': Plante, *Becoming a Londoner*, p. 40.

p.341 'I had managed to design the walk': NS, *An English Garden in Provence*, Harvill Press, 1999, pp. 63–5.

p.341 'I wish that when I was your age': Plante, *Becoming a Londoner*, p. 52.

p.342 'Natasha is hysterical on the subject of Lasky': SS to Nikos, 26 May 1967, CDP.

p.343 'I am not going to have anything more to do with the liberals': Lyndon Johnson to Richard Goodwin, 22 June 1965, in Richard N. Goodwin, *Remembering America*, Boston, MA, Little, Brown, 1988, p. 392.

p.345 'The effect was electrifying': SS to MS, 30 March 1967, CMS.

p.347 King was involved: for the Cecil King plot against Wilson, see Peter

Wright, *Spycatcher*, Viking, 1987, p. 369. Wright describes King casually as 'a longtime agent of ours'.

p.347 'The trouble with this *Encounter* row': SS to Nikos, 14 April 1967, CDP.

p.347 'So I did, dear boy': Sutherland, *Stephen Spender*, p. 451.

p.352 'The whole story': David Plante to MS, e-mail of 15 Oct 2013.

p.352 'You and I may think he has been a little naïf': WHA to NS, 26 May [1967], Berg Collection, NYPL.

p.354 articles were written: see (among others) Max Kozloff, 'American Painting during the Cold War', *Artforum*, May 1973; Eva Cockcroft, 'Abstract Expressionism, Weapon of the Cold War', *Artforum*, June 1974; and Serge Guibault, *How New York Stole the Idea of Modern Art*, Chicago, University of Chicago Press, 1985. I've also tried to connect the Trotsky left-wingers in New York and the eventual CIA in my book on Gorky, *From a High Place: A Life of Arshile Gorky*, New York, Alfred A. Knopf, 1999.

p.355 'Your father is still famous': Jennifer Josselson to MS, 24 May 2012.

p.355 paid a fat sum: NS unpublished diary for 1985, n.d., p. 4, SSAB.

Twenty-six: Romantic friendships before all

p.362 'it makes no difference to S': NS unpublished diary, Saturday 2 Feb 1985, SSAB.

p.363 'S always thinks in terms of himself': ibid., Sunday [5 May] 1985, SSAB.

p.363 'S would always put everything else': ibid., Wednesday 8 May 1985, SSAB.

p.364 'The truth is, if one is not loved': ibid., Thursday 14 Feb 1985, SSAB.

p.364 they'd never *felt* criminal: Plante, *Becoming a Londoner*, p. 73.

p.366 'No . . . but he was very fond of you': David Plante, e-mail to MS, 3 July 2014.

p.368 'You've asked me before': for a biography of Gorky that includes many of Mougouch's stories, see my *From a High Place*.

p.368 his love letters had been copied: for the controversy over the Gorky letters, see Nick Dante Vaccaro, 'Gorky's Debt to Gaudier-Brzeska', *Art Journal*, vol. 23, Fall 1963, pp. 33–4.

p.370 'It just seems to me that somehow': this comes from an undated fragment in my diary of the time. I can't vouch for its accuracy but it sounds like her.

p.371 'I do not believe that writing or any other activity': 23 April 1995, *NSJ*, p. 747.

p.375 'Stephen, sentimental': Plante, *Becoming a Londoner*, p. 159.

Twenty-seven: The right to speak

p.377 His reply was emotional and confused: Jennifer Josselson to MS, 26 May 2012.

p.378 Following the letter: for *Index on Censorship* etc., see Sutherland, *Stephen Spender*, p. 457.

p.379 there were frequent and recurring difficulties with the State Department: I am grateful to my cousin Philip Spender, who worked for *Index*, for emphasizing this point.

p.380 a photo of one man shooting another: this famous photo was taken by Eddie Adams on 1 February 1968.

p.382 'I am beginning to feel': SS to Nikos, n.d. [early May 1967], DPC.

Twenty-eight: Guileless and yet obsessed

p.387 he wrote a 'diary' poem about it: the poem on the birth of Saskia was first published in SS, *Journals 1939–1983*, p. 271. For our Italian life, see MS, *Within Tuscany*, Viking/Penguin, 1992.

p.392 'This last sentence of his': MS diary, 3 July 1975.

p.394 American art was the invention: the earliest evidence I've been able to trace regarding an awareness that American art must take a lead after the war comes from a lost circular issued by the Federation of Modern Painters and Sculptors, quoted in the *New York Times*, 22 May 1942. See MS, *From a High Place*, p. 264.

p.395 'He appealed to me across Arthur's cocktail glass': MS diary, 19 Nov 1975.

INDEX